To Mesopotamia and Kurdistan in Disguise

ELY BANISTER SOANE

COSIMOCLASSICS

NEW YORK

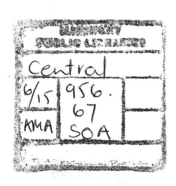

To Mesopotamia and Kurdistan in Disguise
Cover Copyright © 2007 by Cosimo, Inc.

To Mesopotamia and Kurdistan in Disguise
was originally published in 1912.

For information, address:
P.O. Box 416, Old Chelsea Station
New York, NY 10011

or visit our website at:
www.cosimobooks.com

Ordering Information:
Cosimo publications are available at online bookstores. They may
also be purchased for educational, business or promotional use:
- *Bulk orders:* special discounts are available on bulk orders for reading
groups, organizations, businesses, and others. For details contact
Cosimo Special Sales at the address above or at info@cosimobooks.com.
- *Custom-label orders:* we can prepare selected books with your cover or
logo of choice. For more information, please contact Cosimo at
info@cosimobooks.com.

Cover Design by www.popshopstudio.com

ISBN: 978-1-60206-977-0

In Kirkuk they enjoy great freedom from persecution, despite the periodical efforts of Muslim priests to incite ill-feeling against them. Their presence is too necessary to the well-being of the town to make a massacre anything but a catastrophe for the Muhammadan traders, who have been led by their integrity and capability to place great faith and confidence, and often to deposit large sums of money with them. In these qualities if honesty, and an ability for getting on with Muslims amicably without conceding a particle of their behaviour as strict Christians, they contrast very forcibly with the Armenians, Syrians, and Arab Christians.

—from Chapter VI

PREFATORY NOTE

THE following chapters are a plain narrative of a journey across Mesopotamia and in Southern Kurdistan, made up from a journal kept throughout the voyage from Constantinople to Bagdad through those countries.

I think I may fairly claim that I have given here a description of a great deal so far undescribed, also a view of places, already known, from another standpoint.

Several of the situations have made it necessary to mention the fact of a knowledge of Persian, extensive enough to enable the writer to pass among Persians as one of themselves. Lest this appear a needless and offensive boast, I would say that the incidents demand its mention, and it is explained in the course of the narrative.

In the historical portions of the book, in so far as more modern history is concerned, I have been enabled to give some entirely new matter, for that on Kurdish history was supplied me in letters received from Shah Ali of Aoraman, Shaikh Reza of Kirkuk, Tahir Beg Jaf, Majid Beg Jaf, Muhammad Ali Beg Jaf, while a great part was communicated during conversations at Halabja and Sulaimania. This information, then, I think is unique. As to the chapter on Chaldean history, I am deeply indebted to M. Badria, Rais-i-Millat of Mousil, also to his brother Habib Badria, who, having access to old histories in Mousil, were generous enough to allow me the benefit of their information.

There is, I am afraid, an overwhelming use of the first

v

personal pronoun, which I trust may be forgiven, for without it the story would not be a personal one.

The tone of the narrative may betoken, perhaps, a partiality to the Kurds ; and I must admit, that having met from them more genuine kindness—unclaimed—than from any other collection of strangers met elsewhere, I owe them a large debt of gratitude, the least return for which is to throw some light upon a national character hitherto represented as being but an epitome of all that is savage, treacherous, and inhuman.

E. B. S.

MOHAMMERAH.

CONTENTS

LIST OF ILLUSTRATIONS

TO MESOPOTAMIA AND
KURDISTAN IN DISGUISE

CHAPTER I

IN STAMBOUL

WHEN I descended from the train one dismal morning in Constantinople, in a bleak terminus just like a hundred others of its kind all over the Continent, it was with the intention of staying in the Ottoman capital for some time. A long residence in the Middle East had rendered me susceptible to the magnetism it certainly exerts, and at the same time had given me a very thorough appreciation of the comforts and conveniences of the Occident. As I was quite ignorant of the western parts of the Turkish Empire, and entertained the same ideas regarding them as I suppose do most people at home, it seemed that Constantinople must furnish a delectable resting-place, a point from which to look out upon East and West with equal facility, choosing from each the features necessary to a pleasant life that should be within reach of books and libraries, and afford equally a way of escape among Oriental people and surroundings, without necessitating a long journey and longer bill.

Unfortunately I knew neither Constantinople nor its winter climate, nor its inhabitants. I had never had dealings with Turks, and had left out of my calculations the Greeks, who make up thirty-five per cent. of the population of this capital, once theirs by right of sovereignty, and still almost theirs in all that concerns the world of commerce.

1

As a matter of fact, the sum total of my knowledge at the moment I arrived was that Constantinople consisted of three quarters or districts, Pera, Galata, and Stamboul, and possessed an hotel called the Pera Palace, the expenses at which were far too grand for my cottage style of purse.

By some person of doubtful nationality, I had been advised to go to a French pension in Galata, which I was assured was cheap, clean, and comfortable. As French pensions in other parts of the world may be, and often are, all these three, the scheme seemed an excellent one; so having escaped from a weary and bored Customs official at the station, I piled my belongings upon a victoria, and we started to clatter over the knobs of stone, and through the mud-pits that are the roads of Constantinople. Through mean streets we rolled and banged our way where horse trams clanked and crawled, between rows of shops whose wares were just those of the cheap streets of any continental city, to the floating bridge over the water called the Golden Horn, a most perfect misnomer in December, suggesting the crowning sarcasm of some disappointed tourist.

At the approach to this curious bridge, we were halted amid a dense crowd of foot-passengers in the everlasting fez—sprinkled with bowler hats and the headgear of every European nation—and made to pay five piastres (10d.) for the right to pass. In order to prevent any passenger evading the toll, a row of Turkish officials stood across the road, clad in a conspicuous enough uniform—a white smock.

The Golden Horn was of a very ordinary mud colour, and below the bridge, prosaic enough with its crowd of steamers and the busy ferry-boats that ply up and down the Bosphorus and to the Asiatic shore. The wharfs were lined with unbeautiful Customs, port, and shipping offices, backed on the rising ground by the indescribably hideous imitation French and Viennese architecture of Galata and Pera. Tall barracks with rows and rows of filthy windows looked out upon the prospect, and at their *vis à vis* in Stamboul across the water, and, crowning the mountain of wall and window formed by the successive tiers of houses up the hill-side, rose the Tower of Galata, a circular erection topped by a Turkish flag.

The roadway of the bridge being laid with large baulks of timber placed transversely, no two of which ever arrive at a common level, prevents rapid travelling even were the road clear of foot-passengers, who use it in preference to the footpaths. The Galata end plunges into a street absolutely packed with human beings, carts and carriages, where all the money-changers of Galata—Constantinople's business town—seem to have congregated. A turn to the right leads to more trams, and a long and weary cobbled street of shops large and small, along whose pavements saunter the deck-hands of steamers hailing from every European and Levantine port. Greeks of course are in the majority, many in their national costume of blue tights, with a huge and pendulous posterior, coloured shirt and little zouave jacket, and a hat of the "pork-pie" order. Armenians, too, abound, and Levantines of all kinds. Italians, in this Italian quarter of Galata, are everywhere, and the language of the streets is anything except Turkish. Here and there an incongruous group of fierce and savage fellows, with packs of stuffed leather upon their backs—the Constantinopolitan edition of "the Porter's knot"—shout and joke in a tongue understood of none even in this cosmopolitan city. They are Kurds, the strongest, most manly of the population, and the most despised, probably for those very qualities—in this town of sharping and guile.

Leaving this street and crawling up some very steep inclines lined by tenement houses, the carriage reached a long road running along the side of the hill. I suppose it should be called a street, for want of a better, or worse, name; but as we associate the word with another order of thing, it is well to explain that this, an important enough artery of Galata traffic, was—and doubtless still is—a wide alley of cobble paving, with huge holes at frequent and irregular intervals. In the absence of underground drainage, the paving sloped to the middle, and after filling the holes, the excess liquid filth flowed downhill. The solid variety, however, to which every resident contributed with assiduity, lay in heaps and figures about the street, proclaiming in the language of putrescence the quality of the inhabitants. In describing this main street of the Italian quarter,[1] I have described most of Constantinople, excepting only a few excellent streets on the Bosphorus side of Pera, where the wealthy foreigners live.

At the door of a kind of restaurant I was deposited, and no sooner had the carriage stopped than an ancient woman opened the door and welcomed me in fluent Italian. As my knowledge of that language is limited, she called loudly for "Marie," a shrewd and kindly woman of about thirty, who appeared from a sort of cellar from behind the eating-room, and in French informed me that she had a room, told me the very reasonable terms, and asked for a deposit; and very soon I found myself installed in an uncarpeted apartment furnished with an iron stove, a bed, a washhand-stand, and a small table. This was the best room. A powerful and eloquent odour pervaded the house, telling of the thoroughly Italian nature of the cooking, and hinting at the existence of innumerable cesspools on the premises. I found afterwards that there were five latrines in the house.

It needed but a dinner in the eating-room to complete the tale of excellence of this exceptional pension, where one met Armenians and Levantines performing the usual skilful feats with knives and awkward morsels, regarding the fork as an instrument fit only for the inexperienced and timorous.

Next morning I climbed by devious alleys, and through lakes and torrents of filth to Pera, and spent hours trying to find better accommodation at a moderate price; but after being shown the loathsome dens of various Armenians and Greeks, and retiring with the best grace possible before the astonishing charges of every clean and relatively wholesome place, I was fortunate enough to meet a Russian, a tenant of an "appartement"—the Constan-

[1] The Rue Luledjie Hendek.

tinopolitan flat—who wished to find an occupier during a three months' visit to Moscow.

To my great delight the "appartement"—in a new building close to the Pera Palace Hotel, in one of the best parts of Constantinople—was clean and well-furnished, and we closed, with as much satisfaction on his side, I hope, as on mine. At any rate, he insisted upon sealing the arrangement with innumerable "aperitifs," followed by vodkas and liqueurs at various *brasseries* about Pera, and having become friendly with a resplendent lady of Roumania, he bade me farewell and departed with his new acquaintance.

While in Constantinople I never regretted the arrangement, for the place was comfortable and convenient, and being in the midst of Pera, which is nothing but a semi-French town with no more evidence of Turks about it than a few porters and cabmen in fez, and drunken police, I began to forget what I had come for, namely, to get in touch with the Oriental side of the city. As a matter of fact, one made so many curious and interesting acquaintances among the French, Armenian, Roumanian, Russian, Balkan, and other elements, that one's time seemed fully absorbed with them. I quite forgot to commence studying the Turkish language, and acquired a fine proficiency in French, and picked up a little Greek, a language as useful in Constantinople as Turkish. After some time, however, when the execrable weather permitted, I began to make excursions to Stamboul, and avoiding all guide-books, found out the show-places myself, and many other interesting corners, among which I counted the shops of the Persian Turks in the Great Bazaar, where I always was sure of a warm welcome, simply because I affected a liking for their Persia, and hoped with them—perhaps against hope—for her regeneration and independence.

In the Great Bazaar, too, was just a touch of that East in which I had lived, and was to see once more, though the effect was so often spoiled by the interpreter of Mr T. Cook and his train of amiable creatures, seeking the "secret of the mysterious East" in the shops of Greeks.

There, donning a fez, I would stroll, my headgear saving me from the disagreeable attentions of the Greek shopkeepers, the most pertinacious of their calling in the city. For a long time among the natives of Persia in the bazaar I could find none but Tabrizi. Persian Turks often enough know little Persian; but at last I found a native of Shiraz, much to my delight, for a residence of two years among the Shirazi has always been a pleasant memory, and this particular Shirazi, too, seemed as glad as I was to meet a sincere admirer of the Jewel of Southern Persia, "The Pearl among the Emeralds."

At any rate, if kindness and hospitality be any criterion, my Shirazi was certainly pleased to find a kindred spirit.

Great amusement was caused among my friends of Persia by a passage-at-arms I had with the Persian Consul. I had heard that an old acquaintance was second secretary at the Consulate, and one day found my way by the steep and crooked alleys of Stamboul to the dirty red-painted building that flies the Persian flag. Entering the courtyard, I was accosted by the doorkeeper in Turkish, and as at that time I had considerable difficulty in understanding that language, I addressed him in Persian. This was more than he had expected from a stray European, and as his knowledge of Persian was as feeble as mine of Turkish, he passed me on to a suave little "mirza" or clerk, a Teherani.

I asked after my friend Mirza Hasan Khan, and was told that he had left for Persia some time ago, so I turned to leave the place. I had hardly reached the gate, however, than the little man came running after, and in polite Persian asked me to "bring my excellence" to the Consul-General, who desired to see me.

Following him upstairs and through a group of waiting peasants of Azarbaijan, I was introduced into a large room well carpeted with Persian rugs, where sat at a writing-table the Consul-General, a middle-aged Persian gentleman. Beside him upon a couch was his first secretary, a smiling little man from Tabriz.

I was at a loss to know why he wanted to see me, and

could only suppose that he wished to know who I was and what was my business with Mirza Hasan Khan. Entering, I saluted him in the Persian fashion, whose etiquette demands that the entrant shall first salute the occupants of a room. Receiving the usual reply, I accepted his invitation to be seated, and waited for him to speak, again following Persian custom, which forbids the less important of two men to open conversation.

He began by asking if I had been long in Constantinople, whether I intended to stay, how I liked it, and so on, and having exhausted his preliminary questions a pause occurred, during which the two Persians regarded me in a steadfast and interested manner, which I was at a loss to account for, as they are usually far too well-mannered to embarrass a visitor in any way.

After a rather awkward minute thus, the Consul, in an abrupt and official manner, exclaimed—

"Why this disguise? wherefore these lies? the truth were better; tell me your native town."

For a moment astonishment held me; this kind of conversation is possible from a Turk, but from a Persian! To say nothing of being quite at a loss to account for this extraordinary change of manner, I could not at all fathom the reason for such inquiries politely or impolitely made. In my innocence I had imagined myself paying a mere complimentary call, and found myself addressed as a defaulter of some kind, and so waited for further enlightenment.

"Lies?" I asked.

"Yes, lies; it is evident to me that you are a Shirazi, your tongue betrays you, and I wish to know what you have done to render expedient this kind of appearance, and this weak story of being an Englishman."

It occurred to me suddenly that here was the representative of Muhammad Ali Shah who had, six months before, by a coup, replaced himself upon the throne of absolute power, dissolving in the most drastic way the Chamber of Representatives, many of whose supporters had fled to Europe and were travelling about in European dress. Evidently I was being mistaken for one of these.

In this dilemma I bethought myself of my passport, and fortunately discovered it, together with a number of letters, including one from the Persian Ambassador addressed to "Mūsīū Soon," and after some difficulty succeeded in proving my identity.

The Consul's cordiality returned in a moment. With the utmost effusiveness he invited me to a large armchair, produced cigarettes, and called for tea. The visit from that moment took the form of usual ceremonial call upon a Persian. As I took my leave, remarking that I hoped he would not seek to have me arrested as a revolutionist, he said, thinking the whole affair a good joke :

"Well, you shouldn't speak Persian so fluently; you see your countrymen are usually so backward in acquiring our language, that when one appears talking as we do, can you expect us to believe it ? "

I saw him several times afterwards, and he always met me with the air of a man who shares some great and confidential jest with one.

About this time, December 1908, the Turkish Parliament was inaugurated, and amid the discord of Turkish bands and through avenues of flags and festoons, the procession of deputies and foreign representatives fought its way to the House at Stamboul, to sit for a few months and prove its futility.

The attitude of the Persians, who had been the first to experience the pains and penalties of popular representation, was interesting. It was, of course, popularly supposed that the Persian element in Constantinople and Smyrna—some ten thousand people—displayed heartwhole enthusiasm for the Turkish " Mejliss," and if the addresses and congratulations of the Persian political clubs were to have been believed, this supposition would have been true. Persians, however, are always alive to the value of expediency, and obviously clubs which, existing only by the tolerance of the Turks, propagated doctrines only to be regarded as heterodox by the Persian Ambassador and consuls, must display conspicuously their sympathy with any popular Ottoman movement.

In the privacy of their own houses, the sarcasm and deprecation of foreigners so near the tip of the Persian tongue found ready articulation.

As Shī'a, these refugees, to put it but mildly, lack sympathy with any movement of the Sunni Turks, and having seen repeated in the election and the arrangement of the Turkish "Mejliss" several of the errors which contributed to the discord and downfall of the first Persian Parliament, were disposed to look on with supercilious superiority at the efforts of a nation which they ever regarded as rather barbarian. Besides which, bad as Persia was under the old regime, the lot of the peasant and the humbler town-dweller was never so bad as was that of the equivalent classes in Turkey; and if there are degrees in the perfection of corruption arrived at by the administrative powers of both empires, there are few experienced Turks and Persians who will not give the palm for completeness in this art to Turkey, at any rate in her Asiatic provinces.

So the Persians, looking on, seeing all the difficulties to be surmounted, difficulties complicated by the turbulent and treacherous temperame·t of Greek and Armenian, waited to see an eventful crisis, and when it came as they had predicted, the triumphant attitude of "I told you so," for which they had prepared themselves, was intensified by the feeling of having also scored off an old enemy.

The only immediate outcome of the Parliament's inauguration, so far as it affected the dweller in the city, was to provide a number of newspapers with columns filled with reports of speeches—no whit more or less puerile than those provided by our Parliament for the London papers—and a large increase in drunkenness, particularly among the police. The provinces responded with their own interpretation of "Hurriat" by lawlessness of every description, which increased to a point almost unknown in Turkish history, at least in the Asiatic provinces, with which alone this book is concerned.

After all, it was a faithful enough repetition of Persia

in early 1907, when the dying Muzaffar ud Din Shah granted the first Persian Constitution. In that unfortunate country the ignorant mass looked to the Majlis to produce, within a few days, a panacea for the ills that had grown up and become an integral part of the nation during centuries of misrule, and the failure of the people's representatives even to adjust minor matters resulted in the outbursts all over the country which eventually, fanned by Muhammad Ali Shah, enabled him to regain his absolute power for a time.

In the Turkish Empire practically exactly the same thing happened. Needless to say, a very large section of the people was vitally interested in the existence of Sultan Abdul Hamid as a despot, particularly those powerful priests and place-holders who amassed wealth by means possible only when the Sultan was there to consent, and participate. The victims of this large class expected that with the proclamation of "Hurriat" ("freedom") these tyrants would retire swiftly into oblivion, but as time went on and the bloodsuckers (and bloodspillers too) continued their operations with increased vigour, the people, emboldened by the new political doctrines, rose in every direction. Tribes of Arabs and Kurds, who had regarded the new regime as a partial revival of their importance and a return—in a degree—to some of their ancient independence, finding levies upon them of taxes and recruits undiminished, rebelled against the Majlis and Sultan alike—a situation resulting which, at the time of writing,[1] bids fair to give the Turks and their army as much as they can do for some time to come.

It is fair to add that many of these outbursts are said to have been aggravated secretly by Sultan Abdul Hamid, who had submitted with a meekness never seen in the Persian monarch to the drastic changes his people effected. At any rate, his end was the same as that of Muhammad Ali Shah, for after a few months both find themselves deposed and in retirement.

In any case, the politics of Constantinople are too well

[1] Autumn 1909.

known to need ventilation here, so we may as well return to our original subject of Persians.

I learned soon after my arrival in Constantinople that Kurds abounded, but all of the Kermānjī or Zāzā tribes of Northern Turkish Kurdistan, and my hopes of finding a Kurd of Southern Persian Kurdistan seemed as if they would certainly end in disappointment. My reason for wanting to meet one of these people was to complete certain studies to which I had already devoted a year, in Kermanshah of Western Persia.

By chance, however, one of my Persian friends informed me one day that a priest had recently arrived from Sina of Persian Kurdistan; but beyond telling me his title, Shaikh ul Islām, and indicating vaguely where he imagined him to be living, in one of the curious caravanserais of Stamboul, he could tell me nothing; and as the Shaikh in question was a fanatical Sunni, I naturally could not expect my Shi'a friend to interest himself more deeply.

I was resolved to find him, however, and so spent some days tramping up and down the terrible alleys and streets of Stamboul, inquiring at every Muhammadan hotel and doing the round of all the caravanserais I could find, asking for the Shaikh ul Islām of Sina, a question that evoked considerable merriment among most of the Turks to whom I succeeded in communicating my meaning in the few Turkish words I knew. As is always the case in Turkey, inquisitiveness was the greatest impediment and nuisance. Anyone of whom I asked would put a string of questions as to why and wherefore, and who and whence, which my ignorance fortunately prevented my answering.

At last, however, by dint of getting a list of caravanserais, and taking them one by one, I found the Shaikh's habitation. This particular serai was like most in Constantinople, a two-storeyed building of tiny, windowless rooms round a courtyard, amid which a small house was erected, equally containing separate cells. The first floor had a gallery running round it upon which the rooms opened, and I found my man in a corner cell, or rather found where he was when at home. All this time the weather was indescribably awful, daily blizzards, rainstorms and blizzards again, freezing hurricanes from the plains and uplands to the north and west; and I wondered how this native of sunny Persia, a stranger to these terrible days of darkness, could live, and what is more, raise the courage to go forth into the mire and filth of Constantinople streets.

His servant I saw, a Kurd of Sina, who spoke a little Persian, and who was so astounded at hearing a European speak Kurdish that he quite lost his tongue. However, we made an appointment, and two days after saw me once more facing a blinding snowstorm to shuffle for half an hour from Pera through Galata across the Golden Horn, now a funnel where all the winds of all the ice on earth seemed to blow into Stamboul.

Crawling over the heaps of snow in the caravanserai courtyard, where not a soul was visible, I ascended the rickety staircase and knocked at the low door at the gallery end. Some one shouted in Persian " Kī a " (" Who is it ?"), and getting a reply in the same language, told me to walk in—which I did.

A small skylight sufficiently illuminated the place, and at once its arrangements stamped the occupants as natives of Persia. Opposite me, a tin road-samovar sang behind a row of little tea-glasses. Upon the samovar head sat a squat little teapot, and the Kurdish servant was filling a Persian hubble-bubble beside a brazier. Three or four Persian wooden boxes ornamented with brass-headed nails were by the walls, and in a corner were the necessaries of the road, earthen water-pots, tin " af tābeh " —a kind of jug for ablutions—tin wash-basin, and other articles with which every traveller in Persia is familiar. Commencing halfway and covering the floor to the farther end was a gilīm, a kind of carpet, woven in Persian Kurdistan, and seated facing one another, their legs concealed under a quilt apparently supported upon a stool, were two men. Him I sought was a black-browed and bearded priest, an individual surly looking enough to scare away any uninvited visitor. His companion was but an older edition of himself. Their heads were covered by small white turbans, but whether they had changed their native dress for that of Constantinople I could not see, as they both wore heavy overcoats.

The stool under the quilt covered in its turn a brazier of charcoal, and formed the " kursi," which is the Kurdish method of keeping oneself warm. Obviously the heat, which is considerable, is confined to the space under the quilt and does not escape into the room, which in this case was bitterly cold.

The Shaikh had been informed of my coming, and welcomed me in Persian, with just enough Kurdish accent to be perceptible ; and I squeezed my legs under the quilt, which he pulled up to our chins, and spent a few minutes exchanging compliments with him and the older man. The situation might have struck an outsider unused to a " kursi " as absurd : the spectacle of three men apparently sitting up in a kind of a huge bed, for the quilt was an ordinary bed-quilt, and pillows supported our backs— nodding gravely over the top of the bedclothes at one another.

They were much depressed by the weather, but on my telling them that I had been to their Kurdistan and knew their country and language they revived somewhat, and with tea and cigarettes became jovial and communicative, supplying me with a great deal of the information upon tribes, that I had come to seek, but had not hoped to acquire in the first interview.

However, the climate of Constantinople had done sufficient to disgust them with the place, and the Shaikh announced his intention of leaving by the first steamer for Beyrouth, and returning to a place called Halabja, on the Persio-Turkish frontier, in the Southern Kurdish country. Not unnaturally I was curious to know, first, the reason for his leaving Kurdistan ; and second, why he did not propose to return there, stopping short on the frontier at the nearest spot. Tentatively I put a question or two, but

he evidently had a suspicion of all strangers, and I had
to be content with my own theories, which could evolve
nothing more probable than classing him as a political
refugee; at any rate, he seemed pretty miserable in these
strange and squalid surroundings, and, bearing in his
language and manner the strong reminiscence of Persian
Kurdistan, seemed terribly out of place in this town that
aped Europe and all its meanest features.

In all, I had three interviews; he would not be induced
to come over to Pera, which he had heard of as a town
full of European women and shops "à la ferangi," where
he considered his priestly turban and flowing garments
very out of place. So each time I found him under the
quilt with his companion, much depressed, very silent,
sighing heavily, and talking of nothing but places and
people he had left behind in his native mountains.

My acquaintance with him, though little enough, was
the cause of ripening an idea which ever since I had
arrived in, and disliked, Constantinople, had gradually
been springing up in my mind. Though no Kurd, nor
separated from kin and custom, yet as a former dweller in
the east of Persia, I yearned for the freedom of plain
and mountain, the slow march of the clanging caravan,
the droning song of the shepherds on the hills, the fresh
clean air, and the burning sun. His talk was of all this,
and my thoughts of it too. His dialect and his rough
Persian recalled too vividly scenes of a year before.
Irresistibly pictures arose of the plain and hill of
Kurdistan, the glorious sunsets over plain and on snowy
peak, and the more I gave way to these day-dreams, the
more I let the rude accents linger in my ear, the stronger
grew the attraction of the road.

The Shaikh left and I heard no more of him, but I
missed him and his little room, a corner of Kurdistan
in Constantinople, with occupants whose home habits
remained unassailed by all the temptations of the city's
coffee-houses and comforts, and daily I could not help
picturing his progress across Syria, and gradually to the
borders of Kurdistan, the Tigris lowlands. I even hailed

the day he should have got to the first Kurdish town as notable, little dreaming that he had been robbed and nearly killed before he got there—by Kurds.

At last I made a compact with the weather: if it really cleared and warmed by a certain date, I would stay; otherwise, permitting no other consideration to hinder, I would resolutely book a passage to Beyrouth, and find my way to Kurdistan.

Funds certainly were scarce; I could not afford to travel as a European usually does, with servants, paying double for everything and occupying the best quarters everywhere. If I went I must don a fez and pass as a native of the East, must buy my own food, and do my own haggling, must do all those things which no European could or would ever think of doing. In Persia I had had experience of life in disguise as a Persian, and this would be an easier task for I was a stranger among strangers, and any difference in our ways and habits would be put down to that fact. There was a certain attraction, too, in going unattended by anyone, knowing practically no Turkish nor Arabic, across Syria and down the Tigris to Kurdistan. Once there I should be more at home, for I knew two or three dialects and Persian pretty perfectly, which would enable me to pass as a Persian among the Kurds, and to hide ignorance of that habit and custom which are the rule of life in the East. As to Muhammadan observances, I had in Persia learned all that, and as a Shi'a could say my prayers, and dispute the Qur'an with the best of them.

So, all things considered, the scheme recommended itself. It was cheap, I should see much new country, and many new tribes. I should learn many more Kurdish dialects, and when I had finished should be in possession of a truer knowledge of the people, their ways and nature, than a European possibly could in ten years.

So I sat down and waited for the decision of the weather.

CHAPTER II

FROM CONSTANTINOPLE TO HIERAPOLIS

"Chauakānam kaot ba chūl u raikadā
Halmbarī chū be vairān jakadā."
("My eyes were turned towards the solitude and road,
And I rose up and went to desert places.")
Song of the Erzinjan Kurds.

THE weather was not so fond of me as to clear up for the
sake of keeping me, for as the day of decision approached
it grew steadily worse, and it was in a driving storm of
cold rain that I waded down to Galata and booked a
passage by the Messageries Maritimes steamer to
Beyrouth.

There were few arrangements to make; a passport
I possessed; it was but necessary to provide myself with a
document called a "tezkere i ubūrī," a travelling passport
in Turkish, issued by the police. So having obtained an
order from the Consul, I found my way to a collection of
huts, called the "Eski Zaptié," in Stamboul, and after
running from hovel to hovel in order to interview
numerous effendis, whose duties apparently consisted of
making marks upon the application form, I was suddenly
presented with the document from an unsuspected corner
of a dirty courtyard. The writer was absolutely unaware
of my existence in the building, nevertheless I found
myself described in Turkish as of medium height, dark-
haired, and beardless, with black moustache, all fairly
accurate—last and most, of the "Protestant" religion. I
was to pass during most of my journey as a Muhammadan,
and here I found at the outset all my plans checked by a

16

Turkish clerk who described me in his fatuous passport as a Protestant. Naturally enough I protested, and vigorously, against the right of these omniscient police clerks to brand me as of any sect or creed; but they were mildly astonished at my objections, and could not be brought to see any point except that all Turks were Musulman, all Armenians "Kristiän," all French "Kātūlīk," and all English and Americans "Purūtestän." They but regarded these as the religious names of the nations, and could not conceive that an Englishman might be any one of the innumerable dissenting sects. That he could be a Catholic was too obviously absurd, and the increase of their contempt for my intelligence was most marked as I asserted the possibility. So the offending word had to stand, and I resolved secretly to erase or destroy it whenever necessary.

The day of departure was like the preceding months, rainy and cold, and I looked with pleasant anticipation upon the prospect of seeing in a few days the sunny hills of Syria. Our ship was the *Saghalien*, a comfortable and roomy old boat. The early spring season had brought with it the first of the tourists to Palestine. Arriving on board, I heard the first English that had fallen upon my ears since I had left London. The parties were incongruous enough. Four or five Roman Catholic priests escorted a company of pious "bourgeois" to the pilgrimage at Jerusalem, while another and much larger party of manufacturing folk of wealth and accent had been gathered from Leeds, Leicester, and a dozen other of the Midland towns of England. A second party had been formed by some imitator of Mr T. Cook, and included no less than six gentlemen of religious profession, each from a different sect of British dissenters. These were all provincial too. An American and his wife, a Turkish Pasha and his family and attendant effendis, and some unattached and inconsequent Germans and French, pretty well made up a full ship.

As I had to start wearing a fez sooner or later, I thought I might as well begin at once, and pass for a

B

Persian going to Persia, which would excuse my ignorance of Turkish, which no other disguise I could have adopted would have been effectual in doing. In the guise of a native of a far land, and *en route* for places where the name "English" was hardly known, I felt strangely cut off from my fellow Europeans when I heard them talking about their tour, planning expeditions and journeys new— when they should have "done" Palestine and Egypt, and returned once more to their Midland towns—experienced Oriental travellers.

It is strange what a simple exchange of headgear can do. Here was I, by the mere fact of wearing a fez, isolated, looked down upon by types one would pass unnoticed in London, audibly commented upon as "quite a civilised-looking Turk," exciting wonder as to "'ow many wives 'e's got," and such traditionally Oriental questions. The ignorance of these people was wonderful and colossal. We sighted, I remember, Mitylene one morning, and all the force of parsons and tourists hung over the rail with guide-books and glasses, disputed whether the high land was Chios or Rhodes, oblivious of the big chart on the top of the saloon stairs, where our position could be reckoned on the route line at the expense of two minutes' thought. They certainly appreciated the beauties of the glorious archipelago through which we passed, not too quickly, and faithfully enough raised enthusiasm in the places the guide-books recommended. Rhodes, when we did get there, and they were certain it was not Cyprus, created great excitement among them, the controversy anent the Colossus and his legs was heated enough to keep the subject alive quite two hours after the island had disappeared beneath the blue horizon, "quite as blue as the sea at Blackpool," as one Manchester man affirmed, in a spirit of rash generosity.

Before we had been two days at sea, I was drawn into uttering some words of English in a moment of thoughtlessness, and that to a very hearty individual from Newcastle. He trod heavily upon my feet, and as I quite involuntarily replied to his apology with an English phrase, he looked at me in the most utter astonishment, ejaculated, "Great 'eavens, you speak English."

"Yes," I said, "I was brought up in England."

"Oh," he replied, apparently relieved, "that accounts for it, you—er, where are ye goin' to?"

I told him I was going to Persia, and his hasty conclusion saved me the trouble of any equivocal statement for the moment, for he continued:

"Oh, then, I suppose you're one of those Persian gentlemen that's been in England lately for the Persian Parliament. 'Ow d'you like England, what part d'you know best?"

"Kent and Sussex," I replied, perfectly truthfully, ignoring his first remarks, "and all the south, for I have never been farther north than Lincoln."

Here we were joined by one of my interlocutor's friends, and I was introduced with some enthusiasm, my discoverer announcing in the tone of a naturalist who had just found a rare bug,

"This gentleman speaks English as well as you and me, every bit; 'e's a Persian, goin' to Persia."

Well, from that moment, I became very popular among these folk, and found them very hearty indeed, especially when I gave them the information that Persia looked to constitutional England for sympathy and help, and regarded her as a natural and ancient friend; in contradistinction to the Russians, whose Cossacks she detested. The fact of my being a Persian—naturally enough, they seemed to think—gave me a claim to their friendship, and nothing pleased them more than to get me to tell them of my country's wrongs, her aims and ambitions, her history and customs, her religion and literature, and every conceivable subject. On every such occasion I had a sympathetic and interested audience, who asked innumerable questions, and whom I was pleased to be able to enlighten considerably. They had to confess that their preconceived ideas were very changed, and the general attitude they acquired and which they were at no pains to conceal, being genuine and honest, if unpolished fellows, was that of well-informed superiority, which should assert itself on their return to England.

In playing this part I suppose I was playing also a very mean trick, the only excuse for which is that I am a sincere well-wisher of Persia, where I have spent some pleasant years of my life, and this disguise afforded my assertions an extra credence and weight which no Englishman, however well informed, could hope to obtain from his countrymen on so remote a subject as Persia.

So agreeably did the time pass, that I was sorry to see the hills of Beyrouth draw closer and closer. These were the last Englishmen that I should see for a long time, for my disguise quite prevented my being able to call upon consuls where they existed in towns upon my route. With considerable regret I bade them good-bye and saw them depart, led by one of those terrible creatures, a native Christian, the lust of tips and perquisites gleaming in his eyes. As I watched them, helpless and confused, being shoved this way and that, I almost envied them; for they were going to " sail " through Palestine in special trains and carriages, put up at the best hotels, and return in the same lordly fashion to England; while I was embarked upon a very different enterprise, to be conducted always with an eye to the elusive piastre, and a ready, lying tongue.

And so I found myself sharing, with two Turks and an Arab Christian of Aleppo, a small boat, from which we were bundled out into the Customs with a herd of Arabs, Turks, and all kinds of Levantines.

I was recommended by a Syrian who spoke French—like everyone else in Beyrouth—to put up in a small hotel on the quay, and was given a room overlooking the harbour, with a little verandah in front, where one must sit warily, for dirty locomotives shunting in the street had a way of stopping just underneath and firing with a particularly poisonous kind of coal, the while they blew off steam from remarkably noisy safety-valves. This was the terminus of the Lebanon Tramway, which crawls up the hills to a point called Rayak.

The hotel, kept by a Turk, was clean and cool, but to

feed one had to go round the corner to a kind of restaurant, "à la ferang," where an incongruous party of pilgrims of every race returning from Mecca sat uneasily on small chairs, and regarded with distrust the array of knives and forks a Greek waiter set before them.

Beyrouth—once one of the greatest maritime cities of the Phœnicians, when Tyre sent out her ships to the Tin Islands—has grown since then, and is now a flourishing and picturesque city, built upon the slopes of the hills that separate Syria from the Mediterranean. The population is, I should think, mostly Christian, and only in the alleys of a small bazaar does one see the real signs of an Oriental city. For the rest, there are broad and dusty roads, a large public square and gardens, and electric tramways everywhere. The language of the place is more French than Arabic, and English receives good attention at the American college there. Like Haifa and Tripoli on the same coast, it is on a little point of land and faces north, protecting its harbour by a strong sea-wall, enclosing a deep basin.

In the East one looks out as the first preparation for any journey, what the Turk calls a "youldāsh," and the Persian a "hamrāh," or travelling companion. On this occasion and without looking for him, he appeared, in the person of a Konia Turk, who was staying in the same hotel. We were to leave at sunset for Aleppo by the train, and my fortunate meeting with him, though our conversation was perforce limited owing to my ignorance of Turkish, enlightened me to the fact that we should be twenty-four hours *en route*, and must take pretty well whatever we wanted to eat with us. So we made an excursion to the native bazaar, and from the sellers of comestibles in baskets, procured a large quantity of excellent oranges and some bread and various kinds of sweet cakes.

At six o'clock we hired porters and carried our goods to the station, a shed on the quay a few yards away, and having registered our luggage at exorbitant rates, apparently solely by the overwhelming condescension of a military-looking effendi of abominable manners, we took tickets—second class to Aleppo. So well do the French control their employees, that my companion found afterwards that he had been charged two medjidies excess on the luggage and one on the ticket, which the effendi and the booking-clerk doubtless appropriated. I escaped these impositions apparently owing to the attentions of a young Arab porter, who for some inexplicable reason took me under his protection, as he refused all "bakhshīsh" when the train started.

The carriage in which we found ourselves face to face, with our knees knocking together, filled up with ten other persons. As the rolling-stock of this masterpiece of French railway engineering is barely six feet high, and narrow gauge, the temperature rose swiftly with the odour of the occupants. The seats or benches, which I surreptitiously measured, are exactly fifteen inches broad, and in this vehicle we were to—and did somehow—pass the night. Our fellow-passengers were four terribly frowsy Italian employees of the railway, and six uniformed individuals. Turks away from the towns whose inhabitants are Turkish seem always to be uniformed, and it is hopeless to guess at their standing and importance, which is always to be assumed in one's intercourse with the officials of this eminently officious race. These individuals were of course all "effendis," and three of them wore swords, which may have meant anything, as from subsequent observations it seems even a Customs clerk has that right. Fortunately, they were too taken up with their own affairs to notice us, and we consequently escaped for a time the merciless curiosity which emanates from a Turk, private or official.

About four in the morning, after uneasy and very shaken sleep, we were turned out in darkness and desert on the metals. This was Rayak, where the broadgauge line for Aleppo branches. Fortunately our new train, somewhat more commodious, was ready, and we made a rush, our new quarters being less crowded. Having taken our places, and while we were yet waiting, a sound as of flustered people, just arrived, and fearing to miss the train, broke the stillness. The first train had departed and every one was seated, and we apparently were stopping to allow passengers a nap in perfect quietness. The noisy knot of people thus naturally attracted attention, but what was my surprise to see in this Turco-Arabian land the face of an Isfahāni, of Persia, look into our window, glance away at companions following, and shout in the Persian of his native town that there was room.

A small crowd of very worried Isfahānis clad in their national dress came running, and doubtless would have left some of their number in our carriage, but that several effendis pursued them and headed them off wherever they attempted to gain entrance. Most of them knew no Arabic nor Turkish, but were obviously bent on getting to Aleppo. Puzzled at the inexplicable attitude of the omnipotent effendis, refusing place to these poor strangers, who emphatically announced that they had paid their fare, I leant out and asked one in Persian what was the trouble. For a moment he seemed to be dazed, hearing his own language spoken by a fezzed Turk, but his ears at last convinced him, and he poured out his woes.

"Bah! la'nat ullah 'alaihim" ("God's curse upon them!") he shouted. "From Damascus we had second-class tickets. They put us and our women in a cattle-truck, these sons of Sunni dogs; offspring of Turkish prostitutes, and now they refuse us even that;" and even as he spoke I heard a raucous voice shouting in Arabic, "La makān ul 'Ajam" ("There is no place for Persians"), and in the hated Turkish, "Get desharda! keupek oghlu!" ("Get outside, son of a dog!")

The unfortunate men—pilgrims returning from Mecca they were—were hustled from door to door, cursed and reviled for heretics and Shi'ahs, refused room anywhere. No insult was bad enough for these unfortunates, no jibe too cutting.

Suddenly from somewhere a French official appeared, who had as little sympathy with Sunni as with Shi'ah Musulman, and he solved the question by tacking an extra coach on, wherein the Persians were accommodated, and kept separate, their quarters infinitely more roomy and comfortable than those of their oppressors; and so we started and fell asleep, to wake in the early sunlight at Baalbak, a place great with memories of the past, but all too quickly left behind in the present, when the train, that cares nothing for the worship of Baal, pauses but a few moments, and continues its way over rolling plains with low hills in the distance to Homs and Hama, two Arab towns, whose Christian population saves them from the decay inseparable from Turkish rule and Musulman subjectivity.

Within some hours of Aleppo, two uniformed officials boarded the train, and shoving aside a passenger—not uniformed—installed themselves. After a few minutes, one, a fat, squinting person, produced a dirty and ragged little note-book and commenced making marks in it, the while looking at the passengers as one who sketches. Having completed this mysterious operation, he passed it to his companion, who, after reading it, passed it back with a " Pekī 'alā " (" Excellent! "), and both commenced eating oranges, dropping the peel carefully under their neighbours' feet. For half an hour or so they were thus engaged, when one, looking at his watch, remarked that it was late, and departed swiftly out of the door and along the foot-board. Some time after, he reappeared by the same way, and seating himself, reproduced his note-book and revealed his identity. He was a police officer; his duty was to ascertain whether all the passengers in the train might be allowed to enter Aleppo without danger of their inciting political riots or committing crimes of all sorts. This was four months after the inauguration of the Parliament, four months after we had been told that the old restrictions on travel instituted by the Sultan and his spies were absolutely abolished as being an abomination and a relic of despotism and darker ages.

However, this particular effendi was apparently far above such laws, as I found out everybody else to be later on, and insisted on full information. There was an unfortunate German mechanic travelling to Aleppo for the factory of a merchant there; and because he was a European, I suppose, the effendi subjected him to every annoyance possible, affecting to disbelieve his statements, practically accusing him of being a criminal. His profession worried the policeman, too, and I think, probably, exposed ignorance caused the petty revenge he took, for when he asked the European's profession, he was told " Muhandis," an engineer, and did not know the meaning of the word. My turn at length came, and I was in some fear of uncomfortable queries; for to state that I was an Englishman would have been utterly disbelieved in a land where our countrymen travel only in first-class reserved carriages, wear "solar topee" hats, and are attended by servants. To call myself a Persian would probably have satisfied the man, but there was always that damning passport, and of course I did not know but it might be examined in Aleppo side by side with this creature's notes.

So, knowing but little of his Arabi and Turkish, I feigned total ignorance, indicating by signs that I was going to Persia, pointing to myself, the eastern distance, and repeating " B'il 'Ajam ("to Persia"). He asked me innumerable questions, which had I answered would have tied me up in a terrible confusion of contradictions, but at last, failing to get any reply from me he suddenly desisted, finding no amusement in the sport, I suppose, and passed on to a more intelligible victim.

About four o'clock in the afternoon we arrived at Aleppo, or rather at Aleppo station, terminus of that creeping railway, rejoicing in the extraordinary name of " Chemin de Fer de Damas Prolongement Homs et Hama."

To my surprise, no one asked for passports, the only annoyance was that second-class passengers' registered luggage would not be distributed for another hour. While receiving this information I was furiously attacked by a kind of hotel tout, fortunately the last I was to see, for I left both hotels and touts behind with Aleppo. However, I submitted to be thrust into a carriage and found myself careering along a straight, broad road towards the town, whose chief feature is the castle upon its flat-topped mound. Modern Aleppo is obviously an Arab city, the language is Arabic, French has not yet displaced it as at Beyrouth, while it possesses a few broad streets, where the badly written French signs of Greek, Armenian, and Syrian shopkeepers, photographers and hotel-keepers hang. The majority of its ways are stone-paved alleys between high walls, with the lattice-windows always associated in the Western mind with Aleppo. Beyond that it possesses a splendid bazaar, rows and rows of booths in the ordinary Oriental style, whose owners squat within, selling the European and native articles to be met with in all bazaars from Constantinople to Afghanistan. To him who has dwelt in the farther East, it comes like the first step towards the old country again. With joy I roamed through these busy alleys of shops, and purchased my road apparatus, candles, sugar, tea, tin and glass tea utensils, knobs of cheese, fruit, etc., of Arabs sitting behind rows of pendant sugar loaves and tin cans, entrenched among masses of heterogeneous wares.

In point of view of the antiquity of Aleppo, only excelled in Western Asia by Damascus (which after 3500 years of importance, still maintains its premier position), some note of its history is due.

That it was a city of the Hittites is witnessed by the inscriptions in that language within the citadel gates, and at present we know of no antiquity greater in Syria than that of this wonderful empire, that lasted for the enormous period of 3000 years (3700-700 B.C.), and of which there will be occasion to speak later. Though little, if anything, is heard of Aleppo in the ancient chronicles, it is so near to the ancient Karkhemish (Corchemish of the Old Testament), that it probably stood and fell with it during the wars with Assyria, which lasted from 1100-700 B.C., though no mention of it occurs in the stone inscriptions of Nineveh, Kalah, Kuyunjik, and Asshur.

In the storm of nations, Scythians, Cimmerians, Arabs, and—above all—Medes, that raged when Assyria fell,

Karkhemish is forgotten and Aleppo is not heard of till Christian times.

It was probably converted to Christianity about the time St Paul sent his message to Antioch (Acts xi. 19-24), but it is in Muhammadan times that it really begins to play a part in Syrian politics. It was then the see of a bishopric, and was sufficiently important to be contended for in the early days of Islam, when a great battle was fought in the vicinity (A.D. 657). In A.D. 1056 the great conqueror Alp Arslan took it, and a century later saw Saladin defending its castle against the Crusaders. It fell, like all Western Asia, before the barbarian Mongols in 1260, and was sacked.

It has in more recent days produced many theologians and men of Muhammadan learning.

In the Turko-Egyptian war of the middle of last century, fighting took place there, the Egyptian army bombarding the city. A large barrack built by their commander, Ibrahim Pasha, still stands, to harbour Turkish soldiers, just outside the town.

That I was unable to explore the now empty fortress was a great disappointment, but even had it been possible, I could have learned nothing more than the many historians and archæologists who have visited it, and provided the reading public with every detail of its history, past and present. Besides this, Aleppo has been one of the best known of Oriental cities, particularly to English people, for here have lived and died agents of the Levant Company, and our Levant trade has ever had Aleppo for a prominent buyer.

Like Diarbekr, Mosul, and Bagdad, Aleppo lost much of its importance with the opening of the Suez canal, previous to which time it had been on the northern overland route to the East. Still, the advent of the railway, feeble as that is, has done something to restore it to its former importance, though the Turks, as everywhere else that they rule, have cast the blight of their presence upon it. At present it manufactures a large quantity of cotton cloth which is exported very largely Eastwards, and forms the principal dress material for the population of Southern Turkish Kurdistan and Northern Mesopotamia.

I had hardly been in Aleppo half a day, at a filthy place boasting the name of " Hotel de Syrie," kept by an Armenian—a fact which did not prevent Musulmans staying there—when a Turkish coachman turned up willing to take me to Diarbelr, the next big town on my route. I held out for two days' grace, but he, having clients at the other end waiting to be brought back, would hear of no delay, and so after a few hours I found myself mounted in one of those queer vehicles that ply between the cities of Syria.

The concern is rather like a punt on wheels. A wooden or canvas-covered top shelters passenger and driver, and curtains, when they exist, may be let down to guard the traveller from sun and storm. In this all the luggage must be placed, and comfort depends upon the skill with which things are arranged. Fortunately I had little, and putting my only trunk at the fore end I was able to retain a large square space, with a mattress under me to sit or recline upon.

Small articles like water-pots or samovars are tied on outside at various points, and there exist till broken or squashed, their almost inevitable fate. Commissariat has also to be arranged, for the supply *en route* is sometimes uncertain. Travelling light as I was, we only carried flaps of bread, some dates and onions. Fruit was unfortunately not in season in this month of March.

My coachman for some reason took me for a Haji returning from Mecca, and I found this such an excellent disguise, ensuring such civility on the road, that I was content to let it stand, till too late to change, and forthwith wound about my fez the white handkerchief which is a sign of the pilgrim homeward bound. We left Aleppo in our carriage thus one noonday, and a few minutes outside the town and over the ridge, one looked round and saw nothing but the yellow Syrian desert devoid of hills, the surface only occasionally disturbed by Arab villages, like clusters of anthills, the style of

architecture as far as the Euphrates being all of the
sugar-loaf pattern. For some hours our two ponies took
us along the level track—there is no made road—till
nearly sunset, when among a few mounds we suddenly
came upon a village the natives call Bāb. Doubtless
proximity to Aleppo may account for the excellent little
bazaar, cleanly and good caravanserai, in one of whose
upper rooms, overlooking the courtyard full of mules,
donkeys, camels, horses, and sheep, I found a resting-
place. Built of white stone, this caravanserai in point of
comfort was one of the best I have seen in many years'
wanderings. Design it had none—one block of rooms,
some nine feet above ground, formed one side. Opposite
were large stables, on the roof of which was the row of
rooms of which I occupied one. The entrance to the
caravanserai was the usual kind of deep porch with small
chambers on either side, and above the archway of the
entrance the enterprising architect had constructed two
excellent rooms with glass windows, for the wives of
wealthy travellers, opening on to a little fenced space
of roof where they might promenade. The "khanchi"
or keeper of the serai pointed to this with pride.
The rooms, he informed us, were special accommodation for travelling pashas and such great game,
and the chicken-run of a promenade was considered
to be absolutely the last word in the progress of architecture.

The first experiences of travelling in native guise
reveal many little things one never thought of before,
when, as Europeans, we arrived at a stage, had our room
quickly swept and carpeted, camp tables and chairs set
out, and steaming tea swiftly produced. Certainly I
did not have to sweep my room on this occasion, though
subsequently I learned to wield the three blades of grass
they call a broom in these parts. Water, too, the khanchi
fetched. But my small belongings, which it was not safe
to leave in the carriage, I had to bring up, and made
several journeys up and down the narrow steps from
courtyard to roof, laden with mattress, quilt, blanket, and

the bags and bundles without which one finds it impossible to travel in the East.

Then I discovered that I needed tea very badly, so I had to go downstairs with my tin samovar, draw water from a well, fill it, and beg the lighted coal from a coachman whom I saw smoking a hubble-bubble. This done, I retired to my heights again, and after some time enjoyed a glass of tea and some dry bread.

At this juncture my coachman appeared, and expressed his astonishment that I had not followed the custom of travellers arriving in a strange place—to visit the bazaar.

This I had omitted to do, in fact had not thought of it. Now it was just sunset, I had no dinner to eat, the bazaar was closing; and worse, there was nothing, not even bread, in my bags for to-morrow's twelve hours in the desert. By this time I could get on fairly well with Turkish, but suddenly my coachman exclaimed, in a fit of geniality, "Az kurmānjī dazānam" ("I know Kurdish"!), and I found in a moment a new means of communication, for though I did not know the Kermanji dialect well, it is sufficiently near some others I did know, to be intelligible. I found afterwards that from the fact of my hailing Kurdish as an old friend, my coachman, who had been at some pains to find out my native place, a point always to be settled with one's travelling companion in the East, had at once registered me as a native of Persian Kurdistan. So with status as a Haji of Kurdistan conferred on me, I was introduced as such by my friend the coachman to all and sundry.

Here he proved a real friend, for he offered to show me the bazaar and try to get bread and some dinner before closing time. The bazaar was a small one, but fortunately there was a tiny cookshop, where exactly three kinds of very greasy pilau were on sale. From these I selected the least uninviting, and arranged for the proprietor to send a couple of plates of it to the caravanserai. We went into the village baker's, and there I found the great advantage of being, first, a Haji, and next, a strange Haji. At first the man, who was closing his shop, was very loth to serve us; but my guide, in tones of pained remonstrance, mentioned that I was a Haji, and the man hesitated, and finally began to throw bread into his scales. As a means to get full weight, Muhammad, the coachman, threw in the remark that I was a stranger from far away, knowing neither tongue, nor country, nor custom. The worthy baker, with a sententious remark upon the virtue of honouring the stranger and the acquisition of merit, threw in an extra piece and looked to me for the pious expression that was his due, and which I was fortunately able to supply in Arabic, much to his gratification. When we asked him the price, he actually told us the right amount without any haggling, and remarked upon the wickedness of harassing the stranger. This excellent attitude I found in many places, that is, wherever there were Kurds or Arabs. Turks are another race in manner and custom. I found my dinner waiting at the caravanserai, and invited my coachman to partake, for I knew that the humble station I occupied in the social scale was only equal to, if not lower than, that of a coachman.

With frank gratitude he squatted opposite me, and with our fingers we finished the mess. Previous experience in Persia had taught me how to negotiate semi-liquid dishes with a piece of bread and two fingers, or consume piles of rice without feeding one's surroundings. Also I knew the style of ablution necessary, and the formulæ of thanksgiving after eating. This latter was not called for on the road, for religious observance falls into considerable desuetude among the slaves of the desert track. Dinner finished — it took about three minutes—we shared each other's cigarettes, and as he departed to attend to his horses and I retired under a fold of my coat in a corner of the room, I felt that once more I was back in that generous and genial East that I had known before, so many hundreds of miles nearer the rising sun.

Next morning before daybreak we were up and on the way, and the sun rising showed us the same yellow undulating plain with now a range of distant hills to the north of us. We were not taking the usual track across the desert, which goes as a rule more northwards towards Birejiq, a town whose chief feature is a castle built during the wars of the Crusade.

Our way lay towards Membich, a city with almost the most ancient history of the Syrian desert—Karkhemish always excepted. We were traversing the lands which have seen the cultivation of the great Hittite nation that is said to have had its capital at Karkhemish but a few miles from here, about 3500 B.C., an age only excelled by Babylonia herself. From that time till the conquest of these lands by the Assyrians, some 700 years B.C., the king of the Hittites ruled over what was then doubtless a fertile country. It is about the Euphrates banks that some of the greatest battles of the world have raged. Hittite, Assyrian, Greek, Parthian, have all fought for Syria, and won and lost it; and Membich, that had a temple to the goddess Atergatis (of whom more hereafter), existed as a wealthy city, and stood for all these centuries, to be despoiled at the hand of a Roman plebeian, a place-buyer, whose ambition and greed eventually brought him to well-deserved ruin. This was Marcus Lucius Crassus, who in 54 B.C., in a campaign against the Parthians, "entered the shrine, carefully weighed all the offerings in the precious metals, and then ruthlessly carried them off." [1]

The town was not, however, destroyed, for it was ceded by Anthony, some twenty years later, to a deserter from Parthia, who, after holding it for a few months, once more returned to Parthia, leaving it in Roman hands.

To a field of ruined walls, piles of enormous carven stones, mounds betokening ancient buildings, we came that evening. Upon the highest mound is now a little mosque, and the place is peopled by a number of Circassian immigrants, who in their Cossack dress looked singularly out of place among the Arabs around them. On all sides are the remains of ancient buildings, stones too great to carry away. Their principal use to-day appears to be to

[1] Rawlinson, *Parthia*, p. 152.

wall in the fields of grain, and when not too large for transport, to form new buildings in the dirty, squalid village, whose accommodation—three filthy rooms, all that remains of a caravanserai—is in keeping with the tone of the place.

Here we blessed the foresight that had made us bring some eatables from Bāb, for the surly inhabitants refused to supply anything but eggs, which were at the price of six for the equivalent of a penny. The water was bad, our supply being from a shallow well (just outside a particularly odorous cesspool), from which half the village came to draw water.

Since there was no bazaar to go to, nothing to do, nothing to buy and eat, I spent the time sitting on my door-step, for there were too many flies to share the room with, and nightfall and sleep came very welcome.

CHAPTER III

FROM THE EUPHRATES TO THE TIGRIS, EDESSA (URFA), AND AMID (DIARBEKR)

THERE are, I believe, no remains in Membich of the temple of Atergatis which Crassus spoiled, and even at Karkhemish there is nothing but a mound unopened and kept closed by the Turks, to show where a great goddess, probably the greatest goddess of ancient times, was worshipped.

In reading the histories of Chaldea, Syria, Canaan, the Hittites, Israelites, Phœnicians, and Greeks, there appears as the chief goddess in their mythology always a goddess of victory, or love, and it is interesting to trace the course of this deity through the religions of the ancient East. The Chaldean race, which inhabited the lowlands, at the mouths of the Euphrates and Tigris, from ages far beyond our knowledge, had, from earliest times set up a goddess, "Belit," the lady, and it is from her that the later goddesses of other nations, or rather the later names and worship, sprang.

It is now known that the Hittites (for whose history the world is indebted to the wonderful research of Professor Sayce) were an extraordinarily powerful nation, that held the lands of Syria from about 3700 B.C.[1] to 700 B.C., when the Assyrians overcame them. During this period they came into contact with the civilisation of Babylon, and, long before the appearance of the Syrians as a nation, probably adopted the worship of Belit or Ishtar (the same deity), whose name they altered to Atergatis. The

[1] Ragozin, Assyria.

worship of Atergatis was general among the peoples of Canaan (Syria), under the name of Ashtoreth, or Ashtaroth as we find it in the Bible.

The Canaanitic mythology also supplied a fundamental idea of male and female essence in Baal and Ashtaroth, with whom we are familiarised by the Bible stories ; and this idea of the origin of fecundity and power, Baal, the God of all the living principles, according to the Canaanitic peoples, was the deity after whom the Israelites so often strayed; and Ashtaroth, the goddess of motherhood, love, and sensuality, necessarily was coupled with him.

Baal or Bel, or Moloch, the Sun-god, or Dagon, are all names of the same god, according to different tribes and peoples, who adopted this, probably the earliest conception of any worship of the supernatural arising from reverence of the sun and moon as the emblems of day and night, fire and moisture, heat and cold, light and dark, life and death, as twin gods of these antithetic phenomena—in short, the symbols of existence at all.

So we find the goddess Ishtar worshipped by the Phœnicians as Ashtoreth, by the Hittites as Atergatis, by the Philistines and Canaanites as Derketo, the fish-goddess (whose emblem and likeness was that of a half-woman, half-fish, as that of Dagon, the god, was that of a fish-man).

It was of course to these that the high places whereon they erected "Asherah," or places of adoration, were dedicated, and against them that the prophets of Israel were sent.

Thus we find Elijah sent against the priests of Baal (the Syrian version, the fire-god), who called upon their god, since he had in their mythology retained the first principle of fire, to send down that element.

However, Ishtar, or whatever one of her names we may call her, played a more important part in the history of Western Asia than the Sun-god himself. To her, temples were erected by all the nations worshipping, and she retained through all, the suzerainty over the planet Venus, her particular sign and emblem.

Yet even among the Assyrians, who probably exalted her name more than any other nation, she bore a dual character, for we read that she had a temple at Nineveh and another at Arbela—a place dedicated originally to four gods. Now the Ishtar of Nineveh was essentially a goddess of love and luxury, who ruled the planet Venus; but she of Arbela gave victory in battle and strengthened the arm of the warrior.

It was at any rate a powerful and compelling religion this, that lasted through four thousand years of battles, of races that appeared, rose to importance and vanished, of peoples as little in sympathy with natural feeling as the Phœnicians and Assyrians, as the Hittites or Chaldeans. The worship of this goddess went on claiming homage from the mighty kings of the Hittites, the Chaldeans, and the Assyrians, keeping subject the host of nations, great and small, from Persia to the Mediterranean coast.

And now we are told that the Hittite kingdom extended to Ionia, and temples were erected to the goddess at Ephesus and Smyrna. Here came the Greeks as colonists, and, adopting the hosts of female attendants and priestesses as a basis, founded the legend of the Amazons. Not only that, but they adopted and adapted the worship of Atergatis, giving her a Greek name, under which she achieved a greater fame and commanded a greater reverence that any goddess of the pure Greek mythology.

And here, in this hamlet of Membich that was called Hierapolis during Greek supremacy, was one of the chief Syrian temples in the last day of her worship (54 B.C.). When this occurred, the Hittites had been gone into the oblivion of the past some 650 years, but the goddess, and perhaps her temple, an offshoot of the greater temple of Karkhemish, still stood.

For what we know of the Hittites we are indebted, as above mentioned, to Professor E. G. Sayce, who first announced to an astonished world of Orientalists and students, a great Hittite nation, the existence of which had been to that day—not two decades ago—absolutely unknown.

We now know that the Hittite empire lasted for the enormous period of about 3000 years.

The Chaldean chronicles mention them as a nation, in the date 3500 B.C. (*circa*). The seat of the nation appears to have been at Karkhemish, but before that they had been domiciled in the Taurus Mountains and the hills of Armenia, whence they descended, a hardy mountain race, to the lowlands of Canaan.

They were the descendants of Heth, son of Canaan (Genesis x. 15), and once settled in Karkhemish, where the chief temple to Atergatis was built (modern Jerabulus), extended their kingdom from the Bosphorus to the confines of Egypt, with whose Pharaohs they fought long and sanguinary battles.

Like all peoples in the East, even in the present day, they would appear to have been tribal in constitution, but their chief king was he of Karkhemish, with a lieutenant king at Kadesh in the south.

However, their might, long-lived as it was, fell before the onrush of the Assyrians, then but a young race, comparatively newly separated from the Chaldeans and Babylonians, and in 700 B.C. the last of the Hittite kings, who had been for some time tributary to Sargon, rebelled against his stronger neighbours, was defeated, and the last remnant of the Hittite empire, which had grown weak and dismembered, was destroyed and forgotten.

At Karkhemish, the capital through so many centuries of the Hittite empire, and chief city of the worship of Atergatis, there remains now but the great mound. War has again raged over the remains of greater combatants, for the Turks were defeated by the Egyptians there half a century ago.

Its interest to-day lies in the fact that the Bagdad railway is planned to cross the river just by the mound of Karkhemish, so we may look for bulky volumes in German some day, which will give us fuller particulars of this ancient city than we possess at present.

We left Membich very early next morning, and *en route* discovered that several other carriages had put up in the place during the night; for both behind and before were rumbling, swaying vehicles, two or three full of luggage, and the rest carrying passengers. From Membich the country—as barren as ever—began to get a little hilly, and in the far northern distance we could see the Kurdish mountains in the province of Mamurat ul Aziz, at this time of the year well capped with snow.

For a few hours we got along at a good pace among the low hills, till we received a sudden check from a very steep place going down, and as we turned the elbow of a hillock, the Euphrates appeared below us, an angry, rushing river of very considerable width. By devious and dangerous ways we arrived at a broad foreshore, to find half a dozen carriages already arrived, and by the time the contingent from Membich had been drawn up there were twelve all in a line, the horses unsaddled, waiting to be ferried across by a craft rather like a high-prowed long-ship cut in half at the waist. Upon the high stern a man wielded an enormously long steering-oar and two or three others with poles and oars supplied a propelling power. But it was not merely a question of rowing across; there were but two landing-places, one on either side, and the current was of such a force as to render it absolutely necessary to tow the craft about a mile above the proposed landing-place on the opposite bank. Then, shoving off, everybody exerted their utmost strength to get the clumsy craft across the river, and if they were sufficiently quick and strong, they would perhaps hit the spot where the waiting carriages stood. If they came to shore lower down, there was of course nothing to do but tow back again. Necessarily the transit of a couple of carriages and their horses (the utmost capacity of the ferry), counting from the time another party had landed on the opposite bank, took two or three hours.

Our large party of passengers, seeing that delay would inevitably occur, were disposed to come to an amicable arrangement regarding precedence. Unfortunately we discovered that half the vehicles were hired by the Chief of Police of Urfa to transport himself, his goods and women-folk, and though he had—from what his fellow-travellers said—evinced no desire for speed so far, he now turned upon every one of us who talked of arranging an order of crossing, brandished his sword, and upbraided the company in general for proposing any such arrangement in his presence, which should be sufficient to give us the clue to all matters of precedence.

He would go first with all his goods and women, and whoever paid him would follow him in the order of the magnitude of their contribution. The Turkish and Armenian drivers seemed so effectually cowed by his disagreeable appearance and offensive manners, that most of them—ignoring his offer of precedence by payment—retired some distance and began to lunch, content to let him get clear away. Two cartloads of Christians of Urfa, however, intimidated by his continued attempts to extort money, paid and got away during the afternoon.

The remainder of us arranged who should go first, and, making the best of the hours we had to wait, composed ourselves to that which fills up so much of the idle time of the East—sleep.

It was nearly sunset before we finally got across, and found ourselves on the broad plain of the Euphrates valley. With all despatch we harnessed up and set out. Arriving at the caravanserai, we found it full of the effendi and his chattels, and the travellers who had followed him; so, making the best of a bad job, we went on, trusting to luck to find a place to sleep.

We had traversed the plain and were gradually ascending a pleasant hilly country by moonlight, when the driver descried a cluster of sugar-loaf roofs just off the road, and we stopped to interview the inhabitants.

A couple of finely built men came out, apparently Arabs, but they had not spoken half a dozen words to one another before we saw that they were Kurds. This resolved both the driver and myself to stay, for the Kurds, with all their bad reputation, are better hosts than Armenian, Turk, or Arab. Eventually, when a number of children and sheep had been dragged out from what appeared to be a cellar, they told me that the best room in the place was at my disposal. Descending three steps, and passing along a dark narrow corridor, I found myself in a circular chamber whose high sugar-loaf roof was invisible in the gloom undispersed by a tuft of burning brushwood.

The Kurds, with continual joking and merriment, tripping one another up, as they brought in the baggage, eventually deposited all my belongings in the room, and then installed themselves. The hamlet had a population of some fifteen men and women, and within five minutes these were all gathered around my strip of carpet. One of them knew Turkish, and tried it on me, taking me for a Turk; but when I replied in Kurdish, telling them I did not understand Turkish, they evinced considerable satisfaction, and hailed me as a brother Kurd, albeit of some other tribe (these were of the Milli), but nevertheless a fellow-countryman, and to be treated as a guest. And right well did these simple people act up to the fine old Kurdish law of hospitality. They possessed little enough of the world's goods, but their best fowl was sacrificed to the occasion, eggs in numbers sufficient for ten men were produced. Every one of them except the headman, who sat by as host, busied himself about something. One made a fire in the centre of the room, making gloomier the gloom with pungent smoke; another fetched water for washing—they would not let me go outside in the keen wind, to the spring. One heated water for tea, while his companions killed and plucked and commenced cooking the fowl. Surplus eggs they hard-boiled and put up for my journey next day. I felt ashamed to be imposing thus upon these simple and genuine people, only I knew that utter incredulity would have met any attempt I might have made to undeceive them. What could they think of a man whose only means of communication not only with them, but with the whole world of Syria, was Kurdish? I found, however, that the appreciation they evinced for tea and good cigarettes, luxuries unknown to them except by name, quite outbalanced my qualms. The unfortunate driver, who was subject to fits of surliness, finding his protégé in such a state of independence, gave way to a period of disagreeableness which the jibes of the Kurds did nothing to dispel, and finally retired to sleep among his horses' legs. As a race, Kurds are a witty and facetious people, great lovers of practical jokes; but I think these excelled any I ever met in this particular feature. The séance was one continual roar of laughter; despite their inquisitiveness, their personal remarks, their habit of fingering everything, the whole tone of their behaviour was too obviously ingenuous and well meant, possibly to offend any but Turks, whom they cursed and reviled, and made the subject of many unmentionable pleasantries. About ten o'clock the headman, a handsome fellow, doubly important in the possession of the village rifle, told every-one to clear out and let me sleep, and they retired, driven by the butt of the ancient fire-arm.

I was composing myself to sleep when a young woman came in, and began quietly to sweep the room with a bunch of twigs. Not unnaturally I sat up and regarded her with some astonishment, not lessened when she pro-duced from a recess some bedding, which she put down beside mine. I was hardly in a position to make a remark upon her obvious intention to share the room, but the situation was saved by the appearance of one of my friends of the earlier evening. He saw me sitting up, and asked why I did not sleep, as if the proceedings which had just taken place were too ordinary for remark, and I learned in reply to half-formed questions that he was the house-owner, his wife the sweeper, and that owing to the size of the village, which possessed but two rooms fit to sleep in, they were going to spend the night beside me. This method of procedure was propounded by him in such a matter-of-fact way, and was so apparently quite the thing to do, that I could not, nor did I wish, to make any remark upon what was a purely patriarchal custom. What I learned was, that had I been a Turk or Arab, they would have told me to sleep in the carriage; but being a Kurd, and a guest, I must excuse their presumption in occupying the room, which was my exclusive property. The poor man even seemed somewhat ashamed at having possibly broken some unwritten rule of hospitality, but I did my best to put him and his wife at ease, and we literally lay down together.

I was awakened by the wife early in the morning; her man yet slumbered. She herself carried out the small luggage to the carriage, and then two or three villagers turned out and loaded up the heavy things. Last of all the headman appeared, and, as we drove away, the sound of his rough hearty farewells rang in my ears. These were the first Kurds I met, the outposts of a great race, that covers 125,000 square miles of mountain in Turkey and Persia, and who, despite the fact that their outlying tribes are but fourteen days distant from London, are the least known of any Middle Eastern race; albeit they are one of the bravest, most independent, and intelligent of all, cursed only by the black mark of the blood-feud, and a terrible propensity to brigandage.

The way to our next station was across an undulating plain peopled by Armenians, and sedentary Kurds of the Milli tribes. For miles and miles we rolled along between ploughed lands, where the grain was just beginning to send its green spikes above earth. From the north a keen wind came at a temperature obviously lowered by the snow on the hills, about whose shoulders rags of cloud were beginning to collect, to drench the land and the travellers therein but a few days later. In fact, rain had already fallen by the afternoon—when we found ourselves upon a dreary and immense plain of mud, sticky, clayey soil, into which the wheels and the horses sank. Our station, Charmelik, was visible in the far distance, a distance we seemed never to be able to reduce, for the sticky prospect spread out on all sides, and our speed was about half a mile an hour. Sudden showers began to fly round the country. One could count them as they descended from the hills, and progressing swiftly—columns of dark rain descending from dense black cloud-centres—

did the round of the soaked plains, and apparently returned to the mountains and the solid mass of cloud that hung about them.

However, we did arrive at Charmelik at sunset, and put up in a little room. The village is a Kurdish one, and talk among the inhabitants was mostly of Ibrahim Pasha, the famous robber chief who held this country in terror for so long.

So bad a character was he, this outlaw (who adopted his trade in revenge for the Turkish treachery that brought his father to a miserable end), that Kurd and Arab alike disclaimed him; Kurd asserting that he was Arab, and Arab calling him Kurd.

The body of ruffians and thieves that joined him were of every class—Turk, Armenian, Kurd, and Arab. All served under his standard, and by his disregard for the property of any tribe or people he drew upon himself the enmity of his own kinsmen, the Milli Kurds.

But like every astute robber and scoundrel in the Turkish dominions, he bought the Sultan's favour, and could and did ridicule all the efforts of local government to catch him. For the most part he frequented the hills that border on the Mesopotamian plain to the north, but he was also a power in Viran Shahr and Harran to the south, where he kept everyone in a lively fear of him. Not until the Turks arranged themselves into a Constitution was this powerful brigand, by a ruse, caught and killed, and the heterogeneous collection of rascals dispersed.

The villagers of Charmelik related how his men would follow travellers into the village, instal themselves in the best room, order a meal, and having rested and smoked a pipe or two, stroll out, calmly load the traveller's effects upon his own cart and take them away to their nearest camp. So much were their reprisals feared—for revenge upon a village was burning and extermination—that not a single person dared protest. Even Turkish officers and officials had to submit to this treatment, and, so the reminiscent throng round the fire assured me, suffer a good beating in the bargain for being of the detested race.

Altogether, Ibrahim Pasha's was one of the most successful and best organised of the Kurdish raiding parties, and numerically the most powerful. The only other combination, formed solely for the purpose of brigandage and revenge, was that of the Hamavand, whose acquaintance I made later, in southern Kurdistan.

We left this village next morning in a freezing cold, and the sun coming up, found us gradually ascending through gullies and defiles into a considerable range of hills. In that much-abused country, Persia, I have travelled many hundreds of miles by carriage, but I must in justice say, that the worst tracks in that maligned and unhappy country are paved boulevards compared to the carriage-ways of Turkey. Here, within easy distance of the sea and of the influence of Constantinople, the track passes untouched by any of the French-speaking, liquor-loving effindis appointed to look after such things ; whereas in Persia there are excellent roads built by the foreign enterprise that she sometimes welcomes and Turkey discourages ; and where the European engineer has not made smooth the way, the Persian himself, with no other notion than to ease the pains of travellers, has done his best, by clearing stones and putting down causeways.

For hours we ascended ravines, and slid, banging, down hill-sides, boxes and chattels of all descriptions almost taking charge despite their substantial lashings. Do what one might, inconsequent paraphernalia, eatables, small articles, would leap out and roll away, and one had the greatest difficulty in exercising sufficient restraint upon the overwhelming inclination to follow head first. For miles both myself and the driver walked, helping the wheels over rocks, piloting the carriage round corners of rocky zigzags, or helping the horses in desperate efforts to haul up slopes.

Here and there was a little patch of cultivation among the stones, and a spring made green narrow places in almost every valley. As we neared Urfa, our next stopping-place, ancient cave-dwellings, now unoccupied, began to occur, and bits of carved stone here and there lay about. In one flat plain, some two miles across, were the remains of a large square building, of the style one associates with pre-Muhammadan times, when mud did not enjoy its present popularity with masons.

However, our troubles ceased suddenly, for turning a particularly bad corner we found ourselves upon a very well-made road that continued all the way into Urfa. This is, I believe, the only made road in Syria, and was the outcome of a project to construct a military and commercial route as far as Diarbekr. The effort expired a few miles north-east of Urfa. Once upon this, we saw what would have been our fate without it, and I quite believed the driver's statement that, previous to its construction, the passes were not negotiable by wheeled vehicles.

On the way we met with a proof of the curious devotion that leads the Musulman from the remotest corners of Asia to Mecca. An old man, in garments that reminded me of Khorasan of Eastern Persia, overtook us, his stride taking him at a greater pace up the hill than our slow walk. I asked him, as a venture, in Persian where he came from, and learned that he was a pilgrim returning on foot from Mecca to Bokhara. His journey he estimated would have taken him nearly a year, from the time he started from his native town to the time he saw it again. He had the appearance of fifty or more years, but none of the feebleness that might be expected, and marched along—having that day done some twenty miles of mountain—as if he were just set out.

Beside the road, as we neared Urfa, there were, in bad repair, remains of an ancient causeway, the original road to the west from Edessa, as Urfa was known in pre-Christian days. Along the paved way of square blocks of stone the armies of the Roman and the Parthian had passed in the days when men worshipped Venus and Astarte.

Urfa, at the foot of this considerable range, stands upon some hillocks, and once the hideous dwelling of the Governor—built in imitation French style—is passed, the ancient nature of the town becomes evident. The peculiar blackness of the massive walls, whose ruins stand everywhere, the style of the bridges that span the ravine amid the city, the citadel mounds, topped with ruins of buildings all of that blackened stone, tell something of the history of Edessa. And in the hills above the light yellow cliffs that look down, are the innumerable cave-dwellings of the ancients, now occupied by nondescript families of sedentary Kurds.

We drew up at a large caravanserai at the edge of the ravine above mentioned, and I took one of a row of rooms upon its spacious roof, that afforded a promenade from which one could look up at the honeycombed hills, or view the clustered houses upon the hummock forming the Armenian quarter. Contrary to custom, the room, which opened upon the roof, and faced the courtyard, possessed glassless windows, looking down upon the street and a coffee-house. This is not enclosed, but is an extension of the actual coffee-room, the other side of the caravanserai. Along the moat edge, benches are arranged, and trees and matting shelters keep the sun off. Along the strip of road running between this café and the caravanserai walls the town auctioneers paraded every morning, selling every conceivable article, from a handful of cartridges to a horse.

Bids were made by the guests in the café as he passed and repassed singing out the last offer. In many cases his price not being reached, he would hand the horse, or whatever it might be, back to the owner and go on with something else, producing the under-priced animal next morning.

As in nearly all the towns of this empire, half the population of the streets and nine-tenths of all the café and corner loafers were effendis in uniform, who never by any chance appeared to have any kind of duties. In fact, Urfa, I was told, possessed a larger proportion than any other town of these undesirable fowl. Fortunately, they did not worry me: I was to learn their skill in annoyance later. Here the attractions of coffee and pipes apparently outweighed those of the possible piastre of the traveller. The population, apart from these signs of Turkish might, is composed of Kurds and Arabs, and an enormous number of Armenians. The Kurds come from the north, mostly out of the hills of Mamuret ul Aziz; the Arabs are from the plains of Mesopotamia, and probably have the claim to be considered the original inhabitants. The language is Kurdish and Arabic. Kurdish is understood by all, for it has forced itself upon the partially alien population as it does everywhere, displacing older established languages with its extraordinary virility and vitality.

The town is not a large one, but its bazaar is very busy, and its Government House always thronged with people. There is a square with a few trees, and the place is sprinkled with bits of old buildings, some adapted to modern use, and others built into new walls. Under the hills one is shown the Pool of Abraham, who is supposed to have performed various feats here. The water-supply is plentiful, the scenery around beautiful in its ruggedness and the fantastic nature of its hills, and I was told that there are very pretty gardens in the immediate vicinity. It is one of those places one sees so often in Asiatic Turkey, where life could be peaceful among beautiful surroundings and prosperity assured, were it not for the Turks and their misrule.

Urfa, or Edessa as the Romans called it, stood in Assyrian times upon the borders of Greater Assyria, and "the lands of Nairi," the highlands immediately to the north, which are now known as the western end of Kurdistan, and its name does not appear as a city till the time of the Roman invasion, when we hear of it as the capital of the country of Osrhœne, whose kings were always called Abgarus, according to the Roman mutilation of the Semitic name. The people were Arabs; and Edessa, while capital, marked the most northerly point of the kingdom.

At the same time the kingdom was on the northern marches of Mesopotamia, and always being in a position of a frontier state between Roman and Parthian, Arab and mountaineer—either Armenian or Kurd, though it is not known if the Kurds had spread so far west—was subjected to the fury of all its neighbours in wars, and played traitor to each on many occasions.

After the break-up of the Empire of Alexander, about the third century B.C., Mesopotamia fell into the hands of the Seleucid princes, and as they weakened, the northern portion of their kingdom fell before the advancing Romans. It was with Pompey (65 B.C.) that the king of Edessa, Abgarus, king of the people of Osrhœne, made a treaty, and accepted actual if not formal vassalage.

Ten years later, Crassus, as already mentioned, made his expedition against the rising power of Parthia, and was deceived and deserted by Abgarus after being lured into a position of danger.   Thereupon Edessa became allied to Parthia, and incidentally saved itself from the destruction consequent upon conquest.

A century later, and we see the Parthian Empire torn over a question of succession: Meherdates, a Parthian prince, at the suggestion of Rome, proceeds to win his kingdom by the sword from Godarz. *En route* he passes by Edessa, and now the Abgarus, with a ready facility for duplicity, after feasting him, sets him upon a road he knows will end in disaster. His theory was fully borne out by the defeat of the pretender at Erbil.

After the death of this versatile monarch, little is heard of Edessa till A.D. 115, when the Emperor Trajan established himself there, in preparation for an invasion of Parthia. Edessa was a convenient spot for such a step, being within easy reach of the Mediterranean *via* Aleppo, and commanding the road from Syria to the East.

Having prepared his army, he set out southwards; but while he subdued southern Mesopotamia, the reigning Abgarus, taking an advantage of Trajan's absence, promptly rebelled, and ejected the Roman garrison installed in the citadel, whose ramparts and walls still stand on the southern side of the city.

Vengeance overtook this effort at independence, for during the next year (A.D. 116), Lucius Quietus, a Roman general, captured the place and burnt it.

Yet once more we hear of Edessa before it sinks into the temporary obscurity that followed the fall of the Roman power in Mesopotamia. In one of the last attempts of Rome finally to crush the Parthians (A.D. 197), Severus, who came from France to try and recover the territories (Edessa among them) recently conquered by Volgases V. of Parthia, found Edessa on his way to the East, and the reigning Abgarus, always ready to turn a complacent face to the man in power, submitted without a murmur, and handed over his sons to the Romans as hostages.

It was not perhaps remarkable that Edessa, after these centuries of strife between the great empires, that saw the ebbing and flowing tide of Assyrian, Persian, Greek, Roman and Parthian, Roman and Arab, sweep by and over it, possessed a population of which the Roman and Greek element, particularly the latter, was an important section. When Christianity began to spread, the proximity of Edessa to Antioch made it easy for the bishops of those early days to travel there, and so we find as a result of the efforts of converts a college springing up in very early times.

Though there were doubtless many of the Greeks in this college, we are told that it was the Chaldeans who founded it, and made it famous for its erudition, and particularly its knowledge of the medical science. Doubtless Chaldean, Greek, and Arabic were all spoken there; the last certainly, for Arab pupils of the college, natives of the land towards Mecca and Medina, were relations of the early Muhammadan saints, notably Abu Bekr.

This famous school was dissolved by Zeno the Isaurian,[1] and the Chaldeans, with no loss of zeal, transferred it to Susa, in Khuzistan of south-west Persia, whence the now famous missionaries of the Chaldeans to China were despatched.

In 1124 A.D. it had become one of the western strongholds of the followers of Hasan Sabbah, the Ismailis or Assassins of Crusading fame, and when they were finally

[1] Layard, *Nineveh*, vol. i., p. 249 *n.* Humboldt, *Cosmos*, vol. ii., ch. 5.

stamped out, a large number were slain in Edessa, or as it was then called, Urfa; and since then it has taken an ordinary place in 'the scheme of the general history of Mesopotamia, acquiring evil notoriety recently (1895) for the terrible massacres of Armenians under Turkish instigation.

At Urfa I made the acquaintance of three characters, samples of the curious results of the shattering of races and medley of their remnants which has taken place over western Asia. I had noticed two or three times on my way from Aleppo another carriage with three occupants, and at Urfa found them occupying the room next to mine. Their appearance was remarkable. The eldest and leader of the party was a sinister-looking man, with a big hooked nose, and a huge mouth which opened at one corner to display the only two teeth he possessed. Upon his head he wore a turban, and an old overcoat and Turkish trousers, extremely baggy in the leg and tight at the ankles, completed his visible attire.

The next in importance was a Kurdish-looking fellow, dark, but with a humorous twinkle in his little eyes. The headgear was Kurdish too, the style affected by the northern races. A felt basin cap wound round with a blue cloth is the headdress of these people. He had adopted the peculiar form of head handkerchief usual among the mountain Chaldeans; that is, instead of making a regular turban, he rolled his cloth till it made a thick rope, and then twisted it round his felt cap three or four times. He wore also the hairy Kurdish zouave jacket and wide trousers. In fact, to the experienced eye he appeared a Kurd of the Erzeroum district. The third of this trinity was all that the others were not—absurdly fat, his hairless face formed a grinning moon under his tiny fez. As coat he wore a garment reaching a little below his waist, made of shot blue silk, and the bagginess of the upper end of his trousers exaggerated his already ample breadth to the point of ludicrousness.

These queer creatures, when in their carriage, spent a great part of their time chanting in Gregorian tones in a language neither I nor the coachman could make out. Now and then they would sing a Kurdish song or a little doggerel in Turkish. Their conversation was carried on in Arabic and Kurdish, which two of them spoke equally well; only the middle man, who appeared so Kurdish, confined himself to that language. At night, now, in the caravanserai, I had a chance of listening to the crew, and heard them talk in the Kurdish called Kermanji, in Arabic, in Turkish, and then in this dialect of theirs which contained a good many Kurdish words. This was distinctly tantalising, and next morning I made the acquaintance of the one I set down as pure Kurd. He was very hearty; we spoke in Kurdish, and I found that they had already ascertained from my driver that I was a southern Kurdish Haji. I now learned that they, too, were returning from Mecca, and were natives of Sert, a small town south of Lake Van. No sooner had I heard this than the secret of their dialect was out. I remembered tales the Chaldeans of Urumia and Dilman in Persia tell of the mysterious "Gavarnai," who come from inaccessible passes among the Kurdish mountains, Gavarnai calling themselves Christian, but often fleeing from Gavarnai who were Musulman. The solution of the Gavarnai question is as follows:—

The district of Sert and the Gavar (or rock) district of Kurdistan is one of the most inaccessible of the many sealed corners of this mountain country, and it was here that the descendants of the Chaldeans and Assyrians fled before the hordes of the Tatars in the early fifteenth century, finding an asylum among the Kurdish tribes.

Here in the beautiful valleys of Sert they settled, and many became Musulman among the Kurds. Others fled from Sert before the blood-feuds of their own kinsmen, who gradually learned from the Kurds a hardy recklessness and bravery unknown of their ancestors of the towns and plains, and pushed farther into the mountains.

In quite recent times the village of Khusrava, now a considerable town, was founded by a Chaldean fugitive or explorer from the Sert valleys, named Nicolai, about 1780.

This statement I put here upon the authority of a

native of Khusrava, and leave it as it stands, not without remark, however, that the neighbouring town of Salmas was in pre-Muhammadan days a Chaldean bishopric, where there were undoubtedly a large number of Chaldeans among — but not intermarried—with the Armenians of that region.

The language of these Assyrians, sometimes called Neo-Syriac, or Aramaic, has remained and is spoken, though now known as a language of the Christians, by a great part of the sedentary Musulman population of the Sert plain, who, though calling themselves Kurds, are of Chaldean descent.

Such were two of my new aquaintances, the eldest and youngest. My particular friend, though he knew the dialect, came from a hill village, and besides proving his Kurdish origin also carried further proof in his appearance and manners. We became very good friends, and made many excursions about the bazaars of Urfa together, his tongue, always ready for badinage in any of four languages, assuring him a welcome everywhere.

At Urfa I renewed acquaintance with the Kurdish cigarette, which I suppose must be a unique pattern. The form has been evolved doubtless by necessity, for the tobacco produced in Kurdistan could never be rolled into an ordinary cigarette. Instead of pressing, keeping damp, and eventually cutting the leaf, the Kurds dry it, and pound it to a coarse powder, which to the uninitiated but intending smoker provided with cigarette papers would present an insurmountable difficulty. Consequently a special form of paper, affording employment in its manufacture to hundreds of women in Diarbekr and Mosul, has been invented.

The paper is thicker and coarser than an ordinary cigarette paper, and at least twice as long, and in the packets one buys they are already stuck together, forming slightly tapering tubes. A long slip of thick paper 1 inch broad is taken, and rolled into a plug which is inserted in the narrow end, its natural spring retaining it in place. Tobacco is then poured in from the top, and after sufficient coaxing and shaking down, the edges of the paper are turned in to retain the contents. The greatest disadvantage of this style of cigarette is that the tobacco being absolutely dry, and in tiny chips, does not hold together when smoked, the glowing head continually falling off.

Here in Urfa little else was smoked, and as I knew that eventually I must get used to them, I resolved to procure decent cigarettes as long as possible. So I hunted high and low for Turkish Regie productions, and at last found a dozen boxes, the purchase of which impressed my Kurdish friend immensely, for these are the one thing in Turkey of which the price is fixed and about which it is useless to haggle; also, compared to native cigarettes, they are terribly dear. These that I bought were twenty for threepence—still double and treble the price of Kurdish cigarettes. The purchase of these luxuries gained me the honorary title of effendi from my acquaintances, a title that never left me till I got buried in the frontier mountains of Persia.

We stayed two days at Urfa, and my new acquaintances of Sert were detained still longer. So, in departing, I bade them farewell till Diarbekr, where we should meet again.

From Urfa the road to Diarbekr keeps a mean way between ranges of mountains, the Karaja in the south-east and the high Kurdistan ranges to the north-west, called in ancient times Masius and Niphates respectively by the Romans. In many places the track brings one near the Euphrates, and traverses a number of ravines carrying down tributary streams. The general aspect of the country all the way is great rolling uplands, across which wind and rain come with express velocity and piercing cold. I believe the road from Severik to Diarbekr is impassable from December to February. Certainly when we passed in early April, snow was lying in patches not far away. The prospect is always immense, always dreary, for, though there is water to be got in any one of the innumerable gullies of these immense plains, and though the soil is fertile enough, the Turkish blight is upon the land. In the distance, more particularly to the north, are the sullen, frowning masses of the Kurdistan mountains, at this time of the year half hidden in black clouds, and before and behind apparently limitless plains rising gradually to the east, till at the highest point one looks down over the undulating desert with a curious feeling of being left out in the desolation of utter abandonment, unsheltered from wind, rain, and snow, and lost in the immensity of a silent death-like solitude of infinitely sinister aspect.

And these plains and mountains have from immemorial time been the boundaries, natural and political, of the south and north lands. The high dark range over north— Niphates we must call it, since to-day it has lost its general name—gives birth to the Tigris, the "Arrow." [1] It was also the northern boundary of Assyria under the first great Assyrian monarch, Tiglath-Pileser I. (1100 B.C.). Behind its frowning walls lay the mysterious lands of the Nairi, whom the Assyrian monarchs, greater than any of their descendants, succeeded in subduing, or found necessary to keep chastised periodically. The proudest boast of the Assyrian monarchs was ever that they had penetrated the lands of Naira and subdued their petty kings. And afterwards, the lands of Nairi were called "Gordyene," which is "Kurdian" or Kurds, no more and no less, a fact which supports the Kurdish claim to possession of the land ever since the first Aryan in the birth of time came forth from central Asia to people the West.

Here Roman, Parthian, and Greek invader have turned back and set their faces once more to the merciless plains and downs. Those gloomy hill-sides have looked down upon the broken armies of all the greatest Eastern nations, Assyria only excepted, and watched them as they crawled away, to the south and west, relinquishing all hope of penetrating the dread country of the fierce Gordyene, forbear of the not less fierce Kurd of to-day. Strange it is that this sturdy nation, whose name has stood for

[1] The name Tigris, which we adopted from Western historians, is the mutilated version of the Medic "tighra," modern Persian and Kurdish "tir," an arrow.

rebellion, bravery, and untamable spirit, should never have taken rank among the more transitory peoples who never subdued it. Except that they were the Medes—or we imagine them to be—they have no claim to the historian's enthusiasm—at any rate, these western Kurds have not. They remain as ever, indomitable, invincible, proud, unsubdued, broken only by their own quarrels, hating the Powers that nominally rule them. Secure in their defiles and mountains, and in their archaic language, they cede no jot of their exclusiveness, let the West press never so hard.

This digression from narrative is permitted, I hope, by the lack of detail worth recording about the road from Urfa to Diarbekr. Except that for the first half, for two days, the fiendish genius of some Turkish engineer has induced him to scatter boulders and call it a road, and then lay down 3 feet of clay on marshy ground, and call that a road too, the track calls for no remark. There is but one station of any interest, Suverek.

Referring to notes, I find that two objects struck me as remarkable when approaching this squalid town upon the plain. One is a square white building, with rows of glass windows all round, a porched doorway in front, a Turkish flag on top. This is the Governor's house, an example of mean European architecture, isolated, from the small surroundings that give it a spurious importance, looking cold, miserable, hollow, and infinitely shoddy, in that vast landscape of plain and distant hill. The other feature is the mound, like that of Aleppo, upon which are the remains of the Governor's house that the rulers of twenty centuries ago put there, for whose might and whose right, and whose strong hand the country may sigh as it looks there upon the work of a mighty past, and here upon those of a little present.

Modern Suverek is a mean town of one-storeyed houses of black stone, inhabited by sedentary Kurds and Armenians, who are, I believe, permanently on bad terms, as these two races always are. There are no streets as we know them ; the hovels are clustered together, leaving alleys of a particular filthiness between. The traveller perforce puts up in a ruinous caravanserai which is situated fortunately on the edge of the town, and looks out through its broken doorway to the desert. The people are peculiarly surly and ill-mannered, and despite the size of the place nothing seems to be purchasable. When we arrived it was quite within the nature of things to find all my sugar finished, and so, leaving my room in charge of an aged Arab woman I found cupping herself outside in the courtyard, I set out to explore. My first question to the Armenian who acted as doorkeeper, elicited the fact that there was a shop round the corner. So round the corner I waded through pestilential mire, and found the shop. It was an open booth—the shop of the East —and the stock-in-trade just required three glances to sum it up. There was a small boy playing with a grey-hound. Behind, upon a sloping shelf, a bag of stones, called cheese in these parts, where last year's cheese is a delicacy, and the fresh article scorned. Two bunches of onions and a few boxes of matches completed the emporium. So I took my trousers up one more turn, and set forth among the alleys, displacing Armenian infants from mud-baths, disputing the right of way with armed Kurds, and finally finding myself in a mosque courtyard, where I was promptly accosted by a priest, who asked my religion, and receiving the answer " Islam," still doubtful, called upon me to be repeat the creed, which done to his satisfaction I made use of him as a guide, and with his assistance found a shop similar to the first, where the owner was more enterprising and kept not only sugar—and sold at a fanciful price—but tea and cigarettes.

Bread, too, I found, but solely by the priest's goodwill, for, taking compassion upon this strange Haji, he took me to someone's house where bread was being cooked in an earth-oven, and procured for me ten flaps for two-pence.

Fortunately good water was abundant in the court-yard of the serai, where a nozzle poured out a plentiful supply, filling a broken cistern and half the yard. Hither came all the Kurdish women to get their supplies, and I spent an hour sitting on my door-step watching for an ugly girl—and saw none. We had great difficulty in getting away next morning, for the Armenian keeper of the place demanded a mejidie (3s. 4d.) for horse provender from the coachman, and 1s. for my room, which had leaked upon me all night. An hour was wasted in the doorway disputing. Half a dozen Armenian loafers hung upon the horses' heads while we endeavoured to quell the screams and expostulations of the keeper of the place. We were forced to pay in the end, or stay where we were, the only satisfaction being that we passed off a bad five-piastre piece upon them, and gave the trouble of changing a lira. And so we drove away, cursing Christians and pagans in general and Armenians in particular.

Next day we had crossed the high plains and got into the warm desert towards Diarbekr. As we approached, the black walls rose above the horizon, and occasionally the gully where the Tigris runs would be apparent, the yellow of the cliff face showing against the duller colour of the plain. Approaching from the west, Diarbekr is not beautiful nor remarkable. In the middle of a great desert, the river, too, hidden by its cliff banks, Diarbekr appears as a citadel of black stone without any green or vegetation. Nearer views revise the unfavourable first impression, for on the slopes and the lands by the river banks, there are splendid gardens, which in this month of April were dressed in all the delicate hues of blossom and new leaf. The fine bluff upon which the city stands, looking up and down the river, is, of course, invisible from the west, facing the rising sun as it does.

My driver told me to prepare my passport, for he assured me we should not be allowed to pass the gates through the walls without showing our credentials. So I produced my passport and got it ready—that traitorous document, proclaiming me English, British-born, and Christian!

I began to wonder how the " Kurdish Haji " would look if questions were asked of the driver, to whom by now I had employed so many pious Musulman expressions and ventilated such orthodox sentiments, besides conducting myself in the manner of any other travelling Asiatic, that I knew he would swear to my Islamism. Not only that, but the police would certainly never believe that I was a European, my style of travelling, the only language I knew well—Kurdish—being convincing arguments against such a possibility. So it was not that I was afraid of being found out, but that I regarded with some trepidation the possibility of being accused of having stolen another's passport, a very heinous crime indeed. English passports and European correspondence would serve me little among people where Europeans are very rarely seen, in places where the Englishman seldom, if ever, travels, and never in such guise. The weather, too, had done its best to disguise me. I was darkened by wind and sun ; nine days' black beard scraped the chest left bare by a buttonless shirt. My trousers were muddy and torn, and I wore a long overcoat, very much like the robes of any of the myriads of Turkish subjects who affect a semi-European dress.

There was no alternative, however ; one could not stop outside in the plain nor enter unperceived, so we drew up just outside the gate in the massive walls at a police post, and an official demanded my passport. I handed it to him, and held my breath. The coachman who had seen this done a thousand times, and took no interest fortunately, seized the opportunity to descend and buy some cigarettes at a shop near by. The effendi, unusually civil for his class, asked me where I came from, and by what route, and where I was going. Hearing that my destination was Mosul, he seemed to lose interest, but produced a pocket-book and prepared to note particulars of my passport, when I observed that he held it upside down and made illegible marks in his book, and I realised that no art of the Constantinople passport clerk could betray me, for he was utterly illiterate. He asked my name, and still fearing eventualities, I repeated my own name very indistinctly, which he aptly transliterated as Ali as-Sūn, after which all was plain sailing, for he presupposed that I was a Haji, which the coachman confirmed, and I let him know I was a British subject, the supplementary fact that I was Persian-born being supplied by the driver, and so with a polite good-day we passed on.

CHAPTER IV

DOWN THE TIGRIS TO MOSUL

DIARBEKR at first sight strikes the stranger as a remarkably clean, bright, busy city, with streets unusually broad for the East, enormous bazaars, not roofed as in other Oriental cities, but merely rows of windowless shops lining the ways. Two main thoroughfares intersect the town at right angles, with gates at each end, and the whole is surrounded by the huge wall of basalt built in its present form by Justinian. The population seems for the most part Kurd, wild men of great stature, from the north and east, with high felt hats, like those of the ancient Persians of the Sasanian sculptures, their zouave jackets of sheepskin with the hair outside, the scarlet shoes forming parts of a distinctive costume. The fierce look that a Kurd invariably acquires, the thin bony face, the long stride, mark the hillman, who walks in these peaceable, if noisy, streets with a hand on his rifle and dagger.

We put up in a two-storeyed caravanserai, near the north gate, a place clean and roomy, boasting the luxury of glass to its windows, one or two of which contained a chair and table. These were not for Kurdish Hajis, however, and I humbly took my upper room, thankful that I had a window whence I could survey the lordly effendi as he crossed the yard to his "European" room. Upon the board floor (another luxury this, in a country whose floors are of mud) I spread my rag of carpet and threw my bedding, and, following the coachman, retired to a coffee-house outside for a cup of tea, and the ordeal of questions that pour upon the stranger.

The coffee-house was a big barn-like place, black with the smoke of innumerable water-pipes, and furnished with broad benches, just too high to sit on and let one's feet touch the ground. They are, of course, made to be squatted upon. The place was very full, and we had to squeeze in on one already occupied; and I found myself next a holy man, a yellow individual in the long cloak denoting a priest, and the green turban that is the sign of a Sayyid, or descendant of the Prophet. This sanctity of course called for greetings from us, the plebeians, the insignificant, and with humility we tendered our "Salamun 'alaikum," receiving the "'Alaikum as salam·" in sonorous tones before we sat down.

The first questions came quickly enough.

"Whence do you come? whither going? what nationality? why travelling?" which were answered by the responses I had resolved to adhere to.

"From Aleppo to Persian Kurdistan, a Shiah Musulman travelling back to my country."

This I said in Kurdish, for the man was ignorant of Turkish, which became less known as we went farther east.

Himself he was an Arab, a native of Mosul. In the lands of Islam, where knowledge and religion are inseparable, it is the divinity student that becomes the doctor, the lawyer, the judge. This priest was by profession a petty lawyer, and gained a kind of livelihood by settling disputes. To this he added the profession of healer of scorpion bites, which he remedied by applying to the wound the oil extracted from the black scorpion. Conversing pleasantly of this science, he produced a cigarette box and played with the lid as one who waits to finish speaking before taking a smoke. He ceased his dissertation upon scorpions, and nonchalantly opened his box, to display two large scorpions writhing within and scraping their horny legs and claws against its tin sides. He lifted one out, disregarding its furious blows upon his fingers, let the reptile crawl up his arm, picked

it off, replaced it in the box, smiled at me a tooth-
less and sinister smile, slipped off his seat and left the
café.

My coachman had watched the performance. He knew
the man well, he said; he had practised his trades in
Diarbekr for years, always a buyer of good black scorpions
at fourpence each, and a seller of the oil at a mejidie for
ten drops. His remarkable performance with the live
scorpions was possible owing to his practice, when
catching scorpions, of nipping off the sting of the tail
with a pair of scissors.

There was a fresh briskness, a hearty feeling in the air
of Diarbekr, that took the fancy. The new springtime
exactly achieved that mean of temperature wherein man
feels at his best in the Mesopotamian plains, that scorch
the life out, and make the strongest languid during the
long summer.

The place was crowded and busy; the Kurds, released
from their snow-bound mountains, were coming in to buy
summer clothing; the Armenians, who are the craftsmen
of Diarbekr, were enjoying a period of immunity from the
terror in which they often exist.

The broad street of the town, that lets in the breeze
and the sun, gave it a cheerfulness in that season that
many another town, whose winter mud is just beginning to
congeal in dark alleys, lacks.

I took the earliest opportunity to get outside the north
gate, which was but a few yards from the caravanserai
door, to inspect the curious stones that are embedded in
the walls, stones bearing images of birds and beasts, relics
of a wall that perhaps encircled the city during pre-
Christian times. Yet with all the evidence of importance,
with its old church towers turned to minarets, where the
bells that called to the worship of the Trinity are replaced
by the call of them that cry to the Indivisible Unity,
where Roman ruled later than in any other city of the
East, and where the Christian was predominant till Islam,
borne upon the shoulders of Arabs from the south, drove
him out and subdued him: with all this, Diarbekr has

figured less in the ancient annals than many a village and mound that to-day passes unnoticed.

All the nations that passed over the lands have fought for and owned it. Assyria knew it not by name, though if it existed then, it was an outpost of the empire. Armenians, Persians, Parthians, and Romans fought over it, but the chronicles tell us little. In Christian times the Persian leader Kawad (Sasanian) practically destroyed it; in A.D. 507 and in A.D. 1124 seven hundred persons of the Assassin or Ismailia sect were massacred. It fell into Turkish hands in A.D. 1056, when Tughril Bey of the early Seljuq dynasty captured it.

It was not on the main road from Syria to Babylon, nor Europe to Persia; the hosts of invaders and defeated passed too far to the south, and left Amid in her corner, where she trembled at the noise of the battle that sometimes ruined her. Tigran, one of the greater Parthic-Armenian kings, took the place when he subdued Gordyene, upon whose southern borders it still stands, and he built a capital a little north of it, ignoring its claims to importance.

The present city has, as already described, four gates in its massive walls, but the Turks have knocked out a wicket gate in the north wall, and called the Yengi Qapu, "The New Gate." Also, a Turkish governor, offended at the sight of so substantial a monument of a race greater than his—and pagan—attempted to destroy the architecture neither he nor all his kind could ever emulate, and succeeded in defacing a portion of the north wall. Demolition of such a monument, however, proved too great a task for this mean vandal, and he desisted, and has gone his insignificant way. A few of the old churches still exist, which, in my character of Muhammadan, I was prevented from viewing.

The modern population, apart from the Kurds and Mosul Arabs, is composed of Christians, of whom there are more varieties than in other towns of Asiatic Turkey. The Armenians are in the majority, and form the whole of the large section engaged in the manufacture of copper vessels, for which Diarbekr is famous. There are Greeks, relics of the rule of Byzantium, divided into three or four sects, Syrians, or Christian Arabs as they prefer to call themselves, some belonging to the Syrian Church and others Catholics. There are Chaldeans, who glory in the assertion (never disproved) that they are lineal descendants of Nebuchadnezzar and the later Assyrians, speaking an ancient dialect which is nearer to the inscription-language than any other.

The Roman Catholics have been busy among all the sects, notably among Armenian and Chaldean here, and many of both own allegiance to the Pope. Every sect—and none can tell how many there are—is as certain of its own particular salvation as of the perdition of all the others, and a hatred reigns over this Christian "centre" among the various kinds of Christians that puts in the shade any length of the detestation for Islam.

It is unfortunate that the Asiatic Christian is, as a rule, a very undesirable creature, more bigoted than the most fanatical Muhammadan, of a craft and infidelity seldom witnessed in other lands, and of an attitude towards his co-religionists of different tenets that can be only described as traitorous. It may be reckoned a heretical statement to put forward, but the dweller in the East is bound to confess that among the greater part of the peoples of Western Asia, Islam produces a better man than Christianity. The temperament of the middle Eastern Semitic is ultra-utilitarian. The ideals that Christianity puts before him have too slender a hold upon a nature that craves for the substance, and the latitude allowed in daily life by the Western faith accords ill with the temperament that seeks set rule and law, that may govern the manner of his rising and sitting, of his eating and sleeping, and by the observance of which he may accumulate the merit that may secure to him the acquisition of ideals almost mundane. The high soul and spirit required by Christianity is too far above these material minds, and the hazy and ill-understood ideal cannot hold their endeavours as do the needs of life and the almost unconquerable cupidity of the Semitic nature. So we see the spiritual and intangible, the higher head and sign of their religion lost sight of, in the struggles that rage about leadership of their minor saints, and points of doctrine and dogma that tear asunder the Christian community. Islam is material, her ideals are powerful and simple, there is through all that unification of leader and led that all can appreciate. One God, one Prophet, one Book, each in its own rational relation to the other, a simple doctrine, powerful in its direct appeal to the unity, a leader, a prophet who lays down with the despotism understood of the ancient Semitic spirit, law and letter for all things; that is a creed that the Arab mind sees as tangible, if such an expression be permissible; a law for all and a reward attainable by the observance of its well-defined canons, demanding not too much of the man in his daily life, yet holding him— as all who know the East must know—with a mysterious and invincible power that calls upon his life when it wills, and finds it ever ready for the sacrifice.

Persecution has doubtless made the Christian crafty and distrustful, and is often quoted as an excuse for the many undesirable qualities he possesses which the Musulman does not share. Alone among these Christian sects stand the Chaldeans of the north, whose pride of race and tongue has done something to keep them above the Armenians, Syrians, and Greeks they despise, and to preserve alive in their breasts the sentiment of the ruling race from whom they profess to spring, and which saves them from many a littleness which is an integral part of the nature of the other Christians.

The persecution of the Christians—of which Diarbekr has too often been the theatre—excites the sympathy of all nations, and rightly too; for whatever be their quibbles, they hold fast to Christianity through all the massacres and terror that Turkish vindictiveness has incited and paid for. I say paid for, because it is, among the underworld of western Kurdistan and northern Mesopotamia, a common subject of talk in the cafés how much the Sultan and the Government paid the ruffians of the

E

towns to do their dirty work, and how much the Kurdish Aghas presented to the authorities to be allowed to finish unhindered the blood-feuds that existed between themselves and Armenians sheltering in Diarbekr and the towns of Armenia. A very reign of terror overshadows the apparently peaceful and prosperous town.

None ever know when the Turks will permit the looser part of the Musulman population to slaughter, or call down from the hills those terrible Kurds that hold Christian and Musulman alike in fear.

It is impossible not to notice here the universal law that forces the weak to imitate the appearance of the strong, as a protective measure. The Christians of Diarbekr and the outlying country have adopted the dress of the town Musulmans, the long tunic and the waistband, the felt cap surrounded by a blue handkerchief, to such effect that the stranger cannot distinguish one from the other at first, and only learns to pick out the slight difference in the arrangement of the head-handkerchief after some time.

So too at Mosul, where the Christians and Muhammadan Arab are not visibly different, except where the former has adopted a fez; and in southern and Persian Kurdistan, where Kurd and Chaldean dress precisely alike, and where the Chaldean speaks perfect Kurdish, and, happy to relate, is usually on excellent terms with his ferocious neighbours, who have none of the detestation for them that they have for the treacherous Armenians.

From Diarbekr I purposed to travel as far as Mosul down the Tigris on a kalak, or raft of skins and poles. The few Europeans who have adopted this pleasant method of travelling, usually hired half the raft, erected a booth or tent and carried a cook and servants, travelling tranquilly, with no more to do than admire the scenery and take snapshot photographs. In my assumed character I could not go in for this style of luxury, and had to look out for a passage by a kalak carrying cargo, upon the top of which I might be allowed to sit, for a consideration.

However, I was to have a tent after all, and it came about thus:—

I was eating my frugal lunch of dry bread and lettuces one day in the caravanserai, when an aged man in the long garments and felt waistcoat of a southern Kurd came up to my room, and entering with a salutation, sat down, and accepted my invitation to share the meal. He introduced himself as Haji Vali, a native of Erbil, on the western marches of Kurdistan, a Baba Kurd, returning from his seventeenth journey to Mecca. He, like me, sought a passage to Mosul, and came with the news that a kalak was ready; and, moreover, possessed a shelter of sticks and calico which had been made for an effendi now unable to travel, and which could be bought for a mejidie or so. The old man knew a little Persian, and spoke, besides his native Kurdish in which we conversed, Turkish and Arabic. The assurance with which he had joined me at my meal, and the certainty he seemed to feel that I should become a partner with him in our passage to Mosul, I found a feature of all his doings.

He had an abrupt, dictatorial manner, which he tempered with bluff heartiness, and, used to the respect which his seventeen journeys to Mecca had earned for him, was not accustomed to receiving a refusal to any of his propositions. So when he proposed to me—whom he called Musa—addressing me as "his beloved son," that we should share all expenses, I agreed. No sooner was this settled than he departed, to return later with his goods and chattels, some being saddle-bags, and little sacks of charcoal, a tin samovar, and a packet of letters and papers which he entrusted to me, as being more secure in the pocket of my overcoat; for in the fashion of the long tunic of the East he possessed no pockets, but two wallets hanging at his sides, and must needs thrust any valuables in his breast. The kalak owner now appeared with the Armenian doorkeeper as witness and intermediary in the negotiations. This kalak owner was a gaunt Kurd, pretty well seven feet tall, a cadaverous-looking giant who, squatting on the ground, seemed an ordinary man's height. An

impediment in his speech and a single fierce-looking eye
make him a fearsome-looking fellow. He was very easy
to haggle with, though, and started by demanding six
mejidies for transporting us to Mosul, we to be allowed to
use the tent, which should become his property at the
journey's end. We held out for five mejidies, and half the
proceeds of the sale of the tent at Mosul. Eventually,
after the consumption of many cigarettes, and after he
had three several times risen and got half-way down the
stairs in apparent indignation at our inflexibility, with the
Armenian as disinterested go-between, we arranged on
the price of two mejidies each, the tent being the Kurd's
property. The kalak was to start next morning, and we
must transport ourselves and our belongings outside the
town to a spot where a stone bridge crosses the river some
mile below Diarbekr.

In the meantime we must purchase food for some days;
the journey, if we received no checks, would occupy five
days, but if high winds arose or much rain fell we must be
resigned to twelve days or even longer. So we visited the
bazaar. First to a baker's, where we ordered a sack full of
thick flaps of bread, that he would cook by noon, and half
toast besides, making them as it is called, "firni," which
prevents the bread going mouldy. Then to buy sugar, at
which operation my knowledge of "European"—as Haji
Vali called an ability to read Latin characters—was needed,
for the Armenian shopkeeper tried to pass off upon us as
"English sugar" some inferior produce of Austria, and his
surprise and Haji Vali's delight were about equal when I
exposed the fraud by reading the label.

To buy anything was a great nuisance. When I was
alone I never had the patience to beat the seller down to
the last farthing, and would pay an eighth of a penny
more for an article than its proper price; but old Haji Vali
would have none of this. He knew the price of everything
in every city from Medina to Bagdad, and woe betide the
Christian who swore to a false price. At last, however, we
actually did finish our purchases, which, if I remember,
were as follows: a sack each of charcoal and bread, ten

pounds of rice, one pound of tea, three sugar loaves, six
pewter teaspoons, seven pounds of clarified butter, odd
quantities of lentils and pease, three long strings of dried
"lady's fingers," a little vegetable; pepper and rock salt;
some dried fruits. These we carried to the caravanserai,
bent double under the sacks and bags we shouldered.
The purchase of these things took us from nine in the
morning till nearly sunset, and involved as much talking
and argument as a session of parliament.

Having locked up our purchases and tied up our
goods, ready to be taken away next morning, we went
out for a last look at Diarbekr; but the old man, sick of
bazaars, surprised me by a request, unlike what one would
expect from one of a people that usually expresses so little
regard for the aspect of things natural, and the beauties of
the world we live in.

Taking my arm, he said:

"Musa, my son, after the day's toil, let us go outside
the gate to a quiet spot among the trees upon the cliff,
where we can sit and look upon the view."

So, very gratefully, I consented, and we took our way
by the gate, turned to the right, and passing the hideous
military school, came to the cliff that overhangs the
Tigris. We descended a little by a footpath, and found
a clump of trees on a narrow ledge, whence, sheltered from
the view of passers above, we could look out northwards,
across the plain, and to the ever dark hills of Kurdistan.
The old man sat silent for a long time, but at last
expressed his sentiments in one long " Allahu akbar!"
("God is great").

And then he pointed out to me the beauties of the
great rushing stream, the vivid colouring of its yellow
banks, and the light green of the groves of trees that
sprang with a new year's life far below us.

Again he sat silent, and gazed with narrowed eyes at
the far mountains, and when he spoke again, it was the
soul of the Kurd and of the mountaineer that threw the
harsh words of his dialect from his tongue:

"God! and God! and God! He, the Indivisible, His

glories are manifest to our eyes, and His mercies to our hearts and minds. Yet my son, think not that these mountains—upon which the body roams, while the soul, soaring above, meets the Unknown in a medium pure[1] as the snow-field that stretches above—are His masterpiece. For verily, as these mighty hills are the greatest of His works here, yet they are but as the pebble upon their flanks compared to His works in Heaven.

" See this work, how it exists.   Who are we to boast of the power He gave us, Who takes it away after our four days of transition?   See these city walls, the great among us made them, and they shall fall in a space of time incalculably small in His sight, yet the stones of them are His handiwork, and long enduring, have endured, even as those hills.   And when the walls shall sink, one, build-ing the sign of his ambition with the ruin of another's, shall use these same stones, remembering the former builder of walls.

" Ah! that he forget not the Maker of the stones that last, and the hills that endure."

The old man spoke quietly, yet as he spoke, the blue eyes dimmed and the voice shook—indeed there are anomalies in this world, dual personalities, among the sons of the East that one never suspects.

This old man, who had spent his life in an occupation we should deride as hypocritical—for he was a guide to Mecca, and while overcharging the uninitiated, achieved spurious merit—had yet in his old heart a spot where the poetry that lives in the Aryan breast yet lurked, and emanated, ascribing everything to that fearful Omnipotence that the Muhammadan worships.

In the Persian I have often met this dual personality— the hard, cautious man, who descends to any trickery and deception, even crime, for the meanest ends, and in a revulsion of feeling reviles himself, sees himself as others see him, in the purest poetry of language and thought

---

[1] He used the words " Sā o spī wakī wafraka lasar " (" Smooth and white, like the snow above ").

expresses the most beautiful sentiment, and falls to earth again.

The mountains, always the mountains, held the old man's gaze. There is a fascination about them that it is not necessary to be a Kurd or a Persian to be able to acquire. The impassive monuments of old-time glacier and volcanic upheaval, relics of convulsions that rent continents, that rise straight up from the flat, broad plains, may well seize upon all that is impressionable in anyone, and inspire the dullest with that craving to penetrate the mysteries of their deep valleys, and view the world from their blanched heads.

Truly, Diarbekr, that looks out from its fine bluff upon the lands of four old empires—Assyria to the south, Armenia to the north, Media to the east, and Rome to the west, might have much to meditate upon, were it allowed time for meditation between the continual rebellion and persecution that tear it.

Sunset, that meant gates closed, forced us to return, and once within the gates, Haji forgot his mood, and recommenced his talk of the journey, of the prices of our various purchases, of the unscrupulousness of Armenians, and the exaction of the Turks, who sent up the price of everything.

Next morning early we roused up, and while I went out into the streets to find a porter, Haji busied himself arranging the goods for carrying. A sturdy Kurd, whom I found in a mosque yard, arranged to carry our things for five piastres (1od.), and we loaded him up with a box and the saddle-bags, upon which we cast our bedding. The rest we must carry ourselves, for Haji, who would spend as little as possible himself, would not allow me to waste a coin where it could be saved.

It took us a little while to convince the Armenian keeper that a couple of shillings was enough for five days' occupation of his room; but this once done, he helped to load us up, and at length we departed. Haji's load was the sack of charcoal, and a bag containing the rice and some sundries, while I shouldered the bread and suspended

from myself bags containing tea and sugar loaves, odds
and ends of all descriptions, and a charcoal brazier that
picked pieces out of me wherever it struck its many sharp
corners. The whole length of Diarbekr we struggled,
for the south gate was our first objective, and not
till then did I realise the size of the place. The
straight street ran on as it seemed to infinity, but the
gate (so like the gate from Winchelsea to the Romney
marshes) did appear at last, and by some extraordinary
providence the police did not worry. The sun was getting
up at the pace he always does in the East, which I am
sure is greater than anywhere else, and we sweated and
panted as we waddled along, bent double under our loads.
The porter, with the strength of his kind, outdistanced us,
and with his steady march was soon lost among the trees
that border the winding road. Haji's breath gave out
here, and we had to rest, but at last we did get to the
bank of the river, and threw our loads down upon some
bags of apricots that were to go to Mosul.

And now, since we are arrived at the kalak, a description of the ingenious craft is necessary. Briefly, two
hundred inflated goatskins arranged in the form ten by
twenty, are bound to a few thin transverse poplar trunks
above them. Over these again seven or eight more tree-
trunks not more than 7 inches thick, are placed crosswise,
and upon these, to form a deck, is placed a layer of bales.
Between two pairs of these bales a basket-work affair is
fixed, which, with a stake, forms a rough thole-pin. A
pair of enormous sweeps swings on these, and the
oarsmen, standing upon one bale, build a bridge of twigs
across to the next row, and wield the sweeps standing.
Under the sweeps an empty space is always left across the
raft, where the skins are visible between the rafters.

The raft, from its shape and construction, cannot be
propelled, and the *raison d'être* of the oars is for turning,
by which the kalak is directed into the right currents, and
to pull the craft out of the danger that rocks standing in
the stream often threaten. In the upper river, between
Diarbekr and Mosul, particularly during the springtime,

progress at night is impossible, for the side-currents which sweep round the rocky banks at the velocity of a galloping horse would hopelessly smash the raft. Wind, too, naturally exerts a great driving force upon a craft that draws but three inches of water, and its strength, too much for oars to fight against, often compels a halt.

When we arrived, Kurdish porters were loading up the last of the cargo, dried apricots and rice mostly, from round about Urfa. The crew were busy blowing up partially deflated skins with a tube which they inserted into a protruding leg of the skin. Our tent, or "tenta" as the Arabs called it, was wedged between two walls of bales, and entering, we found it had a plank floor laid over the treetrunks forming the raft.

We had two fellow-passengers—one an Arab merchant of Mosul, a man of tremendous piety, who spent his whole time smoking cigarettes and calling on the Lord. The other was as diametrically opposite to him in character as possible: a time-expired soldier, a youth of twenty-three, who was returning from the Hejaz Railway, where he had formed part of the military police guard, to Kirkuk, his native town. Foul-mouthed, blasphemous, a thief, possessing no money and expecting us to keep him, he was a type of what the Turk becomes when the army has moulded him to its standard of ruffianism.

The crew of the raft was composed of two Kurds, little men of the Zaza, a tribe that lives in the high mountains round the upper Tigris valley and headwaters. These people are different in appearance and manners from nearly all other Kurds. They are short men, of a shy, quick temperament, very sharp, and excellent workers, speaking a dialect which, while Kurdish, denotes by its form a very high antiquity. It is possible that these are lineal descendants of the hill-tribes that the Assyrians had so much trouble in controlling, and whom the Parthians and Romans of a later age never subdued. In the high, pointed felt cap and long-toed shoes they still preserve part of a dress familiar from the sculptures of the southern Armenian mountains.

The skipper of our craft was known as one of the most skilful of all the river men, and in the dreadful weather that followed he showed by his ability his claim to that reputation.

We cast off from the bank at ten o'clock this sunny morning, a light breeze from the north both assisting our progress and keeping the temperature at a degree of perfect comfort. Under such conditions, fine weather and a broad river that runs at a steady pace without too many shallows and rapids, there is probably no more pleasant method of travelling than by kalak. As it proceeds, the raft turns round and round slowly, giving a view of every side.

There is an ease and comfort about it all that only the traveller fresh from the road can appreciate. The abundance of cool, clean water is the chief delight of the journey, contrasting with the ever-present trouble of the road, with its water often enough scarce, and always obtained only at the expense of considerable manual labour. The dust and filth, the long, wearying stages, the trouble of loading and unloading and of seeking food in obscure bazaars when one is dead tired, the awakening from a sleep all too short in the dark before dawn, all these are past, and all there is to do is to lie at full length upon the bales and give oneself up to the luxury of pure laziness and enjoyment of the view.

For two days we floated down between flat banks, passing a few villages, all Kurdish. At night we tied up, gathered some sticks, made a fire, and cooked rice. Haji and myself were regarded as the first-class passengers, possessing, as we did, a tent, and living upon cooked food. The others had but dry bread and cheese, of which they had brought a sufficient supply to last. As the custom of Islam generally, and of the Kurd particularly, demands a fraternal fellowship among all travellers, we entertained the passengers and crew at our evening meal every night. The class distinction that asserts itself in every land on earth, whether it be the difference made by breeding, position, or hard cash, became apparent on the first evening. I had cleaned and washed the rice, boiled it, and produced a pilau, turning it out into our one dish, which was but a big copper saucepan-lid. We invited the company to partake, refusing to eat under any other conditions. The crew, however, were too shy, and asserting their own unworthiness, said they would eat afterwards. The Arab merchant, too, hung off with polite phrases, but was eventually forced to join. The soldier needed no encouragement, and would have sat down and begun without waiting for us to put out our hands to the dish, a terrible gaucherie; but for some reason both Arab and Kurd, who had conceived a strong dislike to him, fairly beat him off, saying that he was not of our class and rank, and might wait and eat afterwards. So, with very bad grace, he retired to sulkiness and cigarettes. A hearty appetite, helped by the pity-to-waste-it kind of sentiment, assures the total disappearance of a cooked meal among all the people of road and river in the East, so there were never any leavings, and the washing up of the one dish was always undertaken by the crew. Morning and afternoon, we made tea upon the raft, precedence in the dispensing of it being strictly observed. First myself, for all had given me the title of effendi, on the strength of a fez and overcoat, and regarded me as the aristocrat of the party, then Haji Vali my partner, then the Arab, and after we had each partaken of the regulation three glasses, the crew received their two, the soldier getting his share last of all.

The third day, great mountains began to rise high before us, stretching away across the course of the river, far to the east and west. The second night we tied up at a Kurdish village just before reaching some high cliffs that were the sentinels of the terrific gorges we were to pass later, and here our luck turned. First we learned that a section of the Kurdish tribe in the hills we could see ahead had rebelled, a quite usual occurrence, and to show their defiance of authority, were shooting at passers-by on the river. This was certainly disquieting, but a prospective danger is sometimes dwarfed by present discomfort. In the pouring rain that set in at sunset, we forgot all about robbers and rebels. A strong gale arose, with torrential rain, which wet our tent through, threatening to tear it away altogether. The Kurdish crew, who feared to leave their craft to the mercy of a wind and ever-strengthening current, that might carry it away and shatter it against rocks, were bound to sleep aboard, and in a piercing cold they lay sodden, rivulets running from their thin garments, and tried to sleep. We in the tent were not much better off. All our bedding got soaked, thick cotton quilts which take hours to dry ; our rice and charcoal became pulp and mud respectively. Streams falling from pools in the calico roof spouted upon us, now on our faces, now in the nape of our necks. Pools formed upon our coverings, and soaked through. Our clothing could absorb no more, nor our bedding, and at last we, like the unfortunates outside, resigned ourselves to becoming shivering bodies wrapped in spongy swathings, our only advantage over them being a little shelter from the stinging wind. In the black darkness we had to crawl out over bales of apricots, slippery with the juice and wet that oozed from them, to secure our flimsy house : every few moments a new place had to be found for such valuables as matches, whose ever-changing refuge was invaded by the rain with a malignant persistency as regularly as we devised it.

Morning brought us no relief, and indeed made our case worse, for had we stayed at the village we could have taken shelter in its houses. By an irony of the elements, the wind held off at sunrise, and despite the rain we cast off. An hour downstream, where it narrowed among the hills and ever-rising cliffs, the wind swept down again, and we tied up by a strip of beach under a precipice, and so cut ourselves off from any chance of shelter. For three days and nights it rained and blew. Even our bread, the only thing we had to eat, became sodden. Haji developed rheumatism, and a temper so irritable that I migrated to the bales outside, and slept two nights upon the apricots, covered by soaked and clammy things that, while they kept the wind off, were so chill as to make their advantage problematical.

The fourth morning, however, broke fine, and in half

an hour the clouds had torn to rags, the wind had gone overhead, driving the rack at a tremendous pace; but below, the river ran blue between its yellow cliffs, now a good two hundred feet high, and we steamed in the welcome warmth; and now we saw how the three days' torrent had altered the condition of affairs. Our mooring-stakes were a couple of feet under water, and the river, which from here runs in a gorge through the mountains—a gorge ever narrowing—was flying along at express speed. Our courageous skipper cast off, and we commenced to race along. The river pursues a remarkable course here. The reaches are straight and short, and owing to the similarity in colouring of the opposite banks it is impossible to see the turn—often less than a right angle—till right upon it. Huge hills rise up beyond their lower slopes covered with trees, and above all we could see snow-capped peaks. In these wild gorges, of a beauty of spring verdure, of a magnificence indescribable, we felt—as in all effect we were—but a chip swept along the great river. At every turn the current, setting towards the far bank, would sweep round, roaring against the vicious-looking rocks, and all hands were called to the oars to keep the raft from dashing upon them, and being torn to pieces. The river, narrowing between points sometimes, or running over submerged rocks at others, breaks up in high curling swell, and the current doubles its speed. Here we would experience the greatest excitement in guiding the raft to the exact centre of the converging ridges of waves and shooting through between them at a tremendous velocity, to rush upon the boiling commotion where they met. The raft would undulate, its non-rigid construction prevents its rocking, and waves would roll up, drenching us and our goods, and our half-dried garments, while the raft cracked ominously. At such points Haji and the Arab merchant, grasping the nearest firm object, would ejaculate fervently, "Ya Rebbi! Sahl! Ya Rebbi!" ("Oh God, help! Oh God!"), and passing the danger spot, utter equally fervent thanksgiving. As we proceeded, the hills and cliffs got higher and steeper, great mountain sides rose at a slope apparently impossible to climb, to dizzy heights. Here and there would occur a narrow point of land, around which the stream curved, and upon every such was a little Kurdish village, the house of the head-man, well built of stone, with a loop-holed tower standing up on slightly higher ground. Once or twice shots were fired, but our pace took us far beyond the reach of the sportsmen, almost before they could reload. Seeing these great hills, these constant precipices, it was easy enough to understand why the armies of the old Powers of Mesopotamia in their marches northward always took the westerly plain roads, and left these hills to the tribes that have inhabited them ever since Central Asia poured out its hordes of Aryans far back in the years before history, to people the Western world.

One afternoon, when we were favoured with good weather, we turned into a long reach, and had before us one of the most remarkable sights the Tigris has to offer. The right bank of the river rose in a vertical cliff to a great height, and was faced across the broad stream by fellow cliff not so high, but honeycombed with cave-dwellings. The right hand cliff (which was the result of a hill-side cut off by the river) was broken at one place and continued again, the ravine—but a few yards across—coming down to the water's edge. Upon the summit of this continued portion we could see a considerable town, so high up that human figures looked minute. Behind all, rose precipitous hill-sides, between whose gorges and valleys could be seen yet wilder crags and peaks. In the village or town two or three towers, narrow and tall, of the dimensions of a factory chimney, rose, looking more slender and high from the eminence upon which they stood. But most remarkable of all were the great piers of a once colossal bridge, that, springing from a lower point of the cliff, or rather from a spot upon its slope down to the foreshore, spans the space to the opposite cliff, bridging the Tigris further south than any existing stone bridge. Here the stream is broad and deep, and the mighty piers that tower above and shadow the passer-by in his humble kalak, speak volumes for the perseverance and talent of people past and gone, and, by comparison, the qualities of the Ottomans. And on both sides, on the left or east bank, where the cliff growing ever lower still hedges the river, and on the west, where receding it leaves a fertile foreshore, the faces are pierced with cave-dwellings, rock forts that communicate with one another. Curious chambers, open at the river-side, mere eeries, looked down upon the stream, and it is only a near approach that reveals the mode of access, a passage diving into the rock. From the village above a staircase has been cut, zig-zagging down the cliff-face to where the river laps the solid rock wall.

This remarkable place, far off the track of any road, removed from even the feeble influence of the Turk by its surrounding mountains, is called Hasan Kaif. The name is modern, and tradition says that Hasan Kaif[1] was a Kurdish brigand who established himself there and levied toll upon all river passers, fortifying himself in a place that hardly needs any artificial protection, so well has Nature fenced it about. The bridge is said by most people to be Roman, but later experts than those who started the theory—for want of a better—state that it is Venetian, a relic of the old road to the East. In fact, I believe traces of Venetians have been found also in the town, where there are ruins. It is probable that the Venetians knew the place by reputation and history before they ever established themselves there. The population has probably been always Kurd, the Armenians that existed there before the Armenian massacre having immigrated. Now the Kurds have the place to themselves once more, and under the superlatively corrupt and feeble government of to-day, its old reputation has returned. Here, too, are some Yezidi, those ingenuous souls that, instead of attempting

[1] This legend is unfortunately flatly contradicted by the spelling of the name. Hasan is not the name with which all travellers in Islamic lands are familiar, but an Arabic word signifying an "impregnable castle," a name obviously suited to the old castle on its cliff. Oriental students will appreciate the difference on learning that the second consonant is Sād, and not Sīn.

to curry favour with the Almighty, regard the evil power as more potential in this life, and seek to appease Satan, which perhaps comes to the same thing in effect upon their daily lives. We did not stop here, but allowed ourselves to be swept past, down a wide reach where the hills opened out, and at nightfall tied up where the river grew tremendously broad and turned sharply to the right.[1]

With night rain came on again, once more drowning us in our garments and coverings. So much water had the cargo absorbed that the raft had apparently sunk. At the start the skins were half out of water and had to be constantly sprinkled with a spoon-like instrument of leather, to prevent drying and cracking, but the last two days they had been invisible, and now even the covering beams began to disappear. The apricots, soaked by the first rain, had swollen and grown pulpy, a day's sun had partially dried the outsides of the sacks, and induced a most unpleasant effluvium. Now everything became full of water to its saturation point again, and on this occasion a freezing wind arose, the reason for which we perceived at daybreak, for the hills were covered with new snow.

We cast off at the second hour of daylight, and floated out into a lake of swift-rushing eddies, crashing commotions of meeting streams. Here the Buhtan Su—the largest of the streams that go to make up the full Tigris—enters at a broad place, a bay among some abruptly rising hills. For a mile or so the reach of the combined rivers sweeps along broad and deep, then is forced to take the only possible outlet through a narrow gorge, between where the speed is positively giddy. As we approached the turn, a number of Kurds appeared, running down a valley to the river, and as they neared opened fire upon us, hitting nothing

[1] The old Arab name of the place was Ras ul Qawl, and it was in the 11th and 12th centuries under the government of Mardin. It was ceded in A.D. 1263 to one of the Kurdish tribe of Al-i-Ayub (the tribe of Saladin, famous in the Crusades), which was itself related to the great Hakkari tribe residing in these districts. The place has been in the hands of this family and its descendants ever since. Apparently the castle is of a much earlier date, though we are told that the Al-i-Ayub tribe rebuilt it.

but a bale or two; but their attention was diverted most opportunely by another party, which, appearing on high, commenced a lively fusillade directed at our assailants. Very unfortunately we were not in a position to stop and watch the developments, but as we were hustled round a bend we saw that a brisk fight was in progress. It interested me very much to note the behaviour of my fellow-travellers. The crew seemed to think the affair very ordinary, and never ceased rowing; in fact it would have been impossible to relinquish control of the raft in this corridor full of rocks. The Arab and Haji, too, while very careful to take shelter behind bales, knowing that we must soon be carried beyond reach of danger, were very little perturbed, only the Kurdish blood of the older man boiled to think that he had not a gun to respond. The Turkish soldier disappeared at the first shot, having wedged himself in among the apricot bags and the rafters, whence he at length emerged wet and muddy.

We were not to go far that day, for rain and storm came on again, and we had to tie up; but the morning came fine, and despite the precarious condition of the raft, which was now floating under water, we resolved to go on as far as Jazira, a small town at the foot of the mountains, and reached there completely water-logged, and sinking deeper every minute, a little after noon.

Here our crew were paid off and another couple taken over; the process of handing over being to count everything on board, passengers included, when the new man, entering into possession, looked around and was expected to carry out all necessary repairs, or rearrange cargo and passengers as suited. He wasted no time, and plunged into the chilly water, pulling out deflated skins, blowing up others, replacing faulty ones, and tidying up generally till sunset.

We were to have started next morning, but again the weather came on, and a worse downpour than ever drove all the loafers away and left us forlorn upon the beach, whence we retired to a hole in the ruined wall of the old citadel.

Jazira, or Jazira ibn Umar, once important, is now but

F

a large and excessively filthy and ruinous village, peopled by Arabs, Kurds, Turks, and Christians of various kinds. Its importance is evidenced by the existence of some police, and we were soon made aware of their existence.

When we first arrived, as we were short of a few odds and ends, I went and explored the bazaar, which is good and well stocked, considering the size of the place. There is also a public bath, into which I put my nose and fled. The bazaar sells rope (for which the place is locally famous), dates, desiccated cheese, dried fruit and raisins, and the usual imported articles. I wanted dates, I remember, and had a curious time getting them, for the inhabitants, mostly Kurds, would not believe that I was anything but a Turk, fez and overcoat being inseparably connected with that race in the minds of a people who dress in peg-top trousers of native cloth, shirts of the same, and felt waistcoats.

I had acquired sufficient Turkish to speak by now, but Kurdish came more easily off my tongue, so at the first shop I reached, where I saw dates exposed for sale, I asked the price in Kurdish, and was answered in Turkish. Mentioning the price I professed to be ready to give, I received the assurance of its impossibility in Turkish, with an assertion, not made without pride, that the speaker knew that tongue.

"Very good," said I; "but I don't."

"How? do you only know Arabic, then?"

"No, I don't know Arabic; you must talk Kurdish."

"Where do you come from?"

"Diarbekr and Aleppo and the cities of the West?"

"And don't know Arabic?"

"No, nor would I speak it if I did, to a Kurd."

"Then you must be a Kurd, but your language is not ours; where is your country?"

"My country is one you never saw—Persia."

"Persia!" he exclaimed, and shouted to his neighbours, "Here is a Persian!"

Several collected about, anxious to see me, for it is a curious fact that anywhere along the Tigris above Bagdad no Persians exist, nor ever come, and are greater strangers in this out-of-the-way corner than a Greek.

There was soon a small crowd around, and ignoring my need of dates, the heartier ones took me off to a café, and I was kept there for an hour or two answering questions about Persia, and learning a little about Jazira, the chief feature of which was, according to them, the bridge of boats which crosses the river during the summer only, and a hill upon which the Ark is said to have grounded on its way north to Ararat.[1] I at last escaped, and having purchased dates and rope, was returning to the kalak, when I met our late skipper, who sought me, to say good-bye, as he was returning on foot to Diarbekr.

I was proposing to give him a penknife I possessed, but he saw he had nothing of equal value, and would only accept a handful of dried dates, in exchange for which he gave a cake of sweet bread. He had just received his pay for five days' hard work, which required skill, experience, and probity, the sum of two shillings. No wonder people employ Kurds in preference to lazy and incompetent Arabs and Turks.

The third day an extra row of skins with three more rafters was added to our raft, and half an hour before we were supposed to start, eight soldiers of a Turkish

[1] There is practically no doubt that the story of the Ark's journey is as inaccurate as that of Jonah and some other incomprehensible narratives of the Jewish chronicles. Sir William Willcocks, whose work in investigation of ancient waterways in the Euphrates valley will soon achieve fame, has practically proved that Noah was flooded out in an exceptional season that inundated the whole of the flat plains of the lower Euphrates and Tigris, a district now flooded regularly every year. The Ararat upon which he landed was Ur of the Chaldees, situate upon a mound which, above the waste of water which in flooded seasons looks like an illimitable ocean—would have appeared a considerable eminence. Futhermore, and completely refuting the possibility of a journey to Ararat, is the fact that the strong prevailing wind which blows, has blown for thousands of years during springtime from a northerly direction, would have kept Noah south, even if we can disregard the fact of the rush of water southwards to the Persian Gulf, to say nothing of all the high mountains of Kurdistan and Armenia between Chaldea and Ararat.

regiment from Kharput calmly walked on board, knocking the captain overboard, for he would have protested.   These creatures, by their behaviour and subsequent cowardice and brutality, disgusted us to such an extent that had we foreseen the annoyance their folly and bestiality would cause, I think we should have all got out and walked from Jezira to Mosul.

However, we were trying to coax them to sit in such positions as would not endanger the raft's equilibrium, when upon the ruined wall above two uniformed persons appeared, and a third, who came aboard with a confidential serious air, told us the police required us.   Haji, the Arab merchant, the soldier, and myself, climbed the wall and were ordered in a surly manner to produce passports. The others had not theirs with them, but mine was ready, and I produced it, hoping that affairs would pass off as easily as at Diarbekr.

Not so, the policeman read the whole thing, then turned sharply upon me, and informed me that I had stolen an English tourist's passport, that I was obviously an Oriental, or why this method of travelling, this dress, this acquaintance with Kurdish.   In vain I protested, and he asked me my name.   With horror I heard the voice of Haji, just arrived, answer :

"This is Musa Effendi, a Persian gentleman, for whom I vouch; my very good friend and comrade, a good companion, and a devout Muslim."

The policeman folded up the passport with a triumphant air, and directed his two men to take me to the police office.   A sudden thought helped the situation.   "I am a British subject," I exclaimed; "touch me at your peril; thank God we have a consul in Mosul who awaits me.   If I do not arrive, there will be the devil to pay."

And heartily glad I was that the passport supported the statement of British subjectivity.

"Then how comes it," said the policeman, who never doubted that I was a Muslim, "that you do not bear a Muhammadan name? and are described as Protestant? which all know is a kind of Christian?"

The feeblest bluff saved me; perhaps they distrusted the truth of the details written there.

"As to the name," I said, "the English law recognises only surnames; if you are a native of Mosul, are you not called a Mosulli wherever you go? are you not known among strangers as 'the Mosulli'? so I am described as of 'Elisun,' which is my native place. As to Haji's assertion that I am Persian, why, that is right enough, are there not thousands of Persians born British subjects? and God knows why the Kafir, the heathen Armenian clerk of the passport department in Constantinople, called me Protestant, except that seeing I was an English subject, imagined that, as the English nation is Protestant, I must be also of that schism."

The chief policeman thought it all strange, but I received unexpected assistance from his lieutenant, who had apparently been to Constantinople, and, to air the fact, asserted that he knew well the English habits and laws, and that what I said was quite possible. My now almost silenced assailants had yet one more kick left, and it was obviously quite his trump card.

"Then if you are English by subjectivity," he regularly shouted, "produce your English passport."

I did so, amid the silence that such a curious and formidable-looking document produced, and it saved me. Without a word the Turkish "tezkere" was handed back to me, and feeling now doubly triumphant, for I had proved the disguise of language, manners I had adopted, almost too perfect, and had, at the same time, demonstrated to a crowd of unattached roughs and Turks, that bullying could not extort from me the money which was the sole object of the policeman.

Half an hour later, Haji and the Arab merchant came back, cursing the Turks. The old man had a passport which had been handed him when he left the army thirty-five years before, in the days of Sultan Abdul Aziz, and had been forced to pay a mejidie because it was so old. The Arab had a similar document, and paid a similar sum.

With a feeling of great relief, that even the presence

of our eight soldiers could hardly quell, we cast off and commenced our journey to Mosul.

A few words are necessary here of Jazira. It was occupied for a long time by the Romans, who built the citadel, but before that its position at the entrance to the mountain system of Masius gave it importance as the outpost of the city of Nineveh, in Assyrian times, an importance it retained till quite recently, when Turkish influence has killed it. The ill-fated pretender Meherdates passed here in A.D. 49, on his way south, and the Emperor Trajan, a century later, made it a depôt for the wood he cut in the mountains, to build ships for the invasion of Babylonia, then in Parthian hands. We are told that it suffered much at the hands of 'wild Kurds, and later it has been the scene of many bloody battles. For many years it was owned and ruled by the Khans of the great Hakkiari tribe of Kurds, and was a Chaldean centre while they ruled there. In the world of Oriental literature it claims a position as the birthplace of Ibn ul Athir, a great Arabian historian, who was born there A.D. 1230. To-day the mixed population has a reputation for roguery, treachery, and lawlessness.

Here begins the great plain, which, occasionally broken by insignificant hills, at last, below the Sinjar range south of Mosul, drops to the dead level of the Mesopotamian plain, which, unrelieved by even a mound, stretches right away to the Persian Gulf.

The passage from Jezira is usually, in springtime, reckoned as two days, but we were not to be so fortunate. Our raft, very heavy to row, presented a large surface to the wind, and the day after leaving Jazira, a strong breeze drove us against the bank. We struck with a terrifying crack of tree-trunks, and some skins burst, no serious damage really occurring. It was sufficient, however, for the army. With one accord, crying out curses upon the river and the wind, they rushed to the edge of the raft nearest shore, and despite a 5-foot bank, past which we were skimming at a high speed (for we had not stuck), they leaped off, leaving coats, shoes, and food behind. Two or

three had near escapes from drowning, and all got partially
immersed in the icy water. Scrambling to the top, they
attempted to pursue us, screaming to us to stop—in their
folly imagining it possible—but the thorns and the pace
at which we went, soon convinced them of the uselessness
of haste, and they desisted and were left standing in the
desert—and blaspheming.

We had not come off quite unscathed. A corner of the
raft was badly broken, the loss of skins allowed a considerable portion to sink under water. Moreover, a thole-pin
was wrenched out of place, making rowing very difficult.
Worst of all, the current became very swift, and we could
find no place with water sufficiently slack to allow mooring.
Till sunset we had to go on, when a fortunate side-current—
out of which we foolishly tried our best to row—took us
round the corner to a quiet pool, and we tied up on the
bank opposite to that of the soldiers' desertion.

All night we spent repairing, taking shares in the labour
of walking into the water and bringing ashore the heavy
bags of apricots—spongy with water. At dawn, tired, but
hopeful of a safe arrival at Mosul that afternoon, we set
out, but a side-current of exceptional force and speed
caught us, and cast us upon a rock, against which the
stream fought and broke. We took it broadside on. The
force overthrew our tent and the samovar of boiling water
for tea. Teacups, saucers, and such small fry, leaped out
into the stream, a bale rolled off, then a box—of mine—
skins popped or floated away detached, rafters smashed,
and we sailed away, carried along irresistibly, literally
sinking. The crew and passengers were busy trying to
save the cargo, that threatened to roll overboard. Rowing
was impossible, for an oar was damaged, and we could only
sit and wait for the next crash, which we were certain
would come, and hope that it might be in shallow water.

We were saved this, for, drawing near the beach, the
idea struck our captain to swim ashore with a rope, the
distance being some fifty yards. One man's strength, or
two, was patently insufficient, so three of us, the crew and
myself, stripped and fell overboard with the rope, notwith-

standing the protest against my action from Haji, who thought it *infra dig.* for an effendi, and even wondered how a person of any comparative importance could be expected to help himself in an emergency. We succeeded in getting a foothold about ten yards from shore, and though dragged along, at last pulled the raft in and tied up.

The whole day we all worked, unloading the raft, repairing and reloading, hindered by the soldiers, who turned up, refused to help, and would have beaten the skipper had we not intervened.

Finally, after accusing us all of stealing a shoe that had fallen overboard, they came to blows among themselves, and, assured that we should be repairing for another three days, left for Mosul, cursing.

Next day we ourselves arrived, weary enough, our raft sinking, and an hour or two after sighting the first garden of Mosul, floated down past the sulphur spring and the old wall of the town to the lower landing-place above the composite stone and boat-bridge, and, calling porters, Haji and I installed ourselves in a caravanserai in the bazaar, having been twelve days *en route* from Diarbekr.

CHAPTER V

MOSUL, THE CITIES OF THE ASSYRIANS, THE YAZIDIS

I suppose it must be the proper thing when writing of Mosul, to expatiate upon the antiquity of Nineveh; but so much has already been written upon this subject ever since Layard first uncovered its mounds, and so well written, that to attempt adequately to treat of it here would be presumption. Suffice it to say, that around Mosul, the modern city, which stands opposite the ancient Nineveh, sometime capital of Assyria, are the remains of Nineveh, old and new, while in the neighbourhood are Kalah, Asshur, Hadra, and Khorsabad (Dar Sharrukin), some of which are being excavated by energetic Germans, who publish yearly an excellently illustrated account of their labours.

The traveller to-day is shown by the people of Mosul the mosque and minaret of Nebi Yunis, "The Prophet Jonah," erected in Muhammadan times by Muslims, who had identified the site with that of Nineveh.

Christian, Jew, and Muslim alike pay considerable reverence to the shrine, although the two former are not allowed access to it. All believe in the ingenious story with a blind faith that should shake our modern sceptics. Unfortunately it is practically impossible, in these days of miracles explained, to believe in the fish of Jonah, that either slid across dry land, or, as Mr Fraser[1] remarks, "must have been a clever fish to swim 20,000 miles . . . in three days and nights," unless, as he sagely observes, "the fish . . . according to the Scriptures, had been specially prepared, doped perhaps, as they call it in America."

[1] David Fraser, *The Short Cut to India.*

The Bible, with that protective ambiguity not always absent from its more wonderful tales, says that Jonah embarked from Tarshish.   Now Tarshish, the Phœnician name for Spain, is just exactly the direction in which the unwilling Jonah would have fled in order to escape the tedious desert journey to Nineveh.   We are not told how far they got when the tempest broke out, but there seems no reason why one should not assume it to have occurred promptly, and to have driven the ship back upon the Syrian coast, when Jonah might possibly have landed, if we can ignore the fish.   Certainly the fish is unfortunately assertive, and its curious feat of carrying Jonah to a point three days from Nineveh is explainable only as hazarded above by Mr Fraser.   Also, the Tigris is hardly deep enough even for sharks above Tikrit, many miles towards Bagdad.

At any rate, one explanation is as good as another with so Biblical a history.   It would seem reasonable to suppose that Jonah, finding himself once more in Syria after his shipwreck, set forth for Nineveh, a journey which must have taken him anything between twenty and forty days.

But here, if we accept the foregoing theory, we are faced by another remarkable feat of travelling, for "Nineveh was an exceeding great city of three days journey," which has been taken to mean that Nineveh was three days away from where the fish vomited up Jonah.

But it is a noteworthy fact that the magnitude of the city is mentioned, so to say, in a breath with the distance from somewhere, and this supports a theory which, in all humility, is here advanced.

Those unfamiliar with Eastern colloquialisms cannot be expected to know that in these lands of camel and mule travel, the unit of travel is "one day," and since miles and furlongs do not exist—the parasang is a Persian, not an Arabian measure—"a day" means about twenty miles. Would it not be intelligible to say—when it is remembered that the name of a city still comprehends the cultivated lands about it—" Nineveh was an exceeding great city of sixty miles (in extent)," *i.e.*, with its irrigated lands, around which was, and is, sandy waterless desert.

The following verse[1] then reads intelligibly: "Jonah began to enter into the city a day's journey." He began to enter by the cultivated lands, and assuming the city to be about the centre, would reach it the second day. If, as we used to be told, Jonah was yet two days away from Nineveh when he predicted and cried, "Yet forty days . . ." and so on, the obvious conclusion must credit Jonah with an exceeding great voice, or messengers to carry his word before him, or unavoidably figure him as a fatuous fellow literally "crying in the wilderness."

If, however, we assume that for a day he came along through the fields and cultivations, he would arrive at the city the second morning, and his cry would naturally fall direct upon the ears of the townspeople.[2]

A curious feature of the whole business is that no mention of Jonah is made on the Assyrian monuments, which would surely have been made by those conscientious historians, the rulers of Asshur, if he had acquired such importance before the King of Nineveh as we are told in Jonah iii. 6.

Whatever be the solution of the story, the worthy prophet, who displayed a lamentable temper in his proceedings at Nineveh, enjoys the full respect and admiration of the good folk of Mosul, who in 800 A.D., inspired by the

---

[1] Jonah iii. 3.

[2] Professor Ragozin, in his excellent book on the history of Assyria, mentions a possible explanation of the "Fish," which, if acceptable, disposes entirely of that inconvenient creature.

"The very fable which is such a stumbling-block to the intelligent reading of the whole book becomes most unexpectedly cleared of its hitherto impenetrable obscurity when Assyriology informs us that the Assyrian name of the "great City" is NINUA, a word very much like "nunu," which means fish, the connection being, moreover, indicated by the oldest sign for the rendering of the name in writing, which is a combination of lines or wedges plainly representing a fish in a basin or tank. The big fish that swallowed Jonah was no other than the Fish City itself, where he must surely have been sufficiently encompassed by dangers to warrant his desperate cry for deliverance."

tale that occurs in the Bible, Turah, and Quran alike, erected the present mosque.

The Mosul people, especially the Christians, are very proud of their city and the antiquity of its surroundings. The Christians, regarding themselves as direct descendants of the great rulers of Assyria, assume an autocratic bearing in their relations with the plebeian Armenian, which I believe no one grudges who knows both races.

Mosul itself, crowded on and around its mound, a filthy and labyrinthine city, inspires the modern visitor with a respect for its apparent antiquity and its no less remarkable smells. I remember noting one most pleasing feature of municipal arrangements, which provides a kind of pool by one of the main streets where the superfluous contents of cesspools is emptied. Antiquity cannot claim Mosul as it does many a lesser city, it is only in Muhammadan times that it has come to importance, and held a place in the economy of Mesopotamia.

A modern Persian historian and geographer, Haji Zainu'l Abidin Shirvani, gives the following note upon Mosul, in his work, the " Bustanu's Siaha " (" The Garden of Travel "), p. 569 :—

" The general opinion is that the first person to build it (Mosul) was Zuwayid bin Sawda, and in Persian it was called Ardeshir. After Islam arose, the Hammer Arabs attacked and took it, building therein structures of stone, and a protecting wall, leading water to it, and making gardens."

Its proudest boast, as an Arab city, is that there is no definite record of it having fallen into Persian hands, a fact indisputable apparently ; but it must be remembered that, when the Persians possessed these lands, Mosul, if it existed at all, was a place of little importance.

To-day its most uncharitable detractor cannot say that. Despite its filth, the meanness of its bazaars, its unpleasant climate, and the Turks, it is a very important place, and a populous one, counting 90,000 souls, by a late and reliable computation. If the purpose of this book were to talk trade, it were possible to descant upon its

BAB-UL-TOP AND AUCTION MARKET, MOSUL.

[*To face p. 92.*]

leather craft, its cigarette-paper manufacture, its carpenters and masons; and it is but due to the Christians to say, that whatever commercial importance it possesses is due to their efforts, and to their efforts alone.

Here, of all the cities of Syria and Mesopotamia, the Christians enjoy more freedom from persecution than any other population of the same persuasion forced to live side by side with Musulmans. They themselves attribute this desirable state of affairs to the fact that both Muslim and Christian are Arab in language and sympathy, and above all are bound together by the bond of fellow-townsmanship that is often so strong a consolidating feature of isolated towns in the East. At all events the statement is supported by the immunity they have enjoyed from molestation during all the massacres of Christians that have occurred within the last two centuries.

They affirm that on one such occasion the Turks endeavoured to rouse the Musulmans of the surrounding districts to enter the town and slay the Christians, and did their utmost to incite the Muslim townspeople to assist in the massacre, but so far from their proposals being met with consent, they were warned that any attempts of the kind would see Christian and Musulman combined.

Nowadays, when Mosul is a city fairly well kept in order, when street murders are of not more than weekly occurrence, the place is full of the Turk, who seeks a post in a city where the hostile Kurd and nomad Arab cannot offend his dignity by their disrespect, nor menace his person with their ever-ready rifles. The language of the place is Arabic, but Turkish is understood, as is also Kurdish, for Kurdistan is not far away, and the wild characters one meets sometimes in the bazaars tell of the proximity of the tribes.

Bad government and continual insecurity of the country have done their best to restrain the people from any attempt at permanent buildings, the result being that every bazaar, mosque, and caravanserai is broken down and ruinous; in fact, Mosul strikes the stranger as a squalid city on the verge of disintegration. A few moments out-

side the city one steps into the Mesopotamian desert, and
Mosul, standing there, a mound in a desert, looks every
bit what it is reputed among the Western peoples, a city
buried in a remote and unmerciful wilderness. To
approach it from any side except Diarbekr, by river, one
must pass several days of the almost waterless desert
road. Only to the south-east is the land fertile, and one
understands why it is in that direction that Assyria proper
lay. To-day the distant Zagros Mountains and their
unknown and feared Kurds form a barrier as unconquerable as ever the ancients found them; and to them it was
my purpose to go.

We put up in an upper room of a khan or caravanserai
called Hamad Qadu, and as our ways lay together, at least
as far as Erbil, we thought to continue in companionship.
But Haji found a cousin, who dragged him off to his house,
and so we settled up our accounts and parted. The old
man seemed to have conceived a great affection for me
during his journey. "I never had a son," he said, "for
never did I take to myself a wife, for women are affliction
and tribulation; but now I am old, I realise what it might
have been to have had a son, and I curse the stiff-necked-
ness that ran me counter to the infallible laws of the
Omniscient," and he wept awhile, embraced me, and
departed.

Left alone in my stone cell, I bethought me of finding
a muleteer to take me to Sulaimania, and as the café is
the advertisement medium of the East, I betook myself
there, inquired for a "qatirchi," as the Turks call a
muleteer, and found myself immersed in local politics.
The bearing of them upon my need of a mule appeared at
the end of the story, and may as well do so here.

There are in Mosul a number of Sulaimanians engaged
in trade, besides the inconsequent people who in the East
travel from place to place apparently for the love of it.
There are also soldiers galore—creatures dead to any
feeling of self-restraint, decency of behaviour and manners,
who are a curse to the place they pollute. A brawl
occurred, owing to an assault by a drunken soldier upon a

Kurdish woman of Sulaimania, and as Kurdish blood, even the vitiated blood of Sulaimania, is hot, it boiled, and many Mosul people were killed.

The primitive laws of these parts count the blood-feud as their chief, and here was sufficient to keep the two towns at feud for years. No native of Mosul dared go to Sulaimania, and equally, no Sulaimanian dared show himself in Mosul, though he was safer in a city where sufficient order prevailed to prevent his murder, except under provoking circumstances.

Besides this, even were there not these obstacles to free intercourse, a Kurdish tribe called the Hamavand had cut all communications on the Sulaimania road, killing and robbing all who attempted the passage.

That was why I could get neither mule nor muleteer, and had to face the prospect of remaining in Mosul indefinitely. To this I could not resign myself, and cast about for some means of approaching Sulaimania by another road.

Two days I spent in idleness, passing the time in my room and at the café. The question of food was simplified for me by the excellent dates and buffalo cream in the bazaar, upon which, with unleavened bread, I lived, desiring nothing better.

On the third morning three or four Turkoman natives of Kirkuk appeared, and tried to make me hire mules to that place, which is half-way to Sulaimania. Big, rough men, almost like Kurds, speaking Kurdish fluently, they dilated upon the dangers of the other routes, the impossibility of going to Sulaimania from Keui Sanjaq, whence I had entertained hopes of going. They would not give me transport to Sulaimania, but would undertake to find me mules if any went on, a very safe compact for them had I accepted it. But I resolved to wait a little longer, thinking that perhaps they would, finding cargo scanty, consent to take me all the way.

My patience was rewarded, but not as I expected. That afternoon, returning from the café, I was hailed by a sorrowful-looking individual, who turned out to be a native of Sulaimania and a muleteer. It seemed that he had been engaged to bring from that place a merchant, who had made himself so obnoxious to the natives as to prefer the risks of Mosul to those of Sulaimania. The muleteer, not in any actual danger, was nevertheless somewhat nervous about staying in Mosul, and as all trade was stopped between the two places, could not hope for loads, all of which considerations put him in such an accommodating frame of mind, that he was ready to start at any time, and accept the sum of four mejidies (about 13s. 4d.) for the six days' journey.

So I paid him his earnest money of a mejidie, and sealed the contract by a cup of tea at the café. The Turkomans were somewhat disconcerted when they heard of the transaction, and predicted all kinds of catastrophes, particularly robbery and murder by the Hamavands, through whose country they swore we could not pass.

However, we started next day in the afternoon. The mules were on the opposite side of the river, so porters had to carry the luggage over the bridge of boats and its stone continuation to the flat beach on the other side, where loads were piled, awaiting mules for Kirkuk and Keui Sanjaq. The mules appeared about four o'clock in the afternoon, and we started. My steed was loaded with two boxes, slung at either side ; upon these bedding was laid, and the whole secured by a long girth, and I climbed to the summit of the erection and experienced once more the joys of sitting on a sloping half-yard of bedding through which all the knobs of the pack-saddle asserted themselves. Upon such a seat one has to sit for twelve hours at a stretch very often, and to the inexperienced the question of balance is usually sufficient to occupy attention till the lumps beneath him begin to bruise.

To my surprise, instead of heading south-east, we commenced to go in a northerly direction, but this I found was to reach a good camping-ground for the night. For an hour or so we went through a kind of thicket, and at last, emerging on a little plain where the grass grew high and green, we cast our loads, and the mules were led off to water. Our party was a small one, all natives of Sulaimania, except one muleteer, a Kurd of Halabja, a place I was to see later. The muleteer himself, Rashid, had an assistant, an ancient man of vile temper, and he in his turn boasted a menial youth. There were two other travellers, a servant clad in a long green overcoat and pegtop trousers; and a kind of pedlar. These last strongly advised me to discard my fez for a skull-cap and turban, and provided me with the necessary articles for constructing one.

It appeared that in wearing the conspicuous scarlet headgear I was a source of danger both to myself and the others, for the Kurds, who hate anything and everything appertaining to Turks, have a way of singling out this mark of the beast as a target. Even the overcoat I wore was a subject of deprecation, for we were getting to the land where, if one is not a Turk, it is "aib"—a fault— to wear anything but what custom sanctions.

The costume of Sulaimania cannot be termed Kurdish, though the wearers style themselves Kurds, with what accuracy will be seen later.

It is the fashion to use the striped Aleppo cotton cloth called "Shaitan Baizi" (which means the "white demon") for garments, and a Sulaimanian outfit is as follows:—A pair of white cotton trousers, very baggy in the legs, but gradually growing narrower towards the ankles, which they embrace tightly. Socks are not worn, but the feet are shod with red leather shoes, of which the toe turns up in a point. The back is often taken up to a tapering flap of several inches long. The undershirt is equally of white cotton, reaching to the hips, and fastening at the neck with a knob of cotton made into a button. The sleeves however, a kind of exaggerated surplice sleeve, hang down in a point reaching the ground, and serve for wrapping up money and papers, for drying the face of water or sweat, and cleaning the nose after it has been emptied by the application of the fingers and a powerful snort. Over these garments a long tunic of cotton cloth, open at the front and reaching to the heels, is brought together by a

G

waistband or belt. The sleeves of this are open from the wrists to near the elbow, permitting them to be easily turned back and rolled up, when the superfluous shirt-sleeve is rolled round and tied about the upper arm.

If it be cold, a sleeveless waistcoat of thick felt is worn, and an abba, or camel-hair cloak, is the property of every person of any importance. The inferior classes make their abbas of a thin cloth, of a grey or yellow colour. The head-dress is several blue and white handkerchiefs wound about a skull-cap of black cotton cloth, ornamented with flowers worked in silks. The style of head-dress marks to a great extent the different tribes of Kurds. A heavy dagger stuck in the girdle completes the costume for the towns-man. This is the dress of the Sulaimanian as well of the Hamavand, Jaf, and other extreme southern tribes, who have discarded the old fantastic garments. The real Kurdish costume, which will be described later, is very different.

My dress, however, had to pass somehow, and the muleteer coming up, made the useful remark that if a stranger adopted the customs of a new country, at once he would forfeit the consideration granted him by those he met on the road, which is a very true observation.

By sunset we had the tea ready, the little glasses circulated, and, casting our bread and dates on to a common handkerchief, we dined, and then, wrapping our-selves in our cloaks, lay down in the shadow of ancient Nineveh to sleep, none of my companions aware that where we reposed was just under the palace walls of Sennacherib.

There are, opposite Mosul, the remains of two great cities. The most ancient of all Assyrian palace-cities is Asshur, the city of Tiglath-Pileser, whose name occurs in the Bible so often, that great spoiler of the Israelites, who reigned eleven hundred years before Christ. The ruins of this, now known as Kileh Shergat, are situated on the west bank of the Tigris, some distance below Mosul. Lower down still, where the Greater Zab River joins the Tigris, are the ruins of Nimrud, or Kalah,[1] the royal city of Asshurnazipal, who ruled Assyria from 884 to 860 B.C., and whose campaigns extended, like those of many of the Assyrian kings, to the Mediterranean coast.

North-north-east of Mosul is the place called Khorsabad, a Kurdish name meaning "The place of the bear," or a corruption of Khosruabad—"The Abode of Khosroes," but known to the realm of Assyria as Dar Sharrukin, the palace of Sargon, a great ruler, who carried away the Jews "into Assyria, and placed them in Halah, and in Habor the river of Gozan, and in the cities of the Medes," i.e., in what is the western portion of what is known as Assyria proper. The River Habor is now called Khabur, a tributary of the Euphrates, in central northern Mesopotamia.

Of the great cities of the Assyrians there remain Arbela, to be spoken of later, and Nineveh, probably the most famous of all. This is situated partially in the mound upon which the shrine of Jonah now stands, and at Koyunjik, a mile or two farther north, just by where we camped. This latter is the older Nineveh. Here, Sennacherib in 700 B.C. built himself a palace in the already ancient city in the fashion of his ancestors. Part of his life he spent in the wars with the Jews: he had summoned Jerusalem to surrender, had besieged it, had done his best to resubdue Judah and Israel, when he was driven off by a plague, a fact recorded by Isaiah. From Syria to Persia, from Armenia to the Persian Gulf, in the manner of his fathers, he waged war, and subdued again the ever-rebelling lands, finally retiring to his palace at Nineveh, to be foully murdered by his sons.

His fourth and favourite son, Esarhaddon, succeeded him in 681 B.C., and in 670 B.C. commenced the palace of New Nineveh, the mound of Nebi Yunis, the other side of the brook Kauther, which we had crossed in the afternoon, and which in those days existed.

In these mounds, of which four have been partially excavated, furnishing us with a wealth of precise informa-

---

[1] Kalah was founded by Shalmaneser I., 1300 B.C.

tion and glorious sculpture, there lies yet many a volume, and as yet Arbela, which is as ancient as any of them, is untouched.

Next morning early we arose and loaded our animals, and took a course almost due south. First, we recrossed the historic brook Kauther, passed under the shadow of Nebi Yunis mound, upon whose sides is a large village, and had before us a great rolling plain, entering which we were upon the ground of ancient Assyria proper. To our left ran a range of low hills, and in their folds were many villages, dull collections of mud-huts half-buried in the ground. But they contain two races whose history is full of interest. No Musulman inhabits this plain; there are but Chaldeans and Yezidis, those "Devil-Worshippers," who have been accused, besides worshipping Mephisto-pheles, of adopting and practising the rites of Semiramis, the priestess of the lascivious cult of the worship of the sexual organs.

It is due to these Yezidis to clear their character of this last accusation, for which no reason can really be attributed except the hatred of the Muhammadan and Christian commentators, whose object has been solely to discredit them, and not to enlighten general readers.

The Yezidis, while recognising a Supreme Being, shun allusion to him as forcibly as to the devil, the mention of whose name, or any word suggesting the evil principle, occasions them infinite distress. When the name of Satan cannot be avoided, they use the expression Malek Taus (King Peacock),[1] or Maleku'l Kut (The Mighty Angel). They believe Satan to be chief of all the angels tempor-arily fallen in punishment, but to be restored eventually.[2]

---

[1] Layard mentions the image of the bird, which local tradition has seized upon as a proof of idolatry, but neither he nor any subsequent traveller could gain a sight of it, nor learn more of its use than that it was sent from place to place (being a small object) accompanying important messages among the high priests.

[2] This is the usually accepted theory. The Tiflis Yezidis, how-ever, gave a later inquirer a different version, stating that Satan has, after weeping sufficient tears in seven vessels to quench the seven hells of his seven thousand years' exile, now been reinstated in Heaven.

Next to Satan are counted Gabriel, Michael, Raphael, Azrael, Dedrael, Azraphael, and Shemkiel, seven powerful angels who influence the affairs of this world.

They reject none of the holy books of the various religions, but while placing full confidence in the Old Testament, regard the New Testament and the Quran simply as holy books worthy of veneration.

Christ they consider an angel, and deny His crucifixion,[1] and Muhammad, Abraham, and the patriarchs they reckon as prophets. Moreover, they await both a reappearance of Jesus Christ, and the coming of the Imam Mahdi.

The name of the sect is of doubtful origin, but Layard is inclined to a theory that it may be connected with an old Persian word meaning God.[2] The theory advanced, particularly by Shiah Muhammadans, that they were founded by Yazid,[3] the murderer of the saint Husain, is obviously untenable, and was put forward solely in order to further discredit them. The true origin of the sect is quite unknown, and the peculiarly mingled nature of their tenets makes investigation difficult. The Avesta, the sacred book of Zoroastrianism, about the 6th century B.C., mentions and execrates certain devil-worshippers, and Zoroaster himself had a campaign against similar people in north Persia. There are, in the faith of the modern Yezidis, certain indications of a connection with the ancient faith mentioned in the Avesta as being that of prehistoric peoples—a species of nature worship. But then there are equally indications of the survivals of the old Chaldean or Babylonian sun-worship, particularly in the reverence they pay to the sun, called by them Shaikh Shems, and the moon, as Shaikh Sin, corresponding to Shamash and Sin of the ancient mythology.

Can we assume this important event to have happened since 1839, when Layard was informed of the theory quoted in the text?

[1] Here they have adopted the Muhammadan tradition, see Quran, iv., 156 : "They slew him not, and they crucified him not, but they only had his likeness." [2] Yazd, Yazdan.

[3] Or, that Yazid became a leading member of the sect.

Their customs, like their tenets, display a remarkable catholicity. They baptize, circumcise, reverence the sun and moon, carve Musulman texts upon their tombs, quote the New Testament, allow polygamy, consider wine lawful, and certain meats forbidden, a mixture of the habits of Zoroaster, Assyrio-Babylonian, Muhammadan and Christian worship unequalled by any other sect. They abhor the colour blue, and never use it in their dress nor display it in their houses.

The centre and apparently original seat of these people is near Mosul, and there, in a valley of the Kurdish hills, is buried the Yezidi saint and prophet, Shaikh Adi, who is said to have lived variously in the ninth and eleventh century.

Very little has hitherto been known about Shaikh Adi, the date of his existence is disputed, and his identity has not been even hinted at, except for an ingenious theory put forward many years ago, attempting to connect him with Adde, a discipline of Manes.

So far we have had to be content with the assertion advanced in a Persian work that he was one of the Marwanian dynasty of Khalifas or "Caliphs," an error easily discovered.

I think, however, that the following explanation may be now accepted, the result of investigations in various Muhammadan works, to the authors of which he is well known.

From these the writer has extracted the information that Shaikh Adi was the son of Musafiru' Zahid, of the family of Ummaya, a native of Baalbek in Syria. In the reign of Marwan (early eighth century), he "was transferred" to Mosul,[1] and resided in the towns of the great Kurdish tribe of Hakkari, where his great sanctity gained him a large following among the peoples there residing.

He died during his exile, and was buried in a valley called Lash,[2] which means in Kurdish "the place of

---

[1] Original reads "wa antaqala bi'l Musil" (Taraiq ul Haqaiq).

[2] I made inquiries when in Mosul and afterwards, regarding this place, which is called Keuwi Lash, or The Mountain of a Body—or

a body," probably a name given after the interment.

There are four ranks in the priesthood of the Yezidis: Pir, Shaikh, Qawwal, and Faqir. The first, a Kurdish and Persian word signifying an elder or a saint, are persons of great sanctity and abstention. The Shaikhs (leader, chief), correspond to resident priests, while the Qawwal (speaker) are itinerant, and are expected to sing and dance in the festivals which demand those exercises. The last order, the Faqir (poor, humble), perform menial tasks in attendance upon the tomb of Shaikh Adi, at the valley of that name near Mosul.

The language used is a Kurdish dialect, but Arabic is employed in their chants and hymns.

A great deal of mystery surrounds their origin, and, as reading and writing are considered crimes among them, documents do not exist to help speculation. Layard imagined them to be Chaldean by origin, who have adopted the outward forms of many religions as a protective measure, and incidentally fallen into confusion regarding their own tenets.

They have been regarded from earliest times with execration by Musulman and Christian alike, and have lived ever at hostility with all their neighbours. At one time they possessed some numerical strength, and harassed their enemies very seriously, but a Kurdish chief subdued them and broke their power by a wholesale massacre. Since then they live here and there among the Christians and Kurds, a certain number still inhabiting the Sinjar range of hills, which stretches in a westerly direction from Mosul. They also exist in the Caucasus, near Tiflis and Bayazid.

Since Layard's time they have suffered further persecution from Turk, Kurd, and Christian, and at present are in a miserable state of poverty. Except for the fact

corpse. A Muhammadan priest of Mosul informed me that Shaikh Adi is certainly buried here, and reverence is paid to the tomb by some Musulmans, who, however, are inclined to shun the place, owing to its association with the Yezidis.

that they do not wear blue, they are indistinguishable from the population of Kurd, Turkoman, and Chaldean among whom they live, except by those little marks only a native or a dweller in the land can discern.

South of the range that we passed that second day out of Mosul, and beyond the River Ghazar, they do not exist now. This river we crossed, trending to the east of our morning course, and had great difficulty in passing its ford, the mules several times tottering, rendering the rider's balance doubly insecure. The river is an affluent of the Greater Zab, and flows into it very near the place we passed. In fact, our course, which was towards the Greater Zab River, lay across the point of land, a few miles wide, between the two. We reached the high banks of this historical stream in the afternoon at the same time as the rain, and finding our way half-way down its cliffs by a little path, threw our loads upon a ledge some ten feet wide, and sheltered under a projecting rock.

Across the river we saw the flat plain of the ancient province known as Adiabene to the Parthians and Medes, the most sought-after, the most fertile of all the lands of Assyria, itself Assyria proper. At this time of the year, it was a carpet of rolling green.

Below us, the river, in spring flood, roared around the rocks strewing its broad course, and looking upstream we could see the white peaks of Kurdistan tearing the ragged clouds. Opposite was the village of Zailan, inhabited by a curious sub-tribe of Kurds in Arab dress, of a savage and wild habit and speech. Here, at the same spot that has seen the fording of the armies of the Assyrians, Persians, and Romans, lay the old road from Nineveh to Arbela, which was the sacred city of Assyria, and upon this road the conquering kings of that mighty nation returned to do homage and render thanks and sacrifice to Her of Arbela, the Goddess of Victory. Upon this ancient way we were taking our humble course, and like many of our great predecessors, were stopped at the ferry by the flood. In our times a tiny ferry bark, like those described on the Euphrates, takes passengers across, but it was just loading as we arrived, with some donkeys, and the owners had no intention of attempting another crossing in the storm. While they were employed thus I received a call under my rock, from the chief of the place, an individual in a white hairy cloak. He tried me in Turkish and Arabic, and we conversed in the former for a time, during which he told me that, flood or slack, storm or calm, ferry or no ferry, the village had to pay 600 liras a year to the Government of Mosul as the tax upon that part of their revenue. Moreover, did the natives refuse to work at a scheme so often unprofitable, they were chastised by soldiery. Consequently the price exacted for passengers, two and four footed, was excessive, a donkey paying 1s. 8d. and a mule 3s. These considerations did not seem to affect the Kurds, for in the manner of their kind, they worked like fierce demons, steering and rowing their unwieldy craft with shrieks and laughter. Though called Kurds, and displaying some resemblance to the race, I should think there is a strong Arab mixture amongst them.

We collected a heap of sticks, and sat round a blazing fire, shivering. Sunset was accompanied by renewed wind and rain, so no sooner was it dark than we covered ourselves with everything we possessed, and lay down upon the soppy turf to sleep. The mules were tethered on the ledge, and every now and then one of us would awake suddenly to find a huge nostril puffing inquiring breaths into his face, or to save a quilt or coat being stamped into the earth by his odoriferous neighbours.

CHAPTER VI

THE ZAB RIVERS, ANCIENT ASSYRIA AND
ADIABENE, ARBELA, KIRKUK

REFERENCE to a map will show a rhomboidal space of country with natural boundaries upon all sides, of which the Tigris forms the western. From it spring the others, the two Zab rivers, Lesser and Greater, running up at an angle to meet the Zagros range, which, parallel to the Tigris, makes a fourth boundary. Within these limits lies a land, part plain, part hill, well watered, and of a pleasant climate and extreme fertility, and this was Assyria proper, and the later kingdom and province of Adiabene, whose eastern border, the Zagros Mountains, harboured then, as now, hordes of savage hill people, and formed at once a barrier and a menace, even to the kings of Assyria.

The northern river, that upon which we were camped, is the Greater Zab, known to the Romans as the Lycus. Its proximity to the capitals of Assyria (Kalah was at its mouth) kept it in a protected region during Assyrian times, and the first great battle recorded upon its banks is in 128 B.C., when the Assyrians were but a memory. At the spot where we camped, Indates, general of an army of Fravartish, a Parthian monarch, descending from the Median hills (Zagros), met Antiochus, a Syrian king of renown.

Here a fierce battle was fought, ending in the defeat of Indates, and Antiochus erected a monument upon the spot of his victory, to commemorate the defeat of a powerful Parthian.

106

The Lesser Zab, a smaller river, a long day's journey across the plain, has acquired more fame in battle and history. Tiglath-Pileser I. in 1100 B.C. mentions on the famous cylinder found at Asshur, "forty-two countries altogether, and their princes from beyond the Lesser Zab, the remote forest districts at the boundaries to the land Khatti,[1] beyond the Euphrates, and into the upper sea of the setting sun,[2] my hand has conquered from the beginning of my reign until the fifth year of my rule."[3]

In A.D. 52, during the time of dispute between Parthians and Romans, Vologases, the Parthian king, undertook an expedition against Izates, the tributary king of Adiabene, "the land between the two rivers," but having encamped upon the Lesser Zab, was called back suddenly southwards by rebellions in the cities there.

However, the battles for which the Lesser Zab must be above all events famous, are the battles between the Khurasan forces of Abu Muslim the Abbaside and those of Abdullah ibn Marwan in A.D. 749, and between the same Khurasanis and Marwan himself, in A.D. 750, five months afterwards, in both of which battles, Marwan, the last of the long line of Ummayid khalifas, was defeated. The importance of these battles ranks as high as any in modern Eastern history, for by the decisive victories gained there, an Arab khalifate of immense power was terminated, and replaced by a Persian dynasty, the House of Abbas, of Khurasan, in Eastern Persia.

"It may truly be said that Qadisiyya and Nihavand were avenged on the banks of the Zab," says a great authority, alluding to the battles one hundred and ten years before, when Zoroastrian Persia was broken before the Arabs of the new faith of Muhammad, whose descendants in their time were to become the subjects of those Persians to whom, in the folly of their own ignorance and savagery, they had applied the name Ajam—'the Barbarians.'"

---

[1] The Hittites.
[2] The Mediterranean.
[3] Ragozin's *Assyria*, p. 57.

From our position on the Greater Zab it was a day's journey (ten to twelve hours in the saddle) to Arbela, or Erbil, as the modern style has it,[1] and we crossed the river early, and by sunset were arrived. The situation of the town is in a low hollow at the foot of a small range of hills, behind which rise a higher ridge of the Zagros. Consequently, it would not be visible across the rolling plain, were it not for the huge mound that marks the buried ruins of the city of the goddess Ishtar.

The particular afternoon we approached it was a typical spring day. In the plain we had slight showers, but as we approached the mountains, we began to draw into the region about which the thunder-storms circled. Our first view of Erbil was remarkable. Heavy clouds were driving along by and over the mountains, from which the rain descending in grey curtains shrouded the landscape. Brilliant lightning flashes showed up crags of hills among the clouds, and a rainbow attempted to arch the scene. We were searching among the confusion of showers for a sight of the town, when a heavy cloud and its pendant shower passed, leaving a patch of travelling sunshine behind; and, as a curtain that sweeps by, with the muttering of thunder, this veil swept from before Erbil, and shining red and lurid in the sunshine we saw its mound—mysterious, and indistinct, backed and flanked by tortured black clouds and their downpouring rain. For an instant we saw it thus, and then from overhead occurred a cloudburst. The clouds descending in a funnel-shaped deluge hid the mound, and a din of thunder broke out about it, brilliant lightnings playing the while, making a tumult of the elements fitting in its grandeur to the memory of that great goddess of all, Ishtar of Arbela.

We were just in time to see the little town by daylight. There are no signs of antiquity about it now, except some Muhammadan ruins. All those of Assyria are safely conserved in the mighty mound upon which the modern Turkish ruler has built his castle. The height of the mound is very considerable, rising far above the roofs of

[1] The Kurds call it Haoril and occasionally Haolir.

the highest houses, a mound so great as to appear natural; one would never credit the fact that it covers the works of man, had we not seen the palaces of the Assyrians elsewhere. Here, where was the great temple that during a thousand years and more received the homage of all races and monarchs, there is every reason to believe that the accumulated embellishment and offering must have made there a shrine unequalled, perhaps, anywhere in Asia.

When we arrived it poured with rain, and in the dark we slopped through the alleys of a modern Eastern town, and over a mound to a ruinous caravanserai, where I found a damp, half-inundated room for my belongings. Since nothing, not even wood, was obtainable, I dined off tea and dry bread and a few dates that night, and slept in a pool. My companions had become separated in the dark, and had found asylum elsewhere. Here is the western border of southern Kurdistan; and Erbil is populated by Baban Kurds, a sedentary tribe, speaking a variation of the Mukri dialect.[1] Turkish is also understood, or rather Turkoman, for Altun Keupri and Kirkuk, Turkoman towns, are not far off.

In the tenth chapter of Genesis, 8-12, we read :—" And Cush begat Nimrod : he began to be a mighty one on the earth. He was a mighty hunter before the Lord : wherefore it is said, Even as Nimrod the mighty hunter before the Lord. And the beginning of his kingdom was Babel, and Erech, and Accad, and Calneh in the land of Shinar. Out of that land went forth Asshur, and builded Nineveh, and the city Rehoboth, and Calah, and Resen between Nineveh and Calah : the same is a great city."

Now the date of the building of Asshur's city is at least 1800 B.C., and verses 11-12 allude to the small district of Assyria proper, with its three cities of Kalah, Nineveh, and Arbela. During the whole time of the Assyrian monarchies Arbela took the relation to the reigning king's capital that Canterbury did to London in English history : it was

---

[1] Formerly one of the most famous and powerful families of southern Kurdistan.

always the religious capital, gaining an added importance, for that in Assyria the king was always the high priest of the religion of Asshur. That Ishtar, the goddess Baalath of the earlier Chaldeans, transferred her shrine northwards when Assyria began her separate existence, is probable ; and Arbela (whose name Arba-Ilu means " Four Gods ") was chosen, perhaps as being the shrine of some then existing divinity. So that the Erbil of to-day is at least three thousand years old, and was the second seat of that goddess Ishtar to whom reference was made in Chapter II. The vitality that has kept it in existence since those early days has not deserted it any period, for it has been worthy of mention at least once during the supremacy of every one of the nations that successively ruled it—Assyrian, Mede, Persian, Greek, Parthian, Roman, Armenian, Roman again, Persian, and the Arabs. A few notes arranged chronologically will show this.

Asshurnazipal, 884 B.C., a king who showed the city great favour, calling it " his city," took here a captive king who had rebelled against him, " flayed him alive, and spread out his skin upon the city wall." Sennacherib, a greater king, perhaps the most famous of all kings of Assyria, performed a pilgrimage there in 692 B.C., to pray for success from Ishtar in his coming battle against the Babylonians. He was answered. His son Esarhaddon, but twenty-four years later, being in the northern mountains engaged upon an expedition to avenge the foul murder of his father, is described as having communicated with Ishtar the goddess, and received from her shrine at Arbela messages of encouragement and assurances of victory.[1]

A few years later, in 656 B.C., Asshurnazipal (Sardanapalus), preparing for war against Elam (modern Arabistan in south-western Persia), made a great pilgrimage there, to pray for a sign from the goddess, which was granted. The temple was then one of the most glorious of Assyria. The usurping king, Teumman, was duly defeated, and many captives were brought to Arbela, and, in the brutal manner of the times, flayed alive.

[1] Ragozin's *Assyria*, p. 161.

At the end of that century—in 608 B.C.—the battle of Nineveh finally overthrew the great empire, and the Medes took possession of it, Arbela falling into their hands. The city's sacredness must have ensured a certain immunity from sack or destruction, for it was important eighty and odd years later, when Darius crucified there a petty king, him of Sagartia.

Till Alexander with his army invaded Asia, it remained in tranquillity, but in 331 B.C. a great battle there made it a Greek town.

However, it was but eighty years after that Arsaces I., the liberator and founder of the great Parthian empire, conquered Adiabene, and subsequently the sanctity of Arbela won for it the distinction of becoming the burial-place of the Arsacid kings of Parthia. The Greek and later Syrian kings of the Alexandrian Succession had, however, sufficient hold over the province to make it necessary for the Parthians to fight them for it ; and not till about 136 B.C., did Mithridates, a Parthian monarch, overcome the last of them and possess the country then called Adiabene, ancient Assyria proper. The province became, under Parthian rule, governed by a petty king or "vitaxa."

Armenia in 83 B.C., under Tigran I., the ruling prince, who for some time enjoyed considerable power, possessed itself of Arbela and Adiabene, but was driven out a decade after he entered it, by the Romans and Parthians acting in concert against this insolent upstart. Under the Roman and Roman-Parthian sway the province of Adiabene—always coveted for its richness—attained prominence, for the Romans desired absolutely to possess it and its capital.

So in A.D. 49, Meherdates, a Parthian prince in exile at Rome, being invited by the Parthians to expel the tyrannical Godarz, proceeded from Nineveh to Arbela to meet the usurper, encouraged by the allegiance of Izates, king of Adiabene. He met Godarz near Arbela, and after a long battle, decided chiefly by the desertion of Izates and other fickle friends, he was defeated.

Thirteen years later, A.D. 62, Tigran V., a king of Armenia appointed by the Emperor Nero, attracted by the richness of Adiabene, and by the absence of the Parthian king Vologases I., attempted its invasion. He harassed the unfortunate people so much, that they sent to Vologases complaining, and threatening to earn peace for themselves by giving allegiance to Rome. The Parthian king responded promptly enough, declared war upon Armenia and the Romans, and appointed Manubaz, king of Adiabene, to command of an army, which expelled Tigran and invaded his country.

From this time Adiabene became a bone of contention till the Persians rose up, and smote Parthian and Roman alike, to found once more an Aryan empire.

In A.D. 115 the Emperor Trajan occupied the province, which resisted bravely; but his successor Hadrian, unable to hold it, relinquished it two years later. Severus, one of the greatest of the later Romans, fired by ambition and a desire to chastise the Adiabenians, who had given him great trouble by helping other states to resist him, invaded the country, but Vologases, in A.D. 196, expelled him. Severus, however, made a final attempt a year or two later, and this time added Adiabene to the Roman Empire, establishing his right to the title Adiabenisus, which he had prematurely assumed in A.D. 193.

Arbela under the Roman rule suffered a scandalous and sacrilegious outrage by one Caracullus, who, returning from an expedition against Babylon in A.D. 216, broke into and violated the Parthian royal burying-place, dragged out the bodies, and cast them away.

It had but ten years longer to exist under the foreign tyrant, for Artaxerxes (Ardashir) the Persian, of the new Sasanian dynasty, conquered it, and expelled both Roman and Parthian from that and many other lands.

Under the favourable rule of this enlightened and civilised monarchy the Christians made great progress, obtaining protection and encouragement from the Persian Zoroastrian monarchs, and Adiabene was in A.D. 500 the see of a Chaldean bishopric, including Mosul and Arbela, where the shrine of Ishtar, after having exacted worship for a couple of thousand years, fell into a speedy disrepute.

In the 7th century the hordes of fanatic and savage Arabs swept away the Persian culture that was fast becoming imbued with Christianity, and Arbela and Adiabene fell into those depths that engulfed many a greater city and province. However, Arbela was sufficiently important to be mentioned as one of the larger cities sacked and ruined by the barbarian Mongols of Hulagu Khan in the 13th century. Fortunately the ruins of Ishtar's temple and the old city were then hidden under a covering of earth that time had deposited upon them, and thus Nature has preserved them for Western investigation, from the hands of a human pestilence that respected neither monument of God nor man.

During the centuries the Kurds, who drive out many peoples, have occupied the city, which is still the most important of the province. So powerful is the Kurdish language, however, that in many places whose population is not of that race, the forceful, graphic language has displaced all others; and as in Sulaimania, the people, originally mixed, now call themselves Kurds.

As we entered Erbil at nightfall and left it in the dark of dawn, I had practically no opportunity of seeing its modern aspect, but its mound was visible till we had gone many miles over the flat plain. Starting at four in the morning, we got into Altun Keupri in the late afternoon. To the north of this town the plain gives place to low hills, the valleys of which at this time of the year were a mass of flowers; but the rain once more overtook us as we passed by the pretty gardens outside the little town. Here the Lesser Zab crosses the plain from east to west, marking the boundary of old Assyria proper, and the later Adiabene. Altun Keupri, a place without any particular history, is situated on an island between two branches of the river. From the north it is entered by a long bridge with a turn in the middle, like an elbow. Reaching the entrance to this, one is challenged by an individual who emerges from a hole in a wall, and counting the mules, gives tickets in

H

return for payment of tolls, which tickets enable the passenger to pass the bridge on the south side free of further charge. The place is picturesque enough, standing up upon its island, the house-walls being built in a continuation of the low cliff face, giving it a fortified appearance. One long street runs through the town, which among the river Arabs and in Bagdad is known as Guntara (Qantara), "The Bridge." There is a little bazaar, occupying half the length of the town, which gives place to a coffee-house and a tea-house lower down. Then come the barracks, which occasionally harbour a few soldiers; and lastly the telegraph office, which one passes, to reach another large coffee-house and the foot of the bridge that gave the name of "Golden Bridge" to the place.

"Gable Bridge" would have been more correct as a descriptive title. To ride up or down is impossible, the loaded mules and horses have to be carefully pushed and guided over its precipitous slopes.

As an example of the daringly experimental in bridge design it is excellent, and its extraordinary appearance must have impressed its builder very considerably to gain the name "Golden Bridge": it is of the most prosaic and uncompromising stone and plaster.

I found out more about the place later on, but on this occasion we passed right through it, and in a downpour threw down the loads in a yard among a few houses on the south bank of the river. My companions repaired to a little tea-house near by, and I found a room in a corner of the yard occupied by a darvish, who followed the trade of mat-weaver, a craft unknown in these regions. This room he consented to share with me, advising me not to sit too near the door, which had a habit of falling down occasionally. As I was in a town and my Kurdish head-dress was soaking wet and very heavy, I discarded it for my fez, thereby gaining the title of "effendi" from the darvish, where before I had been but "brother" or "beloved." Moreover he busied himself to attend upon me, asking me in Kurdish the while where I was going. At last he stopped in the middle of puffing at a smoky fire, looked up at me with a half smile and addressed me in Persian. He had detected a Persian word or two I had used in Kurdish. Hearing my Persian he displayed his knowledge of tongues by asserting that I was undoubtedly a Shirazi, and receiving a confirmation of his statement, immediately changed his "effendi" for "agha," the Persian polite form of address. Nor was he content with this adjustment of affairs; he rose, and taking my hands in his, kissed me on both cheeks, ejaculating:

"Bi haqq i 'Amiru'l Mu'minin chashmam raushan shud va ruzigaram bi ghurbat khush!" ("By the right of the Lord of the Faithful[1] my eyes are lighted, and my days in the strange land made pleasant!")

Never did I realise more vividly the truth of the Kurdish saying, that Persian is the sweetest of tongues; or the Shirazi, "that a word of Persian in a strange land is better than a drink of water in the desert." After weeks of harsh Arabic, uncouth Turkish, and rough, if not disagreeable, Kurdish, Persian came like the voice of a friend among enemies. My darvish was a native of Nishapur, the birthplace of the famous Omar Khayyam, and had travelled on foot from there to Mecca, and though it was now three years, had not yet returned, wandering towards it gradually, earning a living by the exercise of his craft. Now he would not allow me to so much as light a cigarette for myself, and sent me out to the tea-house while he swept the room, prepared tea, cooked some eggs, and got some curds and bread.

So I strolled out, and entered the little place where a dozen people were sitting round on high benches, and had a place made for my fez—not me—by a Kurd, distinguishable by his headgear. I found that my companions had already spoken of me, and I was thus introduced as a Persian of Shiraz, by name Ghulam Husain, which the Turks could never get hold of, calling me Husain Ghulam Effendi, or Husain Effendi. My fellow-travellers must have

[1] The Iman Ali, termed only by the Shi'a or Persian Muhammadans, "Lord of the Faithful."

advertised my place and circumstance, for tea was brought, and the Kurd beside me, getting up, took away from before a muleteer a little table upon which to put my glass. It is the custom in Turkey in Asia, and Europe too, to greet a newcomer with the " Marhabba," at the same time raising the hand to the eyes.[1] The habit is, besides being an act of politeness, a very true gauge of the relative importance of newly met persons. By the number of " Marhabba " the stranger gets, he can judge the position he shall take among those assembled. On this occasion everyone, including two Turks in uniform, saluted me thus, and I replied to all in the popular fashion, dabbing at my forehead in everyone's direction, only uttering audibly, " Marhabba, Effendim," to the Turks.

My Kurdish neighbour, I found, knew a little Persian, and had been to Teheran and Kashan. He introduced himself as a Kurd of the Mukri, a native of Sauj Bulaq, the Mukri capital, and lamented the fate that kept him in Turkish territory mending shoes. Here I began to get in contact with the sentiment I found often expressed by Christian and Kurd alike all over southern Kurdistan and eastern Turkish territory, a leaning towards Persian rule and custom, and an emphatically expressed aversion to all things Turkish. Among the Kurds this sentiment takes so strong a form, that many of them set themselves to make a study of the Persian language, and employ it in all transactions requiring writing, never using Turkish unless forced to do so.

Half the occupants of the coffee-house were Turkomans, natives of Altun Keupri, which is one of the settlements which originated in the times of the Seljuq Sultans —in the Middle Ages. They are a pleasant race, and proud of their descent ; nor do they display much sympathy with the Ottoman Turks, whom they regard as plebeian, and their contempt for their mincing and malpronounced Turkish is unbounded. Their own language, which is the

---

[1] This action is an abbreviation of the compound wave, which apparently beginning by lifting imaginary dust, places it upon the mouth, eyes, and head.

same as that of Azarbaijan in Persia, they call Turkoman, and it is a rough, forcible tongue pronounced in the guttural manner the Turkish originally displayed.

After consuming a couple of glasses of tea, I rose and returned to my darvish, whom I found seated behind my tin samovar, tea prepared, the room swept. He had procured a number of flaps of bread, a large bowl full of "dugh" or "airan," as the Turks call it, which is curds mixed with water.

In Persian fashion he rose as I entered, his hands crossed before him, nor sat till I was installed upon my strip of carpet and had requested him to do so.

My muleteer now appeared, and Qadir, one of my fellow-travellers, Kurds both. These sat upon the door-step, and by the light of a candle we partook of tea. These two, hearing myself and the darvish speaking Persian, introduced us to the rhyme which is ever being quoted all over Kurdistan—

> " Laoza laoza arawia
> Turki hunara
> Farsi shikara
> Kurdi guzi kara ; "

a doggerel signifying,

> "Arabic is sonorous, Turkish an achievement, Persian is sugar— and Kurdish an unpleasantness." [1]

The darvish and myself became so engrossed in the reminiscences of Persia in which we indulged, that we quite forgot the presence of the two Kurds. Our conversation outlasted the candle, which guttered out on its end in the mud wall, and by the light of a burning stick the darvish spread our bedding, and we retired, to the sound of a chant which he murmured under his cloak, till he fell asleep, mainly consisting of "Bismillah ar Rahman ar Rahim, al Hamdu'l illah Rebbu'l 'alemin ar Rahman ar Rahim."

---

[1] Persian translation of the last line :—
"Kurdi guz i khar ast."

He woke me next morning by murmuring gently,
"Agha! Agha!" in my ear. To rouse a sleeper noisily
is a breach of etiquette among Persians.

It was just dawn as we crept along the stony road
leading out of Altun Keupri to Kirkuk. There are three
roads between the two places, and the condition of the
country determines which one the caravan takes. This
time we were to take the longest; for to our left, the
east, lay the Hamavand country, distant certainly, but
whence roving bands of Kurds emerged, raiding. By
turning to the right, about ten miles outside Altun Keupri,
we should pass through a long range of low hills which
runs between the two places, and have their protection on
our left as we went south to Kirkuk. These are almost
the last of the ranges, which, rising higher and higher as
the Kurdistan highlands are approached, are the sentinels
of the Zagros range, which itself is the rampart of the
Persian plateau. All along this road, till we put the hills
between ourselves and the east, we could see far-away
snowpeaks beyond Rawanduz, that were on Persian soil.
We found a way through the range, which is not more
that 500 feet high, and came out into a broken place of
foothills, where were a few Kurds grazing sheep, and lower
down some Arabs cutting green barley that would have
yellowed and scorched if left longer. For here is the hot
region; Kirkuk is on the same plain as Bagdad, and
suffers from an even worse climate, the hot winds scorching it during several months of the year. Clear of these
hills, we came out to the flat desert that stretches away
west to the Tigris, and beyond to the Euphrates, and
beyond again to Syria, a dead level over which the hot wind
of summer blows, or where in later spring the air, getting
stagnant, grows hot, and one bakes in the shadowless
waste. Four hours from Kirkuk, whose gardens were
visible as a dark line on the horizon, we passed a ruined
caravanserai, which a native of Kirkuk, jogging along on
an ass, assured me was the remains of a caravanserai built
by Shah Abbas of Persia, some 300 years ago.

Wheat was growing in some places along the roadside, but a swarm of small black locusts covered the road with their hopping millions, which were making havoc among the young stalks. Farther on, we were alarmed by the sight of some black tents, the abodes of nomads, and we were not reassured when two horsemen cantered up from behind a fold in the plain. They were Kurds in dress and appearance, but persisted in talking Arabic as they rode along, probably to conceal their dialect. Our suspicions of course at once made them Hamavands, and the one or two of us who possessed rifles slipped a cartridge in. But they either heard or saw a signal in the hills we had crossed, for leaving us suddenly they put their horses to a gallop, and soon disappeared among the hillocks. We were quite close to Kirkuk, where the roads, short and long, converged, and as we came to the junction, an Arab, who had come from Altun Keupri by the short route, told us that our horsemen were two of a gang which had looted a caravan that morning in the hills. It appeared that this band, an outlying one of the Hamavands, patrolled the long road one day, and the short one the next. Our luck had sent us along while they were engaged elsewhere.

Kirkuk, which lies at the end of this range, is invisible till nearly approached, for, forced by the necessity of getting near the water-supply, it has taken a position by the river-bed (which is dry half the year), and is quite hidden by the hillocks around, except from the east side, where the ground slopes gradually down to it. It possesses a mound, upon which part of the town is built, the remainder being round the south of its base.

We entered an outlying village, passed between gardens to a huge barrack where the garrison is quartered, then by a line of coffee-houses full of idle, uniformed creatures, over a long stone bridge, and turning to the right, plunged into the gloom of a short arched bazaar of extraordinary height and width, and out again along a busy street to a clean, new caravanserai.

This, like so many of the caravanserais in the towns of Mesopotamia, is of a composite nature. Its yard and the stables surrounding afford accommodation for beast, while the rooms which enclose it on three sides, upstairs, harbour both travellers, and residents, who are strangers without women-folk. The entrance to this caravanserai was between two huge cafés, at the back of which the yard lay, and above this long entrance were the offices of the mayor, and the agent of Singer's sewing-machines, an article which has penetrated to the remotest districts of Kurdistan. These offices opened upon a gallery which communicated direct with the rooms set apart for passengers.

Kirkuk is famous for Turkomans, fruit, and crude oil, all of which abound. The town, which must have a population of at least 15,000, is one of the trilingual towns of the Kurdistan borders. Turkish, Arabic, and Kurdish are spoken by everyone, the first and last being used indifferently in the bazaars. Itself a Turkoman town, to its south and west are nomad Arabs, and to its east the country of the Hamavand Kurds. Turkish power is very evident here. Being near to Bagdad—seven days—and possessing a Turkish-speaking population, it is in a position to supply a large number of youths to the military schools, which, half-educating the lads, turn them out idle and vicious, and incapable of existing without a uniform. The result is that they all obtain some post, telegraph, police, or customs, or join the ranks of the superfluous and un-attached army "officers," and return to their native town to lounge in the innumerable tea-houses, and earn a living by tyrannising over whatever unfortunate their position enables them to blackmail and persecute. Consequently, Kirkuk is full of uniforms containing the scum of the town, often drunken brutes—who sap the life of the place, driven to any length of rascality to gain a living, for they are usually unpaid. Despite this plethora of police, I was unmolested, probably the composite crowd of the Kirkuk bazaar makes a stranger too inconspicuous for their attention.

The architecture of the place is purely Arab; the Persian influence noticeable in Bagdad, Mosul, Diarbekr, and other cities of Mesopotamia and Syria is not seen here. Solid stone buildings of no beauty, a few mean mosques and minarets, very solid, but with no ornamentation, and an immense arched bazaar, make the architectural features of the place. The Turkoman population, or rather the commercial section of it, compares very favourably with the people of Bagdad and Mosul. A stranger meets with great consideration, nor is he swindled right and left, nor annoyed, as among the Arabs of the greater cities. Purchasing food and other things in the bazaars, I found everywhere an astonishing honesty and rough goodwill that wins the heart of a stranger, and this, notwithstanding the fact that I was taken for a Persian, and a Shi'a Muhammadan, with whom the Sunni has very little sympathy.

I can quote an example which shows how this hospitable quality often appeared.

Some days after I arrived there I found the soles of my boots flapping under me as I walked, so repaired to a shop in the bazaar where Bagdad shoes were for sale. Selecting a pair, I proceeded to bargain, but not knowing the proper price, I was somewhat at a loss to determine my highest figure. The shopkeeper asked two mejidies or forty piastres, so I proposed eighteen piastres, and brought him down by degrees to twenty-two, when having nearly halved the original price, I thought it sufficient, and assented. I produced a mejidie in payment, and was groping in my pocket for the two piastres remaining, when the shopkeeper extended his hand, saying :

" A mejidie is the real price ; you are a stranger, and did not our prophet command us all to honour the stranger ? Take the shoes, for from you I will not take more than a mejidie, for a Kirkukli the price is twenty-five piastres, but big profits among ourselves do not matter, whereas from you—who I hope will go from Kirkuk with pleasant remembrances—I am content with what a mejidie gives."

This sentiment I encountered everywhere in Kirkuk, except from the Christians ; but that is but natural, seeing that I was in the guise of a Muhammadan. I experienced later the kindness of the Chaldeans for strange Christians in the town.

Besides the Turkomans and other Muhammadans there is a large number of Chaldeans and of Syrian Christians, natives of Bagdad. A few Armenians are also there, employed in Government and commercial affairs, but they are natives of Diarbekr or Armenia. The Chaldean settlement is of considerable antiquity, having migrated here, according to their own traditions, during the time of Alp Arslan, in the 11th century. If Kirkuk is, as the natives assert, a remnant of the Seljuq kings, this is possible, and perhaps even probable. Unlike the Chaldeans of Mosul, they have not forgotten the Syriac character, and while they speak only Turkish, employ these characters in writing among themselves. It is only the Chaldeans who are found living among the Kurds, who have retained their language, both written and spoken. In Mosul, where it is reckoned part of a good education to know it, it has no generality of use, and one has to go to the villages to hear it spoken.

There is a church in Kirkuk administered by priests from Mosul; the Chaldeans are, like nearly all in Turkish territory, Roman Catholics, for the old Chaldean Church died under the unscrupulous assaults of the Roman Catholics, who pursued a Machiavellian policy in bringing over the old Church to Papal allegiance, a change which has been for nothing but the worse.[1]

In Kirkuk they enjoy great freedom from persecution, despite the periodical efforts of Muslim priests to incite ill-feeling against them. Their presence is too necessary to the well-being of the town to make a massacre anything but a catastrophe for the Muhammadan traders, who have been led by their integrity and capability to place great

---

[1] Lest this statement seem unwarrantable, I beg to support it by the opinion of the Chaldeans themselves. They are in most cases fully aware of the circumstances under which their forbears—and contemporaries—became absorbed into the Roman Catholic Church, and there are very few of them whom I ever heard express any sentiment upon the matter save deep regret, the more so that they know now that it was possible to have the much-prized education the Roman Catholics supply without a disintegration of their Church, for the Archbishop of Canterbury's mission has taught them that.

faith and confidence, and often to deposit large sums of money with them. In these qualities of honesty, and an ability for getting on with Muslims amicably without conceding a particle of their behaviour as strict Christians, they contrast very forcibly with the Armenians, Syrians, and Arab Christians.

They are distinguishable by their head-dress and shirt-sleeves alone, for they wear the long, striped tunic reaching to the heels, and the zouave jacket or " salta," which, however, they do not ornament with scroll-work in gold and silver as do the Kurds.

Their shirt-sleeves are tight round the wrist, and do not appear below the long sleeves of their jackets ; while their head-dress, a blue handkerchief round a skull-cap, is worn broad and flat, embracing the head closely, not standing out as do the turbans of the Muhammadans.

Up to recent years they still displayed a partiality for light yellow striped garments, a relic doubtless of the choice of colour forced upon them in the early Middle Ages by the Khalifas of Bagdad, who commanded all unbelievers to wear a distinctive dress, usually honey coloured.

In Kirkuk is a large colony of Jews, the first of the hosts of that race that exist from here eastward all through Kurdistan to Sina of Persian Kurdistan and Hamadan.

It is thought possible that these are direct descendants of the Jews of the third captivity,[1] whom Nebuchadnezzar carried away to Babylonia in the 6th century B.C., just after the fall of the Assyrian Empire.

They use the Aramaic character, and in Kurdistan speak Hebrew, a remarkable fact being that the Chaldeans of Sina in Kurdistan and the Jews of the same place, while survivals of different epochs, speak almost exactly the same ancient Semitic dialect, a conclusive proof, were any needed, of the Semitic origin of the Chaldeans.

---

[1] " In the third year of the reign of Jehoiakim king of Judah came Nebuchadnezzar king of Babylon unto Jerusalem, and besieged it. And the Lord gave Jehoiakim king of Judah into his hand, with part of the vessels of the house of God, and he carried them into the land of Shinar."—Daniel i. 1-2.

In Kirkuk, as in all Kurdistan, the chief occupation of the inhabitants is that of drapers and mercers, the cotton cloth and print trade is entirely in their hands; in fact so far have their co-religionists of Bagdad progressed, that the cottons of Kurdistan are supplied from Manchester by Bagdad Jews settled there.

Kirkuk is thus a collection of all the races of eastern Turkey—Jew, Arab, Syrian, Armenian, Chaldean, Turk, Turkoman, and Kurd—and consequently enjoys considerable freedom from fanaticism, besides being strongly governed by a Turkish governor who possesses sufficient military strength to keep in order almost every element, the Kurds being the only difficult section of the population, with their contempt for all rule and order that does not emanate from their own khans.   Unfortunately this excellent state of affairs does not extend for more than a mile or two outside the town, where Arab and Kurd roam at will, defying all.

In the bazaars one occasionally sees a knot of swarthy fellows, very ragged, speaking a dialect only the traveller in south-western Persia can recognise.   These are the Faili Lurs, Persian subjects, whose presence warrants the institution of a Persian Consul here.   This individual forced himself upon my acquaintance in the following manner :—

The frequenters of the tea-house by the caravanserai, during the first few days of my stay, came to know me as a Persian of Shiraz, and as Persians are rare in Kirkuk, the consul heard quickly of my existence.   I was waited upon one day by a Kurd wearing a Lion and Sun badge, but with no other sign of his office as a consular servant.   He demanded my Persian passport, and could not be convinced that I was a British subject, and consequently not amenable to Persian passport laws.   Nothing I could say could convince him, the very fact of my speaking Persian fluently damned my assertions; but I was inflexible, and he eventually went away.

Two days afterwards he turned up again; but this time I was prepared to prove to him my identity as a Persian-born British subject. To this end I had arranged my Foreign Office passport, which bore the visés of both Turkish and Persian consuls in London. These contained a certain amount of writing in the two languages, and under each of these I wrote in Indian ink, which could be erased by licking it off later, the words " Mirza Ghulam Husain Shirazi," under the Persian visé in the Persian " shikasta " hand, and under the Turkish in the handwriting adopted by Turks. This I now produced with a flourish, displaying with triumph to the messenger and a few of the bystanders with whom I was acquainted the English arms and the signature of Sir Edward Grey—and then turning to the back, the Persian and Turkish visés with my name under each. Perfect success met the scheme, the servant changed his tone and became polite, and the effect upon my audience was to win me many " marhabba " afterwards in the café.

Next morning I was engaged in a little tailoring. My overcoat was getting too warm, or rather, the weather was getting too warm for the coat, and I had no other garment sufficiently long to be dignified, save a thin corded dressing-gown. Perforce I adapted this. I took off the abundant braiding, removed the waist-cord and sewed on some buttons, and produced a garment thereafter called a " labbada " or long coat, such as religious students and Azarbaijan merchants wear.

I was sewing on the last button, when a knock came at the door, and the servant of the Persian Consul stood there bowing, " Would I come and see the Persian Consul on a friendly visit? He was in the caravanserai and very anxious to make my acquaintance." So donning my new garment, I followed him along the gallery.

I found him in a room over the gateway, seated at the upper end upon a small carpet. Below him, that is, against the long side wall and nearer the door, was a collection of varied Kurds, of Sauj Bulaq, Sina, Merivan, and other Persian towns. Their head-dress of handkerchiefs indicated their origin. Standing up near the consul was an elderly, thick-set man, bushy-bearded, wearing the baggy trousers and shirt tucked in, that are typical of the muleteers of the Persian border, but his pointed cap proclaimed him a Mukri. The room was partly taken up with three tables, upon which stood basins and copper vessels containing various concoctions. A tray covered with small sweetmeats, just cooked, stood by an earthen oven in a corner; and a young man was engaged in placing therein a fresh tray full of uncooked confections. Sugar loaves lined the walls, hanging by nails, and a smaller table near the window was covered with bottles of colouring matter and the apparatus of a sweet-maker's trade. Amid all this the consul sat, a grey, fierce-looking man, in Kurdish dress, but he wore upon his head the felt hat and narrow handkerchief of the Kermanshah Kurd.

To this assembly I entered, walking delicately to avoid numerous obstacles on the floor, and all rose, answering my "Salamum 'alaikum" with a sonorous "alaikum as salam," to which the bearded man added the "wa rahmatullah wa barikatah."

The consul made place for me by his side, and in excellent Persian replied to my compliments. The assorted Kurds, who understood very little, began a discussion about some tribal feud somewhere, and left us to a conversation in which the bearded man, who turned out to be the proprietor of the sweet business, and a Persian subject of Sauj Bulaq, joined. This old fellow, Haji Rasul, was a darvish of a sect of the Shi'a Muhammadans.

Our conversation turned inevitably upon politics, and thinking my companions must be Nationalists, as are most Persians nowadays, I began to describe some of the doings of the Majlis in Teheran during 1906 and 1907. They listened in silence for some time, offering no opinion, but when I ceased, the consul began with great enthusiasm a flowing eulogium of Muhammad Ali Shah, cursing in the most powerful language the revolutionary movement that tended to put power in the hands of mean schemers, plebeians, and heretics. His arguments hung upon the nail of fanaticism, as I am afraid most of the Royalist arguments ever did in those days, and warming to his subject he read me a homily upon the evil of allowing my young mind to be led away by the specious arguments of them who called upon the saints to witness the right of their evil actions. Apt quotations from the Quran he poured out upon me, growing ever more excited, and at length ceased suddenly, out of breath, and hot. I managed to steer him away from this subject, and he began to relate his difficulties and the qualms of conscience he had had in the matter of his late wife, whom, suffering from some terrible internal disease, he had taken to Mosul to the English doctor there.

"This matter," he said, "is a constant source of anxiety to me, for I have not the satisfaction of knowing that God sanctioned the means by the end attained, for she died. I took her from Sulaimania to Mosul in a palanquin, and laid her before the European's door, together with presents of gold and silver, and a bottle of brandy I had bought specially, knowing such things acceptable to the Christians. And he was moved to pity, for he was a generous man, though an infidel, and, refusing the presents, took her in. And many days he spent, labouring with all his knowledge to cure her. Despite the shame of this discovery of her nakedness, and the ridicule it might pour upon me, I persisted, but He who knows took her life. And I yet think that her death was perhaps an expression of the Almighty displeasure, for though but a woman she was a Muslim, and the wife of a Muslim, and the procedure was not in propriety."

He seemed relieved when I was able to quote him the case of a High Priest's wife in Shiraz who had been cured by a European doctor.

After this the meeting broke up, and he departed, and I after him. I subsequently learned that with the appointment of consul he combined the craft of watchmaking, and was known as Mirza Saatchi—"Mr Watchmaker." The old man, the proprietor of the sweetstuff shop, had something to say before I left, and he addressed me in his feeble Persian mixed with Kurdish:

"I am an old man," he said, "and by many cities have I wandered, from Salonica to Basrah, and Trebizonde to Mecca, but never have I missed the opportunity of cultivating the acquaintance of a Persian or Shi'a. Let us not forget one another. We are both strangers, both of that land that is the fairest of all the earth, where mercy and charity overspread the land, where Muslim treats Muslim as a brother and not a foe—like these Turks. Let it not, therefore, be said that I, Haji Rasul, though I am but a poor Kurd, have violated the tradition of Islam, Persia, and the Kurds alike. Here I work by day, and in the verandah I sit at night, alone; help to relieve my loneliness by your constant company while you are here."

The old man was so evidently sincere, and expressed himself so fervently, that I felt forced to promise to come and see him that evening.

There was a long bench in the verandah from which we could look down at the crowd below and the operations of the police, whose headquarters was just opposite. Here, too, every morning an auction was held, amid a crowd that sat upon high benches under a tree, drinking tea or coffee, discussing local politics, and hatching plots against their neighbours.

The crowd that frequented these coffee-houses—there were four of them round the caravanserai door—were the idlest collection of creatures it is possible to imagine.

Being near the mayoral office, police court, and one or two other public offices, the attendance of uniformed parasites was enormous, and these, appearing about the twelfth hour (then about 7 A.M.), sat till the second hour, then lounged away to their houses in the town, appearing again at an hour to sunset, and sitting there chattering and rattling the everlasting tasbih, the Muhammadan rosary, till late at night.

The newcomer in Kirkuk, who would buy bread, experiences difficulty unless he can find the special bread-sellers, who hawk. this necessary comestible about in shallow baskets. Desiring dates, I purchased some the first day I arrived, at a shop, and noticing next door a basket of bread, attempted to buy two flaps, but the owners would not sell it. Nor would they consider the question unless I bought something at their shop. This I refused to do, and launched out in some indignation into a tirade against such a habit, which annoyed and harassed the stranger, leaving him hungry in a strange land. This induced them to attempt to make a gift to me of two pieces, which pleased me less, and at last they consented, very unwillingly, to sell me what I wanted. The sale of bread alone, by shopkeepers, is rare all over Sunni Mesopotamian country, and among the Turkomans, and they will—as in this case—give it rather than sell it. This is probably owing to the habit in these patriarchial lands, of making bread in the house which is given freely to all who request it; the sale of such a necessary is looked upon as rather degrading.

One evening at sunset I joined Haji Rasul where he sat meditating on his bench. He had a companion and assistant who performed the labour connected with their daily life, cooking, cleaning their room, spreading the bed-clothes and the carpet upon which we sat. This youth was a native of Smyrna, a simple Turkish lad, the best specimen of his race I ever met. He was a rarity in Muhammadan lands, a Sunni converted to Shiism, for the old Haji had converted him in Smyrna. Despite his travels he could talk nothing but Turkish.

A constant companion of this strange pair was a small white cat, to which they were both strongly attached. Having been with them since kittenhood, it fully reciprocated their affection, and had developed a high degree of feline intelligence.

The old Haji had brought it from Aleppo, and it possessed a little cage in which it performed its journeys. Its food was specially cooked for it by the youthful Turk, and it had regular time and its own dish, for meals.

Spotlessly clean it was, and very exclusive, desiring no intercourse with the roof-prowling cats of the caravanserai, whom it ejected from its neighbourhood.

I

Both Persians and Kurds have a strong liking for domestic cats, and in the bigger towns of Persia it is a sorry household that does not possess one or two, as petted as any in Europe.

It was a strange sight to see the rough Kurds who sometimes came to see Haji Rasul, gravely rolling cartridges for it to pursue, or stroking its arching little back with a lighter hand than they ever laid upon anything else, the while talking seriously to it in their rough tongue.

Haji Rasul himself talked Arabic, Turkish, Kurdish, and a little Persian. He had acquired these during his twenty years' wandering. From Sauj Bulaq he had started twenty years before, and had walked |via Kurdistan and Anatolia to Constantinople. There he had learned the art of making sweets. Saving a little cash, he embarked for Jedda, whence he performed the great pilgrimage. From Medina he walked to Damascus, and finding employment, rested there. Later he went by ship to Salonica, and thence to Smyrna, where he remained some years collecting money to make the long journey to Kazimain and Kerbela, near to Bagdad, the most holy shrine of the Shi'a Muhammadans. It had taken him two years working by slow stages to get from Smyrna to Kirkuk, and he was attempting to collect enough cash here to get him to Bagdad. At any rate he could not have gone when I saw him, for the Hamavand had closed the road to Bagdad by their raids.

Fanatical he was to a degree I seldom have seen. He observed the letter of the law regarding Christians, and was most careful to have nothing to do with them, yet I found him a just, charitable man, very kind hearted, and willing to take the greatest pains to help or make me comfortable. If a Christian said Salam to him, he would not reply by the same salutation, displaying thereby the haughty fanaticism of the most bigoted Shi'a ; yet, as every sincere Musulman must, he deplored the decadence of Islam and cursed more violently the backsliders of his own religion than the reprobates among Christians, "for," said he, "these have the law and the book, and the light of the saints before them; while those have ever been in a mistaken path, and know no better."

In all his dealings he was just, nor would he favour the Musulman more than the Christian in a matter of business.

He had a habit of dropping into deep meditation. One night he asked me my name; hearing Ghulam Husain, he repeated several times:

"Ghulam Husain, Ghulam Husain," he murmured, "The Slave of Husain, may I be his sacrifice! Ah! Husain, Husain, shall we not rise up and smite the Sunnis, for that they slew him, him the pure, the sinless, betrayed, and murdered by the evildoer—ah, what a name, The Slave of Husain, and what a life to live up to, Husain! Husain! . . ." and he would drop into a reverie murmuring now and then " Husain "—reviewing doubtless the details of the tragedy of that holy man, whose character bears comparison with that of any Christian saint, and whose self-sacrifice and resignation was no less heroic.

A Kurd himself, he deplored the levity of the Kurds, who are much given to dancing and singing. Each night the Kurdish muleteers would collect on the roof of some rooms in the courtyard, and chant their interminable "Guranis" or folk songs, dancing hornpipes of ever-increasing fury and joining in roaring choruses. Sometimes they would engage in wrestling matches, and cast one another about the yard, the exercise often terminating in a display of hot temper, when knives would be drawn, to be sheathed as an onlooker made a jest that called forth laughter from all.

We were hopelessly detained in Kirkuk. Behind, on the road we had come, the Hamavands had closed in; towards Bagdad it was the same, and to the east where our course lay was their own particular country, across which not even companies of soldiers would dare to go.

Every day it was announced that a certain army accountant, whose presence was needed in Sulaimania, would attempt the passage with a hundred soldiers, armed with Mauser rifles, and a number of mules were engaged;

but the good man never seemed to make up his mind to go. Rashid, my muleteer, had engaged all his spare mules to the Government for this purpose, and a daring Chaldean merchant prepared fifty loads of sugar for isolated Sulaimania. Sixteen days we waited, and at last the order came to load at midnight, and collect just outside Kirkuk—that is, to join the main caravan and the guard. The leader was one Shefiq Effendi, a Kurd of the Shuan or " Shepherds," a large tribe inhabiting the hill country south of the Lower Zab River. By his influence and that of the hundred soldiers, we hoped to pass safely these terrible Hamavands.

By law they were outlawed, and orders existed that any entering the town were to be shot on sight; but such was their reputation for daring, that I often saw them strolling in the bazaar of Kirkuk, caring nothing for a knot of Turkish soldiers, who followed them round, afraid to molest them, for the people of Kirkuk, armed though they were, and protected by a regiment of soldiers, feared a sudden raid of revenge from this intrepid handful of Kurds.

Hearing that I was resolved to go, Haji Rasul did his utmost to persuade me to stay. For they were Kurds, he said—Kurds, more savage than the Jaf, or the Guran, more daring even than the Mukri themselves. He took me by the hands, beseeching me to stay, nor risk the life God had given me for a mere mundane consideration of time.

" Time," said he, " is long, and your life is young ; what matter if you stay another month, two months, nay a year, if you are enabled to preserve the body God has entrusted to your care. Have I not been twenty years wandering, and do I complain that I have not yet got back to my native place ? "

We were seated round a mess of a kind of porridge at the time, in which we dipped our bread, eating it with our fingers.

" See," he said, " I eat this morsel not because I delight in its flavour, for it is of the poorest, nor because I crave a plenishment of belly, but I am performing that duty which is incumbent upon all of us, even pagans, the conservation of the flesh, which God has given into the keeping of our intellects."

Though the restless spirit of the Western had been long calmed within me, yet it was not quelled, and here asserted itself. For sixteen days I had remained in Kirkuk. The weather, with that suddenness of progress to hot and cold that it exhibits upon these dry plains, had grown oppressive; the plain which, when we arrived, was covered with green, if scanty grass, was now a bright yellow, the dried stalks were scorching, and the mules' daily expedition to the plain to graze was almost a farce. In that peculiar way that marks the approach of summer, the sun shot up at a high velocity from behind the crimson hills towards Kurdistan, climbed to his ever-mounting zenith, hung there, it would seem for twelve hours or so, and as quickly descended ; the hours of cool daylight were but three. Towards sunset the decrease in temperature was hardly appreciable, for the world was heating, and it took an hour or two of darkness to make it reasonably cool. As has been said before, the town is situated in a position that in our climate we should call "sheltered," which in these lands means extra hot and stifling. The afternoon hours were approaching that temperature which induces sleep behind closed doors, and the one occasion upon which business called me outside, at about three in the afternoon, showed me an empty town, and also scorching heat of the sun in Kirkuk in May.

Besides, the fez, the most utterly ridiculous headgear man ever invented, protecting neither from heat nor cold, acts with such calorific power as to make one's scalp regularly boil in sweat under a hot sun.

Flies, too, were breeding like microbes. My daily journey to the bazaar took me past some butchers' shops, and I noticed one morning that the never-cleansed beams upon which the meat hangs were unrelieved black in colour—flies, solid, and overlaid with flies, that hardly even moved when the butcher swept his long knife along, squashing hundreds, to cut meat next moment without even wiping his blade.   Fortunately the custom of the country doubtless prevents a great deal of disease that might result from such condition.   Butchers' shops open in the early morning till about the second hour; one sheep only at a time is killed, and until that is sold another does not appear.   Consequently owing to the short time during which it is possible to purchase meat, there is a great rush of buyers, and the flesh of the sheep and goats does not remain long enough than to have one thin layer consumed by flies.

Water was becoming scarce too; the river, which had run fairly full as we entered the town, was now the merest trickle, and all the water was obtained from wells.   To waste such a valuable would have called upon the stranger the wrath of all in the caravanserai, so a scanty rinsing of hands and face was all that could be attempted, and that only when I could by stealth draw a potful and convey it unseen to my room.   There are public baths in Kirkuk certainly, but even the natives, bound by tradition and custom to extol all indigenous institutions, admitted that they were not very nice.   Nevertheless it surprised them that I did not patronise the "hammam"; but what upset my neighbours was the fact of my shaving myself, which I had attempted to do in private, knowing the prejudice against it.   For the East reckons a barber as a very mean fellow, and to perform upon oneself, if it be the beard, a transgression of the Quranic law, and if it be the head, a dangerous folly.   And whether it be the result of this repugnance to the trade or a naturally despicable nature that consents to the odium, it is a fact that Oriental barbers are as a class very mean fellows indeed.

Through the offices of my friend the consular watchmaker, I was taken one day to see a notable of Kirkuk, one Reza, called by the Muslims Shaikh Reza, and by the Christians, who hate him, Mulla Reza, an inferior title.

This worthy is the principal priest of the place, and though a Sunni, and a fanatic at that, has no objection to seeing and being polite to the dissenters of Islam, the

Shi'a, among whose ranks both myself and the watchmaker were classed.

He inhabited a house adjoining the mosque wherein he officiated, one of the best houses in Kirkuk. His court-yard was laid out in flat beds in the Persian fashion, and a few mulberry trees veiled the bareness of the high walls. He received us in a long room, well carpeted, and was alone. A very reverend seigneur this indeed; the frown of sanctity sat blackly upon his brow, unlightened by his white turban. At his elbow on the floor was a gramophone, from whose trumpet a raucous Arab voice had just ceased to shriek verses of the Quran—to such uses are European abominations adaptable! Hearing that I was from Shiraz, he at once began to quote Hafiz and Sa'di, for he spoke excellent Persian; and then, producing a manuscript book, read some of his own poetry. He versified in four languages—Turkish, Arabic, Persian, and Kurdish; but preferred Persian to all of them, having a just contempt for the majority of Turkish verse, consisting as it does nearly all of Arabic and Persian.

He complained bitterly of the progress Christians were making, and doubtless would make under the *régime* of constitutional government; in speaking, his eyes flashed, he grew excited, the latent fanaticism in him boiled, and he longed to see the blood of these infidels spilt. With cries of disgust against the lukewarm sentiments of the Turkomans, he denounced Musulman and Christian alike, and frankly declared that he would like to see the heads of the latter adorning the barrack walls. This creature, who had naught but notoriety to gain from such a catastrophe, has several times attempted to harass the Christians, but they have found sufficient protection, and he sees himself foiled, and his proposals ignored every time he would rouse feeling against these harmless people. It took him the whole time of drinking three cups of tea to exhaust his fury, and we took leave of him, expressing no opinion upon his sentiments.

The watchmaker gave me an example of his hot temper, as we sat in the coffee-house afterwards. At his house he

was visited one day by the sub-governor, a Constantinople
Turk, and the talk turning upon poetry, the shaikh, who
has Kurdish blood in him, was extolling the merits of
Persian and even Kurdish verse, and expressing his scorn
of Turkish. The Ottoman officer naturally objected, and
rashly quoted a long poem terminating with the words :—

"Furukhta am bi sham' u kafur u san sin."

"Ah!" exclaimed the shaikh, seizing a perfect opportunity, "Furukhta am" is pure Persian, and "sham' u
kafur" are Arabic, and what Turkish remains, but a miserable insignificance? "u san sin," the point coming in with
the meaning of the Turkish—"and thou art it"—the
miserable insignificance.[1]

About the tenth day of our stay there, the muleteer
Rashid came along in great glee, saying that we should
leave next morning, and that I had better lay in a stock
of provisions for the journey, though, as he remarked,
"God knows whether we shall eat our bread, or the
Hamavand's."

Four regimental doctors had turned up from Mosul,
appointed to Sulaimania, and they were to have as escort
a "tabur," or four hundred soldiers. The usual fiasco
occurred to prevent our going, for the army, not having
been paid for months, went on strike, and two hundred
more appointed to replace them flatly refused to go, fearing to face the Hamavand, who had so barbarous a habit
of thirsting for the guns and blood of the Turkish troops,
and such a capacity for quenching the thirst. So we
stayed.

As an instance of the self-imposed duties of the unattached Turkish officer, I may quote the following
episode :—

Haji Rasul and myself were sitting in the dark one
evening smoking our cigarettes, and conversing upon the
usual topic of Persian politics, when a highly uniformed

---

[1] A little editing was unavoidable here, the shaikh's words being,
"Wa bir parcha pukh qaldi, va san sin."

individual rolled up, and between hiccups gave vent to a
hoarse "Salamun 'alaikum." Without invitation he sat
between us, and introducing himself to me as a major in
some regiment, proceeded to bully Haji. It appeared that
the old man had had some high words with one of the
people, whom he employed to sell his sweets, and this
officious busybody, overhearing, inserted himself between
the two, constituting himself an arbitrator. Haji had
naturally refused to have anything to do with such
matters, but his opponent, seeing a chance of winning his
case, commenced pouring out his woes to the officer. The
old man in disgust had departed, leaving the pair, and
laid his case before the mayor of the town.

The major, meanwhile, had settled the affair with the
other litigant, arranging to receive two mejidies as a fee,
and finding that Haji did not accept his mediation, came to
try and bully him into acquiescence. Needless to say all the
intimidation he could bring forth did not scare Haji, who
threatened to throw him downstairs. He solved the question himself by falling over asleep, after a pause for the
thought which his fuddled condition made difficult. Such
are some—I hope not all—of the Sultan's officers. This one
had passed through the military school at Bagdad, but as
I afterwards heard how this feat may be performed—being
literally little more than a passage through the establish-
ment in the case of certain favoured individuals—I understood how he had become a military officer.

One morning I received a polite note in Turkish from
the postmaster—with whom I was not acquainted—asking
me to come and see him. So I took my way along the
dusty hot road, past the innumerable cafés full of hunch-
backed, uniformed Turks, till I found the office. To-day
not being post-day, the postmaster reclined in an armchair behind a table, smoking cigarettes. On my arrival,
he saluted me very politely by my name, talking Turkish.
It was, of course, not to be expected that he would state
his business till after some small talk, so we conversed
about various subjects till he worked round to that of
antiques, upon which he was an enthusiast. "Antiques"

in this country mean coins, and Assyrian cylinders, little cylindrical pieces of stone with images and figures carved upon them. He had invited me there to benefit by the opinion I must have formed upon the value of antiquities, for Ferangistan to him was a place where half the world sought antiques, and consequently anyone who had been there, as he heard I had, must know the value of such relics as were to be found near Kirkuk.

Having thus prepared me, he shut the door, and produced with *empressement* a small bag of coins and seals from his stamp-safe. These were for the most part early Muhammadan, a Parthian or two, and a few Assyrian pieces. The greatest treasure—to him—was a George III. five-pound piece, upon which he put a fabulous value. Beyond telling the probable date of his antiques I could not help him, but he pressed so hard—thinking my unwillingness to mention prices was due to an idea of purchasing—that at last I proposed some values which I was pleased to see highly gratified him. In these regions there is always a good market for antiques among the Turks and Christians, who buy them, gradually collecting a stock, and then take them to Constantinople in the hopes of selling for a fortune.

Coming back that morning I remember buying some lettuces of an old man, who cleaned and washed them for his purchasers. The price, which gives a good idea of the price of vegetables and fruit, was two lettuces for three "pul," seven of which make a "qamari," which is equivalent to three-farthings, so the lettuce worked out at about the twenty-fourth part of a penny each.

In this stands explained the tenacity with which two persons will haggle for an hour over fractional sums, for the acquisition of a farthing means a considerable part of a meal gained.

One morning early, the muleteer Rashid came along and woke me. The effendi under whose wing it had been arranged for us to go had suddenly made up his mind the day before, and was now ready. So hurriedly we loaded up, and barely getting time to bid farewell to Haji Rasul, who commended me to God and the saints, we filed out into the yet empty streets to the meeting-place outside the town. Just as we got there and saw ahead a collection of mules, foot-passengers, and soldiers, the day broke, and we bade farewell to this remote corner of Turkey for a time.

CHAPTER VII

CHALDEANS

THE course of our narrative will take us on into Kurdistan, and among peoples different to those we have met in our journeyings from the Mediterranean and the eastern border of Mesopotamia. We have had occasion to notice various races and peoples in passing, but of all these, those who have by their high antiquity of descent the premier claim to description are the Chaldeans, to whom up to the present we have not given more than casual notice. As we are about to pass out of the land of their ancestors, into the hills and mountains of the semi-independent Kurds, this opportunity for adequate remark upon the interesting Chaldean race cannot be passed.

The traveller of to-day, once he passes Urfa to go east, meets, besides Armenians and Christians of Greek descent, large numbers of the non-Muhammadan population who, in various places, go under a variety of names—Nestorians, Nasara, Kaldani, Jacobites, Catholics, New Chaldeans, Inglisi, Amrikani, and Protestan—the last three in northwest Persia. These varied sects are all branches of the Chaldean and Assyrian race, lineal descendants of the two nations that occupied the Tigris valley as far from the mouth as Jaziri ibn Umar; and the lower Euphrates valley, or Babylonia.

It is now 2500 years since the Assyrian nation broke up, and but a little less since the second Chaldean period was brought to an end by Alexander the Great; and since then, the Assyrians or Chaldeans (for they were the same race) have been in subjection to alien rulers, though the powerful and tenacious nature of the Chaldeans has won for them a premier place in the civil life of all ages, and is to-day the means of furnishing a great part of western Asia with a class of merchants and villagers on a far higher scale of civilisation and culture than the peoples among whom they live.

Many writers, and many residents in the countries inhabited by "native" Christians have given unrestrained exercise to their pens in describing their disgusting character, their deceit, their petty spirit, their unfaithfulness, and so on. Nor can any deny that this is only too true in many cases. Certainly the Christian who comes in contact with the European is often a very disagreeable character, but it would be but fair to him to mention, if possible, any member of any Oriental race or faith—particularly Semitic—whose moral standard was not debased by intercourse with Europeans, and the usual imitation of European vice, consequent upon a mistaken idea of Western catholicism and progress. It will be readily appreciated that the Christian naturally follows this line of conduct sooner and with more facility than the Muhammadan, the intrinsic aloofness of whose faith holds him off from a ready adoption of Western habits, good or bad, particularly in the case of the Semitic Muhammadan.

Our sources of information upon the origin of the Christian Church in Mesopotamia are unfortunately extremely scanty, and it is only by references to passing events that occur in purely secular works that we are enabled to follow the course of dissemination of the doctrines of Jesus Christ in the Middle East. To adherents of the English Protestant Church the history of the Chaldean or Eastern Church should have a special interest, for the old Chaldeans followed a scheme of tenets more similar to those of the English Church than of any other section of the much-divided Christian religion. Sir H. Layard, who stayed among the Chaldeans of Mosul in 1840, in his work on Nineveh remarks: "To Protestants, the doctrine and rites of a primitive sect of Christians, who have ever remained untainted by the superstitions of Rome[1] must be of high importance."

We have no ground for any assumption, such as has been made, that Christianity was carried by the old road through Urfa and Nisibis, to Assyria by a follower of SS. Barnabas and Paul to Nineveh, or one other of the cities which still stood upon the sites of old Assyrian capitals. Nevertheless, in A.D. 410, when Yezdijird I. of Persia reigned, Christianity was a recognised part of the social structure of Assyria and Persia. Obviously for such progress to have been made as to render Christianity one of the accepted religions in those regions, points to the fact that preachers and priests must have commenced their itineraries a great while before A.D. 400.

It was the Assyrians, or Chaldeans, who as a nation adopted speedily the tenets of the new faith. Doubtless after the demolition of Assyria, and then of Babylonia, the worship of Bel and Ishtar, the ancient gods, had fallen into abeyance or even total desuetude, and the remnants of the old nation seized upon the new religion to satisfy the spiritual need that every people experiences. Their prelates and dignitaries soon became a very important part of the Christian organisation, and it is interesting to note the sympathy of the Persian Sasanian kings for this new religion, and the success Christian effort met among the Persians. This ancient and highly civilised people, whose character contains a great deal of the speculative, has always been ready to consider the claims of new Deistic theories, and has, in Muhammadan times, found an outlet for its speculative tendency in the adoption of Shiism, which it has made a purely Persian section of Islam. The early Christians looked, perhaps with a warranted hope, upon the field of Persia, for here were no feats of iconoclasm to perform—no Diana, no Jove, no Venus, disputed with Christ the right to men's adoration.

---

[1] Ichabod! the proud day of that statement is passed away, and so is the greater part of the Chaldean Church—"the superstitions of Rome" have captured the Chaldeans, though not, I fear, in fair contest.

In Persia they found a tolerance broad as her mighty plains, a dualist theory that provided only for principles of good and evil, as sharply defined as her barren hills, a splendid isolation of thought far above the turmoil of degraded passion that then represented the pantheistic doctrines of the Greeks, Romans, and Assyrians themselves. High ideals, spiritual aims of an altitude unknown to the Western materialists, found themselves in singular harmony with the ascetic idea of early Christianity.

We must understand that of all places, near and remote, it was Persia and the Zoroastrian people, the Perso-Aryans, and probably the Medes—or races inhabiting modern Kurdistan—that welcomed Jesus Christ's doctrines, and hailed their purifying influences with the delight of the neophyte to whom the master's knowledge is revealed. So we are told by a Chaldean bishop, writing in A.D. 400, that Yezdijird I., king of Persia, was a merciful and good ruler, just and kindly.[1] And so after, it was the known sympathy and support of the Persians that gained for the new Church the name of " The Persian Party."

This name was given after Nestorius himself, excommunicated from the Byzantine Church, had found asylum under Yezdijird, and the support given by this king was extended also by his son Firuz (A.D. 459-484), who took under his protection later dissenters from the Western Church.

In A.D. 410 the great dissension between Nestorius, Patriarch of Constantinople, and St Cyril, upon various points of doctrine, arose, and resulted in the split which gave birth to the new sect called the Nestorians. Throughout the controversy—resulting in the General Council at Ephesus in 431—Nestorius had been supported by the Eastern Bishops, and it was natural that after the rupture, the Chaldeans, who sent them, should join the ranks of, or rather become themselves, the Nestorians.

[1] "The good and merciful King Yezdijird, the blessed amongst the kings, may he be remembered with blessing, and may his future be yet more fair than his earlier life! Every day he doeth good to the poor and distressed."—Browne, *Lit. Hist.*, vol. i., p. 135.

The doctrines of Nestorius were not by any means novel, nor, to those who would regard Christianity as a whole, sufficiently important to cause a split, or occasion such venom as has unfortunately always been characteristic of the militant sectaries of the religion of peace. The Bishop of Tarsus, Diodorus, had already promulgated Nestorius' doctrines among the Western Assyrians, and as they were gradually accepted, their upholders gained the name of the Persian party, partly because of the situation of the new sect, and partly on account of the sympathy of the Persian kings.

From this time the tenets of Nestorius, stamped out in Syria and western Asia, became exclusively identified with the Chaldean nation, and the first existence of the Nestorian Church or Assyrian Church began about A.D. 450, or earlier.

From now till the advent of Muhammad, the Church may be said to have prospered. It had vicissitudes certainly, for it was not in such a position as to dictate to rulers and kings. It is, again, a sorry feature of Christianity that we are told that during that time all the persecution they suffered was from the Christian Byzantine Empire, and all the sympathy and protection they obtained from the Zoroastrian monarchs of Persia.

Among these stands out the exception of Kawad, king of Persia, who is described by Chaldean priests of the period as a monster; war also did its work in harassing the Church, but we have no reason to believe that it did not harass the idolaters as well, for the Persians, whose armies continually scourged Mesopotamia, were not admittedly of the religion of any of the invaded peoples, while inclining to the doctrines of Christianity, as we have seen already.

During these times the great college of Edessa (Urfa), which the Isaurian Zeno had closed on account of its Nestorian doctrines, was transferred to Jund-i-Shapur, near the modern Shushtar, in Elam, into Persian territory, for there the Chaldeans were sure of protection and sympathy from a people whose talent has ever been for literature and learning. And the hope of the exiled priests was well justified. The place of exile became a cherished home, and the medical college of Edessa grew at Jund-i-Shapur to a great missionary and educational centre.

From Jund-i-Shapur, already in the territory of the Persian shahs, missionaries were sent out to every Eastern country, Chaldeans by birth and tongue, speaking Persian, and their enterprise carried them to India, Turkestan, and China. So great had become the hold of Christianity upon Persia, that at a very early date the country was divided into bishoprics.

This college was established about A.D. 550 by Nushirvan the Just, shah of Persia, one of the last of the Zoroastrian kings, and of the Sasanian dynasty. Through all the later ages of Persia and Arabia he has been the subject of eulogy, by Christian and Muhammadan alike, for his great justice, a virtue more highly esteemed in the East than by us, because so much rarer. Although he never became confessedly Christian, his sympathies with the Christians were such as to induce him to make a Chaldean woman his queen. Her son was brought up as a Christian, and by his zeal he provoked admonition from his father, whose policy seems to have dictated an impartial attitude toward all faiths.

Had his relationship with, and just bearing towards, Christians been insufficient to gain their gratitude and esteem,[1] he would have won it by his persecution of the peculiar sect of Mazdak, which the Christians had regarded with loathing and horror.

It is difficult to come at a true appreciation of Mazdak's character and doctrines, for all we know of either has been recorded by sectaries of other religions, Christian, Zoroastrian, and Muhammadan, and such reports are naturally prejudiced.

[1] Browne, *Lit. Hist.*, vol. i., p. 168, quotes the gratitude Christians bore Nushirvan, for they "gave a touching proof of their gratitude for his favours a century later, when they would not suffer the remains of his unfortunate descendant Yazdigird III. . . . to lie unburied."

K

In general the scheme was a communistic idea which involved mystic rites; the property of men, even to their wives, was common to all, and certain regulations for daily life were imposed, notably the prohibition from eating flesh and shedding blood, which last law excited the extreme abhorrence of priests of other faiths.

The sect arose and was favoured in the reign of that Kawad before mentioned, who probably earned the execration of the Christians and Zoroastrians alike by his favouritism of the Mazdakites, perhaps induced by hopes of quelling the great power the Zoroastrian priests had acquired.

Nushirvan, however, while yet Crown Prince, instituted a policy of repression that ended in a massacre of Mazdakites, and the execution of Mazdak himself, at which some Christian Persians and the court physician, a Christian priest, were present. This occurred only after Nushirvan (then known as Khosru) had exposed to his father the king, the means by which Mazdak performed his miracles. During the long and glorious reign of this prince, perhaps the most peaceable and tolerant period of that age, the Christians made great progress in Persia. Nushirvan, though refraining from any committal of his own convictions, imported to his college Greek philosophers and adherents of Nestorius, and went so far as to make with the Byzantines a treaty which protected them.

So at this time, the latter end of the 6th century, we have a pleasant enough picture of Persia excellently ruled by a monarch of broad views, whose queen and eldest son were Christians; whose courtiers, doctors, and advisers counted in their ranks men of the same faith; whose principal college, the glory of his life, was a Christian institution. Small wonder, then, that the Chaldeans looked with high hope upon the future, when Zoroastrianism should pass away to give place to a Christian Persia.[1]

[1] None can tell, naturally, what would have been the condition of the Middle East had Muhammad never appeared, but while it would quite possibly have been Christian, it would have been a very debased

But while Nushirvan dreamed of empire, and the Christians of religious supremacy, there was born he who would sweep before him the Persian Empire and the priests of Zoroaster, leaving but a remnant in their original domains. For Muhammad Mustafa—"The Prophet"—was born about this time, and mentioned it himself later—" I was born," said he, " in the time of the just king," i.e., Nushirvan, shah of Persia.

Nushirvan died 578 A.D., and was followed by a number of weak monarchs till the ill-fated Yazdijird III., last Zoroastrian king of Persia, who, defeated at Qadasiyya by the Arabs in A.D. 635, died, an exile, in Khurasan, in A.D. 651.

At this, one of the most important turning-points in the history of the East, and the occasion of the inception of a doctrine that numbers among its adherents a large portion of the total population of the world, it is advisable to turn aside for a moment from the history of the Eastern Christians to ascertain in what condition the Church was at that time. Most commentators upon Islam and the Christianity of this period agree that the Church of Jesus Christ had, by its adoption of various heterodox ideas, become split up into little more than a widely spread religion, which, while nominally one in faith and aim, was actually nothing more than a number of sects at war with one another upon points of dogma, and generally sunk in corruption. This certainly was the case among the Christians of the West under the Byzantine Emperors, and the Syrian or Arab Christians of Western Arabia and Damascus. In such confusion was the Christian Church in these parts that Muhammad in seeking between the two great faiths of his land, Judaism and Christianity, for material wherewith to compile the Quran, turned away from the involved and contradictory views of the

---

faith ; for even in those days before Islam, wherever the Christian Church had wandered far from Chaldea, it had become terribly corrupt, and doctrines crept in that almost took from it the right to be called Christian.

Christian priests, to the more comprehensible doctrine of the Jews.

But we are concerned with the Nestorians alone, and of all the sects, or schisms, this was the least corrupted in fundamental idea, and we find that it compared very favourably in organisation and unity of purpose, with the almost idolatrous sects of the Syrian and Coptic Churches.

Secessions and heresies occurred in Malabar, Socotra, and Diarbekr, but the original Nestorian idea seems to have been generally retained, namely, that of the dual nature of Jesus Christ, one personality the man, and the other the Word of God, and the refusal of the title of " Mother of God " to the Virgin Mary, who, they said, was the carnate vessel, albeit purified, that received the purely material seed communicated by a miracle, and therefore the mother of the man Jesus, the carnate individuality.

At any rate it may be seen that such doctrines, in themselves the result of speculation, are by no means bound to be the final expression of speculation, which is ever progressive, and it is hardly remarkable that many sub-theories should have sprung into existence among the Chaldeans. Yet we notice that the Chaldean Church existed, homogeneous, through the great bulk of its immensity from the year 410 till about the 17th century, a fact which speaks as no argument can for its unity of idea and teaching, as compared with the lamentable condition of the degraded Christian institutions of Syria and Greece.

In the first years of Islam there was more tolerance for Christianity than ever afterwards, as well as for Jews. Even Zoroastrians met with a certain consideration owing to a half-reverence Muhammad had accorded to their prophet. The Christians and Jews, however, were " People of the Book "—that is, people of a revealed faith—and as such entitled to more merciful treatment than pagans and idolaters. Moreover, Muhammed was considerably indebted to Christians and Jews for a great part of the Quran ; and a Nestorian priest, Sergius, is said to have assisted him in the compilation of certain chapters. In answer to an accusation by the Arabs that he was assisted by a foreigner, the passage in the Surah ul Nahl (The Chapter of the Bee) was " revealed."   " We also know that they say, ' Verily a certain man teacheth him to compose the Quran.' The tongue of the person to whom they incline is a foreign tongue, whereas the Quran is written in the perspicuous Arabic tongue."

So, while Muhammad displayed the greatest abhorrence for all Christian symbols, execrating above all the cross or crucifix, yet he did not force them to retract their beliefs, and arranged a special code of treatment for them, particularly exempting them from military service, in lieu of which they paid a poll-tax, or "jaziya."[1]

In the case of towns and countries which submitted to the Islamic army, the generals of Muhammad entered into covenants of protection in some cases, agreeing to protect them as long as they paid this tax, and there is ground for believing that the treaty between Muhammad and the Chaldean Church, of which an exact copy was published in A.D. 1630,[2] but the authenticity of which is doubtful, existed in some form. By the terms of this treaty the Nestorians were protected and exempted from many vexatious taxes.

The Chaldeans now entered upon a second period of prosperity, which lasted 200 years, and during which under the early Khalifas they attained premier positions in all matters of philosophy, learning, and even statesmanship, causing more than once complaints from the less gifted and, consequently, the less favoured Musulman Arabs. The 2nd century of this period, from the time of the battle of the Zab (see p. 107), when a Persian dynasty reigned, was as well the golden age of the Khalifate as of the later Chaldean Church. Under the

---

[1] An enormous amount of feeling has been recently roused upon this subject in Turkish dominions, by the resolve of the new Turkish Majlis to abolish the jaziya and make Christians and Jews serve in the army.

[2] *Testimentum Mahometi* (Paris : Sionita, 1630).

beneficent rule of the earlier Abbasid Khalifas (among whom were the renowned Harun al Rashid and Ma'mun) the patriarchate was transferred to Bagdad, and a new bishopric was founded at Kufa, the very heart and centre of Islam. Under the Khalifas Ma'mun and Harun al Rashid particularly, the Chaldeans found themselves in the greatest favour. Their colleges were protected, and as they were versed in many languages and sciences, their priests and philosophers were given the translation into Arabic of books from the Greek, Persian, and Chaldean languages. It is to the Chaldeans of this time that Islam is indebted for many of the Greek authors' works, particularly Aristotle, whose philosophical treatises have been ever popular among the Arabs.

Undoubtedly, both Arabian letters and the Chaldean Church reached their highest point in the period A.D. 809-813, the Khalifate of Ma'mun, and we may here remark upon the extent of the Church at that date. There were then, or soon after, as many as twenty-five bishoprics all over Asia,[1] for the missionaries sent out in the 5th century had not been idle, as we shall see later.

However, this, the brightest period of Islam and Christianity, was sadly darkened by the accession of one of the monsters of history to the Khalifal throne. After the Khalifa Ma'mun came Al Mu'tasim, a famous ruler also, who transferred the capital to Samerra, higher up

---

[1] The Bishoprics were: 1. Elam (Arabistan of south-west Persia); 2. Nisibis (north-east Mesopotamia); 3. Basra (Persian Gulf); 4. Assyria (tract between the Zab rivers); 5. Beth Qurma, in Assyria; 6. Hulvan, in western Persia (now called Zuhab, a Kurdish province); 7. Persia; 8. Merv; 9. Herat; 10. Arabia; 11. China; 12. India; 13. Armenia; 14. Syria; 15. Azarbaijan (north-west Persia); 16. Ray and Tabaristan (northern Persia); 17. Dailam (south coast of the Caspian Sea); 18. Samarqand (Transoxiana); 19. Kashgar and Turkestan (Tartary); 20. Balkh and Tucharestan; 21. Sistan (eastern Persia); 22. Khan Baligh (Pekin); 24. Tanguth (Tartary); 25. Chasemgara and Nuachita (Tartary).—(From Layard, *Nineveh and its Remains*, vol. i., p. 257.) From the twelfth bishopric were descended the Christians of St John of Malabar. That of Persia included the Bishopric of Hormuz in the Persian Gulf, said to have been founded by one Theophilus, about A.D. 350.

the Tigris than Bagdad, and he was followed by Al Wathiq, and then by Al Mutawakkil in A.D. 847, who degraded the high office he held as much as his greater predecessors had exalted it.

One of his first acts was to favour the very brutal Turkish soldiers and ruffians in his service, abasing the Persians and Arabs who had served his brother and predecessor. It was not sufficient for him to degrade thus the faithful servants about him; he went on—in the excess of orthodox zeal he displayed as a counterfoil to his drunkenness and debauchery—to defile and destroy the graves of the martyrs of the Shi'a section, to cause to be disgracefully ridiculed the memory of Ali, a saint revered by Sunni and Shi'a alike, and to murder countless adherents and admirers of those martyrs. Every degradation and disgrace he could thrust upon the Jews and Christians he did, causing them to wear garments of conspicuous and unpleasant hues, "particoloured badges, and caps, and girdles of certain ignoble patterns, to ride only on mules and asses, with wooden stirrups and saddles of strange construction, and to have placed over their houses effigies of devils." [1]

The college of Jund-i-Shapur, that Nushirvan had founded, was deprived by him of all its rights, and the director, one Bokht Yishu, banished to Bahrain. The churches of the Christians were destroyed or used as mosques, and various rules prevented their proclaiming their religion while living by any signs, or when dead by tombstones.

In the long record of philosophers, literati, and authors of the earlier times of Islam it is hardly surprising to find almost a blank between the years 847 and 861, when Mutawakkil was murdered during a fit of drunkenness by the Turks, whom he had preferred to all others.

All the persecution the Christians now suffered was not enough to extinguish their influence, and they partially regained their position in the 11th century under the Seljuq monarchs, and right up to the time of the terrible scourge

[1] Muir's *Caliphate*, pp. 521-2.

of the Mongols under Chengiz Khan and Hulagu Khan, they still occupied positions of some importance, and were as yet a cognate church of some extent. Far beyond the bounds of Islam they were busy; busy upon a scheme which they hoped would crush Islam and exalt Christianity all over Asia, from Pekin to Syria. This scheme was no less than the invasion of Asia by the Tartar kings of Qarakorum, whose power was growing fast, and whose thirst for land was growing keener. The Christians, meanwhile, strove to make the religion of Jesus Christ the national faith before the day of conquest dawned, and had certainly made great progress among various Mongol people when the hordes poured out westwards.

It will be remembered that in very early days missionaries had been sent to China and Turkistan, and they had acquired considerable influence over the Khans of Tartary, some of whom are said to have been converted to Christianity. The famous Prester John, whose name has been obscured behind many absurd legends, was one of these rulers.[1]

The campaign carried on from Merv, the see of the Chaldean Bishop of Tartary, succeeded to such a degree as to win to Christianity a large number of the female members of the ruling families, and an important nomad tribe called the Keraite, whose capital was in Qarakorum, in the Altai Mountains. Yet, of the actual invaders of the West none were won over, being frankly pagans, making a policy of equal freedom for all religions, but adhering to none. Thus, while several were of Christian mothers, and were even baptized in infancy, receiving Christian names, they retained no sign of their origin when come to power, changing the names of their infancy to Tartar titles, and forgetting the religion of their childhood.

In China the missionaries had had equal success, as is witnessed by the tablet found at Se-gan-fu, which described the favour which had met their doctrine from both king

---

[1] A very interesting letter regarding the state and pomp of this khan is quoted in Layard's *Nineveh and its Remains*, vol. i., pp. 250-4.

and country, mentioning also the names of Chinese Christian bishops and mandarins of that faith. From this interesting tablet it was first ascertained that, up to A.D. 781, the date of the inscription, the Chaldeans had pushed so far as China, and the revelation of the existence of a recognised Church there was so astonishing to the critics, as to throw discredit upon the monument for some time.[1]

Towards the fall of the Khalifate, the Chaldeans, seeing their Church in Persia almost extinct, and in Mesopotamia confined, and melting before the gradual absorption by Islam, turned the eyes of hope towards these Mongol states, aspiring to find in them a weapon to drive out Islam. That it acted against Islam, dealing it almost a death-blow, is well known; but the too sanguine Christians did not foresee that it would be at the hands of two of the Mongol Khans, one a baptized Christian, that the Nestorian Church should suffer persecution and massacre, and its remnants be forced to save themselves by flight to the inaccessible mountains of the Kurds. For it was not at all a zeal for Christianity that urged the Mongols on, though the reports by Chaldean priests of Western wealth may have excited the greed of the Khans. Just at the period before the great invasions, the opening of the 13th century, missionary effort had redoubled, and Roman Catholics for the first time appeared on the scene, many courageous monks daring the dangerous voyage from Europe to the unknown East. The tolerance of Chengiz Khan, first Mongol emperor, was responsible in a great measure for this renewed enthusiasm, which was the more sanguine in remembering that Islam does not proselytise.

But the terrible invasion of Hulagu Khan, that swept great and small, faithful and infidel, before it, broke both Christianity and Islam for a time, striking at the heart of

---

[1] *Vide* Layard, *Nineveh*, vol. i., p. 245, for a full description of the monument and a part translation. More recent discoveries in the 20th century have confirmed this inscription, which was first seen in A.D. 1625.

both, Bagdad, which was reduced to ruins among scenes of the most terrible inhumanity ever witnessed.[1]

Hulagu, himself pagan, acknowledging no power, superhuman nor human, but himself, was followed by successors who first embraced Buddhism and later Islam, most noteworthy of whom was Ghazan Khan (A.D. 1295), who destroyed thousands of Christians all over Tartary, Persia, and Mesopotamia.

Now Islam had gained over the devastating Tartars, and began to revive as a religion, though the high degree of culture of former days was obviously not to be looked for under the rule of barbarians. But Christianity, persecuted, despised, and detested alike by Mongol and Arab, waned, and its adherents became obscure and humble. Nevertheless, though the great Chaldean Church no longer existed as before, its amputated members in China and India being separated from the central Church, its headquarters demolished, and its priests scattered, yet a great number of Christians still lived in the domains of the Mongol Emperors till the second period of invasion, when Timur-i-Lang (Tamerlane) emulated by his ferocity the earlier and pagan invaders. Among the many cruelties he committed was the massacre of Christians. From the first (A.D. 1380), he made a point of persecuting these people, his design being obviously to exterminate the whole race and religion. Not content with destroying what remained of their churches, he pursued them in every part of Persia, Chaldea, and Babylonia, till he had driven them out of the lands of their ancestors, and their panic-stricken remnants found refuge among the remote valleys and hills of the Kurds, whom even Tamerlane could not assail.

The patriarchate, which had been removed to Mosul, was now transferred to Julamark, a village in the very

---

[1] From the accounts that are to be read of the invasion of Hulagu Khan, we learn thousands of details of the revolting and bestial nature of the inhuman Mongols, and of the ghoulish ingenuity of cruelty they displayed. These are fully described in the books of Planocarpini, Guillaume de Ruÿsbroeck, d'Ohsson, and others.

heart of Kurdistan, out of the reach of any but the Kurds, who lived upon terms of friendliness till the Turks and priests ousted the fine old princes who ruled them there, and induced them to turn against the Chaldeans, in 1839.

The Roman Catholics had, through their missionaries, become aware of the existence of the great Chaldean Church, and now—to their eternal discredit be it said— they actually combined with the Turks to persecute the Chaldeans who yet remained in the foothills and plains near Mosul.

"By a series of the most open frauds, the Roman Catholic emissaries obtained many of the documents which constituted the title of the Chaldean Patriarch, and gave him a claim to be recognised and protected as the head of the Chaldean Church by the Turkish authorities. A system of persecution and violence which would scarcely be credited compelled the Chaldeans of the plain to renounce their faith and unite with the Church of Rome." [1]

However, these unsavoury operations took some time in development, and meanwhile we may see the progress of the emaciated Church—now at enmity with Muslim and Christian alike, finding only sanctuary from its foes among the savage Kurds, the terror of whose name kept the Turks away from the mountains.

The patriarchate in the 15th century was at Al Qush, not far from Mosul, but persecution growing more persistent, and many being forced into the Catholic ranks, the existing patriarch Mar Elias was ignored by the orthodox Chaldeans farther east, and the patriarch Mar Shimun at Julamark was elected, whose descendants, always bearing the name Shimun, are still the leaders of the now almost extinct old Chaldean Church.

In the 16th century the Roman Catholics having by the means employed sufficiently subdued the Chaldeans nominally Catholic, nominated a patriarch, and founded thus a patriarchal line in the name of Yusif, whom they

[1] Layard, *Nineveh and its Remains,* vol. i., p. 259.

established at Diarbekr, placing him over the Catholic Chaldeans without in any way consulting their wishes.

While this Catholic Chaldean section continued, by the exertions of missionaries, to enlist more recruits from the Chaldeans of the plains, the orthodox party in the mountains was gaining strength and confidence. Among the rough and fierce Kurds they became, too, warlike. Adopting Kurdish dress and habits it was almost impossible to tell them from the hereditary mountaineers, with whom they lived upon the best of terms. Inaccessible as were their villages and castles, the Turks were forced to leave them independent, though they nominally admitted the Sultan as lord of the soil they inhabited. It was not till 1839 that the Turkish Government officials encouraged the revengeful spirit of Nurullah Bey, a Hakkiari Kurd, who was at blood-feud with some Chaldeans, and Badar Khan Bey, who was better remembered than the greater man.

A very significant fact in support of the assertion that the Kurds were incited to rise, is the treatment of Badar Khan Bey, when, after the repeated protests and considerable pressure from Europe, the Sultan was forced to capture him. The officer deputed to this task, one Osman Pasha, made such lenient terms with the Kurdish chief as made it practically certain that he had not been acting without the acquiescence of the Turks. Nor was any part of the Kurdish territory invaded, except in the expedition against Bader Khan Bey, after which the troops were withdrawn. The opinions of contemporary Chaldeans, as expressed in some old letters I saw at Mosul, confirm these views, and state that the Kurds, although ever alive to the supposed wealth of the Chaldeans, had been always on fairly good terms with them; indeed, as we have seen, for over four hundred years they had lived side by side without any disturbances occurring.

The Mar Shimun of the period fled, during the massacres, to Urumiah, where were settled a number of Chaldeans, but returned later to Julamark, and was pensioned by the Turkish Government, thereby giving up the last remnants of any pretensions to independence that his people might have preserved. His successors have further weakened their positions by giving way to an overwhelming passion for intrigue, and, occupied with these discreditable operations, in which they try to involve American and Protestant missionaries, they have lost most of their hold over the Church, leaving the field open to the energetic assaults of the Catholics.

In January this year (1909) a new massacre of old Chaldeans occurred in the neighbourhood of S'airt, near Bitlis, a district where the Chaldeans have sunk into such a position of degradation, physical and moral, as to leave them little more than savages. Their priests are in some cases not sufficiently instructed to say the ordinary services, and the people are reported as complaining bitterly that they do not know whom they are supposed to worship, nor what is the significance of the word "Christian." This condition of affairs has obtained for a long time now. For many years, under the vitiated governmental system of Turkey, the Kurds have been allowed to do as they please with the possessions of the Chaldean peasants, no steps ever being taken against them by the Turks, at once complaisant and afraid. It is a noteworthy fact that under the Shi'a rule of Persia the Chaldeans have prospered, and the miserable creatures they call "Gavarnai," who come, naked and hungry, fleeing down the mountain slopes from Turkish territory, are almost a different race from the educated and progressive Chaldeans of Urumia and Salmas in Persia.

The Roman Catholic Chaldeans in Turkish territory have increased in numbers since the split in 1550, all those about Mosul and in Diarbekr being of that persuasion. However, Roman Catholicism received a shock in 1869, when the Bull of Papal Infallibility was issued, and a section was led by Thomas Ronkus, the Mutran Mallus, and Kas Jacob Naaman, afterwards Archbishop of Bagdad—which was called the New Chaldeans, that split from the Roman Catholics.

The clauses of the Bull to which these objected were :—

1. That a bishop cannot be made without Papal sanction.

2. That three candidates for archbishoprics must proceed to Rome, of whom the Pope will choose one and reject two.

3. All the revenues of the Church are to be sent to Rome.

It appears that the Mutran Mallus, who had been sent by the Patriarch Yusif Odo to Rome, at first accepted the Bull, but that upon the Armenian Catholic Church splitting on the same subject, the Patriarch Yusif Odo and his mutrans seceded, and betook themselves to Al Qush, and in the village of Dar el Sayeda appointed four mutrans without interrogating Rome. One of these, Elie, however, deserted to the Dominicans at Mosul, and was made a full priest, afterwards becoming Bishop of Jazira ibn Umar. In 1875 Yusif Odo re-entered the Roman Catholic Church, leaving the New Chaldean sect under the Mutran Mallus. After the decease of the Yusif Odo, which occurred shortly after his desertion of the New Chaldeans, Elie was appointed in his place, and at once directed his energies towards regathering the little sect into the Catholic fold.

He was assisted in a measure by the departure of Mallus for Malabar, and after his return, finding his people wavering, came with them to Mosul and re-entered the Roman Catholic Church.

One of the principal strongholds of this sect was Tel Kaif, a large village near Mosul, which had been one of the first to turn Roman Catholic.[1]

The Old Chaldeans have made several attempts to regenerate the old Church, and have appealed in every case to England for the assistance, for they have always

[1] This village, whose inhabitants would seem to have a special aptitude for river work, supplies deck-hands to the steamers of Messrs Lynch Bros., on the Tigris and Karun rivers, to the Turkish boats, and to the "Nusrat," a Persian steamer on the Karun. By this means the Chaldeans find themselves once more back in their ancient country, and there is now a priest at Ahwaz, not far from where his forbears taught in the great college of Jund-i-Shapur.

considered themselves more in sympathy with the English Church than with any other.

In 1843, the year of the last massacre under Badar Khan Bey, communications were opened with Archbishop Howley, but no result was forthcoming. Previous to this, two gentlemen had visited Urumiah at the instance of the Society for Promoting Christian Knowledge and the Royal Geographical Society, to report upon the condition of the Nestorians.

No substantial reply having been received to their appeals, the Chaldeans became discouraged, and it was Archbishop Tait in 1868 who received the next appeal, and after sending a clergyman to report, in 1881 he sent out a minister. Several years later the Archbishop of Canterbury's mission took form, and a complete staff came out to Urumiah, and was hailed with delight and gratitude by the Chaldeans; for it had come, not to win them over by force or persuasion to another faith, but to help them regenerate the ancient Church upon the lines of their own belief and tradition. Schools and colleges have been opened, as well for ordinary instruction as for priests and deacons.

Among the annals of self-sacrifice and hardship cheerfully endured must shine the name of the Rev. W. Brown, whom Mrs Bishop the traveller met in 1887, at Jula-mark, tramping from village to village, discredited and harassed by the Turks, living in the lowest poverty, and often going hungry and cold in the mountains. This priest exerted his endeavours to pacify the Kurds, who were exhibiting great hostility towards the Chaldeans, and he succeeded in preventing a massacre.

Meanwhile other proselytising bodies have not been idle. The Americans appeared in Urumiah and Turkish territory about 1818, and have a mission in the Urumiah district, a branch of that at Teheran, and a body of Chaldeans has left the old Church to follow the American Presbyterians, gaining for itself the name of Amrikani among other sects. The mission in Urumiah has distinguished itself by an ability to keep on good terms with the Kurds, one of whom was so friendly with Dr. Cochrane in 1880, that when Shaikh Abaidulla invaded Persia, he spared Urumiah at the intercession of the missionary.

Not long after the Americans the French Lazarists appeared, and established themselves near Salmas. The original priests, Fathers Cluzel and Darnes, experienced some difficulty and were nearly expelled, for the Russians induced the Shah to issue a "farman," or royal command, prohibiting Christians from changing their religion. However, the mission survived, and has now schools and priests at Urumiah and Khosrova, near Dilman.

At this latter place the inhabitants, while nearly all confessing Roman Catholicism, lament the fact, for they assert that the means adopted by the missionaries have been underhand and deceitful in a degree only by those of their predecessors in Turkey. Certain it is, that they have by intimidation, by working upon personal disagreements, and by other even less creditable means, quite captured the population of the place, and obtained for themselves the best gardens and buildings, even constituting themselves arbitrators and lords of the water-supply, which they condescend to hand over to the five thousand odd inhabitants only after they have used so much as to ensure the success of their extensive crops, and their consequent enhanced price when those of the villages fail.

Such briefly is the history of the Chaldeans and Assyrians since their nation was broken up. At present they exist, as we have seen, in Urumiah of Persia, in central Kurdistan, in Mosul, and latterly in the new colony at Ahwaz.

Particular mention must be made of the colony in the old capital of the Ardalan princes of Kurdistan, Sina, where, under the enlightened rule of that ancient family they were originally granted refuge, and subsequently so protected and encouraged as to have made them what they are now, a wealthy and powerful, if not numerous body, living on terms of the greatest cordiality with the Kurds of the Persian province of Ardalan. Here

ON THE PERSIAN FRONTIER, S. KURDISTAN.

[To face p. 160.

they possess a handsome school, the greater part of the money for which was subscribed by the Kurdish nobles of Sina, and at which many of the Kurdish lads receive instruction side by side with their Christian fellows.

There are also large colonies in Tiflis, and a considerable number have now settled in America, where they have generally been very successful.

The doctrine of Nestorius, that of the dual existence of Jesus Christ, has already been noted, and we may here briefly detail the tenets of the old Chaldean Church. The Creed is as follows:[1]—

"We believe in one God, the Father Almighty, Creator of all things which are visible and invisible.

"And in one Lord, Jesus Christ, the Son of God, the only begotten of His Father before all worlds: who was not created: the true God of the true God: of the same substance with His Father, by Whose hands the worlds were made, and all things were created; Who for us men and for our salvation descended from Heaven, and was incarnate by the Holy Ghost, and became man, and was conceived and born of the Virgin Mary; and suffered and was crucified, in the days of Pontius Pilate; and died, and was buried, and rose on the third day, according to the Scriptures; and ascended into Heaven, and sitteth on the right hand of His Father; and is again to come to judge both the living and the dead.

"And we believe in one Holy Spirit, the Spirit of Truth, who proceeded from the Father—the Spirit that giveth light.

"And in one Holy and Universal Church.

"We acknowledge one baptism for the remission of sins, and the resurrection of the body, and the life everlasting."

There appears to be some doubt as to the number of sacraments, but seven is supposed to be the number.

In use and ritual there is a nearer approach to the proceedings of the English Church than to any other.

---

[1] Layard, *Nineveh and its Remains*, vol. i., pp. 262-3.

L

Confession, transubstantiation, the existence of purgatory, exhibition of images, are the main points that are denied or prohibited; while they administer both elements to communicants who have been confirmed. The clergy were formerly all allowed to marry, and it was only the highest functionaries who discontinued the custom.

There are eight orders of clergy: Patriarch, Archbishop, Bishop, Archdeacon, Priest, Deacon, Subdeacon and Reader. As we have seen, the Patriarchal office is hereditary, and certain restrictions regulate the diet of the mother before the child's birth as well as his own diet during his life, when all meat is forbidden.

The fasts and feasts are extremely numerous, and all Chaldeans—Roman Catholic, Orthodox, or otherwise—are extraordinarily strict in the observance of such days in their respective sects, besides being very strict Sabbatarians.

CHAPTER VIII

BY THE HAMAVANDS TO SULAIMANIA

Al Akrad Tāïfatun min al jinnī kashafa 'llāhu 'inhumu 'l ghitā'.
("The Kurds are a race of Jinn from whom God drew back the curtain," and revealed them.)

WE left Kirkuk soon after daylight one morning, and joined a large caravan going to Sulaimania under the protection of one Shefiq Effendi, an "askar katebi" or military accountant. As this was the first caravan for some time, a large number of persons availed themselves of the chance of getting to Sulaimania. Few merchants had dared the passage. The travellers were poor people on foot, various kinds of Kurds, a shopkeeper or two of Sulaimania, and a number of officials whom duty called. All these last were taking their womenfolk, and a spirit of fright hovered over these unfortunate females which communicated itself to some of the effendis. For even with the escort we had, it was a highly dangerous undertaking to attempt the passage across the Hamavand country. Their fears were well enough founded, for we had but seventy foot-soldiers, and armed though they might be with Mauser rifles, they could not hold their own against even an equal number of Hamavands, and they knew it.

The marching kit of these sturdy fellows was eminently practical. In these lands, where a man does not look for hot meals three times a day, nor fear sleeping in the open, the ordinary traveller makes his way under conditions which European soldiers would consider hard. So the soldier cannot be expected to carry multifarious knapsacks of field fodder. In fact, he differs from the rest of us merely in the possession of a good rifle and plenty of cartridges. For the rest he wears what shoes he pleases, none at all if it please him better, and he sleeps in the clothes he walks in, as does everybody else, not troubling about what he lies on nor what he pulls over him. We had among us two Christians, a Greek army chemist and his wife, a Chaldean of Kirkuk. He rode upon a donkey, or rather walked and let the ass carry his bedding, for it refused to carry him as well. His wife was perched upon their belongings high above a mule. One effendi was an army officer returning to Sulaimania, his native place, for he was a Kurd, and he had several Kurdish women with him, one on horseback and others astride laden mules. There was the usual number of small boys and babies in arms, and a Jew or two taking printed cottons to Kurdistan for sale.

Our mules carried some boxes of ammunition and a load of books—the new instructions of the Parliament for the regulation of rent contracts and municipal affairs. The muleteers were highly amused at this load, commenting upon the waste of money involved in sending regulations to a town where order never existed, and if it did, rent contracts and municipal affairs were unknown, even by name.

As one looks east from Kirkuk towards Kurdistan, a low range of red barren hills shuts out the view, and over these runs the road to Sulaimania, and after crossing the plain behind, through the only gap in a second range to the plain of Bazian, the centre of the Hamavand country. This gap is the place where the wild horsemen have always assaulted caravans going east, and two months after our journey to Sulaimania, attacked and totally defeated a body of soldiers, killing several, and capturing every arm and cartridge in their possession.

But two days before we had started two ragged fellows had come in from this gap to Kirkuk—two long days' journey—and described the sack of a small caravan there; so prospects for us were not bright.

Judge, then, of the joy when our leader, the Shefiq Effendi, struck off the road and began taking a course among some low hills almost due north. For by so doing he left almost behind us the Hamavand country and headed for that of the Shuan Kurds, a powerful but peaceable tribe engaged in the keeping of flocks and herds—as their name implies.[1]

By noon we were appreciably rising, the hills were closing in, and we could never see far ahead, for the track wound in and out among steep downs. We passed a Kurdish village, a collection of huts upon a mound, about this time. The women, unveiled, bright in coloured robes, turbaned as only Kurdish women are, came out to stare and to inform men within of our arrival. Soon mounted men came galloping over the hills, appearing from apparently deserted corners of the landscape, and approached our leader. Coming up to him they dismounted and took his hand, greeting him with affection, and then we discovered that he—the military accountant—was a chief of the tribe. And no sooner were we away from Kirkuk, than away went the fez from off his head, to be replaced by a Kurdish handkerchief. Despite the invitation of these villagers, our leader would not stop, and we continued our way through the valleys. Here in some places, surrounded by hills, the wind dropped, and the sun's heat became so intense as to make the hardiest of these inured folk complain.

We entered one of these valleys, or rather, small flat plains between hills, and here the heat became intense. No breath of wind stirred, and the unfortunate soldiers began to look very sick and weary. Everybody carried some water, but it was quickly finished, and to add to the annoyance of the intense heat, myriads of small

[1] Kurdish "shuan"—a shepherd.

agile flies buzzed about the head, settling in eyes and ears
and sticking to the lips. One of the women fainted,
and fell from her mule; those of the men that had turbans
spread the handerchiefs that composed them, holding
out corners to shade their heads. Around us, sitting
upon the edge of some cliffs, were rows and rows of
solemn vultures, a fitting feature of this landscape,
where were but the bare stones of the valley, not an
inch of shade, nor a blade of grass, nor a drop of water,
and a silence and repose more deadly than the uproar
of the worst storm. The sweat ran off down the face
from the hair, down the chest it rolled, to soak through
the clothes into the bedding one sat on. The mules
sweated and stank, and the dust rose, choking one's
already parched throat.

For two hours we wound along the flat thus, till we
reached the end of the valley, where the hills closed
in, and the track mounted here. For another half-hour
we crawled up, zig-zagging along a steep and stony
path, and all at once met a breeze—and a view.

For before us were the higher hills of the Shuan
downs—great green ridges and hill-sides, waving with
long grass and bright with flowers. Deep, steep valleys
lay in the shade between them, and in the distance,
dim even in this clear air, rose the snowpeaks of the
Zagros—and Persian Kurdistan.

We were now well within the Shuan country, and
so long as our road lay in it we were safe, for the
Hamavand would not come out of their own country
into that of the Shuan, with whom they are friendly,
besides having a goodly respect for the strength of
this pastoral tribe. So we stopped at the first stream
without thought of robbers, and threw our loads for
a while. There was but a trickle, or rather, three
pools in the bed of the stream, at the bottom of which
a tiny spring bubbled up, and it was a long time
before we all got a drink. There was one tree, too,
in this delectable gully, and the soldiers promptly
bivouacked under it, striking and beating other equally

weary foot-passengers who would have shared the shade. Our particular party, which consisted of the original travellers from Mosul, fared better in the matter of water, for one of us discovered a fresh spring about a quarter of a mile lower down, whither we repaired with drinking-basins and earthen water-pots, and made an excellent meal from this and bread and dates. We were sleeping soundly—the sleep that comes quickly to the dweller in the open air, oblivious of the sun and flies—when the order came to load up; and as the effendi insisted upon our all starting together, there was a terrible rush.

Mule-loading is an awkward business, requiring at least two men. First the creature has to be brought alongside his load, which is two packages of equal weight, one to be suspended each side of him. These are already roped together, and to load, the two halves are lifted together to the top of the pack-saddle—about five feet six high. Then one of the men must run round to the other side, take the off half, pull it down and work it this way and that till it exactly balances its fellow on the opposite side. Then if there be a passenger, his bedding is thrown on top and a long girth thrown over and round all. This is quickly enough done under two conditions—first, that the mule be near his burden when the time comes for loading; and second, that he can be induced to stand while the packages are being lifted up and placed against the saddle. At this moment he has a habit of sidling away, and the load falls to the ground. Needless to say, after loading some sixteen mules, as we did twice a day, at express speed, a rest is very welcome, but one often has to walk a few miles over stony ground, urging the beasts when they lag, and the steep hill-sides frequently force everyone to dismount.

Out of the valley of the stream we came to a higher one between two long ridges of hills, and for three hours made our way northwards along it till we came to a village of the Shuan, prettily situated by a stream and several clumps of willows, and threw our loads upon the beaten ground round about.

The first proceeding when arranging for the night, is to arrange the loads in a kind of wall, and behind these one spreads felts and coats. Meanwhile the mules are led off to water, brought back, and the pack-saddles removed. The muleteers then clean the animals more or less with a rattling tin currycomb, replace the saddles, which act as blankets, and, tethering the beasts to a long line upon the ground, give them their barley.

In the meantime one goes off to the village—if there be any near—to find provender, which in the Kurdish country is a commodity called "du," the Persian "dugh." This is curds and whey watered to the consistency of milk, slightly sour, and always cool, for they keep it in porous skins—it is the most refreshing drink possible. Among the Kurds it is considered a mean action to sell such a thing, and this village was no exception to the rule. I undertook the task of getting for our party, and set off, entering the village through a broken courtyard wall, for there were no streets. After poking my head into several houses I found a good woman who was pouring out "du" into a wooden bowl, and demanded some, saying that there were several of us to share it. Without a word she handed me the skin, a bowl, and a deep spoon, and with all this a handful of flaps of new bread, answering my thanks with the Kurdish "Khwashit bi" ("May it pleasant to you"). Among the Kurds no one thinks of objecting to strangers walking into their houses, nor seeing the women, who walk about unveiled; indeed, they possess no veils. Perfect freedom of inter-course exists, and the womenfolk pause in their journey-ings to and fro to chat and joke with all and sundry, beggar and effendi alike.

In the early morning, long before daylight, the sound of people moving woke us, and we rose to find marching orders already issued, and half the caravan

loaded. One of us ran off to fill the water-pots at the
stream, where the village women were already similarly
engaged, while the rest of us fell to and loaded, and
after a few minutes the caravan started. Dawn found
us just topping a ridge, and at the fork of two footpaths. Expecting to take that leading east, and
towards Sulaimania, we were headed off by the soldiers
to the northerly track, which eventually led us round
the tops of some high hills, and along a steep ridge
from which the ground sloped away with almost the
gradient of. a precipice. Beautiful gullies with running
water and groves of trees branched off down below, and
gave upon a broad plain where we could see the broad
stream of the Lower Zab River flowing. Sulaimania
now lay almost due south, and we could see its position
by the great landmark of the Pir-i-Mugurun Mountain
that rises to its north, a precipitous bluff about ten
thousand feet high. Amid all these beautiful glades
and this verdant pasture-land we saw nobody but a
couple of parties of distant horsemen patrolling their
country.

By noon we were very high up, in amongst the
rolling hills, and suddenly coming upon a steep decline,
we saw below us a large village protected by a strong
castle upon a mound. This was one of the chief places
of the Shuan tribe; and reaching it—by a devious and
steep path—we threw our loads under some mulberry
trees. This arrangement of breaking the journey half-
way through the day is not unusual in Kurdistan, but
I have never seen it done in Persia, where the stages
are shorter.

The effendi went to a banquet already prepared for
him in the castle, for runners, taking short ways over
the hills, had advised the head-man of his arrival, and a
sheep had been killed and roasted whole. The rest of
us, after foraging for "du," lay down to sleep till the
time should come to load once more.

This village is in a very remote corner of the Shuan
country, off any main track, and the natives were so

impressed by the size of our caravan, that they all came out upon their flat roofs to watch us depart. Indeed, so small is the traffic, that there was no path beyond the village, and a horseman accompanied us to show the nearest way to our next halting-place. The track took us up the flank of a precipitous hill, and once there, down a long, steep spine. Here the slope was so great that it was impossible to sit even upon a donkey, and the women, unused to much walking and hampered by unhandy garments, were in almost as much danger when on their own as upon their steeds' legs, of falling headlong down the steep to the stream that ran three hundred feet below.

At the bottom we had to face the next ridge, and over that another and steeper one, on the opposite side of which was a beautifully situated village, almost hidden amongst trees, with a couple of torrents running down between the houses. This was about the highest point of the Shuan lands, and from its summit we could see all their country, miles of hills, green with the spring verdure, stretching away south and west. Before us lay the Zab valley, and the whole view, north-east and south-west, was shut in by range upon range of high, steep mountains, the Zagros. We camped in the open that night upon a steep hill-side opposite a village. Some of the villagers had migrated to our camping-place to be near some growing corn, and were living in palisades which they had erected upon the summit of the ridge.

From here our road lay almost south to Sulaimania. We had come through the country of the Shuan Kurds, and we had no other course but to go down through the Hamavands to Sulaimania. By coming so far north we had turned the flank of the Bazian hills, and would now enter the valley that ran north-west and south-east from its upper end. This is the Hamavand country proper, one long narrow valley between precipitous hills, where no traveller dared venture, and of which even the odd foot-passengers who accompanied us had no knowledge, in spite of their ramblings all over the country. A poor man can of course go almost anywhere on foot without fear of molestation, for he neither excites the cupidity of the Kurds by possessions, nor their enmity by weapons. A thick stick and a dagger are his armoury.

Of this mixed collection, who carried all their belongings upon their backs, a very large number knew Persian, and delighted to air it whenever possible. They were all Kurds, from all parts, Sina, Sauj Bulak, Keui Sanjaq, and even Kermanshah, which is quite cut off from Sulaimania by very precipitous mountains and savage tribes.

Among them were two Aoramani, members of a tribe inhabiting the border mountain of Aoraman, a steep wall of rock nine thousand feet high, in whose valleys the Aoraman tribe lives. I was very anxious to learn something of them, for their own tradition assigns to them an origin in northern Persia; they speak a dialect not Kurdish, and now I saw that they possessed a physiognomy and manner also foreign to the Kurdish peoples. They both spoke modern Persian, and one was quite well read, reciting long stanzas of the Shah Nama, a Persian epic very popular among them. They would not admit a Kurdish origin, calling themselves " Farsan i kuhangahi," Persians of the olden time—and their language, which I afterwards learned, and saw written in several manuscripts, is certainly not a Kurdish dialect.

Our start that morning was delayed, for Shefiq Effendi, our leader, had caused some messengers to be sent to the first Hamavand village, with a letter from the resident Shuan chief, informing the tribe of Shefiq Effendi's arrival, and the displeasure that any raid upon him would arouse among the Shuan.

Notwithstanding this warning to them, and a guard of twenty Shuan horsemen who accompanied us as far as the brook marking the limit of their country, there seemed to be no certainty that we should not be attacked, for the soldiers were, after all, not in the same category as harmless passengers under Shuan protection, and it was feared that a body of Hamavand might descend, and cutting off the soldiers, fall upon them. Consequently mounted scouts from the escort were sent out on every side, particularly ahead, and the Kurdish horsemen displayed considerable skill in the way they galloped up narrow gullies to steep hill-tops, and keeping up with the caravan below, despite the detours they were often forced to make. Every member of the caravan wearing uniform was instructed to reverse his coat or cover it with an aba, or cloak, and conceal his fez in a Kurdish head-dress. The caravan itself was kept together, the soldiers marching in the middle of it!

For some hours we crept round the face of cliffs that debouch upon the Zab valley, and at last, turning away from the river, climbed through several beautiful valleys, enclosed by precipices, to a plateau. We were now in Hamavand country, and a keen-eyed scout descried a little body of horsemen some distance away. These kept parallel with our course, while one of their number went at full gallop in the direction our road would take us.

There is great danger among the tribes when two bodies of horse approach, for it is a custom to fire from the distance at the new arrivals, to ascertain whether they be friend or foe. In the former case they refrain from answering, and wait for the others to approach, which they will do either at full gallop, or taking cover behind hummocks. Within earshot, greetings are exchanged, and recognition takes place, by face, difference of dialect, or turban, when subsequent proceedings are determined.

For some hours we went thus, among the hills which succeeded the plateau, till we arrived at a valley where, upon the hill-side was a large village standing by a river. This is the village of the sedentary Hamavands, which, with its groves and gardens, is a pleasant sight.

Upon the flat roofs the population was gathered; the richness of their clothing and the general idleness telling very plainly the triumphant story of two years successful rebellion and raids. From out this village another knot of horsemen appeared, but refrained from approaching, keeping to the opposite side of the valley.

Not wishing to rest so near the village, we kept on for some time till a turn of the hills hid us, and then in a depression by a basin where the grass grew knee-high, we threw the loads under some trees. Hardly had we done this than from every gully in the hill-sides horsemen came galloping down. Handsome men these Hamavands. As they rushed along, the silk head handkerchiefs of many colours streamed behind them; their long tunics, covering even their feet, rose and fell with the horses' action. The stirrups of many were inlaid with silver, contrasting with the scarlet upturned shoes. Their zouave jackets they had ornamented to the highest degree. Weird designs in gold braid and thread covered the pale blue cloth. Most were armed with Mauser repeating rifles, taken from the Turkish soldiers by force, and they made no pretence of hiding such evidences of their predatory predilections before the numerous soldiers and officers of our caravan.

Altogether there were about fifty of them, and not-withstanding the attitude of the soldiers, who had entrenched themselves behind bales, covering the oncomers, they rode straight up to the encampment, heedless of the disconcerted army that rose from behind its cover, looking foolish. As they approached near, each one ostentatiously opened the breech of his rifle and emptied it of cartridges, then slung it on his back, thereby announcing at once their friendly intentions, and their scorn for the soldiers. It was evident that the Shuan messengers had been well received, for the Hamavand head-man was there, a lad of about twenty, gorgeous in silk raiment, even to the undershirt, of which the long pointed sleeves hung to his feet. Remarkable, too, was the spotless cleanliness of these people. Despite their rough lives and constantly being in the saddle, not one showed a soiled shirt. Later, I discovered that the predatory Kurd, the more wealthy he becomes, insists ever more upon clean clothing—a feature peculiar, I should imagine, to the Kurd of these parts—not that the race can be called dirty, as the standards of Persia go.

The Hamavands, members of a race famous for bravery and lawlessness, have made a name for themselves among their countrymen, outdoing the wildest in foolhardy raids, and the bravest in their disregard of any danger, and a hostility to the Turks that has broken out continually ever since the powers of the old pashas of Sulaimania were broken. These years of outlawry seem to have had an effect upon their physiognomy. While not possessing the fine features of the Kurdish race, they have an alertness in their sharp dark eyes that comes of their mode of life, and a hostile manner that even among friends they cannot always control. We learned gradually, by the news that filtered from the tree where they were gathered round Shefiq Effendi, that they had received our messengers, and would see us as far as their chief's tent in Bazian plain, but we must take the chances of his decision. They could not guarantee that he would not resent the appearance of so many soldiers, nor be able to refrain from molesting them. It was suggested by the local chief that the soldiers should pack their arms upon mules and go back to Kirkuk, when we were assured that the chief would welcome us as followers of Shefiq Effendi. The Hamavands were very frank and very honourable. They refused to accept any food from the effendi, for they might be called upon to fall upon him and his soldiers that night; but after he had exempted them of all responsibility, they consented to partake of his tea.

However, they insisted upon certain conditions in the case of the soldiers. The bugle which had been used in the Shuan country was handed to the Hamavand leader, and one of his men at once tried to blow a call,

a melancholy failure that provoked the sarcasm of his
fellows, not only at him, but of the fools that had to be
led by a braying brass pipe and could not understand
the hill calls. The soldiers were to march wherever the
riders directed, before or behind the caravan, and at
night must camp where told, and be prepared to be
shot at if they moved about at night. The conditions
were of course agreed to, despite the disgust of the
commanding "bimbashi," a Turk who had to have
Kurdish translated, and who began to realise at last
what Kurds might be.

These conditions arranged, a number of the troop
left us to advise the chief, and taking a steep mountain
path were soon out of sight. We loaded up slowly and
resumed our way through some of the prettiest country
I have ever seen in Kurdistan. Water and trees were
abundant, valley after valley was carpeted with flowers
and deep in grass. Sheep and cattle grazed in every
place, guarded by small boys and girls, young Hamavands as yet not enlisted in the fighting forces—I
include girls under this heading, for the women fight
when necessary.

Towards sunset we topped a ridge and saw before
us the long and narrow valley of Bazian, the centre of
the Hamavand country. It is specially favoured with
water, an abundance of which flows down from both
sides. The two ranges appear to pour out all the
moisture they possess upon the Bazian valley, for the
plains that run up to their feet outside are waterless,
and each range while presenting, upon their inward or
Bazian faces, green, if steep slopes, show to the outer
world precipitous faces of bare rock.

Consequently Bazian valley, for the whole of its
narrow length—it is only two miles across—is a green
field, wherein herds of sheep and cows, like our Guernsey
breed, graze all the year round. The Hamavands had
also an eye to self-defence in selecting this secluded
spot, for, shut in at both north and south ends, its
eastern and western walls have no break in them

except the Bazian break in the western range, and a depression in the same range lower down at Sagirma. These two passes are admirably commanded from the steep spurs above them, and have never yet given way to an invading force.[1]

In a corner of the eastern range we came at sunset to a large black tent, the spring residence of the chief of the Hamavands, Hama Beg. From it emerged a number of men, who springing upon their horses came to meet us, and pilot us to our camping ground—for piloting was necessary. The leader of a tribe in rebellion must, even in his own country, be wary, and this chief had placed his tent in such a position that, while at his back was a precipice, on the other three sides a deep bog stretched, passable only by one narrow and slushy path. In the midst of this bog was the firm island upon which he lived and had allotted to us a camping place. The ground, to a stranger, appeared all firm, for a uniform covering of long grass stretched from the rocks' foot right across the plain.

Apparently the chief had decided upon letting us pass his country unmolested, for he came outside his tent and welcomed Shefiq Effendi cordially enough, leading him inside, where tea and nargila were produced.

Up to this point every one had been in a state of trepidation, for there was almost an even chance of being robbed and even slain. And this solely because of the soldiers, upon whom everybody looked with the loathing naturally to be displayed towards—not a single one—but a host, of Jonahs. These unfortunates, besides suffering from a most demoralising fear, were quite subdued, displaying none of the exuberant brutality usually typical of the creatures. Almost in silence they lay down on the damp ground allotted to them, nor objected when a dozen Hamavands formed a circle about them.

---

[1] In the opinion of the Sulaimania Kurds the word Bazian means in Kurdish "the place of defeats," but they have overlooked the fact that the word "bazi" and "bazian" is a common one in Kurdistan, with the significance "prominent hills."

Despite the friendly attitude of the chief, he gave away none of his native caution; it is just possible that he suspected, or saw the possibility of treachery, for while we had a hundred soldiers, there were but thirty or forty of his men there. At any rate, horsemen kept appearing in twos and threes from every direction, unchallenged so long as it was light, but approaching warily, calling their mates by name, after sunset. By midnight there must have been a hundred and fifty men there, sitting wide awake around their chief's tent. Their horses, saddled, with bits removed, grazed near by, ready at any moment.

It was an understood thing that anyone standing up or moving about was liable to be shot at, and one incautious soldier, trusting to the moonless darkness, stood up and moved, and learned to his cost that Hamavands do not sleep when on guard, and moreover can make very close shooting in the dark.

I do not think many of us slept that night. The muleteers were in a terrible fright for fear the Hamavands should quietly lead their mules away and loose them upon the hills, where none but Hamavands could recover them. The soldiers feared sudden slaughter; and the passengers, looting.

Our hosts, too, were on the alert all night long; the glow of the cigarette ends and the grumble of talking went on, and at dawn it would seem that none had slept. It is a remarkable power that Kurds possess of night watching. Time after time I have seen men turn night into day thus, sitting by a fire all night almost motionless, but wide awake, ready for action, and by daybreak mount and ride thirty or forty miles and repeat the same proceeding. They seem almost tireless, possessing a power of endurance that continual danger has taught them. It is at any rate an achievement that makes the Kurd almost impossible to take by surprise in night attack.

The Hamavand tribe, which has brought all the arts of raiding and guerilla warfare to perfection, has a

M

reputation of long standing for its daring and independence. Geographically speaking, they are not strictly within the borders of Kurdistan, but upon its western marches, and owing perhaps to the isolation of their country between its two ranges of hills, have kept aloof from all their neighbours for years.

They themselves claim Arab origin, a pretension not unusual among some of the smaller Kurdish tribes, and unsupported by any evidence for, and contradicted by much against, its possibility. For some years past they have allowed the Kurdish shaikh, or religious leaders, of the Qaradagh, their district, to attain a great ascendancy, and these have, by continual urging and exhortation, achieved their end of saddling the tribe with an iron-bound habit of religion quite foreign to the real Kurd of the mountains. Religious fervour, among Sunnis in particular, is inseparable from a great respect for Arabic language and lineage, with which the Sunni Turk and border Kurd almost invariably evinces a desire to identify himself; very much as Mr Smith or Mr Jones seek to prove a pure Norman descent which their names and antecedents do not necessarily indicate.

So we see Hamavand, Baba, Shuan, and Jaf, all claiming Arab descent for their leaders, while yet very proud of being Kurds to-day.

All these tribes are fond of indicating their dress, an adaptation of that of the Arabs, which they have adopted to the exclusion of the old and fantastic Kurdish dress, and point to it as being something to show their connection with the Arabs.

On the other hand, however, there are far more weighty evidences to prove that they are Kurd and nothing but Kurd, chief of which is their dialect, which is a well-defined and pure Kurdish tongue, the only Arab words in which have been imported. These words are usually the names of implements which, before the crafts of the Arabs were known to them, may not have existed.

From earliest memories of south-western Kurdistan

the Hamavands have been in rebellion against the ruling
power. Like every other small tribe, there is but the
most meagre history to be gleaned, and that of the
most recent only. They came originally from Persian
territory, where they lived near the frontier at Qasr-i-
Shirin. Here they became such an intolerable nuisance
under their leader Jawan Mir Khan, that the Persians,
in a vain hope of keeping them quiet, offered them the
post of Wardens of the Marches at a fixed salary. This
Jawan Mir Khan accepted, and redoubled his raids,
becoming so unbearable that he was captured and
executed. He was succeeded by his son Hama Beg.
Upon his accession to the chieftainship the Turks claimed
the tribe. Needless to say, the Persians gladly handed
over this thorn in their flesh, requesting the Turks to
remove their subjects with all expedition. They were
then given the present country in the Qaradagh district.

In 1874 they made a raid southward and commenced
harassing the frontier towns, actually laying siege to
Mandali, an important border town. Beaten off by
troops and other tribes, they retired, and a number conducted a successful raid as far north as the Christian
villages around Bayazid, returning, so report says, laden
with spoil, and unassailed, though their chief weapon was
but the lance.

Five years later they fell upon Sulaimania, and the
town was only saved from wholesale looting by the
arrival of a battalion of soldiers. Shortly after this
exploit, the Turks having by treachery trapped some of
the petty chiefs, a section was deported to the district
of Tripoli, in Africa, whence they returned. Six months
are said to have elapsed on the journey, and it is still the
boast of the Hamavands that they looted Arab and
Turk alike upon their return journey. Later again they
encroached upon the territory of the great Jaf tribe, and
were warned off by the Pasha of these powerful Kurds,
under pain of incurring blood-feud.

About 1900, or earlier, incited by the shaikhs of
Sulaimania and Qaradagh, they fell upon a large caravan

of Persian pilgrims near Kirkuk, destroying two hundred of these unfortunates. Up to this time Sulaimania, Rawanduz, and Keui Sanjaq had enjoyed considerable revenues from the pilgrims who passed from Persia, *via* Sauj Bulaq, to Bagdad, but after this the traffic ceased, and the shaikhs have lost for their neighbourhood a source of considerable wealth in satisfying the fanatical impulse to slay Shi'a Musulmans.

In 1908 the Hamavands crowned a campaign of two years' indiscriminate looting by announcing themselves in rebellion, and between the autumn of that year and summer of 1909 made good their assertion by stripping the Governor of Sulaimania, stopping all traffic, ending with the feat of attacking a "tabur" of Turkish soldiers, killing twelve (including a colonel and other officers), wounding forty or fifty and depriving them of all their possessions, including Mauser rifles, several loads of ammunition, clothing, daggers, uniforms and animals, leaving the miserable survivors thirty-six miles to tramp into Sulaimania. During this period they threatened the town several times, and always kept bands moving round about, so that corpses had to be taken out under a strong guard for burial, and often only with Hamavand permission.

All the summer of 1909 troops were collected at Chemchemal, a small town upon their borders, some eight thousand troops gathering by degrees. But secure in the knowledge that they could not move until a reluctant commander arrived, the Hamavands came up to the camp at night, dammed the water-supply, and picked off incautious sentries, disappearing before any sortie could be made. The soldiery was unpaid and demoralised, the officer supine and incapable, and the commander detained in Bagdad by various reasons of corruption and idleness. Two local governors—of Sulaimania and Kirkuk—were called to Chemchemal to form a court to judge and sentence the Hamavands when caught.

These individuals, together with the commanding

officers were being paid by the Sulaimania shaikhs to refrain from action, and the non-existence among the soldiers of any steeds, mule or horse, made operations at that time impossible.

So the Hamavands gaily continued raiding, retaining the posts, burning them, cutting up the telegraph lines. The Sulaimania governor when first called to Chemchemal refused to go—he could not venture outside the town. So the Chemchemal authorities obtained three hundred mules by the simple means of appropriating them in Kirkuk, and sent three hundred of their best soldiers thus mounted to bring the Mutasarrif of Sulaimania. With this escort he made a rush, getting to Chemchemal in seven hours, but not without having been chased by the Hamavands and losing some riders.

As the utmost mounted strength of the Hamavands is two hundred and fifty men, scattered in small bands about their country, their assailants probably did not number more than thirty or forty, but the brave three hundred fled.

At last merchants in Bagdad, Mosul, and Sulaimania made so much fuss, and the Central Government—partly ignorant of the reason for the delay of the proceedings—became so pressing, that the commanding officer started from Bagdad. Simultaneously the Hamavands, informed by their own spies, leisurely packed up their tents and their goods and retired over the Persian border to the territory of the Sharafbaiani Kurds, a little tribe the other side of the Sirwan River, upon the frontier.

The commander-in-chief arrived with much éclat, and with orders to pursue the Hamavands in his possession, and to invade Persia if she could possibly be accused of receiving even a Hamavand child over her borders.

The troops at once started to ascertain the whereabouts of the Hamavands, and finding no one in their country, had the satisfaction of eating the growing vegetables and burning the wooden roofs of some deserted villages. For two months they made quite certain that no

Hamavands lingered, catching every now and then a poor stranger Kurd and mutilating him on suspicion.

This heroic task was proceeding when I left Sulaimania, and till now I have reason to believe that the happy gathering at Chemchemal still exists, six months after they arrived to march against two hundred and fifty horsemen.

Some day they will retire, as soon as food gets scarce, and the Hamavands will reappear suddenly, to commence another period of raiding and defiance.

When we were among them on this occasion, as yet no move had been made against them, and the universal opinion was that no caravans after ours could pass. This was the case, for it was not till late August, when the tribe had gone away, that caravans once more went between Sulaimania and Kirkuk.

A large number of horsemen escorted us next morning, and we left their country after about two hours' journey, under the western side of their eastern range of boundary hill, finding at last a path over a neck.

From the summit of this we could see a long range of hills on the opposite side of an undulating plain about twelve miles broad, and far away to the east a great snowcapped wall, the Aoraman mountain, and Persia. This is the plain of Surchina, on the eastern border of which Sulaimania lies. At the foot of the pass the Hamavand escort indicated the spot where they had lately looted a caravan, killing all the military escort and destroying a large number of despatches and Government accounts. The scraps of these still lay about, and one could decipher upon them the tag-ends of sentences, a diversion which occupied some of the travellers for a considerable time. The recognised territory of the Hamavands extends a little way into this plain, and a large number were encamped by a stream in their black tents, and their flocks covered the hill-sides.

Approaching Sulaimania, we came to a region of hillocks where had originally been extensive gardens. Now they were but deserted patches of land where the

few trees remaining were dying for want of water.
Around Sulaimania the country is excellently watered
by a river and a number of streams, but the terror of
the Hamavands in troublous times, and of the Government and the shaikhs in days of peace, has effectually
ensured the desertion of what was once a richly cultivated
country. Right up to the outskirts of Sulaimania are
the same melancholy relics of past prosperity. At
present there are no gardens around the town, and it is
supplied with fruit at exorbitant prices, from villages
on the other side of the hills, which are out of the range
of the Hamavands.

Sulaimania lies on the lower slope of the hills
between two spurs, between which an abundance of
excellent water flows. The town is totally insignificant,
possessing no large buildings nor anything conspicuous,
except a minaret recently erected. From outside it
appears but a homogeneous mass of flat mud roofs,
relieved here and there by an upper room of a larger
house. It possesses no walls nor fortifications, and one
entered it abruptly from the desert, its outskirts being
small one-storied houses, in the courtyards of which
may be seen the idle, handsome women engaged in
their constant and only occupation—smoking cigarettes.

The proximity of Persian Kurdistan is very evident
here, the style of building in the poorer dwellings is
that of Sina and Sauj Bulaq, and in the better houses
that of any western Persian town. We threaded our
way through some open bazaar streets to a caravanseri,
where I had resolved to put up. This was constructed
entirely in the Persian style: a row of rooms round a
courtyard, which opened on to a low verandah.

I secured a room, and throwing into it my goods,
dismissed the muleteer, who was demanding a present
for having conducted me safely through the Hamavands
to Sulaimania.

CHAPTER IX

SULAIMANIA

SULAIMANIA, from which the Aoraman range that marks the frontier may be seen, lies actually about sixty miles from the nearest point of Persia, and one hundred from the Aoraman peak, which is visible from the town. It lies at the foot of the Azmir system of mountains, which support the Persian plateau at this point. It is also the largest Kurdish town of southern Turkish Kurdistan, but despite the importance, commercial and political, that it once possessed, it is a place without any noteworthy history.

It owes its origin indirectly to one Mulla Ahmad, who 350 years ago assisted the Turks in a war. This person, a Kurdish priest, was a native of the village of Dara Shamana, in Pishdr, north of Sulaimania, and a member of the Nuradini branch of the Baban tribe. For his services he was granted certain lands and villages by the reigning sultan, and established himself at the village of Qal'a-i-Chwalan, now called Qara Chulan, a village north of the Azmir range, a day's journey from Sulaimania. Here he reigned till his death, and his successors became powerful rulers, semi-independent, ruling over Surchina, where Sulaimania is now situated, and the lands about Qal'a-i-Chwalan. These chiefs were, like so many of the frontier chiefs of Sulaimania, by no means too faithful to the Turks, and transferred their allegiance to Persia when it suited them.

184

AORAMAN.

[To face p. 184.

In 1779, in the time of Sulaiman Pasha of Bagdad, the government was transferred to the site of the present town, and a government house and other buildings were constructed, and the new town called Sulaimani—not Sulaimania.

Now a dynasty of Kurdish pashas ruled, beginning with Ibrahim Pasha, and followed by his descendants. These governed until the time of Abdulla Pasha, who was contemporary with Namiq Pasha of Bagdad.[1] The Sulaimani ruler, having come to Bagdad to visit the Vali, was seized, together with his brother Ahmad Pasha, and sent under a guard to Constantinople. This was in 1851, and was the end of Kurdish rule in Sulaimania. One Isma'il Pasha, a Turk, was appointed Qaim Maqam of Sulaimania, with a garrison, and Sulaimania has remained a Turkish government ever since. The two Kurdish pashas died about thirty years ago, and their sons live as pensioners in Constantinople.

The Kurdish Ibrahim Pasha, having gained the chieftainship of the district of Sulaimania, and Qaradagh to the south-east, built for himself a large house upon the hill-side—where the modern governor or Mutasarrif now resides. Around this and lower down, the town began to form. The old family of shaikhs, or religious leaders, established itself there also, and the construction of a bath and mosque gained for the place a certain importance. Kurds, however, are not good settlers, and the population of the new town began to form of the various classes of people who habitually follow trade. These are, in these regions, Turkoman of Kirkuk, Jews and Christian—Syrian and Chaldean, mainly the latter. It is said that out of a thousand houses constituting the town in 1825, eight hundred were occupied by Christians, Jews, and Turkomans,

As the neighbourhood is entirely peopled by Kurds of the Marga, Shuan, Hamavand, Bana, and Jaf tribes,

---

[1] Also during the few years in the first half of the century that Sulaimania was in Persian hands.

the language of the place was from the first Kurdish. The shaikhs at the same time exercising their power for evil and fanaticism, made life so difficult for Christians and Jews that a large number each year deserted their own faiths to escape persecution, adopting after conversion the dress and speech of the local Kurds. From this very mixed material a people has sprung whose ancestors were the children of races widely different in sentiment and nature, mixtures of Aryan, Semitic, and Turkish stock, that possesses almost every one of the unpleasant qualities of each race, and a very lively fanaticism that has—under the inflammatory action of the shaikhs—never weakened, gaining for Sulaimania a name for the ignorant and savage isolation that has now brought about its own ruin.

Nevertheless, under the strong rule of the old pashas the priests were unable to gain or exert the malignant influence they ever hoped to do, and the town made very considerable progress, becoming an important market for the wool and skins of the tribespeople, and an entrepôt and distributing station for all goods imported into western Persian Kurdistan from Mosul and Bagdad. There was, on the land specially in the Qaradagh and Shahr-i-Zur, a population of Chaldeans and Jews, and these, whether retaining their own religion, or becoming included and intermingled with the Musulman population, furnished a keen and progressive business instinct.

The pasha always kept on good terms with the chiefs of the great Jaf tribe, and kept a sufficient number of armed and able horsemen to secure peace within his own borders; and accordingly Sulaimania became one of the most important of all the border towns.

During the wars of the early part of this century, the place with Shahr-i-Zur, its adjoining district, became Persian, as it had anciently been; but it was recovered by the Turks, and by the treaty of 1847 remained in their possession.

About this time a great massacre of Christians all
over southern Turkish Kurdistan had occurred, in this
part originated by a member of the shaikh family.
Following this, the power of the independent Kurdish
chieftains became very much decreased, and the Turks
succeeded in preventing the continuance of their sway,
as we have seen.

From this point, where the healthy restraining influence of the Kurdish pashas over the priests ceased,
the members of the family of Sulaimania shaikhs began
to make for themselves a position so strong that
governor and governed alike lived in awe of them.

So long as Sultan Abdul Aziz lived—till 1876—the
comparatively good order of his rule kept the Shaikhs
in subjection, and they contented themselves with gaining
a reputation for sanctity, and acquiring lands and villages
by purchase. Shaikh Sa'id, the leader of the family,
succeeded in these aims so well that he gained possession of lands all round Sulaimania, and spread abroad
the assertion that he possessed the power of divining,
and the knowledge of the invisible and the future.[1]
The former he possessed, certainly, by one of the most
perfect systems of spies and communications. His
prophecies were usually such as could be fulfilled by his
secret agents with dagger and bullet. Not unnaturally
his name became feared; such an exaggerated reverence
being paid to him, that men would salute his horses.

Upon the death of Sultan Abdul Aziz, and after the
accession of Sultan Abdul Hamid, this astute priest
began the system of self-aggrandisement and enrich-
ment that finally became the cause of his murder in
1909.

Seeing the Sultan corrupt and avaricious, and his
entourage unusually sycophantic and treacherous, he
made a journey—together with another famous priest,
Shaikh Qadir—to Constantinople, and by a large present
secured for himself and his family the Imperial favour.
Also by his remarkable gift of plausibility, and by the

[1] "Amru, 'l ghaib wa 'l mustaqbal."

aid of the religious obligation and law that he brought
to support all his arguments, he became practically the
religious adviser of Sultan Abdul Hamid. The final
and triumphal stroke of genius was when Shaikh Sa'id,
the Sultan, and Izzat Pasha—of evil memory—actually
formed a ring for the exploitation of Sulaimania district,
a combination whereby the trio became enriched. Izzat
Pasha guaranteed to supply inefficient and corrupted
officers for the local government, the Sultan would reap
a yearly income besides taxes, and Shaikh Sa'id, without
being in any way responsible officially for the situation
in Sulaimania, was free to crush the people and squeeze
the province till there remained but himself and his
family, enormously enriched, contemplating the exhausted
and ruined town and country.

At the moment of Sultan Abdul Hamid's accession,
Sulaimania was probably more important than it has
ever been, before or since. It had become a market
for the produce of all southern Kurdistan. The carpets
of the country came here for sale, to be taken to Mosul
and Bagdad. Gum tragacanth from Bana began to be
sold here in preference to Sina, and a large number of
Chaldeans of Mosul carried on an extensive and profitable business in the cotton cloths of Aleppo and the
fabrics of Europe, which they sold in Sulaimania and
exported even as far as Hamadan of western Persia;
certain crafts found a place in the extensive bazaars,
notably shoe- and saddle-making, and the manufacture
of daggers and rifles. The begs and pashas of the Jaf
tribe built caravanserais and bazaars, and entered into
relations with Sulaimania merchants whereby all the
produce of their large tribe—skins, wool, tobacco, and
butter—passed through this market. The Bagdad caravan left and arrived every fortnight, and to and from
Mosul at the same intervals. Frequent caravans, too,
served Bana, Merivan, Sina, and Sauj Bulaq. The
governorship was raised to that of Mutasarrif, and
nominally a larger garrison was stationed at the place.

I was told that in 1880 there were fifty Mosul

Chaldeans and twenty Hamadan Persian merchants established there. These last were so important a part of the commercial population as to occupy a special caravanserai, to which the name of Khan-i-Ajam ("The Persians' Caravanserai,") was given, a name it has retained to-day though not a single Persian remains in Sulaimania. The trade — exclusive of local supply business — was estimated at over half a million liras annually; a total it never reaches now, when the highest figure is supposed to be four hundred thousand liras on a good year, and that decreasing.

In 1881, the shaikhs' tyranny, in concert with that of the Government, which extorted iniquitous taxes, led to a revolt upon the part of the people, and they summoned the Hamavands to besiege the town, and expel the governor and shaikhs. The town resisted for four days, and was upon the point of falling, when a battalion arriving from Kirkuk saved the situation, and at the same time delivered the town into the hands of the revengeful priests. Shaikh Sa'id commenced a campaign of open robbery. Large sums of money were extorted from merchants without any pretext whatever, and the prompt murder of the few who resisted these demands effectually intimidated the others. At the same time a policy of patriarchal hospitality and patronage was instituted. Any person presenting himself at the shaikhs' house received food and became considered a retainer. In this way all the worthless members of the population became adherents of the priests; and as many opened shops in the bazaar, a new class of supporters arose which finally embraced nearly all the tradespeople of Sulaimania. In these days it was dangerous to express an opinion about the priests. In every shop, in every corner, were spies or adherents who reported to their masters the actions of everyone, and these individuals were aware of the private life and proceedings of every single individual—Christian, Jew, or Musulman—in Sulaimania. Murder became very frequent, for the disappearance of a "disaffected" person caused no comment for fear of consequences, and murderers had but to acknowledge allegiance to the shaikhs to hear commendation of their excesses in place of condemnation. Through it all, it was the merchants who suffered. The Persians, being Shi'as, suffered from the fanaticism of the Sunnis; none the less because the shaikhs were unable directly to oppress them, for the fear of Persia is still considerable in the border countries: nevertheless sufficient injury occurred to their business to drive them from Sulaimania.

The shaikh family had purchased nearly all the gardens about the town which supply fruit and vegetables, and now, in conjunction with the town authorities, new taxes were instituted upon out-turn and produce. Then the shaikhs commenced a system whereby three hundred per cent. special entry duty was charged upon loads of fruit coming to town. Within two years every cultivator had set fire to his fruit-trees, destroyed his irrigation canals, and fled to Persian soil, there to cultivate tobacco. Subsequent to the events of 1881, when the Hamavands so nearly succeeded in taking Sulaimania and destroying the family, Shaikh Sa'id realised the importance of the tribe and its possible use as a weapon. In order to gain control over it, he, by a series of judicious marriages, bound it to him by ties of relationship, which he strengthened by entering into cordial relations with the priests of Qaradagh. This policy succeeded so well that in 1908 the tribe found itself unable to disobey the shaikhs, when ordered to declare itself in rebellion. For the object of the family was now not only to acquire the wealth of Sulaimania, but to prove their power so great that the Government should be forced to make them the rulers of Sulaimania, in despair of obtaining peace and quiet by any other means. The "coup" at Constantinople of July 1908 had just occurred, Turkey was declared constitutional, and the shaikhs saw the possibility of a loss of their power, and even less pleasant to contemplate — retribution. The Sultan, however, had

considerable power—more than the observers in Europe
ever suspected—which he hoped to augment, and he
was not averse to the outbreak of rebellion, which
should increase the difficulties of the reformers' task.
The old power, corrupt as it was, was, notwithstanding,
none the less effective, particularly in the remoter parts
of Asiatic Turkey, for the Sultan had always on his
side that most powerful section that increased for him
his revenues through the means of robbery and brigandage,[1] and when the interests of these persons coincided
with those of order—as occasionally they did—justice was
prompt and effective.

Needless to say, abandonment of the old *régime*
meant alienation of these forces from the standard of
the Constitutionalists, and it was this condition of the
situation that at once gave hope to the Sultan and
despair to the Majlis, which could not bring enough
power to bear upon any anarchy or rebellion, the more
that the new Government was no more able to meet
the arrears of army pay than Sultan Abdul Hamid had
been willing.

Particularly the Turkoman and Kurdish levies in
the army were extremely disaffected, refusing any duty
that appeared to them repugnant. Therefore, the
Hamavands were perforce left to raid and spoil undisturbed. The situation was growing so bad in Sulaimania, however, that the shaikhs could no longer be
disregarded by the new party at Constantinople. The
merchants were now suffering doubly and trebly. If
they did not lose their goods at the hands of the
Hamavands, the Customs authorities, shaikhs, and town
officials effectually ruined them. Repeated appeals
arrived by wire from Sulaimania; and at last, the
Government, knowing the impossibility of employing
force, induced Shaikh Sa'id to come to Mosul, with
some other members of the family. Here he was

---

[1] A notable instance of this peculiarity of Abdul Hamid's policy
was Ibrahim Pasha, the Kurdish rebel of Harran, whose history is set
forth in Mr Fraser's *Short Cut to India.*

detained, and shortly afterwards the riot occurred in which he was murdered. The mystery of the criminal's identity has never been cleared up. The disturbance arose among the people of Mosul regarding their own affairs, and after some time they were dislodged from the scene of the opening brawls. With one accord, apparently under directions received, they made a rush for the house of Shaikh Sa'id, and forcing it, a number entered, and the old priest was murdered.

This was the signal for redoubled anarchy in southern Kurdistan. Shaikh Sa'id had, as has been shown, acquired a reputation for unusual sanctity, and this, coupled with his power, gave reason for loudly expressed indignation on all sides. The representative in Constantinople, Shaikh Qadir, made a series of inflammatory speeches demanding in the name of all the laws of Islam, summary and awful vengeance upon the murderers. The younger members of the family in Mosul were allowed to return to Sulaimania after they had sworn an oath of vengeance upon the merchants of that town, for they chose to assume that the murder had occurred at their instigation.

In wrath they returned. The town of Sulaimania was forced to go into the deepest mourning. All gramophones and musical instruments were taken by force from their owners and destroyed, and any celebration at weddings was brought to an abrupt and melancholy termination. Shaikh Mahmud assumed leadership of the family, and displayed an ability for violence and crime unequalled by Shaikh Sa'id in the days of his greatest power. A number of the most important merchants were murdered for the sake of what could be extorted from them under the pretext of vengeance. Robberies and burglary occurred in every direction. To express an opinion of even a scullion of the shaikh, was to meet death the same night. And after every new outrage the police and governor received their commission, and the miserable people, wringing their hands, whispered the name of the criminals, and "Piaoi shaikhana" — "They are the Shaikh's men."

The Vali of Mosul was now ordered to proceed to Sulaimania for two reasons. To attempt an investigation of the troubles there, was one; and to punish the robbers of the Mutasarrif, who had left the town and had been assaulted by the shaikhs' horsemen, nearly losing his life, was the other. The shaikhs were, of course, the delinquents; but there was no possibility of fixing the crime upon them, for the people were too much intimidated to utter any complaint openly, and the few Government officials remaining in the town were bought.

The Vali speedily settled upon a line of proceeding that should not place him in conflict with those he could not subdue, and that might at the same time result in pecuniary profit to himself. While yet at Chemchemal, a station on the western border of the Hamavand country, he succeeded in communicating to the shaikhs his idea of "strict and impartial investigation and report."

As is the custom, the population of Sulaimania rode out some distance to meet and greet him, and in that meeting the merchants realised that their hopes were useless. The two parties, shaikhs and merchants, had ridden out, and encountered the approaching Vali near the river which crosses the Surchina valley. The shaikhs, spurring forward, were received with the politest of greetings, the most solicitous enquiries; and the Vali, joining their party, rode ahead with them at a canter, passing and ignoring the waiting merchants.

Within twenty-four hours a summons had been issued to all of the merchant class, demanding their presence at the Serai, or Government House, to answer why they had caused so much trouble and strife in the province by their attitude of opposition to the bereaved and mourning shaikhs. Despite this peremptory message, couched in the most abrupt terms of the naturally uncouth Turkish language, these Kurds displayed a little of their native courage, and refused to reply to charges

N

so basely unjust, or even acknowledge the existence of so corrupt an official by coming near his residence.

This afforded the Vali the opportunity he awaited. He now reported that he had called a conference to discuss the matters of the province, to be composed of merchants on one side, and shaikhs upon the other, at which each might state their grievances and produce evidence. The shaikhs had duly appeared, but as the merchants had refused to come, he could but assume them to be the guilty parties, the instigators of rebellion, the malcontents and malignants, now too ashamed to even attempt to justify their backslidings. The priests had, on the contrary, appeared, and laid before him well-substantiated complaints against the merchants, and provided him with evidence implicating them in the murder of the venerated Shaikh Sa'id.

Having pocketed a large sum,[1] the Vali bid farewell to the Sulaimania and returned to Mosul, satisfied with himself and the shaikhs, and leaving them in undisputed possession of right and might.

A new governor was sent, not a creature of the Vali, with a staff and a new commissioner of police. These were bought immediately upon their arrival. The few troops allotted to Sulaimania were distributed as usual along the frontier guard-houses, and at Panjwin, Bistan, Gulambar, and Halabja, leaving not more than one hundred and fifty undisciplined ruffians and natives of the Kifri and Kirkuk district — Turkoman and mongrel Kurd. The situation grew worse. Now the Hamavands were called up to the gates of Sulaimania, and threats of instant sacking kept the population subservient to the will of the shaikhs. The Majlis at Constantinople had now become a more recognised institution, and at least possessed enough power to control the appointment of Vali of Mosul and Mutasarrif of Sulaimania. Moreover,

---

[1] I regret that I cannot state the amount, which was variously put at five, six, seven, ten, twenty, and thirty thousand tomans (Persian money). It would appear from most reliable evidence that the amount was about ten thousand, or roughly, two thousand pounds.

Sultan Abdul Hamid's days as ruler were coming to an end, and the shaikhs knew it. Izzat Pasha was in exile in Cairo, and Shaikh Qadir at Constantinople, in disrepute. So the shaikhs opened a campaign against Government. The efforts of the Hamavands were directed against authority in the shape of the army. Here and there small bodies of soldiers were cut to pieces and their arms taken. The roads from Kirkuk to Bagdad, Kirkuk to Sulaimania, and Sulaimania to Bagdad, were closed entirely ; and now Sulaimania, already impoverished, shut half its bazaars for want of goods to put in them, and the few merchants who still had the courage to keep their offices open sat in empty rooms and idleness. Then the talk of " ta'qib " (pursuit and punishment) of the Hamavands arose, and we have seen how it was carried out. Corruption everywhere thwarted the best designs of the Majlis, and the Hamavands got away while the shaikhs sat in Sulaimania unaccused, and still maintaining an attitude of injured righteousness that called for justice.

This was the position in August 1909, when I left Sulaimania.

At that time the merchants were awaiting the collection of outstanding debts to leave the province, which they saw would never recover from its ruin so long as the shaikh family exists and is allowed its iniquitous power. Trade has deserted Sulaimania to a great extent. Merchants are going to Persia, which in its worst times never tolerated such a situation as this, and where business—decreased and weak—yet finds a way. Now the Customs duty, increased to the figure of fifteen per cent., will assist the ruin of its trade, which is now reduced to the import of produce from Persia, notably gum and carpets. Transit trade will of course continue to a certain extent, but as a great proportion of the business originated with migratory tribes, its transfer to another place is possible.

When I arrived in May 1909, affairs were bad. Our caravan had excited the greatest interest by reason of its having been able to get through from Kirkuk whole, and news was eagerly sought of all who arrived, particularly regarding any possible amelioration of the situation. However, worse was to come, for no other caravans came through.

I had taken a room in the caravanserai of Ghafur Agha—who was then the Mayor—and found there no other residents save an old Arab gentleman, a native of Tripoli of Africa, who held a post of "mudir" or petty governor of a village, whither he could not proceed, as the village in question had not hitherto possessed such an official, and the Kurdish inhabitants would have slain any one bold enough to attempt to establish himself there as their ruler.

My neighbour, Mustafa Beg, was a courteous and well-educated old man, whose life had been spent in the Mediterranean ports and consulates at Malta, Trieste, and such places. He spoke Arabic and Turkish perfectly, but knew no word of Kurdish; nor could his well-bred and gentle nature at all cope with the rough manners he met in Sulaimania. A more complete example of the absurd disregard of suitability of man for post could not have been seen. Failing the opportunity of assuming his duties, the old man lived alone in a miserable room in the caravanserai. He possessed no covering for his floor; his only furniture was a couple of boxes containing his clothing, a coffee-boiler, an old spirit stove, one coffee cup, and some bedding. He slept at nights in a disused palanquin whose owner had been killed, and it was partly owing to this habit that he met his ghastly death some months later.

In the entrance to the caravanserai a merchant, half-owner of the place, had an office, and some Jewish pedlars stored their wares in two rooms. The rest remained empty, their bare walls testifying to the condition of Sulaimania. The courtyard lay deep in dust and scraps of paper, and a stagnant pool stank in its midst. Desolation was near it, and by the shaikhs' agency eventually lay upon it.

I arrived at about half an hour to sunset, and being foodless, locked my door—that slid like a shutter, up and down—and went out to find something. Bread was naturally the first thing needful, and this I found of two kinds, one very thin flaps and the other thick round cakes, each being sold for two "pul"—the pul being a copper coin of Persia worth about a seventh of a penny. Three flaps (or a pennyworth) was enough for my needs, and this, with two lettuces—at a farthing each—a sticky lump of dates, very dear in this cold country, and a bowl full of watered curds, or "du," made an excellent dinner.

Buying anything at first was rather an ordeal, for Sulaimania has retained the Persian currency, though it is many a long year since it belonged to that nation, no Turkish coins except the mejidie being accepted. Thus old names and coins remain, while the names of Turkish coins are applied to the currency as well, resulting in confusion. There are three actual tokens: the copper "pul"; the silver "baichu," or Persian "panj shahi"; and the ordinary two-kran piece of Persia, here called "tihrani." But we encounter such names as "charkhi," "jout," "deh para," "ghazi," "qamari," "qran," and "qran-i-rash," besides these.

Everything is reckoned in "qamari," and this imaginary coin is worth four "pul," and the "baichu" (which being the actual token must be handled) is worth seven pul. For larger amounts the tihrani is quoted, consisting of five baichu and one pul, or nine qamari; and the stranger plunges about in despair, not lessened by the fact that in Kirkuk they call the baichu a qamari, and the tihrani a qran.

I quote an example of the working of this system, which, it is to be hoped, is not more confusing than the unexplained situation. When I would go to where fragments of a sheep suspended from a pole constituted a butcher's shop, to ask the price, I was informed "thirty-two." I must know that this means thirty-two qamari, or three qrans and five qamaris, which is in tokens, three qran and two baichu and six pul. This is the price

of a Sulaimania "oke," or as the Kurd calls it, "huqqa."
Every town in the East fixes its own scheme of weights;
and being asked, the Sulaimanian will, with excess of
lucidity, explain that the local huqqa is four-fifths of
the Panjwin huqqa, five-fourths of a Tabriz "man," two-
fifths of the Halabja "man," and will not, till the last
moment, give the information that it equals two and
a half of the Stamboul "oke," which passes as a base
for calculation throughout Asiatic Turkey.

Thus, receiving the reply "thirty-two," one arrives,
or is expected to arrive, at the knowledge that the amount
of meat necessary, usually a quarter of a huqqa, costs
eight qamari, which must be paid for by four baichu
and four pul. At the same time is discovered the fact
that the huqqa—like a Persian "man," which it really
is—misnamed, is divided into four hundred dirhams,
and that all fractions of the huqqa must be expressed
in Turkish and not in the native Kurdish.

It was a great relief to find that nearly all the
population knew some Persian, for the northern and
eastern Kurdish I knew was not current here, and to
the population less comprehensible than Persian. At
first, and before I became recognised, the fact of my
wearing a fez gave everyone to think that I was a
Turk; and those who possessed any would air their
little Turkish upon me, and, it must be said, show considerably more gratification at the opportunity of
talking Persian.

Among other customs strange and stupid, is the
one which forbids a woman to appear in the bazaars at
the risk of loss of her good name[1]: why, seems hard to
say, for there never was a more moral town than
Sulaimania. Possibly it is for the same reason that
reckons it improper for a man to wear ornamented
socks, or bows on his slippers, or to remain in his house
by day or treat his wife as a woman, and a hundred
other pranks of caprice which are hard and fast rules
of Sulaimania society and life. And the infringement

This custom has been adopted from the Arabs of Mosul.

of any one of these little rules is met by a horrified look and the hackneyed old expression, "Aiba Bokum,"[1] which has worked so hard here, and is used to prevent so many actions, that any progress or improvement is always stifled by that terrible "Aiba Bokum."

If I would speak to my own wife in the street, if I would bare my head to a cool breeze in a public place, if I would be too friendly with a Christian, or speak civilly to a Jew, these are all "Aiba Bokum," and but the least of them. But would I in rash moments of philanthropy and idealism suggest killing the flies on the putrid meat of the shops, or ridding the town of fraudulent beggars, or building a sanitary house, or cleaning a street, or doing anything of any benefit to myself or others, then I should become a raving lunatic from hearing day and night the pained protest of "Aiba bokum"; if, indeed, I were allowed to remain in the town.

In this, Sulaimania is only too like the rest of the Muhammadan East, particularly those parts farther removed from the West, whose creed is, "That I do as did my fathers, and leave undone that which they did not, and curse the innovator."

Nor is this creed to be set aside lightly, even though it mean inconvenience to the people themselves. Some years ago a doctor of some skill came here, hoping—as he was the first arrival in a town full of dirt-diseases—to make a speedy fortune, as others have done among the Kurds.[2] Two months after he had established himself he left for Persian Kurdistan, carrying his implements upon his back, his head ringing with the phrase "Aiba bokum."

After him came a photographer, who at first was fairly successful, but a Sulaimanian of profound knowledge unearthed the saying of a holy man that repre-

---

[1] Kurdish, "It is a fault, little father."

[2] It should be remembered that the population of Sulaimania town, though they have adopted the language and part of the dress of the Kurds, do not entirely belong to that race, as has been shown in the descriptive note upon these people's origin.

sentations of persons must have the head cut off with
a penknife, or the artist's soul would annoy that of
the portrayed, appearing in his likeness in the last
day. So the unfortunate Sulaimanians beheaded themselves on paper and expelled the photographer. After
a time came the phonograph, the most popular of all
Western inventions in the Orient, and this was taken
up by some individuals, and stopped upon the death of
Shaikh Sa'id as an impious instrument.

This habit of mind, and constant abhorrence of all
that is new, explains why the Sulaimanian still walks
about in the costumes we see in prints of books of
travellers to Persia in the 16th century, why his
shirt-sleeves hang to the ground, why the skirts of his
tunic wipe the filth along the streets as he walks.
These are the conservators of the bad old customs,
would-be slayers of the Jews among them, ignoring the
tie of blood that binds ninety per cent. of them to
that race. The custom and law relating to clothing is
so strong that strangers living among them, if they
would hope to live without annoyance, must adopt
their style of raiment and reject the more convenient
garments of their own lands.

Their isolation has made them very suspicious of
all strangers, and from this suspicion has developed an
inquisitorial bearing almost intolerable. It is the right
of every Sulaimanian to enquire closely into the aims
and identity of every new arrival. Fortunately he does
not resent equally close enquiry, even rather welcoming
it as affording an opportunity for self-aggrandisement
and a self-righteous exposition of his own respectability.
Also, the intense suspicion with which they approach
the stranger renders it quite immaterial whether lies
or truth are given in answer to their queries. Incon-
sistent as it may seem, once their questions are
answered, and the information disseminated about the
town, the stranger is accepted at his own valuation
and becomes part of the population.

Having learned somewhat of these matters, I was

not surprised to receive a visit from a gorgeous individual, who came to see me at the caravanserai one morning. This person was enveloped in a fine cloak of camel's hair, the right-hand side of the back of which was covered with gold thread work: between its folds stuck out from the waistbelt the sheath of a huge knife, and as he entered he removed from his feet a new pair of Bagdad shoes. He saluted in excellent Persian, and having accepted a cigarette, commenced without preambulation his queries, which I answered as briefly as possible.

The dialogue was somewhat thus:—

"Where is your native country?"

"Persia."

"Which town?"

"Shiraz."

"Are there any Sulaimanians in Shiraz?"

"No, nor ever were."

"Are you going to Persia?"

"I do not know at present."

"Why do you not know at present? How shall a man not know his destinations?"

"Because my plans are not formed."

"Stay here, it is the best place—good water, good air, and a kindly population. What are you by trade? Are you a doctor?"

"No, why?"

"Because of your European style of dress, which for any but a doctor is an impropriety here. Are you a merchant?"

"Yes, I might be."

"What are your wares?"

"Cloths and such like."

"Have you also scented soap?"

"No; why do you ask that?"

"Because a merchant came from Mosul twenty years ago with scented soap, but it is an impropriety here."

"Why?"

" Because it was never used formerly ; besides, children always die when they smell it."

" Then do the children of Sulaimania fear sweet or clean smells ? "

"Yes, they are not accustomed to them.   Where did you buy those shoes ? "

" In Kirkuk."

" Here they are improper, having laces."

He cast about for a new question, then suddenly :

" What is in these cases ? "

" Clothing."

" Have you no things in them to sell?   What kind of merchant are you without wares and loads ? "

" I await samples, no wise man brings new goods unless first proved saleable by samples ! "

" You speak truth, but what is in your boxes ? "

" I told you, clothes."

" Where did you buy those trunks ? "

" In London."

" In London ; why did you go there ? "

" I had business."

" What business ? "

" My own business; every man has his own business and affairs."

" Quite true ; but I came here to tell you, as a friend, that you should not sit in a caravanserai, it is not proper."

My patience came to an end, and I reversed the order of things, and started an inquisition of my own.

" Why do you wear a torquoise ring ? "[1] I enquired severely.

" What ? "

" I say, why do you wear a torquoise ring ?—it is improper in my country."

" I came here as a friend, why do you ask such unkind and ridiculous questions ? " he asked in a hurt tone.

" Because," I replied, " in my country of Shiraz there

[1] Practically every Kurd and Persian wears a silver ring with a torquoise, which is a recognised part of dress.

is a saying, ' He who annoys the stranger by inquisitiveness, seeks after such abuse and ridicule that ill-manners
may call forth from the tormented ! ' "

Frowning with indignation, he gathered his gay cloak
about him and departed swiftly, not even deigning to
answer my farewell. Five minutes afterwards the
caravanserai keeper came to the door somewhat perturbed,
and informed me that he who had come as a friend and
gone as an enemy was owner of the place and mayor
of the town, Ghafur Agha himself.

In those first few days there, I found out how the
Sulaimanian deems himself entitled to treat the stranger ;
and to complete the lesson, the day before I left for
Halabja, I was hauled up by a seller of enamelled-
ware plates, sherbet glasses, matches, and pedlary
generally.

" Ra wussa ! " I heard in stentorian tones behind my
ear.

Obedient to the summons I stopped, and turning,
found myself face to face with an apparently outraged
and obviously outrageous individual, who demanded in
the fiercest tones the eleven krans I owed him. In the
idiom of his native Kurdish, and with no excess of
politeness, I denied the debt, and he advanced with half-
drawn dagger ; but finding that I neither fled nor paid,
stopped, a little at a loss as to what his next step
should be.

For a moment he glared at me, then with a con-
temptuous laugh, retired behind a pile of his tin bowls
upon his booth, and stood lost in contemplation of the
arched bazaar roof. I was told afterwards that this is
but a little joke of the Sulaimanian, who occasionally,
before the Turks frightened them away by their gross
cupidity, would catch with the trick a meek pilgrim *en
route* from Khorasan to Kerbela.

One of my first acquaintances in Sulaimania was a
Syrian Christian of Mosul, one Matti Tuma. At that
place I had experienced some difficulty in the matter of
transporting the money I had brought with me, but

finally found two Christians, known as Safu and Samu, who were prepared to give me a bill upon their correspondent in Sulaimania. This I took, having the draft made payable to Ghulam Husain, the Persian, under which name I was passing. This draft was at seven days after sight, but the first morning after my arrival an elderly man appeared, dressed exactly like the Sulaimanians, except for his small turban, and introduced himself as Matti Tuma, giving me the welcome information that he had the money ready waiting. His quiet manner, coupled with the assurance of his desire to assist me in every way, induced me to tell him more or less my plans, without, of course, hinting at my identity.

It was the first time he had met a Persian in Sulaimania since the Hamadan merchants had left. In order to facilitate my life in Kurdistan, where an aimless wanderer is but an object of suspicion, I had resolved, before starting, to open relationships with several firms, and was now in a position to talk about various samples, and enquire into the prices of local products.

Upon these points I found Matti very ready to inform me, at the same time giving me some sound advice regarding the purchase of whatever I might need, and inviting me to use his services and experience of Sulaimania—where he had been for twenty years—without hesitation. He strongly advocated my settling in Sulaimania for a time, for he said that there was yet hope of improved trade. As I expressed my intention of seeing more of Kurdistan, ostensibly with the idea of ascertaining what business was a profitable one, and where the commodities of the country were best purchased, he offered no further opposition, and even told me to leave in his hands the matter of finding mules for my journey.

He then took me to his office, which was at the caravanserai called the Khan-i-Ajam. The office was a long narrow room, opening upon the raised verandah of the serai courtyard. Round the walls were shelves bearing the usual wares of the Mosul merchant, packets of cigarette papers, cottons, prints, calico, Aleppo cloth, cheap tapestry; and two large bags of nails, which, imported from Europe, find here a ready sale.

The floor was carpeted with rugs of Hamadan, and Matti sat upon one by his doorway, in front of a big Russian iron box that opened with a key as large as that of a stage jailer, and rang a bell three times in the process.

As in most caravanserais in Sulaimania, the rooms are really nothing more than deep recesses across the front of which a wooden screen in three sections has been built. These sections open by sliding up, and are held in that position by a piece of iron hooked across the groove in which they travel.

Matti's immediate neighbours were also Mosul Christians, and opposite—for the office was in a long arcade that entered the serai—were the rooms of three Kurdish merchants, to whom I was introduced by Matti. In the custom of the place they had boldly come to enquire who the newcomer might be, and I had to answer a string of questions. These people spoke Persian quite well, and fortunately accepted my own version of affairs as true, and I became known there and then as Mirza Ghulam Husain of Shiraz.

I was also introduced to one Habib Badria, a Mosul Christian, a man of extraordinary appearance for a man of Arab race. Fair and freckled of skin, his hair was that particular hue called "carroty," and his moustache the same. His blue eyes and generally Scotch appearance made him appear most incongruous in his Arab dress and fez. And as if this had had an effect upon his nature, he evinced the most progressive ideas. Immediately he heard that I had been to Europe, he asked me to write for a snapshot camera, scented soap, a French dictionary, and some other Ferangi articles. He professed disgust with the clothing custom forced him to wear, and sighed for the delights of collar and cuffs. Despite these affectations, however, he turned out later to be an excellent and sincere friend.

My way back to the caravanserai of Ghafur Agha lay through a large part of the bazaars, and I could not help noticing the deserted appearance caused by rows and rows of shops left empty by proprietors disgusted and disheartened by the evil and oppression of Sulaimania. As I entered the serai I was greeted by the merchant-owner, whose office was in the entrance. His habit was to sit outside his room in the verandah, upon a bench whence he could look out down the arcaded entry to the street outside and note everyone who passed in. He invited me to a seat upon a bench, and when I had mounted there, asked if he could assist me in any way by the loan of household utensils or furniture till I settled down. I informed him that I was going to Halabja, and he at once displayed unusual interest. I could only give him perfectly logical reasons for wishing to visit the place, for he knew Uthman Pasha of Halabja quite well, and had done business there himself. So I talked of seeing the Pasha's lady with reference to the cultivation of silk (which I knew she wished to undertake), and to gain her influence in order to buy the products of the mountains in her territory. Learning this, he told me that the Pasha himself was in Sulaimania and would be coming to pay him a visit in the afternoon, when he advised me to be present.

At about three that afternoon he arrived and took his place of honour upon the carpeted bench. My friend, the merchant, introduced me as a trader of Persia desirous of visiting Halabja, to which place the Pasha invited me in excellent Persian, and then relapsed into a silence which I afterwards found to be typical of the Jaf chiefs.

I had thus good opportunity to examine a man whose name is respected throughout a great part of Kurdistan, and who is chief of a large part of the great Jaf tribe, and governor of Halabja and Shahr-i-Zur.

His dress was that of his tribe, but of the best quality. Except his white waist-band, no garment was not of silk. The long tunic of striped honey colour, the zouave jacket embroidered with gold thread, and the white undershirt, were all of the finest silk. A richly ornamented dagger was thrust in his belt, and a little Browning pistol hung by its side in a red-leather case. His feet were thrust into Kurdish top-boots of scarlet leather, with upturned points; and his head was enveloped in many silk handkerchiefs, rolled into a turban bigger at the top than at the bottom.

He had the narrow, hooked nose and bony face of the true northern Kurd, and his little eyes looked out from under bushy brows going grey. An enormous moustache hid his mouth, but not the firm lines of jaw and chin. His normal expression was fierce and cruel, and when he spoke, it was in short sentences, in the roughest of the dialect of his tribe.

Several ruffians attended him: two grooms, twenty riflemen, a pipe-bearer, and various other servants, all armed, all fierce in looks and nature, picked men of a tribe noted for bravery and savage warfare.

These stood, not very respectfully, in the courtyard, and did not hesitate to join in the conversation whenever it seemed good to them to do so, nor were their interruptions at all resented by the pasha. This old man has kept up the time-honoured traditions of the Kurds. While rich and powerful, he does not separate himself in any way from the lives of his people, nor count himself socially greater than they. As a consequence he is in closest touch with their sentiments, and what is more, aware of their every action. While we sat there, a rider arrived from Halabja in haste, and producing from a saddle-bag a basket, presented it to the pasha. He had ridden hard all the way from Halabja to deliver the first cucumbers of the season! Immediately one of his own riders was despatched to Halabja to bear his thanks to his wife, who had caused these delicacies to be sent to him.

After this he took his leave, and I also retired to my room, where I was joined shortly after by old Mustafa Beg, my neighbour.

He expressed the greatest regret at hearing that I was going to Halabja, for he had found one, he said, whom, both as neighbour and as friend, he had begun to value as only a lonely stranger can prize the acquaintance of another stranger. He did not attempt to dissuade me, for he himself had been to Halabja and had partaken of the hospitality of the Lady of Halabja—the wife of Uthman Pasha, whose name is famous in Kurdistan. The less did he lament my departure for Halabja, he said, that he knew the climate of that place would induce me to return to Sulaimania, when we should again meet.

The old man loved to talk of Constantinople and the West, and found in me the rare traveller in Kurdistan who had seen these places, and could converse about them as one familiar with the subject. These topics had drawn us together, and he was soon pouring out his woes to me. He had been appointed accountant of Halabja when in Constantinople. Travelling thence, alone, *via* his native place, Tripoli in Africa, he had reached Halabja four months after he had started. The Kurds would not consent to his presence amongst them, for he was a Turk, and they found the means to make him leave. Speaking not a word of Kurdish or Persian, he found himself among a hostile people, with whom he could not even communicate. So he returned to Sulaimania, and was appointed "mudir" of Gulambar, the old capital of Shahr-i-Zur. This post also he could not take up, for the Kurds equally refused to have a Turkish official in their midst. He also became very ill, and lay, alone, in his cell in the serai for six weeks, living upon a little curds and bread, brought to him by the serai-keeper. He was now appointed mudir of Serajiq, a village east of Sulaimania, but the state of the country and a lack of the necessary instructions kept him in Sulaimania; and all the time he had received no pay. He lived upon a little bread, and an occasional "kebab" from the bazaar, making his principal meal the dinner he found in the public guest-room of the shaikhs' house, to which he went every evening. His days he spent in praying, and washing, and mending his clothes (he was scrupulously clean), making coffee, and wandering round the town, calling upon the Turkish officials and clerks.

At times he would sit, melancholy, almost weeping, thinking of the distances and deserts that separated him from his native place and his family, and wonder how he, with the feebleness of advanced age upon him, could go back again. His only wish was to see the Mediterranean once more before he died; and he would tremble as he thought of the savage people among whom he was thrown, and the ridicule with which they met his attempts at intercourse with them.

Our friendship was like to have been a little shaken by the discovery that I was a Shi'a Muhammadan, and I was subjected to close examination upon the tenets of "The Sect of Twelve" before he would be convinced of the fundamental orthodoxy of my faith. His greatest objection was to seeing me pray with my arms beside me instead of folded before me, and to the perfunctory ablution which passes as sufficient among the Shi'a.

He produced a Quran, and finding our opinions did not differ upon it, reinstated me wholly in his affections, with many ejaculations of: "The stranger shall be merciful to the stranger."

CHAPTER X

SHAHR-I-ZUR

AFTER four days' stay in Sulaimania I rose early one morning, in answer to the summons of a muleteer, and, having packed my belongings and laid in a small stock of bread, mounted my steed, bade farewell to old Mustafa Beg, and set out in the dusk before sunrise upon my journey to Halabja, the place I had come all the way from Constantinople to see. The road from Sulaimania to Halabja was one of three safe routes out of that town, being away from the Hamavand country, but even here the presence of robbers belonging to the shaikhs rendered it impossible for any but a large caravan to travel. We were therefore to join a main caravan outside the town. This Halabja caravan is a weekly affair, and goes very regularly, being conducted by natives of that place.

It was impossible when traversing the town not to notice how much Persian architecture has influenced the buildings of Sulaimania. All the older and better houses are built upon the Persian model, the upper rooms with glass doors giving the place the appearance of a town of Persian Kurdistan. Everything is very ruinous now, and the perennial insecurity effectually prevents any attempts at improvement.

Leaving behind us these decaying streets and houses we came out under the graveyard on the hill, where it had been arranged that the caravan should collect. However, we found no caravan, but only three women squatting on the ground clasping bundles; and a half-dozen Jaf horsemen, bound about with three or four cartridge belts each, and carrying rifle, knife, and revolver, sat among the young wheat their horses were cropping. One by one the travellers turned up—men on foot, on donkeys, on mules, women perched high upon platforms of bedding hiding everything save the heads and legs of their steeds.

We were accompanied by an officer going to Khaniqin *via* Halabja, and he had been granted an escort of twenty soldiers as far as the latter place. These at last appeared, and assuming the dignities of escort to the caravan, blew a bugle several times in the hopes of inducing it to start.

Our caravan was a large one; half of its members were women returning from Sulaimania to their native places, villages along the Persian frontier—Kurds all, except for three blatant Bagdadiennes accompanying their husbands, Turkish officials, to Khaniqin. The little party to which I was attached had also its female element, an elderly woman of the mountain lands of Aoram, mother-in-law of the muleteer, and as such allowed to ride free of charge upon a minute ass, which expressed its unwillingness to proceed by sitting down frequently, in streams for choice.

Once under way over the rolling spurs of the Azmir mountains, our military escort began to display that zeal for duty which they never fail to exhibit. Their duty, however, when on the march and in towns has always seemed to me and to the inhabitants to begin and end with a practical study of the science of combined annoyance and roguery, theft and violence, as bearing upon the populace, and in this they attain remarkable proficiency.

On this occasion their first action was to cast from their donkeys three or four inoffensive Kurds, and appropriate their animals. An hour out from Sulaimania the sun began to grow hot, and the soldiers thirsty, and the water-pots of all travellers were emptied despite protest, and because of it in two instances, where the soldiers wantonly broke the pot and spilled its contents.

There was considerable talk of robbers, for the road skirted the country of the rebellious Hamavand Kurds, and the sudden appearance of some horsemen upon a hillock caused the guard some uneasiness and alarm. Being armed with Mauser rifles, they were forced to show some spirit, and retiring precipitately to a depression they fired a volley at the riders, fortunately hitting no one. The perfectly peaceable enemy stopped and shouted something sarcastic, and by their dress and dialect were recognised as fellows of our own half-dozen horsemen. On learning this the condition of the army became piteous. Some six or seven, whose fear of tribal reprisals overcame the influence of military discipline, made off at the double for town, forgetting the men they had fired upon. These, seeing from afar the situation, set off after them with shouts of well-assumed fury. The remainder were penned about by our own horsemen and were receiving a merciless pounding with the butts of rifles wielded wisely and ably from the superior position of horseback. The "yuzbashi"[1] screamed in vain Turkish for bugler and "bash chaush."[2] But both lay, one squashed under a horse's heel, and the other senseless beneath the belly of a donkey that answered the yuzbashi with vociferous braying.

Had it not been that among us were a number of people of the Jaf tribe, into whose lands we were entering, the riders would have now left us, and entrenched among the hillocks farther on would have attacked and looted the caravan. Fortunately their anger soon subsided, and the remaining soldiers, bruised, torn and pitiful, once more resumed their slouch towards Halabja, keeping as far as possible from the rest of us. Under the mounting sun we put the hillocks and gullies of Sulaimania behind us, till ascending a last long slope the plain of Shahr-i-Zur lay before us, a broad valley dotted with the black tent encampments of the Jaf tribe,

[1] Yuzbashi=major.　　[2] Bash chaush=sergeant.

and the many mounds that stand there, relics of ancient inhabitants and recent villages destroyed by the order of a famous shaikh, a Sulaimanian saint and notorious scoundrel.

The eastern edge of this mountain-bound plain lies under the shadow of the great mountain wall of Aoraman, frontier of Persia, a wall bounding the countries of the most secluded and perhaps mysterious of the tribes of Kurdistan, Aorami and Rizhoi, and of those worshippers of the Muhammadan saint Ali, who call him God.

Halabja, or Alabja, as it is written, a speck on the far-rising slope of the plain, was perfectly visible thirty miles away, and between us and it was the perfect desolation beloved of the Turk. His hand here nowadays is but feeble, and this district, once a fertile and prosperous Persian province and still Persian in everything but name, is entirely under the control of Uthman Pasha, head of the Jaf Kurds, who own little or no subjectivity to the Turkish Government, and with the worst possible grace tolerate the presence of the few Turkish officials at Halabja. Post and telegraph they abolished long ago, refusing to pay money for patches of paper to stick upon letters they could carry themselves, and finding a use for telegraph wire in the manufacture of chains and bullets; so that now, while Halabja possesses a full-blown post and telegraph master, the office is as much a sinecure as that of the tax collector, who sits in Sulaimania and begs crumbs of pay from Uthman Pasha.

This Shahr-i-Zur, whose mounds are full of the coins of Sasanian Persia and the tokens of Assyria, was till a few decades back the old sub-province of Gulambar,[1] "The Amber Flower," from all reports one of the most beautiful of all the beauties of Kurdistan.

Thickly inhabited by Aoramani tribesmen and Chaldeans, it possessed innumerable fruit and flower lands, had, and has still, a fine supply of sweet water, and cool

---

[1] The Kurds have corrupted the name, in an appropriate way, to "Khwolmur," "the Dead Land."

breezes from the high mountains to temper the heat
of the plain.[1]

But the Turks gained possession, and, blight that
they are, killed everything, so that now its only people
are the Jaf nomads, who pass and repass every spring
and autumn. All this I had learned, and so looked
with more than usual interest upon the scene till we
were hurried up by the horsemen, who had descried a
large body of Hamavand riders in the distance. With
bustle and hurry we fled to the shelter of a cluster of
tents, the residence of a tiny tribe—the Muan—whose
village, deserted in summer, lay half a mile distant in
a grove of willow-trees.

Here we threw our loads upon the plain, and each
little party built about itself a barricade of its own
belongings. Wheaten bread being unknown at this time
of the year among the villagers, we had brought our
own, and this we supplemented by a big pot of "du,"
the national drink of Kurdistan.

With nightfall came rain, and unsheltered as we were,
all of us became very wet. Scorpions, which abounded,
having, too, an aversion to damp, took shelter under us,
and what with wind, thunder, rain, scorpions, regiments
of fleas, and intermittent firing, we slept very little, and
were not sorry to load again in the cool early morning.
The muleteer's mother-in-law had fared; worst, for she
had acted as sentinel all night, her chief duties being
to drag slothful pack-animals from off our bedding,
upon which they would stand and stamp, adding another
nuisance to the night. The soldiers, tired and disgusted
with life, were very dismal this second morning.
Drenched and footsore, stiff from their drubbing of the
previous day, a walk of thirty miles through the heat
of Shahr-i-Zur appeared a gigantic affliction indeed.
Half-way across the plain, where the stagnant air soaked
up warm vapours from the water standing in the
depressions, we came to a great goat-hair canopy, sur-

[1] The district is mentioned in some ancient works as Siazurus,
and was an important district of Holwan in Sasanian times.

rounded by minor establishments of the same material. This was the encampment of Mahmud Pasha Jaf, the most powerful man in these parts, and the only signs of his magnificence were the glorious carpets, the rows of leather trunks, and the silk quilts hanging in the sun to let the fleas escape.[1]

We reached Halabja in the afternoon, a little town set among gardens. It is distinguished by three great houses, those of Adela Khanum, whose name is best translated as "Lady Justice"; of Tahir Beg and Majid Beg, her stepsons. These, with a clean and well-built bazaar, give Halabja a distinction it totally lacked fifty years ago, when it was an insignificant village. The stranger in Halabja usually has to accompany his muleteer to the house where he stables his beast, for there is as yet no caravanserai, though one will be built soon. But I had made friends with a merchant of Halabja who knew, as all the inhabitants of Halabja must, Lady Adela, and he insisted that my "knowledge, learning, breeding, and politeness" would gain me a warm welcome from this renowned lady; and that were I to instal myself in a private house she would be offended when she heard, as she of course would do, of the arrival of a Persian, that rare traveller in that part of Kurdistan.

He told me to go boldly to the house of Tahir Beg, which was connected by doors and a bridge to that of Lady Adela, and state that I was a Persian scribe and merchant travelling through her lands, and relying upon her favour. This I resolved to do, and entering a great deserted courtyard, I rode up to the raised verandah and dismounted. A couple of servants strolled up, looked at me and my belongings, and asked who I was. I introduced myself as I had been advised, and

---

[1] An unusual dirtiness of habit must not be attributed to the Kurds because of the mention of the excess of fleas. The plains of Mesopotamia, Syria, and Kurdistan breed millions of these vermin in the sand and dust, and quite as many are found in the desert places as in the habitations. They disappear in July, to reappear in the spring.

they invited me to a seat while they informed Lady Adela, who was in the other house. Her they found just risen from a siesta, and returned shortly with a message expressing her pleasure at having the opportunity of meeting a Persian from Shiraz, the first ever seen in her country, and granting me an upper room in Tahir Beg's house, whence I could look out over garden, plain, and mountain. Here carpets were spread, tea was brought, with cigarettes, by men who spoke a little Persian; and two saucy Kurdish maids, their turbans cocked at a rakish angle, submitted me to a cross-examination while they smoked cigarettes.

Lady Adela, shortly after, sent another message to say that she would see me next morning in private audience, a comparative term in this land of retainers and patriarchal custom. Dinner was brought in upon two great trays, pilau, sour meats, curds, a sweetmeat and sherbet, and followed by a man with a roll of new bedding, upon which I was glad enough to stretch and sleep.

Before proceeding with the narrative, it is advisable to give some note upon the family and tribe of the Jaf, and more particularly upon the extraordinary woman in whose house I was a guest—a woman unique in Islam, in the power she possesses, and the efficacy with which she uses the weapons in her hands.

The Jaf tribe is an ancient one, and has from the earliest history of Kurdistan been powerful, and renowned for the manner in which its chiefs agree and hold together. This trait of character—coherency—so rare among the greater Kurdish chieftains, has won for the tribe wealth and power, so that now various chiefs own such important towns as Panjwin, Halabja, and Qizil Rubat, besides numerous villages and lands, which they have acquired by purchase.

These, the property of individuals, are not connected in any way with the " Jaf land "—that is, the country over which the migratory tribe has the right of passage, domicile, and cultivation, and which is theirs by ancient right, gift, and conquest, belonging to the tribe as a whole.

From the time when Bagdad returned to the hands of the Turks in the 17th century, the Jafs have been in contact upon the west with that nation,[1] and have for about two hundred years recognised the Sultan as their overlord, as well as the Khalifa, or spiritual head of Sunni Islam, to which section they belong. They have, however, as a tribe, maintained more than semi-independence up to the present day, Mahmud Pasha holding himself responsible only for a yearly sum payable to the Sultan. In the 18th century, when the bulk of the tribe left their old lands in Juanru of Persia, two sections of the tribe seceded and took up their quarters with the Persian Guran tribe, with whom they still remain. These are the Jaf-i-Qadir Mir Waisi, and the Taishi. Within more recent times, another section—under one, Fattah Beg—separated and retired to Persia, in the Kermanshah province.

Except for these insignificant sections, the great Jaf tribe is as united as it ever was. From time to time it is called upon to undertake the chastisement of smaller tribes who may misbehave, and act for the Turks as Wardens of the Marches, unmolested by their sovereign ruler. The tribe itself—that is, the people who wander every spring from Qizil Rubat to Panjwin and Saqiz— are under the immediate supervision of Mahmud Pasha, who accompanies them. His elder brother, Uthman Pasha, is, as mentioned before, appointed by the Sultan's ruler, or Qaim Maqam, of the district of Shahr-i-Zur. This is a government of some considerable importance, and is a frontier one, necessitating the possession of armed power upon the part of the ruler. Uthman Pasha, who can call upon the tribe, of course possesses this.

But here we must make a slight digression to bring in Lady Adela, who comes from over the border. The Persian province whose land runs up to the borders of

---

[1] By the Turko-Persian Treaty of 1639, the Jafs were reckoned part Turkish and part Persian subjects.

Shahr-i-Zur is Ardalan. This Ardalan was formerly a
kingdom under a dynasty of petty Kurdish princes who,
though they were virtually independent, yet acknow-
ledged the suzerainty of the Shah of Persia. For five
hundred years these princes reigned, holding court at
Sina, which is still the capital of Ardalan.

Under their enlightened rule, art and literature grew
at Sina,[1] literature of a Persian and Kurdish nature,
which is just being discovered now,[2] the town was
beautified with fine houses and gardens, and Sina
became a place the records of whose beauty are conspicuous in the books of all travellers who have passed
by it.

However, dynasties die out, and this was no exception to the rule. The Ardalan Khans (as the rulers
were called) made a defensive alliance with the ruling
dynasty of Persia, the Qajars, and one married a
daughter of Fath Ali Shah, who ruled over Persia at
the beginning of the 19th century. This lady succeeded
her husband, and ruled over Ardalan with a firm and
just hand. After her came her son, and after him,
Persian Governors—for Nasir ud Din, Shah of Persia, a
strong ruler, whose aim was to bring all the old semi-
independent states directly under his rule, forbade the
succession upon the death of the last Vali of Ardalan,
Ghulam Shah Khan, and replaced him by his own fierce
relative, Mu'tamid ud Douleh.

Side by side with these Sultans and Valis there grew
up and existed another powerful family, that of the
Vazirs, or ministers of the princes, who owned the town
of Duaisa, near Sina. This family was not exterminated
nor even deprived of office, but continued in place till

[1] There was even a special court language, the graceful and
euphonious Guran dialect, an ancient Persian tongue, which is still
spoken by the Aoramani tribe and certain of the Guran settled
people. The common people spoke the Kurdish, which is to-day
the language of Sina town.

[2] There is in the British Museum an uncatalogued manuscript
of poems which the author has identified as being a collection of
works of famous Kurdish poets of the court of Sina.

to-day, when the chief accountant of Kurdistan, as the province is now called, is a descendant of the old family of Vazirs.

The old Jaf Pashas had been forced to keep upon good terms with the dynasty of Ardalan, and from time to time marriages were effected between the Jaf and Ardalan chiefs and petty chiefs.

These alliances were looked upon with great disfavour and some alarm by the Turks, whose keenest desire is to see the Jaf on bad terms with their neighbours in Persia. Consequently when Uthman Pasha in 1895 announced his intention of marrying into the family of the Ardalan Vazirs, some futile opposition was offered by the Turkish Government. However, he proceeded to Sina and brought home to Halabja, then an insignificant village, as bride, a lady of the Vazir family whose father occupied an important position in Teheran.

Once installed at Halabja, Lady Adela proceeded, aided by the prestige of her family, to assert her position, a procedure not opposed by Uthman Pasha. She built two fine houses, finer than any edifice in Sulaimania, upon the Sina model, importing Persian masons and artificers to do the work. Her servants were all Persian subjects, and in Halabja she instituted in her new houses a little colony of Persian Kurds, and opened her doors to all travellers from and to that country, and kept continual communications with Sina, five days' journey away.

Gradually the official power came into her hands. Uthman Pasha was often called away to attend to affairs, and occasionally had to perform journeys to Sulaimania, Kirkuk, and Mosul on matters of government. So Lady Adela, governing for him in his absence, built a new prison, and instituted a court of justice of which she was president, and so consolidated her own power, that the Pasha, when he was at Halabja, spent his time smoking a water pipe, building new baths, and carrying out local improvements, while his wife ruled.

She built a bazaar in Halabja, a square construction having four covered rows of shops connected by alleys of more shops, all covered in and domed with good brick arches, and trade flowed in to Halabja, which grew to considerable importance. Such importance did the place attain that the Turks actually grew jealous, and to obtain a hold over it, put up a telegraph line, to which the tribesmen objected, and expressed their objection by cutting down the wire. At the same time Lady Adela advised the Turks not to repair it, for she too objected to the incursion of Turks upon her territory, and warned them that as fast as they built up telegraph wires her people should cut them down. And so to-day Halabja possesses no telegraph line, though a uniformed official lives there and rejoices in the title of Post and Telegraph Master. Every summer, when the climate of Halabja becomes oppressively hot, the court of Lady Adela repairs to a little village in the hills, or to a town in Persian territory, where some three or four months are passed.

In and around Halabja Lady Adela has instituted the Persian fashion of making gardens, apart from the gardens around the houses, and now outside the little town are several of the graceful and thickly treed gardens which are only seen in Persia, gardens which are wildernesses of large shady trees, with unsuspected bowers and flower-beds in their shady depths.

So here, in a remote corner of the Turkish Empire, which decays and retrogrades, is one little spot, which, under the rule of a Kurdish woman has risen from a village to be a town, and one hill-side, once barren, now sprinkled with gardens; and these are in a measure renovations of the ancient state of these parts.

Shahr-i-Zur, or Sharizur, used to be called by some Shahr-i-Bazar, and until recently its capital was a place called Gulambar, which is under the Aoraman mountain, and there is a legend to the effect that at earlier times a village called Ahmad Kulwan, across the northern mountains, used to be the capital.

However that may be, in the Sasanian times of
Persia, when Qasr-i-Shirin was built, and Farhad hewed
at the mountain of Bisitun, there was a great town
named Hulwan. This was about the year A.D. 400.
Hulwan and its territories extended up to what is now
known as Shahr-i-Zur, and behind the site of the
modern Halabja, in the hills which form an amphi-
theatre behind it, there was a large town called Sasan.
Here were great stone buildings, and their ruins still
stand, ordinary walls and pillars of the great Sasanian
age of Persia. There is every indication, besides legend,
to show that a great city existed here, and in the
Shahr-i-Zur plain below were a number of villages
whose inhabitants cultivated its rich and well-watered
soil. To-day there are but a number of large, high
mounds, a sure indication of ancient inhabitation.
Shahr-i-Zur was so well protected by its hills, that it is
no wonder that the ancient kings looked upon it as a
specially favoured spot, and favourable to development
and commerce. Around all sides is a high ring of
mountains, except upon the north-west, and besides its
ring of hills a swift, strong river shuts them in upon
the southern side.

Across this, from Sasan, a great bridge was built
into the territory of Hulwan, a part of which still
stands. Shahr-i-Zur means the "Strong City," and
Shahr-i-Bazar, "The Market Town"—both equally
appropriate names, but there is no proof as to which
was originally employed to designate the plain.

Among the hill villages, high up in the ravines of
the frowning walls of Aoraman, religious shaikhs lived
and died, and there are to-day several holy individuals
living in little villages perched thousands of feet up
under the mighty and frowning wall of the great
mountain. In the plain, Kurd and Christian lived in
peace, till the ascent to power of a certain Abdul
Qadir, a fanatic, and slaughterer of all who displeased
him. Shahr-i-Zur possessed in his time (about two
hundred years ago) a mixed population, and its Kurdish

people still spoke the ancient dialect known as Shahr-i-Zuri, a tongue of old Persia, rejoicing in grace of form and sound, now only to be heard in Aoraman, much corrupted.

This fanatic was the cause of a massacre of Christians, and the Chaldeans inhabiting the plain fled to the mountains, to Kirkuk, and to Bagdad. The Shahr-i-Zuri, who were upon bad terms with some of the local ruffians employed in the massacre, dispersed and disappeared, and left Shar-i-Zur a waste. Gulanbar, a small town, was deserted and laid bare, with its villages along the mountain foot. These have become partially reoccupied, and are now shadows of what they formerly were.

In 1821 or thereabouts a Persian prince, Muhammad Ali Mirza, invaded and took it, but in a subsequent battle fought near Halabja he was mortally wounded, and retiring across the river, left it in the hands of a Turkish pasha of Bagdad.

Nevertheless the Persians claim Shahr-i-Zur, for it was once theirs, and they conquered it again and again, and to-day it stands upon the strip of land, a debated territory within the borders of which, an international commission has sagely remarked, " the frontier may be assumed to exist."

When Sulaimania was yet under the rule of the descendants of Sulaiman Pasha, Gulanbar was made the seat of a Qaim Maqam, and the necessary three "mudirliqs" were instituted in the plain. So matters went until Uthman Pasha, who is chief of the section of the Pushtamala Jafs, settled in Halabja, and as has been shown, proceeded to make it important. Gulanbar never recovered its ancient importance and prestige, and Halabja began to outstrip its neighbours across the plain, until the Qaim Maqam, now Uthman Pasha, was transferred to Halabja, and Gulanbar was made the residence of a subsidiary "mudir."

At the time of my visit, there were settled in Halabja, besides Uthman Pasha and his wife, Majid Beg and Tahir Beg, sons of the pasha's former wife. Majid Beg has now succeeded to the chieftainship of the Pushtamala, for the old man died in October 1909 and was buried in Biara, a mountain village reckoned very holy in these parts.[1]

It is not more than about a hundred and twenty years since Uthman Pasha's section of the tribe has been settled in Halabja. Originally the Jaf tribe lived in a country to the south-east of Halabja, in Persian territory, called Juanrud. Here they were independent, until the Vali of Ardalan succeeded in capturing the chief, his son, and brother, and executing them. Fighting ensued, and the Jafs, who had made themselves very unpopular with the Ardalan princes, first by the fact of their independence, and second by their arrogance and hostility, were expelled. The nomad section, called the Muradi, fled, some 50,000 people in all, to the pasha of the newly rising Sulaimania, and he conferred upon them the land they now occupy, which extends from Qizil Rubat, in the south, to Panjwin, upon the Persian frontier, in the north. A certain number of sedentary Jafs remained upon the ancestral lands, but suffering under the rule of the son of the Ardalan prince, deserted to the Guran tribe, and became part of them, submitting to their sultans.

Certain others remained, undismayed by the defection of their fellows, and still live in Juanrud—Persian subjects who have forgotten that they were ever Jaf Kurds.

Meanwhile the Muradi section, of which the chief sub-tribe was the Pushtamala, flourished and increased. The Pushtamala, the aristocratic section, continued to be that from which the chief was drawn until after the time of Muhammad Pasha, who, when he died, left three sons—Uthman, Mahmud, and Muhammad Ali. These separated the territories, while keeping close

---

[1] Later information tells of the death of Majid Beg also.

touch and living in harmony. Mahmud Pasha took charge of all the tribe, with whom he travels while it is upon its spring and autumn migrations between the mountains and the lowlands. Uthman Pasha took Gulanbar and Halabja and the Shahr-i-Zur lands, and, increasing in power and wealth, eventually gained the government of the district. Muhammad Ali Beg, the third son, remained at Qizil Rubat, where he owns many lands and gardens, and lives a life of ease and content.[1] Under these three sections of the Pushtamala there are the sub-tribes of 'Amala, Jaf-i-Sartik, Jaf-i-Tilan, Mikaili, Akhasuri, Changani, Rughzadi, Terkhani, Bashaki, Kilali, Shatiri, Haruni, Nurwali, Kukui, Zardawi, Yazdan Bakhshi, Shaikh Isma'ili, Sadani, Badakhi, Musai, and the Tailaku.

The tribes still left in Persian territory upon the ancestral lands are the Qubadi, Babajani, Waladbegi, Ainakhi, Imami, Daprishi, Dilataizhi, Mirabegi, Daitiri, and Namdar Begi; while those who took protection under the Guran tribe, and have become Guran in name, were the Qadir Mir Waisi, Taishai, Qalkhanchagi, Yusif Yar Ahmadi, Kuyik,' Nairzhi, and the Gurgkaish. These are, of course, Persian subjects, and resist the attempts of the Turkish Jafs to induce them to come over the frontier and join the great tribe, for they are quite content to call themselves Guran and be Persian subjects.

The horsemen at the disposal of Mahmud Pasha, Majid Beg (successor of Uthman Pasha), and Muhammad Ali Beg, is 4000 men, who are always armed with Martini rifles, and are ready at a few hours' notice to fight for their chiefs. This and a light tax paid to the Turkish Government are the only obligations the tribesmen have to their chiefs; and of course, while nominally under the control of Mahmud Pasha, they are really

---

[1] The writer stands indebted to Muhammad Ali Beg Jaf for a large portion of the historical matter relating to the Jaf tribe, in all matters concerning which this well-read and well-informed Kurdish gentleman is an enthusiast.

independent in their actions, looting and raiding without
fear of retribution, for they conform to tribal rule by
acknowledging Mahmud Pasha, accompanying the rest
of the tribe, paying their taxes, and providing fighters
when necessary.

It was natural that when Uthman Pasha married
into the aristocracy of Persian Kurdistan, the Turks
were much offended, for his first wife had been recommended by the Turkish Government, a person of whom
they thoroughly approved, and through whose influence
they hoped to make Uthman Pasha more Turkish in
his sympathies than before. That he should have, upon
her death, married a member of the contumacious
Ardalan nobility, who had always been, and ever are,
loyal to Persia, was a blow to Turkish prestige in
Kurdistan which the effendis have resented ever since ;
and when Lady Adela acquired much of the power they
had given to Uthman Pasha, they furiously bit the
fingernail of impotence, and thought of many futile
schemes for breaking her influence.

This lengthy diversion from the narrative was
necessary to explain the nature of the people among
whom I found myself at Halabja, a place unique in
Turkish Kurdistan, in being the residence of such powerful Kurdish people as Uthman Pasha, Lady Adela,
Tahir Beg, and Majid Beg, and in being absolutely
in the possession of the three huge mansions in which
they lived.

The morning after my arrival broke to the sound
of clinking tea-glasses outside the door of my room, and
opening it I was confronted by a couple of retainers
bearing the apparatus of tea "à la persane," a big brass
samovar, a basin to wash saucers and glasses, and the
little waisted Persian tea-glasses and china saucers
themselves.

The bedding was rolled up and carried away, and
hot sweet tea served, three glasses being the orthodox
number. During the space between the glasses one
smoked, and a decent interval was allowed to elapse

P

between their presentation. The ceremony over, the paraphernalia was carried away, and the day being officially commenced, I set out to see Lady Adela.

In the manner of Kurdistan this was a private interview, so I found no more than twelve servants, retainers, and armed men standing at the door. The room was long and narrow, two walls of which were pierced with eight double doors opening on to the verandah, the other walls being whitened and recessed, as is done in all Persian houses. The floor was carpeted with fine Sina rugs, and at the far end stood a huge brass bedstead piled high with feather quilts. Before and at the foot of this lay a long, silk-covered mattress, and upon it sat the Lady Adela herself, smoking a cigarette. The first glance told her pure Kurdish origin. A narrow, oval face, rather large mouth, small black and shining eyes, a narrow, slightly aquiline hooked nose, were the signs of it; and her thinness in perfect keeping with the habit of the Kurdish form, which never grows fat. Unfortunately, she has the habit of powdering and painting, so that the blackened rims of her eyelids showed in unnatural contrast to the whitened forehead and rouged cheeks. Despite this fault, the firmness of every line of her face was not hidden, from the eyes that looked out, to the hard mouth and chin. Her head-dress was that of the Persian Kurds, a skull-cap smothered with rings of gold coins lying one over the other, and bound round with silk handkerchiefs of Yezd and Kashan. On each side the forehead hung the typical fringe of straight hair from the temples to the cheek, below the ear, and concealing it by a curtain of hair, the locks called "agarija," in the tongue of southern Kurdistan. The back hair, plaited, was concealed under the silk hand-kerchief that hangs from the head-dress. Every garment was silk, from the long open coat, to the baggy trousers. Her feet were bare, and dyed with henna, and upon ankle and wrist were heavy gold circlets of Persian make. Upon her hands she wore seventeen rings, heavily jewelled, and round her neck was a necklace of large pearls, alternating with the gold fishes that are the indispensable ornament of the Persian Kurd, and of many of the Persians themselves.

A woman fanned her, while another held cigarettes ready, and a maid waited with sherbet and rose-water. As I entered, Lady Adela smiled and motioned me to a seat beside her on the mattress, and gave me the old-fashioned Kurd greeting:

"Wa khair hatin, wa ban i cho, ahwalakitan khassa shala." ("You are welcome; your service is upon my eyes; your health is good, please God.")

And it was in the peasant tongue of Sina, her native place, not the sloppy, mouthing dialect of Sulaimania; and I replied in the same, grateful to hear the language with which I had grown familiar a year before in Persian Kurdistan.

Her tones were peculiar, not those of a woman, and though not deep, were clear and decisive, and abrupt. Persian she understood perfectly, though a little shy of speaking it before one whom she only knew as a Persian. After asking me particulars of my journey, and news of Shiraz and its people, that she knew of by repute, she asked me to read her a letter in Persian that had just come from Teheran, and was so taken with the accent of Shiraz, that she was not satisfied till I had repeated the epistle three times, remarking to her servants:[1]

"Bravo! that is the true Persian speech, the sweetest of all God's languages."

After that she refused me permission to speak Kurdish, and insisted upon Persian, exacting long explanations of any Shiraz idiom new to her.

For an hour or more the interview lasted, then she rose and earnestly desired to know if I was quite

[1] Lest this seems an unwarrantable claim to a knowledge of Persian not to be expected of a European, the author would mention that he has lived among the Shirazi, as one of themselves, without their knowledge that he was other than a Shirazi.

comfortable, gave orders for new carpets and better
bedding for me, and then retired, and for the first time
spoke Persian as a farewell, bidding me return to the
official " divan," which she held every afternoon.

I was returning to my room, when a serving-man
told me that I must go and call upon Tahir Beg,
second son of Uthman Pasha by his first wife, who
lived in the other end of the big house wherein I had
my room. This chief, who owns some land at Halabja,
has acquired a reputation for considerable literary skill,
and speaks besides Kurdish, Persian and Turkish, in
the former of which he writes a good deal of poetry.
He has also a slight knowledge of French.

As is the habit among such people, he keeps open
house, and callers arrive at all times of the day and
interview him.

I found him in a great three-sided room, or summer
portico, which opened upon the roof of the entrance
lobby and some rooms attached thereto. From the
open side a magnificent view of Shahr-i-Zur and the
Azmir Mountains spread before one, clear and rose-
coloured in the morning light. Round the portico were
ranged wide, high benches, upon which it is possible to
sit, dangling a leg that does not reach the ground, or
to squat in the Oriental fashion. Carpets were spread
upon the ground and over the benches, and just outside, on the roof, a number of armed Kurds stood in
attendance. Tahir Beg sat meditating, upon a bench
covered with a fine rug, apparently oblivious of an old
sayyid, a scowling priest in a great turban, and a
Turkish bimbashi in full uniform. He was a wild-
looking man. His heavy eyebrows shaded the bulging
blue eyes of an opium-smoker, but the vacillating
expression was mitigated by the strong aquiline nose
and firm chin. His mouth was concealed by a heavy,
fair moustache. He wore the usual Kurdish garments—
long, flowing, striped silk robes—and in his belt carried
a Colt repeating pistol and a great dagger. His headgear was that of a Jaf chief—fringed silk handkerchiefs

wound in a turban broader at the top than at the base,
and the fringes hung about his ears and forehead,
giving him a wild and ferocious appearance.

He had been informed of my arrival, and replied
to my greeting in perfect Persian, without a trace of
Kurdish accent, inviting me to a seat beside him. He
asked a few questions, whence had I come, and where
going, and did I speak French, answering to my
affirmative with " Et moi aussi, je sais un peu," a
surprising utterance from a Kurdish chief who has
never quitted his native hills.

As if this effort were too much for him, he subsided into silence, and thus we sat for a space, the
quiet unbroken save for the service of coffee " à la
turque," which the servants handed round. Once he conferred a mark of his favour upon me by handing me
a cigarette from his box, and lighting it for me
himself.

Presently another Turkish official, arrived from
Khaniqin *en route* for Sulaimania, came in, and being
a loquacious fellow, insisted on carrying on a conversation, which was confined to short Turkish monosyllables
on Tahir Beg's part.

He cut the interview short by suddenly rising and
retiring to a private room, whereupon we dispersed.

I had yet another call to make. When I had left
Sulaimania I had purchased two bills for two hundred
and fifty and one hundred and fifty krans (about eight
pounds), upon a Jew of Halabja, and I had been
recommended by my friend Matti, the Mosul Christian,
to go to one Mansur, a native of Sina of Persian
Kurdistan, and a Chaldean. This person was a petty
merchant, and agent of a greater than himself in Sina,
known as Haji Khanaka. As he was from the native
place of Lady Adela, he had from the first installed
himself in a lower room of her house, and for years had
lived as her guest, paying no rent, owning no furniture,
and buying no food, for her kitchen supplied him with
his excellent meals. In return for this hospitality he

performed certain small duties, as a correspondent to merchants and Chaldeans in Sina with whom Lady Adela had dealings, and procured for her any special stuffs or cloths she might require. He was indistinguishable from a Kurd of Sina, for he wore the short tunic, plaited Persian frock-coat, and a turban wound about a felt skull-cap, which is the costume of Ardalan.

He spoke Kurdish, too, absolutely perfectly, and knew Persian quite well. He had already received a letter from Matti regarding myself, and welcomed me to Halabja, putting himself entirely at my service. He lived in a dark lower room, furnished with a couple of carpets and some felts. Upon either side of the far end were the beds, that served their own purpose at night, and during the day were used as couches. They consisted of but a mattress upon the ground, and a roll, composed of pillow and coverlet. Between these beds, exactly at the head of the room, was a large Russian iron box, the mark of the merchant, and above it upon a mud shelf a little heap of devotional books in the Chaldean language. As I entered, Mansur was sitting before the iron box smoking a Persian water pipe, and he rose as I came in, advanced, and with ceremony bowed me to the bed which occupied the highest position, that is, the left-hand far corner of the room as one enters at the opposite end.

He lamented the unfortunate times that had fallen upon Turkish dominions, for he had suffered very considerably in pocket from robberies of his goods in transit from Sulaimania and Kirkuk.

He had also lent a certain amount of money to Uthman Pasha, and cursed the Turks, who, by keeping the Pasha in Sulaimania, prevented his collecting his personal revenues to pay his debts. In Halabja itself he had but little business, except in spring and winter, when the Kurds brought from the mountains the valuable skins he purchased and sent to Sina, whence his co-religionists take them to Nijni-Novgorod for the fair every summer. It was his habit to go home to Sina every year and stay there the summer; but this year, owing to the amount of debts with Lady Adela and the Pasha, he had been ordered by his employer to remain till some wheat had been harvested, or some tobacco sold, when he could press for payment.

After partaking of tea, he proposed that we should take a stroll in the bazaar and see the drawees of my two bills; so we set out, quitting the courtyard by a low, insignificant door which gave on to a *cul-de-sac* leading to a narrow and dirty street. This in turn became a kind of open square, one side of which was occupied by a row of booths, where the occupants were busy roasting "kebabs," cutting up sheep, and purchasing fruit from peasants newly in from the gardens. This was the food bazaar of Halabja, and Mansur told me that but seven years before, there was but waste ground here, where now almost the centre of the little town lay.

The bazaar was entered by a great door, and its wall formed a third side of the little square, a good, solid wall built of the best brick. The entrance gave on to one side of a long, vaulted passage, each side of which was occupied by shops, and which turned at right angles at short distances from the main doorway.

The plan of the bazaar, designed by Lady Adela, is more that of what we understand by a market. In shape it is exactly square, with an entrance at the middle of each side. An avenue of shops runs round inside the walls, and another passage connects two of the doors, cutting the parallelogram into two equal halves. The shops are raised upon a brick platform, or rather are at a height of two feet from the ground, and have a brick platform of that height before them, upon which the proprietor squats or puts his wares. The shop itself is but a great cupboard, the front of which takes out, being made of panels of wood, or shutters. Within are shelves upon which the goods are stacked, and if the proprietor be a Jew, an iron strong-box in front of the equipment.

There are in the Halabja bazaar fifty-two such shops,

and probably twenty of these are occupied by linen-
drapers and cloth merchants, chiefly Jews, who are the
principal part of the commercial population.

The bazaar, where all the news of the town and
district are brought, and whence culled by the curious,
had already heard of my arrival, and as I entered in
company with Mansur I found myself greeted by Kurd
and Jew alike. This cordiality did not, however, extend
to business, for to my disgust the Jew upon whom I had
purchased my little bills refused to meet them, and I
found that the Sulaimania seller had promised to send
goods to him for the value of the bills, but being short
of money, had drawn the drafts and sold the goods on
his own account in Sulaimania. Matti, who had in Sulaimania procured them for me, had fortunately guaranteed
them, so I was not more than temporarily inconvenienced,
for, as Mansur said, "He who stays with Lady Adela
has no need of money."

It appeared that I was the first Persian they had
ever seen in Halabja, and considerable curiosity was
evinced as to my native place. Sitting upon a carpet
before the shop of the Jewish merchant, a little crowd
of interested Kurds and Jews collected, endeavouring with
some success to talk to me in Persian, and one and all
descanting upon the beauties of Halabja, utterly refusing
to believe that the Shiraz whence I came could be larger
or finer, or that Kurdish was not understood there.

Most remarkable was the space Lady Adela took
up in their affairs and conversation. She had, in building this bazaar which attracted trade and was a source
of profit to merchants, at the same time done the best
thing for her own pocket that she could possibly have
devised, for she was heavily in debt to the occupants,
and had naturally the widest option as to when she
should pay. It was reported that she always did pay
in the end; and for this reason, and also the excellent
reason that makes a tenant submissive to a powerful
landlord, no one attempted to limit her purchases, which
in cloth and stuffs were really enormous. The prices

these Jews charged to her, too, were exorbitant, and they excused themselves for this by an account of the interest lost by delay, much as one's tailor must do.

We spent all the morning in the bazaar, and returned for lunch, which appeared about noon. In the afternoon, about the time tea was served—for the Persian invented afternoon tea long before Europe—we went to the divan of Lady Adela. The long room this time was crowded to its fullest. Near the mattress of Lady Adela two others had been put, one for Majid Beg, the Pasha's eldest son, a man of forty-five or thereabouts, and Tahir Beg, both of whom usually called in the afternoon. The former was already there, a stern Kurd, totally unlike his rakish-looking younger brother. A much bigger man, his grave face was much more of an English cast than any other Kurd I ever saw, though an immense number of them have the features and appearance of the Saxon races.

Blue eyes, a fair complexion, short, straight nose, stubbly moustache and square chin, were the facial features one noticed at once; and he sat, hand upon hip, making no remark to anyone, occasionally nodding in reply to something Lady Adela said. All the Jaf chiefs have this characteristic of silence, and will sit for hours sometimes without uttering a syllable. Round the room, squatting against the wall, were all sorts and kinds of Kurds. Natives of Halabja and the district were there; two stray Hamavands, on goodness knows what business, sat there silent and awkward, dark-featured, wild-looking men, who kept their rifles in their hands and their alert eyes ever on the glance this way and that, from sheer force of habit. A black-browed priest from Pava, a village in Persian Kurdistan, three peasants from Sina, and various merchants, went to make up a collection of all sorts of southern Kurds. Every one, even to the shopkeepers and the priest, carried the large Kurdish dagger. Menservants stood about round the door and by their mistress and master, and a stack of guns in the corner represented the property of a number

of the assembly. Outside the room in the verandah the
overflow pressed their noses against the glass doors and
occasionally shouted remarks, often enough in answer
to Lady Adela's comments. Rakish-looking handmaids
in flowing robes and turbans set askew, stood about, or
brought cigarettes, fanned Lady Adela—for the room
and the day were warm—or fetched scissors and tape
for the silk cloth she was inspecting. A Jew of the
bazaar was displaying to her his wares, taking huge
orders for all kinds of stuffs, and squatted before her,
making notes in Hebrew on a dirty scrap of paper. The
maids advised, criticised, and chose cloth and stuff for
themselves, which Lady Adela would promptly refuse,
or occasionally grant them, for she treated them remarkably well. The audience made remarks upon the proceedings, often enough chaffing Lady Adela regarding
her purchases, when she would retort in quick Kurdish
with the best humour, everyone joining in the laugh
which not infrequently was against her. A shopkeeper
arrived with a bill long overdue, and she endorsed it on
the back, making him the owner of a quantity of wheat
when the harvest should be in, for she possessed no
hard cash, or professed to own none. While she yet
measured silk, two riders still in their scarlet riding-
boots, rifle on shoulder, stumped in, leading between
them a wretched Arab tribesman, clad in the traditional
raiment, the single shirt that has gained for the Arab
the nickname " Trouserless " from Kurd and Turk. His
head was bare, for he had lost his " kefia " and " agal,"
and he shrank and shivered as he was thrust forward
into the assembly. Never had he seen so wild and
fierce-looking a gathering. Even Lady Adela, in her
bright garments, her eyes flashing from under a big
turban with hanging tassels, set askew, had the
barbaric and ferocious Kurdish appearance of the
stories, and the sight of so many of these big-boned,
armed men cowed the miserable Arab, used only to
ragged creatures like himself. Nor was his discomfort
at all eased by the laughter that greeted his appear-

ance. His guards, too, seemed to regard the affair as a
joke.

Lady Adela asked the cause of this apparition, and
the guard, with the air of one who relates a funny
story, told how the captive had attempted to rob one
of the villages of Shahr-i-Zur. It appeared that for
some reason he had gone to Sulaimania with camels,
and having become separated from his mates, was
attempting to find his way back to the lowlands *via*
the Khaniqin road. He had begged for, and been
granted shelter and food at the house of a Kurdish
peasant, and was put to sleep in a shed where a
donkey was stabled. He had stolen from here a chain,
and having no place to conceal it, wound it round his
waist under his shirt, and made off in the dusk of the
early morning. The peasant, spying his flight, on
principle pursued him, when the accelerated pace and
the weight of the chain together shook it from its place,
and, falling about his ankles, tripped up the unfortunate
Arab. The Kurd caught him, and finding nothing
handier than the chain, bound his legs with it and left
him to stew in the sun, till two of Lady Adela's riders
coming up, he handed over his capture, and he was
brought into Halabja, running at the horses' stirrups.

The chain, retained as an evidence of his guilt, they
had hung around his neck; and as he fell upon the
floor weeping and trying to crawl to the feet of Lady
Adela to kiss them, the company failed to maintain
their seriousness, even the stolid Majid Beg joining in
the general laugh.

An interrogation of the culprit should now have
taken place, but no one appeared to know Arabic,
except the one word " Uskut " (" Be quiet "), which was
used, and not without need, for the fellow's wails and
weeping filled the room.

The only remark Lady Adela felt called upon to
make was one against her own people, and which was
received in good enough part:

" What shall be the fate of him who would steal

from a Kurd? Are not the Kurds supposed to be the worst robbers on earth? Take him away and loose him."

As they hauled him to his feet and dragged him from the room, his wailing redoubled, for he must have thought he was going to execution instead of to liberty.

As he went out, Tahir Beg was announced, and everybody got up on his feet while he entered, slowly followed by a string of people, who found places somehow among the throng. Tahir Beg himself picked his way among them and took a seat upon the mattress near by, urbanely inviting me to a seat beside him, when he commenced a conversation about the merits of French and Persian.

After his arrival the divan did not last long. First Majid Beg left, then Lady Adela, rising, retired to an inner room, and the company was dismissed. Tahir Beg asked me to come to his evening reception upon the roof, which took place every night. Returning to my room, I found a caller in the person of a clerk or scribe of Tahir Beg, who was smoking one of my cigarettes and gazing out of the window. Like most of the inhabitants of this queer household he was a Persian subject, native of Sina, but wore the long Jaf dress and zouave jacket. He, however, refused to part with the Sina head-dress, and still wore the low skull-cap surrounded by fringed silk handkerchiefs. He had several matters to discuss. First to recommend a man who had applied for the post of personal servant to me—him I arranged to see in the morning; next, to ask me the right price of a Browning pistol, which he had purchased for seven liras; and lastly, to know if I possessed any books in Persian. I had an old torn copy of *Saadi*, and this I gave him, and he sat there reading it indifferently and going into rhapsodies over verses he barely understood, but whose sonorous syllables and broad vowels appealed to the Kurdish ear. It must also be remarked that among the more cultivated Kurds of the south it has always been the fashion to affect a passion for Persian, which is the reason of so many of the Kurdish poets writing almost solely in that language, and neglecting their own language, which lends itself to poetry of the ballad type very excellently.

This young man, Hasan by name, had, I heard afterwards, the reputation of being the "blood" of the place, and a rhymester, doubtless in imitation of his accomplished master, whose verses it was his duty to write down at dictation. He had, it appeared, killed someone in a fight at Sina, and had fled to Halabja for Lady Adela's protection till the affair could be settled. He had then fallen in love with a maid of his patroness, by name Piruza, a pert girl of Sauj Bulaq, of the Mukri—also a Persian Kurd. I had the pleasure later of witnessing their somewhat hoydenish flirtations. This is one of the most remarkable features of Kurdish life. Among other Muhammadan nations, whose women are strictly secluded, marriages can only be matters of arrangement by third parties; but among the Kurds, where the women are practically as free as in any European country—except that they do not go to the bazaar—free intercourse between the sexes is the rule, and the result is a large number of love marriages, which is all for the good of a race so simple in habits and life.

Hasan attempted to fix upon me the profession of doctor, for someone had already hinted that a man and a Persian who had seen Europe and possessed a large trunk, evidently hailing from far lands, must be a doctor. With considerable skill he led the conversation round to medicine and illnesses, and involved me in a long discourse about them, and finding my opinions apparently sound, left me, to confirm the rumour.

Having dined, I found my way in the dark to beyond Tahir Beg's portico, and found three benches arranged so as to make three sides of a square upon the roof. Upon the middle one Tahir Beg sat, silent as usual, and upon the others an equally silent company of merchants, a couple of priests, and two Turks in uniform. I was given a place by the host, and wrapping myself in my camel-hair cloak, gathered my feet under me, and added my silence to that of the others after I had received the greetings of the company and returned them one by one.

After some time a Turk who was opposite me, addressed me in his own language, asking if I had been to Constantinople, and receiving an affirmative reply, began to question me as to where I had stayed and how I had liked it. I was forced to say I had lived in Stamboul, for I feared that if I said that I had been in Pera he might wonder, and justly, what a Persian was doing in that exclusively European quarter. Fortunately my excursions to Stamboul had been frequent, and I knew it well, and he, thinking he had found in me a sympathiser, launched out upon an eulogium of that city, and cursed the fate that exiled him to the farthest corner of Kurdistan. He spoke disparagingly of Halabja at last, led to it by his comparisons of Turkey and Kurdistan, and immediately Tahir Beg awoke from his silence, and in a curt sentence asked why he had not stayed in Constantinople, which would have conduced to everybody's comfort. Finding the atmosphere hostile, the official— a bimbashi unattached—took his leave without further conversation.

Tahir Beg then began to ask me about various places, and drifted into a political conversation, in which he discussed the Balkan and Cretan questions, showing himself remarkably well informed, indeed far more *au courant* with the subject than myself, who took little interest in such things. However, I could give him information upon points nearer home, upon the northern frontier, where the Turks were encroaching upon Persian territory. Great interest was evinced by all those present in the current political events, and, like most Kurds, they showed themselves more in sympathy with the Royalists than with the Popularists, whom they regarded as a number of mischievous busybodies without any talent for ruling their fellows, an opinion very true to a great extent. The feeling against the Turkish Parliament was strong enough too, for Sultan Abdul Hamid had always regarded the Kurds more mildly than his predecessors, and had done his best to bring them into touch with the semi-civilisation of Constantinople, without capturing their chiefs by treachery or imposing undue taxes. Was it not also Sultan Abdul Hamid who had given to the northern Kurds arms and ammunition, and a uniform, and called them Hamidie Cavalry, and let them loose to loot and raid where they pleased?

The system of government by representation is repugnant to the Kurd, whose rule has always been by hereditary chiefs, in whom the ruling instinct is born, and who are undoubtedly the fittest of their race and tribe to be at its head. And if the Kurdish nomad is reckoned unfit and not sufficiently intelligent to know what is best for him, what then of the Turkish peasant, an oaf of the understanding of a cow, and as inferior to the Kurdish peasant in wits as the sloth is to the horse. Thus these Kurds argued, and argued truly, making yet a very good case for despotic government in Eastern Asiatic Turkey and Kurdistan.

While we were drinking coffee out of little Turkish cups, someone started the question of where Lady Adela would go for the summer months. There was some difficulty this year about it, for the Pasha had been kept in Sulaimania by Government affairs, and still remained there, so the necessary arrangements for moving the great household were as yet unmade.

Lady Adela generally went to a hill village in the Aoraman Mountain, or to a little place called Merivan, in Persian territory. Tahir Beg usually followed, or went to his town of Panjwin, three days' journey from Halabja, where a great gathering of Jaf chiefs and tribes took place each year, a sort of summer conference;

and the other Kurdish leaders came in numbers to spend a short time there, to hear what passed, and to keep up friendly relations with the Jafs. From Sina a large number of "Begzada," or aristocrats, came to see Tahir Beg and talk Persian poetry; and more serious chiefs from Persian Kurdistan came too, but not to Tahir Beg, for their business was with the powerful Mahmud Pasha, who had come with the tribe to Panjwin by June.

By the time this discussion was finished, and no one the least bit more enlightened than before, it was late, and Tahir Beg rose, and by departing broke up the party, which dispersed.

Next morning Lady Adela sent for me to read some Persian to her. I found her busy with correspondence, and she handed me several letters to read to her, and at her dictation I took down several replies, correcting her Persian where it departed from the proper idiom. While thus engaged, one, Amin Effendi, was announced, and followed close upon the heels of the servant. He was a curious man to look at, for he had not the Kurdish appearance at all. A tall, broad man with a huge face, little blinking blue eyes of the colour one sees in north Germany, pale straw-coloured hair, a long, prominent, bony nose, and a smirk that apparently he could not banish from his wide mouth.

He was well-dressed, and carried in his hand a little roll of paper, as if to indicate his superior position. With considerable assurance he came in and took a seat upon one of the large leather trunks ranged round the room. Lady Adela, to whom he was evidently some kind of dependent, asked him what he wanted; and he replied, that hearing of my presence he had called now, hoping to meet me. He had heard, he said, that I had been to Europe, and could speak French and English, and was moreover a doctor, and could take photographs. All these qualifications and achievements he dwelt upon, implying untold congratulations upon their possession, his servile smirk never leaving him.

Lady Adela ordered him to speak French with me, and he, to my surprise, addressed me in that language, which he had some difficulty in speaking, continually inserting Kurdish words in the conversation. He told me he had known it well once, and it appeared certainly that it was more a case of having forgotten than ignorance. But what forced itself upon the attention was the remarkable accent with which he spoke French, for had we been in Europe, he would have announced by his pronunciation a German nationality. One did not expect that of a Kurd speaking French, and I naturally asked him where he learned it, and received an evasive reply. In answer to my question as to his trade and occupation, he informed me with some pride that he was Lady Adela's doctor, and wanted to know where I had graduated for the profession. I disclaimed any knowledge of surgery, and told him that whoever might be responsible for the rumour of my qualities as a physician, it was not myself, at which he appeared somewhat relieved, and told Lady Adela what I had said, while I followed it up with strong confirmation. Soon after, he took his leave and I mine.

So much curiosity had the man aroused in me that I went to my new friend, Mansur the Christian, to ask who was this Amin Effendi—the very name was not Kurdish.

"That creature!" he exclaimed, with a snort of disgust, "may the curse of Iscariot be upon him!" and then, hastily remembering he spoke to a Musulman, fell to a sudden silence.

"Well," I said, "why?"

"As you can see," he replied, "he is no Kurd. He is by birth a German of Constantinople whose father sold pills, but who was forced to leave the city owing to some crime he committed. He had two sons, this Amin Effendi and another. These came to Bagdad, and there did that which was wrong, and had to fly. Fate brought them this way to Halabja, when finding themselves upon the borders of Kurdistan, they feared

Q

to go forward, and having no means of going back, threw themselves upon the mercy of the Qazi, and turned Musulman. Uthman Pasha protected this one, and the other one went to the patronage of Shaikh Ali of Tavila, where he now is. They took the names Amin Effendi and Ali Effendi, and are both renowned for the meanness of their nature, their petty intrigues, and their ignorance and idleness. This Amin Effendi professes to be a doctor, but whatever a man or woman may submit to him for cure he has but one remedy, to sell them at a high price the Epsom salts he buys in the bazaar from the Jews. So none go to him, and he lives by the bounty of Lady Adela, who sometimes gives him a suit of clothes and allows him to pretend that he is her doctor."

" He has heard, by the way, that you are a doctor ; and as you have been to Europe he will think that you are accomplished, and will use every means in his power to discomfit you, so I warn you to be on your guard against him."

This surprising account I heard with interest and also with some little feeling of apprehension, which, however, left me when I thought how long the individual had been here, and how he must have completely for-gotten Europe. Nevertheless, there were certain things he might easily have made the subject of awkward enquiries had he been so disposed. For instance, my box had upon it in large letters, E.B.S., quite a sufficiently remarkable fact for one who knew European characters, and me as Ghulam Husain. Hitherto the initials had raised no comment, for I had ever since Diarbekr kept the trunk in a canvas bag, which made it appear— *en route* — like a bale of goods ; but here, to get at something, I had taken it out, and there it stood, an obviously London trunk—obviously English.

How truly Mansur had spoken of his mean spirit was proved that very evening. I had eaten my dinner, and was quietly smoking, when a tap came upon the door. Now a Kurd does not know what it is to knock at one's portal—he either throws it open, or shouts from the other side; and so I knew it must be Amin Effendi. I unlatched the door, and he came in with the air of one who comes surreptitiously upon some errand of importance. As he entered he glanced over his shoulder, and disregarding my invitation to the carpet, sat upon the box, his abba covering it effectually. He began to speak in French, the peculiar nature of which would have rendered intercourse difficult had I not known Kurdish and been able to discount his German accent.

"Che voulez," he commenced, "un . . . un . . . wurd, petit, peu de nitrate d'argent pour des darman . . . medecang, c'est très nécessaire."

This I understood to be a request for nitrate of silver for medical purposes, but I speedily assured him that I had none, and he as quickly passed over what had evidently been an excuse for coming. Drawing his cloak close about him, he leant forward to where I sat upon my carpet, and lowering his voice, in halting phrases told me the subject of what I put down here.

"You are, sir, a civilised man; I too am a civilised man, for I was not always thus;—my father was a distinguished doctor in Constantinople, and I was his eldest son, educated in the best schools and colleges. It was ill-fortune that sent me to the East, and an execrable stroke of bad luck that landed me here among the savages of Kurdistan. It is now thirteen years that I languish here, and I have lost the power, did I possess the means, to go back to Europe, which I have forgotten, and whose customs and language I only remember as one remembers a beautiful dream. Ah, sir, what folly induced you to leave civilisation and comfort and trust yourself among these cut-throats, these brigands?"

"Why," I said, "my country lies much farther yet, this is but a stage upon the way, and I am well content to stay awhile where I find kindness, as I do from those whom you call barbarians."

"Have a care," he whispered, "you know not the depths of duplicity and insincerity in which the life of this place is sunk. Even now those who smile upon your face, frown at your back and seek to destroy you, and it is for that that I am come to warn you. There is a rumour, spread by I know not whom, that you are a Persian of the revolutionary party, seeking to spy out the land here, and disaffect the chiefs against the Turks. And with such they have a short way here. There was last year a foreigner who came from Sina, and he told us all he came to collect the ancient dialect of Aoraman. He was, he said, a Dane, but I tried him, and he could not speak German. But not desiring to be a party to his discomfiture, I warned him that he was upon dangerous ground, and that I knew him for a Russian, for he had books in that language in his possession, and I saw maps in his tent; for he was very friendly, and invited me to sit with him. So I warned him, but he persisted in his assertion of innocence. Well, one morning he was looking at a distant hill through a pair of field-glasses, and I was struck by their strange appearance, and taking an opportunity to examine them found a small camera concealed within. At this time Tahir Beg began to be suspicious, for he more than any of the chiefs resents the appearance, nay the very name, of a Ferangi, and he communicated with Uthman and Mahmud pashas. These each gave the traveller a note which he might show to the head-men as he passed their villages. It permitted him to stay half an hour in any spot, but upon the thirty-first minute he was to be shot. In one day he was out of our lands and far away. Now, I would not draw any comparison between yourself and that spy, for I am convinced of your *bona fides;* but Tahir Beg has suspected you, and has advised Lady Adela to keep a watch upon you. There is a feeling against you, and I warn you that the consideration would not be granted you that was accorded to the Russian, for you are but a Persian, and a bullet would settle all affairs simply

and quickly. This morning Tahir Beg was for having
you examined and shot; but I, knowing your excellence,
and weeping inwardly for you, pleaded and gave my
own guarantee that you were but what you professed
to be, a perfectly innocuous person. Till at last I so
prevailed that he relinquished the subject; but if you
will take my advice you will not extend your stay.

"Ah, sir, you know the old German proverb, 'The
mountain looks fine from afar, but how disappointing
when under it.' Such is but too true of this place.
From afar, where the traveller talks of the hospitality
of Lady Adela, the great houses, the gardens, the
bazaar of Halabja, he forgets the savageness, the
incredible treachery and insecurity which makes life
here a tremulous fear. Ah, these people, they but seek
to squeeze out of a man what he has, and then kill him.
Think not that they will give you anything here, nor
treat you kindly except you pay for it tenfold. Take
my advice, my friend, flee from this nest of scorpions
before yet they sting you to death, quit this town of
hungry vultures while the flesh remains upon your
bones and before it grows on theirs. Look at me, what
do I possess? I walk about in these wretched clothes
seeking only to protect even them from the rapacious
appetite of some predatory Kurd."

"Yet," I said, "it seems to me that since the day
you arrived from Bagdad, a fugitive, possessing less
even than this, you were worse off then than now, when
by the Pasha's beneficence you possess house, clothes,
wife, children, and the wherewithal to keep them all."

"Ah, you do not understand," he protested feebly, and
was silent for a while. Then once again he took up his
tale of alarm and warning, but I had had enough, and
to get rid of him began to ridicule him for a European
turned Musulman, and to ask him where the sect of the
Sunnis was a whit better than us of the Shi'a—
questions he funked—and departed.

It had not sufficed to alarm me, all this rigmarole,
but I was made aware of the existence of a mean and

cowardly enemy at Halabja, whose favourite weapon was obviously slander. Fortunately this was that Kurdistan where it is the habit to shout one's affairs upon the house-tops and hill-sides, and slander has a short life, usually terminated by an unexpected bullet.

So, upon the house-top system I resolved to go straight to Tahir Beg, pretend a high and mighty resentment of such treatment of a guest, and bid him an abrupt farewell. By this means I should be able to tell exactly by his manner what his thoughts were. If he suspected me, he would raise no objection to my departure.

So, groping my way along the dark verandah, I found him upon his roof among the usual cronies, and took my place upon his right among the silent throng. After some time he asked whether I had made any arrangement for staying here awhile, as he was very anxious to study French with me. I put on a resentful air, and answered that I was leaving Halabja in a very few days; and in reply to his question why, told him that a guest was not accustomed to receive night messengers of evil, speaking evil of his host, and that if the ancient Kurdish law of hospitality were to be thus violated I had better leave at once. At this the company pricked up their ears, and at the mention of Kurdish hospitality a black look crossed their faces, and a murmur went around, partly of astonishment at my audacity, and partly of censure and resentment at such a statement in the Jaf house. It also roused Tahir Beg, and he not unnaturally demanded immediate explanation of such statements, whereupon I frankly told him all that had occurred.

To my surprise the company showed considerable amusement, and even Tahir Beg himself nearly smiled; but before he could offer any reply, old Sayyid of Barzinjan, a privileged elder, said: "Dost thou not know this foolish creature Amin Effendi, nor know that this is what he does for every stranger here, thereby ruining our name and alarming our guests. Take no notice.

He is a mean man among the meanest, and being an incompetent fool, naturally fears that you, whom he knows only as a doctor, will cut the ground from under his feet, and gain his dismissal. Wait till to-morrow, go to see Lady Adela, but do not mention the affair to her."

Tahir Beg, making no assertion contrary to this, added that I must take no notice of the creature—a renegade, the meanest of the mean, a deceitful and little-minded individual who could only disgrace those who supported him. He then, as if to make up for the resentment I had felt, devoted himself to a long and cordial conversation upon various subjects, and showing me such attention that it was clear from the behaviour of the company when I left that Amin Effendi's attempt to get rid of me had but improved my position, with Tahir Beg at any rate.

CHAPTER XI

NEXT morning with the tea, an individual whom I had not hitherto seen appeared and assisted. He seemed to be a servant, but the garments he wore did but little credit to his employers. To enter by the low door he had to bend nearly double, and when he had fairly straightened himself out he was a good six foot four. A ragged tunic reached half-way to his knees, the length proclaiming him a Mukri Kurd of Persia; and were this not sufficient, he wore the sharp-pointed cap of that race, around which was a blue cotton handkerchief with the two corners hanging about his ears. Under the tunic he wore nothing, except his ancient and patched trousers; it was his only garment, and displayed a triangle of broad chest burned to a brick-red. He had no trouble of removing shoes as he entered, for he possessed none. While I was having tea, the scribe of Tahir Beg entered and partook with me, and upon my asking him who the man was, explained that one of his objects in coming at this hour was to introduce him. He was a poor Mukri out of employment of any kind, and sought service, and as he was known to Lady Adela, Tahir Beg, and Mansur, he recommended him as a servant for me. "For," he said, "you, as an important person, should not go servantless; it will be advisable to employ a local man while you are here, and he, too, will travel anywhere you like, and is desirous of seeing Persia."

The applicant meanwhile stood by and looked foolish, and as I was not sorry to have at any rate one adherent in a strange land, I agreed to employ him, upon terms not unusual among natives—a new suit of clothes, his food, and the sum of one toman a month—about three shillings and sixpence, or tenpence halfpenny a week. His food included cigarettes, an inexpensive item, for they were thirty-five for the equivalent of a penny, and by purchasing tobacco it was possible to make as many as fifty for the same sum, a " baichu " in the dialect of southern Kurdistan.

During the conversation I was called to Lady Adela, and now, followed by my servant—whose garb reflected little credit upon his master, as he had not failed to tell me—I obeyed the summons. In the audience was a group of maids laughing at what amused them as well as the armed retainers outside. Standing near the door was Amin Effendi, protesting; and sitting in her usual place on the mattress, Lady Adela in her deep contralto tones called him every vile name in the vocabulary of Kurdistan. As I came in she renewed her abuse, called Heaven to blast a creature who had violated all the tradition of the Kurds, who had blackened the face of the Jafs before a stranger, who had presumed to alarm a guest under her protection, and finally commanded him to apologise to me there and then in the words of humblest degradation. He obeyed with a bad grace. " Mud is upon my head, filth upon my eyes; I have eaten ordure and my heart is vile; I kiss the hoofs of the ass thou ridest, and clean the shoes of thy servant, whose slave am I; I go abased before all men, a speaker of lies, and I am not fit to attend the womenfolk," and so on, and yet again and again. He was reluctant at first, but the sound of a cartridge clicking home in a Martini breech and the feel of a knife-point at the back of his neck made him voluble, to the great amusement of the company, and at last I begged Lady Adela to let him go. So she allowed him to creep away, while the maids, unrestrained, advised him to try Epsom salts for the ills of his soul. I had not looked for this kind of revenge, nor desired it, but everyone present seemed to think that I had achieved a considerable victory over one naturally at enmity with me, and I was, despite emphatic protests, put down as an accomplished physician, from the fact of Lady Adela discomfiting her old retainer for my benefit. The rough but sincere congratulations poured upon me by man and maid alike demanded some diversion of object, and suggesting a cup of tea at the coffee-house, I left with a score of men-at-arms to accompany me and retail the story of Amin Effendi to the public there, who by that mysterious telepathy of the East had already got wind of the tale.

It may be remembered that in the first chapter reference was made to a Kurdish priest I had met in Constantinople, and whose talk of his native land had resolved me upon taking my journey. During the time I was making my way across Turkey, I had not forgotten him, and had news of him in Kirkuk, where I heard that he had been robbed by the Hamavands. At Sulaimania I again made enquiries, and had indeed expected to hear that he was there, but was told that he had gone back to Sina of Persian Kurdistan. This news gave me very considerable relief, for I had begun very seriously to consider a matter which I could not put off, namely, the explanation of my identity should I meet him and be recognised. When in Constantinople he had told me, in conversation, that should I as a Christian come to Kurdistan and there turn Muhammadan, he could find me a pretty livelihood in photography, quack surgery, and medicine and teaching; but this was only the style of inducement typical of the priest, and meant nothing more than a nicely put compliment. If he were to encounter me now, passing as a Musulman, and a Shi'a at that (he would have made a Sunni of me), the situation would have been extremely difficult, and all his distrust would arise at seeing before him one in a guise so different from that which he bore in Constantinople, and who had so strangely chosen exactly this spot to journey to for no particular reason, and that after enquiries concerning trivial affairs which had been made in Constantinople.

So I had thought of this possible predicament, and had done my best to guard against it. I must, in order to explain how I was enabled the more securely to adopt my disguise of Persian, ask the reader to pardon me a momentary retrospect, which gives a view of Shiraz four years before. Here I had, after a preceding three years' study of the religion of the Persians, became converted to Islam. I am not here to state to what extent I was convinced of the truth or otherwise of Muhammadanism, nor whether I was convinced at all. Unless I became outwardly Muhammadan I could never learn properly the language, which is so inseparable in its idiom from the religion. So after some interviews with a priest whose name to-day I remember with feelings only of the greatest admiration and respect, I was made a member of the congregation of Islam, and undertook a course of theological study. Under the tuition of my priest and his confrères I acquired considerable knowledge, and was able to hold my own in the theological discussions and arguments which are at once the profession and diversion of so great a part of the populace of Shiraz. By the merest stroke of chance I was prevented from going, as I had planned, to Kerbela and Mecca, and found myself rushing to England on a P. & O. steamer instead of creeping up to Jeddah as a deck passenger on a "ditcher." Thus I had acquired a good knowledge of my subject, if I may so call it; and while away, received many letters from my priestly friends in Shiraz, addressed to Mirza Ghulam Husain, which not unnaturally I kept, and had preserved till now, when I found myself in Kurdistan.

I had resolved if I were confronted by the Kurdish priest, the Shaikh ul Islam of Sina, to produce certain letters wherein it was mentioned that I had been "under the guise of an European, but, thank God, a walker in the paths of peace, and a chooser of Islam and no pagan, such as appears to be." With these letters and my knowledge of Islam, I hoped to be able to prove that I was a Persian and a Musulman, and if he believed that, it was but an insignificant affair to point out what he already knew, that a Persian going, as I had been, to London, must adopt European dress to go there, which would explain my appearance to him as a European.

To return to Halabja, I was talking to my new-found servant a morning or two after his engagement, when it occurred to me to ask him if he had seen the Shaikh ul Islam at Sina. He had not, and for the very good reason that the priest had never returned there. It appeared that he had got as far as the domains of Lady Adela, and had, in a stormy interview with her, demanded armed assistance to destroy Sina, and put to confusion his enemies there—the Government and religious authorities. Lady Adela, whose sympathies with him were very limited, absolutely refused, and forbade him to enter Persian territory, lest she warn the Government and have him imprisoned. So in a fit of rage and chagrin, he betook himself to a holy place in the great Aoraman Mountain, where, upon a steep valley-side the Shaikh of Biara had built for himself a "takia," and entertained sundry darvishes and wanderers upon monastic fare.

From this quiet retreat he did not stir except to pay occasional visits to Halabja, where he was tolerated but not welcomed. At such times he would put up in Tahir Beg's house, sometimes even in the room I was now occupying. Hama, my servant, made some enquiries regarding his intentions, and ascertained that he purposed coming to Halabja very shortly, in fact, as soon as the Pasha returned, to pay respects to him. As the Pasha was expected daily, I was feeling a little uncomfortable, for up to now I had enjoyed the confidence of all the Halabja people, had made friends of some, and had, in the way of the East, become accepted by the place as part of itself. And what was more, in order at once to provide myself with a little money and show my *bona fides* to the people in general, and Lady Adela in particular, I had advanced certain moneys to a Jew to go to Juanru and buy me four mule loads of that valuable cargo called "run," or clarified butter, which in Kurdistan has such a delicate perfume, and tastes so well that one does not scoff at the native description, that "the run of Juanru takes the scent of the flowers the sheep graze on."

Thus there were reasons not a few why I should wish to lead an undisturbed life in Halabja so long as I elected to remain. And so I bethought me of some scheme whereby I might forestall an untimely arrival of the Shaikh ul Islam and the public curiosity, and perhaps animosity when he should express his surprise and doubts.

The only thing I could think of was to go and see him quietly, saying that I was making a pilgrimage to Biara, to which place it was the fashion to journey now and then, calling the jaunt a pilgrimage. It took me some days to make up my mind to this course, for I did not want to hurry, nor to go sooner than was necessary; and meanwhile the days passed in idleness, attendance at the divans of Lady Adela and Tahir Beg, and walks with Mansur the Christian, in the late afternoon, to a garden just outside, where he would squat in the grass, and producing a little bottle from his pocket, consume his araq accompanied by nuts or melon seeds, as is the habit of drinking in Persia. His greatest efforts were to induce me to join him, asserting that it made him miserable to drink alone; but I did not wish to open any possible channel along which thoughts might flow detrimental to the excellence of my Islamic orthodoxy, and which might on occasion become words.

When I had mentioned to Hama that I was going to see the Shaikh ul Islam, he was somewhat astonished, and very much hurt because I would not tell him my business; for such a lack of confidence was unusual he said, between a master and his servant, and reflected upon the latter's integrity. So I bound him to great secrecy, and told him that the Shaikh ul Islam owed me money and I was going to try and recover it, but did not want to wait till he came here, as he was a man of uncertain temper and contumacious nature, and might endeavour to injure me if he found his creditor suddenly installed, so to say, on his doorstep. This was sound Kurd sense, and Hama extolled my reasoning, and advised the purchase of four loaves of sugar as a present for the Shaikh, for it is a fault to go and see such a person without something in the hand.

So one fine morning, having hired for the day for four krans (or one shilling and eightpence) a mule, we loaded it with the four sugar loaves in a saddle-bag, and set forth, having provided the usual bread and cigarettes for consumption on the way. The road lay east from Halabja, towards the great wall of Aoraman, and at the base of the hills south of Shahr-i-Zur. For half an hour we passed along a level road, looking out upon our left across the great depression, imagining what a sight this hill-girt basin of a plain must have been when Nushirwan the Just ruled the land, and gardens and towns covered its still fair face. To the north, in a blue distance soon to be dispelled by a fierce sun, lay the piled-up mountains of the Azmir, behind Sulaimania, whence faint wreaths of blue smoke from the burning grass ascended like the fume of an offering to the sun, as a vindication of the ancient religion of Zoroaster that had its fires upon these same mountain-tops, a votive duty forgotten by man and perpetuated by Nature.

As the road left the level we passed through the village of Anab, where, under a grove of willows, a group of Kurds smoked the morning cigarettes beside a great tank into which a brook bubbled. Here we were joined by an old man, who greeted us, asking where we were going. He spoke in Turkish, knowing no Kurdish, and said he was bound for Biara like ourselves, to visit the retreat of the Shaikh. He was a native of Roumania, and a Russian subject. On foot

he had gone to Mecca, thence to Damascus and Bagdad.
Now he had come to Kurdistan, and was visiting every
one of its little shrines and holy places, after which he
would walk to Roumania again. My name, which was
one only encountered among the Persians—Ghulam
Husain—gave him some difficulty, for he had never
heard the first word of it, and so suited it to his own
liking, and called me Husain Effendi. We climbed our
way over a number of succeeding ridges till we came to
a stream and a tree by it in the little valley. Here
we halted awhile and shared our bread, making a
frugal meal. The old man here became more friendly
yet, and in return for a little cheese I had given him,
presented myself and Hama with four little amulets,
scraps of paper sewn in a triangular piece of cloth.
These he had purchased in Sulaimania from a kind of
hedge-priest with whom he had travelled, and he said
he kept them, sometimes selling one to a villager, or
giving in exchange for food or a night's lodging.

Hama, whose edification at meeting so virtuous a
man was considerable, accepted the amulets with a
gratitude not quite free from a certain awkwardness
noticeable about the simpler Kurd whenever he comes
in contact with any of the stock-in-trade of religion.

After resting awhile we resumed our journey, drawing ever nearer to the great mountain wall, and
crossing ridges that grew larger and larger as we progressed, the descents into some of the valleys being
almost precipitous. It was upon a ridge that we met
a little squad of people, four soldiers, a sergeant, and
a muleteer. In the custom of suspicious Kurdistan
they enquired where we were going, and betrayed
themselves by their accent as Turkomans of Kirkuk.
We passed after exchange of greetings, and each had
descended to his separate valley, when a bullet whistled
by, and we saw one of the soldiers running full speed
after us. We ourselves possessed not one of the
weapons of defence, nor could we escape the pursuer,
for we were kept to the track by our mule, and he

could scramble straight up the hill-side. So we stood, and he came up at a run, without a word seized my bridle, and with the other hand started to explore my pockets. All he discovered was a watch and twenty krans; not much, certainly, but enough to provoke an attempt at resistance on mine and Hama's part. This infuriated the robber, or appeared to do so, for he drew his long dagger and stabbed me in the arm, making a nasty wound. Then he jabbed his rifle-butt with considerable force against Hama's nose. Meanwhile, the old Roumanian was calling upon God. He then explored the saddle-bag, but was told by the old man that this was sugar ordered by the Shaikh of Biara, too influential a person for even a soldier to offend, so he left it and started to return. Hama had not seen him take the watch, and on hearing it from me, set out at a run after the soldier, who was now some distance away. Hearing him coming, the thief stopped, and Hama, with true Kurdish skill, made a swift leap and threw him, not, however, without encountering the knife, in the shoulder. I could not hear what he said, but he was remonstrating with the soldier, and after some time, having recovered the watch and the money, he started to come back, when the robber knelt and, taking careful aim, fired. The bullet passed just over the top of his head and carried away the little tassel on the peak of his high cap, but Hama did not hasten his pace, nor appear at all perturbed. The old man had taken advantage of the incident to escape over the brow of the hill, and was no longer visible, and as Hama came up we proceeded upon our way, the soldier watching us from the opposite side of the valley. Just over the ridge we came upon the old darvish, sitting behind a rock, very disturbed in mind, but overjoyed to see us with no worse wounds than the knife had inflicted. We now bound these up, and when Hama had to a degree stopped the flow of blood from his nose, we proceeded.

In another hour we came to where a sheer wall of

mountain rose above us, to where we could see large
fields of snow, and we turned to the right up a narrow,
ascending valley, or trough, at the foot. This had a
stream running down it, and the sides were thickly
covered with gardens and fruit-trees. A little path ran
among these, and we gradually ascended, the temperature dropping as we rose. As we went we made a
good meal from the hanging mulberries, black and
white, which were just ripening. Some miles up, a
narrow ravine branched off, as if to go straight into
the face of the Aoraman Mountain, and we turned into
it. Here the trees were thicker, and the gardens,
terraced upon the hill-sides, were divided by stone
walls, the alleys between them being often brooks
which rushed down to join the main stream. We
struggled through the mud, and in places thick under-
growth, for an hour or so, then crossing a bridge of
tree-trunks over the stream, came to a rambling stone
house set in the hill-side.

Above us the valley narrowed yet, a little village
hung to its sides, and above, not a quarter of an hour
away, it became but a furrow in the great mountain-
side—and Persian territory. We could see nothing of
the house but a thick stone wall above us, and had to
clamour at a small door set in it. This was opened,
and upon Hama proclaiming a visitor for the Shaikh
ul Islam, we were allowed up the stone staircase upon
which it gave. Ascending this we found ourselves upon
a broad terrace, the retaining wall of which had stood
above our heads a minute before. We crossed it and
came to a cistern of rough marble set in the pavement,
which was here of the same stone, and seeing that at
its edge all shoes were removed, did likewise, and
entered from it to a little room at the end of the
house. From the far end of this yet a smaller apartment opened, and I was shown into it, and my greeting
of "Salamun Alaikum" fell upon the ears of its occupant,
the Shaikh ul Islam, who squatted beside a little un-
glazed window, smoking a cigarette. He returned my

R

greeting, invited me to be seated, and then recognising
me, exclaimed:

"Ah, it is thou!"

I sat down and asked after his health, to which he
replied in a surly way, keeping the use of the second
person singular, a somewhat unmannerly method of
addressing a visitor, and then he relapsed into a
silence, which was broken by Hama appearing with the
four sugar loaves, which he set down near the door,
together with the saddle-bags.

The Shaikh ul Islam asked, "What are these?" and
Hama replied, somewhat taken aback by the sour tones,
that we had brought them as a greeting present, unworthy as they were, but the Shaikh turned to me and
with a heavy frown said the rudest thing possible:

"Take them back whence they came, consume them
yourselves, sell them in Halabja; I have no need of
such things, nor are we such friends as to warrant this
style of civility."

Then again addressing Hama, he said:

"What is your master's name?"

"Agha Mirza Ghulam Husain Shirazi," the poor
fellow answered, astonishment and dismay showing in
every line of his great form.

"And yours?"

"Hama."

"Whence?"

"Of the Mukri, of Sauj Bulaq," and here he bridled
a little, as should a man of a great and powerful tribe.

"And where did you find him?" I was asked.

"In Halabja," I replied.

I was wearing a new aba, or camel-hair cloak, and
this next attracted his attention:

"Was that given you as a mark of esteem by Lady
Adela?" he queried, with a sneer.

"No," replied Hama for me, his ire rising; "my
master seeks favour of none, and pays for what he
obtains with his own, good Persian money."

"Once more I say, take those away, I want no sugar;

take them out, and you"—to his own servant—"go away, what affairs are these of yours?"

Still Hama refused to take up the sugar, till I turned and told him to take and give them to the poor, the usual means of signifying that one has no use whatever for a rejected gift.

So the room was clear of servants, and the Shaikh ul Islam turned to me and recommenced his unpleasant remarks:

"So you are that Englishman of Constantinople; how does a European find his way from there to here in this guise, unattended, speaking Kurdish, and using Persian as his own language? When I was in Constantinople you were my guest and I could say nothing, though I knew what you were; but here I can speak freely, for we are both strangers. And that explains why I cannot accept your presents; I wish to do you no discourtesy, but I am living here in a retreat of darvishes, where our diet is but buttermilk and bread; nor do we indulge in any luxuries, therefore I as a guest in another's house cannot accept presents from any.

"Yet, because I bear you no ill-will, though you have doubly deceived me—coming there in false guise, and here too, perhaps—I beseech you to be frank and tell me who you are—what, after your close enquiries at Constantinople, your business is here upon the frontier."

"It is evident," I replied, "from what you say that you had suspected in Constantinople that I was a Persian, and your surmises were correct, and as a proof I will hand you letters from my native place, Shiraz, covering a long period."

These he perused and handed them back.

"Yes," he said, "that is all very specious, but how am I to know these are not forgeries. And at any rate, what brought you here to see me?"

"When I was in Constantinople," I said, "you were kind to me and lightened the monotony of many a dark day there, it is only natural that I should come to see you when I hear that you are here now."

"No, no," he replied, with the air of a man who despairs of extracting the truth, "it was not that; tell me what it was. Remember, you have placed yourself in an awkward position. If I like, being a priest and holding a judicial position, I can cause you to be examined, and if the truth is what I suspect, it will be very awkward for you. It is useless to tell me you are this or that, for you have lied badly either then or now. It occurred to me in Constantinople that you were not a European, and I first thought you were a Kurd, for none but such know the names of places and tribes as you did; but you spoke Persian as a Persian, and not like a Kurd—like I do, for instance. I suspected then that you had some ulterior motive, and now, can you not see how suspicious your presence looks? As to your letters, they are or are not genuine. One thing remains, you are a native of Persia, that I feel sure; and now, if you would make a friend of me, tell me what you did to be expelled from Persia. Abandon all lies, my son, and cleave to the truth."

I could do nothing but humour his delusion, so I described how I had been mixed up with political troubles in Teheran during the days of Muhammad Ali Shah, and my subsequent flight to London. Whether he believed this or not I do not know, but he pretended to accept it.

"And so you fled to escape the imprisonment or death that was the fate of some of your countrymen about that time," he said with a smile.

"Yes," I said, and could not resist the temptation to add, "like yourself from Sina not so long ago."

"Dogs," he cried, "the Persians, with their crafty tongues; you are one of the accursed breed, for you have the tongue. How I wish all those Persians would slay one another in their squabbles."

"Well," I replied, "such being your opinion of us, it is useless to make any statement, and I volunteer none;

if you ask me questions you must accept what I say, or refrain from asking them. Your right to cross-examination I deny, not being a Turkish subject nor a co-religionist, for like all my countrymen I am Shi'a, and there the affair ends. I came to call upon you, and find myself suspected, and my country insulted!"

"That is very well," he said, "but you do not realise that in this retreat, a resort of darvishes and pious people, I have but to say that I suspect you of being an Armenian or even a Shi'a, and you would not reach the bottom of the valley alive. As it is, I am convinced of your identity, and there is no need for anyone to talk about it. How you explain your presence here I do not know, and shall not ask; let me only tell you this, that if you seek favours from the Halabja family I shall oppose you, for I have all my suspicions. Let us now dismiss the subject. So long as you remain in Halabja I shall treat you in a friendly way, for we are both strangers, and each is bound to assist the other in a strange land. If you would stay here the night, do so, and I shall be glad to act as your host. The way back to Halabja is far, and you may not arrive by sunset."

"No," I said; "I will return, and hope to get back safer than I came, for I was robbed on my way here by one of these Turkish soldiers."

He called for his servant, and told him to bring food, for he insisted upon my eating with him once, and I did not refuse; for thereby, if he were a true Kurd, he would lay upon himself in a measure the obligation of hospitality, and the fact of my having eaten in his house would tend to soften in him whatever enmity he might feel. So when they brought a simple meal, of bread and buttermilk, I joined him, dipping from the same bowl. He excused the frugality of the meal, saying that here this was their diet, and this alone, and when I had finished allowed me to bid him good-bye. I stood before him, bidding him the lengthy parting words of Persian, and he took my hands in his, and looked up for a moment straight into my eyes, as if he would see truth there.

Then he smiled, and said, "My son, the ways of the world are hard, and the stranger brave who comes to the unknown, as you have done. There is that in you I like, for you are not afraid; but you lie, like all your countrymen. But I am sorry for you, yes I am truly grieved for you, poor lad!" and with that he let me go.

At the threshold, however, he called me back in his slow tones, unused to Persian, and I halted in the doorway. He had gone to the opposite side of the room, and now hastened across and pressed into my hands a small sum of money, saying, "Take this; thou wert robbed within our bounds, and we at any rate can give back."

"But not to me," I said; "you refuse a gift and seek to give? No, I hunger not, nor do I look for favours from any; keep it, it is a fit mate for my sugar loaves."

The priest smiled, and patted me on the shoulder. "A good test, a good test," he cried; "Persian, ah! Persian of the Persians, pride forbids you to take it. You are from the south, and not like the Teherani, who would take a kran from his wife's murderer because it was money. Now give it to the poor for me, and we shall both acquire merit, nor seek by imagining to make out why I gave it."

I called Hama, whose long form I could see in the yard, and giving him the money before the priest, told him to scatter it to the poor, and so I scored again, for I knew the old trick; he sought to make me take the money, and relying upon a native cupidity, had presented me with a trust which gave me the power of retaining the cash. He saw that I had seen the catch, and smiled quietly, looking at me in a curious way, and I, waiting for no further comments, left him.

Outside again I mounted the mule, and the emptiness of the saddle-bags recalling to mind the rejected sugar, I asked Hama what he had done with it.

"Why," he said, "when the dog refused it, I took it

to the coffee-house here, and pretended I had brought
it from Halabja for sale. They bought it for seventeen
krans, and here's the money," and he showed me the
krans in his hand, and expressed his satisfaction at so
profitable an ending of the affair. Yet he was boiling
with indignation at the reception I had met from the
Shaikh ul Islam, and upbraided me for wasting my
time upon such a person, recommending me rather
than suffer the indignities he had put upon me to
relinquish my quest of the unpaid debt—a piece of
advice I told him I would take with pleasure.

When I arrived at Halabja in the evening, I found
that Uthman Pasha had arrived from Sulaimania with
all his suite, and that Shaikh Ali of Tavila had also
come in with a huge procession of hangers-on, from
Gulanbar, where he had been staying. So full was
the place now that I was glad that I had, two days
before, shifted my quarters to a room below the recep-
tion-room of Lady Adela, where in a back verandah
I lived a secluded and peaceful life, undisturbed by
anyone except the people of Lady Adela coming to
fetch me for secretarial duties, which I had taken up
almost regularly for her by now.

By this time I was hoping to be able to leave
Halabja soon, for there was nothing to do save act as
Persian writer to Lady Adela and the Pasha, which I
did not particularly want to do, as it would make
departure more and more difficult as time went on.
I had enquired into the possibilities of making a corner
in "run," and had partially succeeded, being now
possessor of the bulk of that commodity in the district.
It was not yet, however, delivered, so I made Mansur
the Christian my agent, and began to look around for
fresh occupation elsewhere. When I announced my
intention of leaving to Lady Adela, she protested loudly,
as did Tahir Beg, and swore that she would keep
me. She wanted me to teach Persian to her two
young sons—rowdy boys of twelve and sixteen—who
never rested at home a day, being ever in the saddle

or in the mountains. Then Tahir Beg, too, had his
obstacles to place in the way. As a final inducement
Lady Adela tried to keep me for the purpose of entering into a business agreement with Uthman Pasha, a
lure which also failed, though so well meant, for I was
not disposed to create a responsibility from my part
to other persons which might hold me when I wanted
to leave the country. So I engaged a mule in a caravan
shortly to leave for Sulaimania, and began to take
farewells of my acquaintances. I was the more resolved
to go, seeing that some little time before, when I had
had the idea to go to Khaniqin to buy sugar wholesale
I had been opposed by the same arguments as were
now tendered to keep me from Sulaimania. But the
caravan delayed and delayed, and every morning's
promise of departure became a new dalliance at noon.
Meanwhile the Shaikh ul Islam turned up suddenly,
and came to see me. I was hardly disposed to receive
him civilly, and Hama was for openly insulting him,
but this was obviously undesirable, so he was received
with as much reserve as possible. I had expected to
see him in a revengeful mood, for he would have heard
by now how well I got on in Halabja, and his jealousy
would—if his antagonism were actuated by that feeling
—flame into possibly open opposition. But I found him
all honey and smiles; he was meek, and a little inclined
to be servile. Why he adopted this attitude I did not
see, except that he must have resolved to accept me
at my own valuation, and, finding me popular, submitted
to public opinion. At any rate it was not worth while
to go into such details and theories, as I was leaving,
and told him so. Immediately he raised a hundred
objections: I should find trade bad in Sulaimania; I
should be harassed by the Government; I should lose
in my transactions with a people noted for their craft
and deceit; I could never live among so rude a populace,
and so on, to which I gave no reply. Hama supplying
one in the vigorous manner in which he was roping a
box the while.

So at last the priest took his departure, and I was relieved. As he went out the muleteer came in, and swore he would get away to-morrow early, if he left half his goods behind him. I was taking back to Sulaimania several loads of "run," worth about fifty pounds in all, contained in sheepskins. As the weather was warm the stuff was semi-liquid, and we had to sew the greasy skins in gunnies for transport. Each skin was slipped into a coarse sack, of which the mouth was sewn up. Then an edge each of two sacks was sewn together with strong cord, and a kind of saddle-bag thus formed, which it was possible to hang over a mule's back. This job took till fairly late, when the Shaikh ul Islam suddenly came rushing along like a madman.

"I thought my counsels had prevailed," he said, pouring out the words; "I imagined you were remaining, and now I hear you are leaving to-morrow. It is better far to stay here, why leave comfort and peace for the rush of Sulaimania? Will you not stay? Will not the counsels of reason prevail against your impetuosity?"

"No," I said, "for I am going. I have hired the animals, and did I wish to stay it would now be impossible."

While speaking, I was leaning over a saddle-bag of "run," and he stood behind me. For two or three minutes he stood thus, and then muttering a good-night, departed as swiftly as he had come. The muleteer afterwards told us that he had tried to induce him by every means in his power to abandon the idea of going, or refuse to let me have the animals I had hired. What his reason was for wishing to keep me I never discovered, nor could Hama, whose wits usually supplied a reason for everything, offer any solution of the affair.

So next morning early we rose, and collected our goods by the light of candles, conveying them to the edge of the wide verandah, whence we dropped them upon the mules' backs. Mansur, who had consented to look after my interests, came as far as the gate and assured me of his diligence in my affairs; and at last when it was quite light we moved off. As we passed

out of the main doorway, Hama directed my attention
to the Shaikh ul Islam, who was standing upon the
roof, where he had slept with Tahir Beg's household,
gazing down upon us. So we left Halabja.

As a mark of regard or from excess of politeness,
Lady Adela had provided me with a guard of four
horsemen, two stalwart fellows of her tribe under a
little wiry man, one Rasul Ahmad, who was noted in
Halabja for his bravery and integrity. His three
underlings were big, well-set-up men, typical Kurdish
horsemen of the south, with long tunics, which, as they
sat their horses, shaded their bare ankles from the
sun. Rasul Ahmad alone wore the scarlet riding-boots
of these parts. I noticed that one of them had a very
poverty-stricken appearance. His horse was a veritable
Rosinante, and he matched it. A great hole was worn
in his tunic where the butt of his rifle had rubbed
as he carried it over his shoulder, the leather of his
saddle-peak was sadly damaged by the gun, from
long carriage across his knees. These are the two
positions in which a Kurd usually carries the arm :
the first when it is known that it will not be necessary
at short notice; the second preparatory to carrying it
almost upright, the stock resting upon the saddle. His
bare feet, innocent of shoes, were thrust into rusty
old shovel-stirrups. His rifle was an old Snider, not
the smart Martini carbine as carried by the others,
and his melancholy face seemed to reflect the seediness
and unfortunate appearance of his gear. He had the
heavy, square jaw and small blue eyes of the Kurds
of the Shuan and Hamavand, and spoke little to any
of his fellows. Once, however, one of them made a
joke at his expense, and the sorrowful cavalier charged
down at him with rifle aimed, but as he fired, Rasul
Ahmad knocked the gun up, and as no harm was done,
the incident was regarded in their rough manner as
a joke.

Finding him riding alongside, I asked him concerning himself, when he informed me that he was of

the Hamavand and not of the Jaf, though he had taken service with them, and he explained the reason. It appeared that after several raids upon caravans with his tribe, he had attempted to hold up some travellers unassisted. In this he had been unsuccessful, and a bullet through his horse's shoulder had brought him to earth, to be caught. To make matters worse, he discovered that his victims were themselves Hamavands, and relations of his chief. Stung by their ridicule, for the affair was regarded as a joke, and urged by the fear of ultimate retribution, he fled on foot to the Jaf country, and took service as a mounted messenger and guard.

His melancholy, he averred, was due to his separation from his own hills, and his wife and family, and the loss of loot that he suffered by his absence from the tribe. He drew a pathetic comparison between himself scorching in the heat of Shahr - i - Zur, while his wife sat upon her roof in the hill village, clad in silk and satins, under her the finest of Persian rugs, round her a wall of rolls of cloths and stuffs from which she chose new garments, the while she listened to the hissing of the tea samovar and held her face to the cool breeze.

By such talk we whiled away the time, and made Sulaimania in one stage, halting during the night for a few hours to rest the animals, and snatching a nap on the hard ground.

A little excitement was caused during the afternoon, by a skirmishing party from a tent village discovering our presence and mistaking us for robbers, and we saw the spectacle of village Kurds calling to horse. We saw the village calm and quiet in the heat of the afternoon, and next instant, men—a moment ago asleep—darting forth at a gallop in twos and threes upon horses kept ever saddled and bridled, to take up positions around us and prevent attack. Rasul Ahmad was able to convince them at a distance that we were but the Pasha's people, and they came down and invited us to tea.

As Lady Adela had put me in the charge of Rasul

Ahmad, I was fain to bide by his counsel for a resting-place in Sulaimania during the night, and adopted his suggestion of staying at the house of a woman, Piruz, a relation of his, who possessed a small house. This, too, was conveniently placed upon the edge of the town, and afforded a resting-place for him when in Sulaimania.

As this was a type of the humbler houses of Kurdistan, it may be well to describe it briefly here.

Round three sides of an irregular square courtyard were built rooms of mud, three of which had no wall on the courtyard side, making a shady, cool place to sit in the summer. The winter rooms, with doors opening from these chambers, possessed each but a single glazed door barely five feet high. One of these, the best, was whitened with gypsum, and the rest plastered with the mixture of chaff and mud that is the chief ingredient of the mason's trade in the Middle East. The floors were of unmixed mud, smoothed as well as the stamping of bare feet could do it. In the midst of the yard a stream of cold, clear water bubbled up from a hole, filling a cistern of plaster and brick nearly level with the ground, under a large willow-tree that made a shady place to drink tea in the morning and afternoon. The landlady, as owner of this mansion, worth fifty pounds, was reckoned wealthy according to the Kurdish idea. She let the rooms to a couple of families for a total of half a crown a month, and having relations and friends who kept her supplied with flour and oil, lived comfortably. Here, where bread is made in the house, and is the main article of food, living comes cheaply enough.

Here I rested awhile, passing the time in conversation with the woman of the house, a good-looking Kurd of not more than thirty years, who by the sensible custom of Kurdistan is free to go about unveiled, and hold all her dealings with men as if she were a reasoning being, conducting all her affairs herself, a type of the only Middle Eastern race whose women are almost as free as the women of Europe, their only restriction being that they shall not go to the bazaar, or if they do, they must cover their heads. In Persia, or among other Musulmans, for two strange men to live in a house full of women, as was this, would be an unheard of atrocity, but here it was thought no more of than such a thing in England.

After eating a lunch of new bread, fresh from the oven, in leaves two feet across, with some "kebab" Hama brought from the bazaar, I set out to find Matti the Christian, who had shown himself so friendly before, and discovered him in his office with his younger brother Ismail, who assisted him. I had not been there a few minutes before Habib Badria appeared, and took his seat upon the bench outside the office, from which he could converse with the inmates; and I was introduced to a much older man, Antoine, and a younger one, Bihnan, who spoke French remarkably well. These were all the Mosul Christians in the caravanserai, and being just as inquisitive as anyone else, took the first opportunity of making the acquaintance of a stranger. They were quiet, well-mannered men, and finding that I had business, strolled off to their offices, with the exception of Habib Badria, who remained, being a special friend of Matti.

Both of them advised me, as I had merchandise, to take a small house near the bazaar for a time, and live with my goods, and they both shut their offices and prepared to take me on a hunt for a suitable house. Apparently they were well informed, for, passing out of the caravanserai we traversed a bazaar, turned up a blind alley, at the end of which we came to a house which they wished to show me, and which I agreed to take. This was vacated by the death of the owner, a merchant who had been murdered by Arabs on the way to Bagdad. He had left in charge, when he left, his old mother, a pure-blooded Kurd, who gloried in her uncontaminated descent, constantly asserting that she was not a converted Jew like the rest of the Sulaimanians.

Her house was built in imitation of Kurdish architecture as developed in Persia, a type common and growing commoner in Persia.

The door opened from the street into the corner of a stone-paved courtyard, and one came under the shelter of a couple of square yards of mud roofing supported upon pillars. Behind the door were a couple of articles like big earthenware shovels, upon the ground. This was the kitchen. The strip from here to the opposite end of the yard was occupied by flower-beds containing hollyhocks and roses, and a cistern raised a foot above the ground-level.

The house, standing opposite, was a two-storeyed one of three rooms below, each opening from the yard by a door, too low for a boy of twelve to enter erect. The best of these rooms, the centre one, boasted a second pair of doors, glazed, and the ceiling was made of short boards, the remains of sugar-boxes. The interior was washed in pinkish mud over the yellow underneath, and the ground was as that of the unpaved alley outside.

Upstairs, however, the architect had shown his skill. The best room, which jutted out from the frontage line some six feet, was whitened entirely with burnt gypsum, and ornamented by fresco and dado in raised patterns of that material.

The pillars between the wall-recesses bore inlaid mirrors, and the ceiling was painted in flowers and stars with scraps of looking-glass here and there in patterns. Three double glass doors with the glass set in huge fretwork patterns looked out over the yard, and the fourth, a wooden door of walnut and oak, opened into the middle room or verandah, from which steps of remarkable inequality descended to the yard. The supporting pillars of the roof of this portico—which replaced the fourth wall—were tree-trunks enclosed in narrow walnut planks, making them octagonal, with long narrow mirrors a foot high inserted at eye height. The ceiling was boarded. The third room would have been like the best one, had not the owner died before he could finish his house, and it had remained in yellow mud and beamed ceiling; and the doors, put in afterwards, were of plain white glass.

The old lady, Baji Raihan, allowed us to look over the little place, and offered to rent three rooms, two below, and the unfinished one above, for the equivalent of seven shillings a month—not an exorbitant sum, as the house was near to all the bazaars and business caravanserais. She herself occupied the room under the finished upper chamber, and would continue to do so. We, therefore, finding it reasonable, decided upon the place and made our way to a coffee-house. This, like all the coffee-houses of Kurdistan, was an edifice of high arches or domes supported upon heavy pillars, ingress being effected anywhere. High benches were ranged around, and in a recess was the apparatus of the place, two large samovars, and tea-glasses, and saucers, which stood upon a wide shelf made of mud and brick. The floor was bricked, and a water-carrier, his skin over his shoulder, came in every two hours and sprinkled the ground to keep the place cool. Here we found a large number of merchants, Christian and Kurd, and I was introduced in the manner of Kurdistan, my name being announced to those who asked it, after they had greeted me with the "Marhabba" of these parts.

The talk was mostly of the punishment of the Hamavands (for which the Turks were supposed to be collecting an army at Chemchemal), of local politics, or of harvest prospects. Here, in the coffee-house, the news of the place is exchanged, prices of merchandise discussed and fixed, bargains made, sales and purchases effected. It was announced by Matti that I had fresh "run" from Juanru, and a little man, whom Matti informed me was a respectable grocer, came forward and made an appointment to come and see the stuff next morning. We sat for some time, and I acquired an idea of the difficulty of the intricate Sulaimanian dialect of Kurdish, one of the most peculiar of all.

We then dispersed to our respective houses, and I

found Hama in the widow's house making tea, which, as I did not require it, was handed round to the women. As the evening was close, I had my carpet put in the yard on the ground, and having eaten, sunset being meal-time in Sulaimania, I sat upon my bed-clothes smoking and chatting with the women, who had disposed their sleeping apparatus upon the floor or on the roof, to which they ascended by a rude ladder. Their conversation was of the shaikhs, but as they appeared nearly all to be related to the Shaikh family, they only deplored the recent murder of Shaikh Sa'id, and I was constrained to enter into a flow of pious expressions of regret. They also touched upon the question of marriage, but I hazarded the opinion that a Shi'a could not ask in marriage a Sunni woman without trouble occurring with the relations, and they were nonplussed, thinking of no other suggestion to make, than that I should turn Sunni, an action which, as a good Shi'a, I repudiated, and rising said my prayers, as well to finish the argument as to convince them of my sincerity.

Rest, however, was rudely interrupted by the sudden rise of the hot north-east wind, here called the " rashaba," which blows from the hills with the force of a gale. This, coming suddenly, and across newly mown fields, smothered us with chaff and dust, which was followed by a sharp rain-shower which drove us to shelter, and we did not finally sleep till the sky was clear, about midnight.

CHAPTER XII

LIFE IN SULAIMANIA

MATTI came in early next morning, and with porters we took away the goods and deposited them in the new house, where we found two or three buyers of my merchandise waiting. These chose the skins of "run" they desired, and having at last settled a price which gave me a profit of some twenty-five per cent., we repaired to the shop of one of them to have the goods weighed by a public weigher. When we arrived that functionary was not forthcoming, so I installed myself in the grocer's shop, high up above the raisins, almonds, walnuts, and spices that he sold, and smoked cigarettes while he vended and attempted to carry on a conversation with me in Persian, of which he knew a little. It had often been a mystery to me how a retail grocer made his money; but now, being a wholesale dealer in an article he sold retail, I saw the game, which he was frank enough to display. His scales were not of the fairest, to start with, and when weighing, he would, when possible, leave in the pan the heavy wooden spoon with which he ladled out the grease. If a large amount were required there would be a haggle over the price, and the buyer probably got his purchase at a reasonable weight, but the small buyer who came for a few ounces was invariably defrauded, either by the calculation of the price, which he probably could not work out, or by the deficient amount given him. And so with three shahis worth of raisins, or the kran's

S

worth of almonds, which the grocer handed to the buyer in a long spoon which reached the remotest basin without necessitating his moving. In no shops in Kurdistan, except the drug and spice sellers, is anything wrapped up, and this habit makes a handkerchief the most essential part of a man's gear. To buy in the bazaar one goes provided with at least three handkerchiefs, if the mixing of dates, meat, and fruit in one handkerchief is to be avoided.

Hama at last found a weighing man, who appeared with an immense steelyard supported upon a long pole, to carry which two porters had to be called, each with an end upon his shoulder. The weights were entered in a little book, and the names of the buyers, sellers, and material under them. We then made up the account, and having paid the weighing fee, half each, settled down to counting out twelve hundred krans, in two-kran pieces, a process that took half an hour, with the examination for bad and cracked coins. This done, we left, with expressions of esteem on both sides, the money wrapped in the ever-necessary handkerchief.

We banked it with Matti, who locked it with the rest of my money in his iron box, and then we sent for "kebab"—scraps of meat cooked over charcoal—and with these and bread, made what is called the "merchant's lunch." All the afternoon I sat outside the office making the acquaintance of the Kurdish merchants round about. One of these, a certain Hama Ali, spoke Persian extremely well, and was very proud of having been to Kashan in Persia, where he had unsuccessfully attempted to trade against a ring of Persian merchants; and while cursing their business astuteness, praised their nice manners and hospitality, and that to a Sunni, who is hated among the Persian Shi'a.

The evening meal was a frugal affair of boiled rice and meat, and a cucumber or two procured for me in the bazaar by the old dame of the house; and an hour after eating I turned in upon the stones of the courtyard, that being the coolest place, for the nights were stuffy.

Early in the morning I received a visit from the old Mustafa Beg, Mudir Effendi, my companion in the caravanserai on my first arrival at Sulaimania. He expressed genuine pleasure at seeing me again, and stayed for an hour or two, drinking the morning tea. He lamented, as always, the lack of his appointment, which he could not take up, and cursed the ill-luck that had transplanted him from Tripoli in Africa to Sulaimania. He had learned no Kurdish, had found no new friends, and passed his days as he had done before, visiting the official Turks, sitting in the post-office, and dining at the shaikhs' house. His old fingers, white and well-kept, trembled so much that he could barely sew on the buttons of his garments, a task he was continually engaged upon; and his pride, that kept him respectable and clean, necessitated his getting up in the night to wash his own garments in the caravanserai cistern, for he could not be seen doing such work, nor had he, indeed, another change of raiment.

He was somewhat avaricious, I discovered, for he had enough cash to purchase more clothing, and at length I gained his consent to buy the material for another shirt and trousers, so we repaired to the bazaar. My costume of those days, in town, was one which gained some respect for me among others, and should, perhaps, have lessened my own for myself.

I wore an old pair of pyjamas under the dressing-gown I had adopted in Kirkuk, and a good abba thrown over these gave me a peculiar appearance, which apparently passed among the Sulaimanians for distinction.

In the bazaar we spent a long time before the old man could decide what quality of white cotton to buy, and a great curiosity was roused among the shopkeepers as to who he could be, for he made himself conspicuous by his arrogance and his loud tones of an Arabic, so different from the dialect of Bagdad, the only Arabic known to Sulaimania. So while he haggled, I accepted the invitation of a Kurdish shopman on the opposite side of the alley, and joined him in a cigarette, answering his questions as a return for his hospitality. The vociferating old man caused him some amusement, as it did the others; and his ignorance of their native Kurdish bent them the more upon driving a hard bargain, for he bore the mark of the Turk, and was to be detested accordingly.

At last, however, he completed his purchase, and we came back to the house and arranged with a sempstress found for us by Baji Raihan, the old woman of the house. For the sum of nine "baichu" (or about ninepence) we arranged with this rakish girl, with the big turban cocked over one eye, to sew the shirts. It being noon by now, we lunched in the upper portico, and the old man left for the caravanserai, while I, in the custom of the country, lay down to sleep for an hour or two.

In this way several days passed. Each morning or afternoon I spent at Matti's office, chatting to the idle merchants, for the Hamavands held the road and no business was done. Habib Badria, who was reckoned as one of the more progressive of the Mosul Christians, and who, in token of the fact, had discarded the Christian turban for the fez, delighted to talk of Europe, and would hold great discussions as to the possibility of his making a living in Paris—the aim and end of his desires. After a while he displayed a great interest in municipal affairs, and would converse for hours about motor dust-carts, underground drains, and such things, never dreamed of in Sulaimania till he heard of them from me. It was a hard task to convince him that London was bigger than Paris, and he regarded it as even a little unmannerly to hint at such, while he obviously forgave me for exaggerating about a nation of which I was a subject; for though I was known as Ghulam Husain the Persian, I had taken care to spread the fact that I was a British subject, to avoid annoyance at the Turks' hands.

Mustafa Beg as a rule avoided the Christians, and

though perfectly friendly towards them, did not consider it quite compatible with his dignity to be seen sitting with them. He had almost remonstrated with me on the subject, but he checked himself as he observed with an unction I do not think hypocritical, "Well, well, you say your prayers like a good Muslim, for I have seen you many a time, and what harm if an infidel give you entertainment?"

The old man came each morning for his tea and cigarettes, and the idea struck me one day to ask him if any of his Turkish acquaintances would like to purchase a Mauser pistol I possessed. He inspected the weapon, and taken with its neat appearance, promised to do his best. In the afternoon he returned, and apologising for coming at an unseemly hour, said that he had not succeeded in finding a purchaser for my pistol, but had discovered a new friend for me. He went on to describe how he had enlarged upon my merits and knowledge of Persian and French to the mudir, or director of the Military School of Sulaimania, an affair run by the Government, and attended by the sons of the Turkish officials in Sulaimania and of a few of the Kurds employed in the local government. This individual Mustafa Beg was extremely anxious for me to meet, and urged me to accompany him to the school, where the mudir lived all day, although lessons ceased at 11 A.M. in this warm weather, having commenced at 6 A.M.

The school was upon the outskirts of the town, in a high enclosure. Half of this formed a pretty garden, and the rest a playground, while the building itself was but a row of neglected rooms along one wall. The European style of culture and education supposed to be imparted to the pupils was evidenced by a high horizontal bar, the sign of gymnastic exercises never performed. Over the doors were the signs "Birinji," "Ekinji," "Uchinji," "Durdinji," and "Baishinji"—first, second, third, fourth, and fifth classes. At the edge of the garden strip was a large tank of clear water, and above it a canopy of boughs had been made, to form what the Kurds call a "chardaq."

Here upon a high bench sat the Mudir Effendi, a fat little man duly decked with tin stars and strapped trousers, an insignificant Turk of Sivas, who spoke no language but his own, if a few words of French be excepted. A younger man was seated near him in a chair, playing with his sword, and he was introduced to me as the "Ekinji Mu'allim," or second in command of the school. His linguistic accomplishments included a slight knowledge of Persian and Arabic, and a good knowledge of Kurdish, for he was a native of the Kirkuk district. The mudir received me very graciously, not being able to refrain, however, from the Turkish habit of showing an overwhelming inquisitiveness as to my nationality, reason for coming to Sulaimania, what I was doing, and anything else he could think of to afford a question. Mustafa Beg, however, made capital of his queries, and made them the occasion of an eulogy of my accomplishments, adding as a final and convincing proof, that I had lived several years in London, and had seen Bombay, Constantinople, and Teheran. These qualifications immediately gave me a position, and having readily answered some schoolmaster questions as to the population of London and Paris, and the strength of the British Army, I was admitted to terms of the greatest friendship. The little man had never been nearer to Constantinople than Smyrna, and like all Turks in the uncongenial climate of Kurdistan, lamented his presence there. He was good enough to compliment me upon my knowledge of Kurdish, a tongue he confessed he could never acquire, and besought me to teach him Persian and French. Being a military man, his thought ran upon matters martial, and his questions soon came round to the subject. He could not comprehend how a State like England could possibly hang together without compulsory service, and expressed the greatest surprise that I could have escaped it. What upset him more than anything else was the obvious fact that without

military service no man in Turkey could carry his
"tezkere," a document all must have, and without which
the subject is liable to suspicion and annoyance, and he
failed to see why a British subject, not being liable to
service, could possess one.   In fact, he lamented the
system which only gave a passport to the subject when
he travelled in certain foreign lands, and considered
such a lack of control over the individual to be a lively
cause of anarchy and rebellion.   After partaking of tea,
and some Regie cigarettes which he produced specially for
my benefit, we made our excuses and asked permission
"to be excused."   As I was about to leave, a note
arrived from Hama, who was at Halabja, and its
contents caused me to go down to search for Matti,
whom I found in the bazaar.

Hama had gone to Halabja soon after I had come
to Sulaimania, to receive a large consignment of " run "
which I had contracted to buy.   The transaction had
been one common enough in these parts.   Under the
guarantee of Mansur the Christian I had advanced to
one Makha, a Jew (with the fiercest red head I ever saw
on any one), a sum to go out into the highways and
byways of Kurdistan and purchase gradually of the
Kurds, who had been storing up the precious oil as
they prepared it, waiting the advent of such a buyer.
So having arrived at Sulaimania I had to send Hama
back, for the time was near when the Jew should return,
and my man must be there to receive the merchandise
and arrange transport.   Hama, however, had not liked
the idea of going to Halabja empty-handed; like all
Kurds who have come in contact with trade and
business, he was keen to experiment.   So after a
consultation with Matti and Habib Badria, the former
of whom did not quite like the idea, it was arranged
that he should take with him a load of shoes and a few
odd things, for sale to the shopkeepers of Halabja.
Accordingly, before he left we went to the shoemakers'
bazaar.   Here is a long street with wide and deep
booths on either side, occupied entirely in the manu-

facture of shoes. These are of three designs: a red
leather shoe turned up to a blunt point, a black one
of the same shape, and a female shoe, a slipper with
only a toe-cap ornamented with steel beads, and a long
high heel—which is added only after the shoe is bought,
and which is put on by a man whose trade it is to perform
only this part of the shoemaking business.

Here in one of the shops we took seats and waited
while the shopman collected from his neighbours' and
his own stock a sufficient number of shoes. In order
that dispute might be lessened to a certain extent, a
Christian was called in who, being not of our religion,
might be assumed to be free from prejudice against, or
favour for, any one of us. He tested the shoes and
examined them, and through him we conducted all
the negotiations. As each pair of shoes had to be
bargained for, the process took some time. Custom, too,
demanded that a certain formality should be observed.
The owner would first mention a fancy price, and to save
time the other holders would, instead of arguing, solidly
ejaculate the phrase, "Warra la khwaru!" ("Come
down!"), repeating it till almost the right price was
reached, when the arbitrator would step in, and after
a short argument would settle a price about midway
between the buyer's and seller's figure, and which both
were bound to accept. In this way, in the space of five
hours, we purchased some fifty pairs of shoes, and having
paid the money, Hama carried away all the footgear
in a sack. These, with a sample of cigarette papers
and a dozen rosaries, made his stock, and he left next
morning.

I now had a letter from him, and from Mansur. The
former told me of his successes with the shoe-selling,
which had, while not great, been satisfactory, and the
latter attempted to explain why Makha the Jew had
not returned from Juanru with the "run." Matti was
rather inclined to regard my efforts with disfavour, and
would, I think, have tried to dissuade me, for he knew
that I was not experienced in trading. Habib, on the

other hand, was extremely keen that I should open an office in their caravanserai, and in this he was strongly seconded by one Antoine, a merchant of twenty years' standing in Sulaimania, and two bankruptcies during that time, a feature of Oriental trading which sometimes betokens considerable acumen and astuteness rather than commercial inaptitude. Antoine was a buyer for certain merchants in Bagdad and Mosul, and when I made his acquaintance, was purchasing gum tragacanth. Now I, too, was quite willing to buy tragacanth, but he had become alarmed, and had managed to form a small ring which had little difficulty in shutting me out. I attempted even to make Antoine act as broker for me, and in an interview when Matti was present as witness, forced a promise out of him, but he repudiated it afterwards. Yet he would constantly come along as I sat outside Matti's shop, and in his queer Persian exhort me to buy skins, or wheat, and affirm that he had made great profit in deals. He had a younger brother who assisted him, a big honest lad, who stood rather in fear of him and his wily ways. For years he had been in close touch with the Musulman merchants, and was considerably disliked by his co-religionists on account of his habit of doing business on Sunday—a day which the Arab and Chaldean Christian observes as strictly as is done in Scotland, and passes in as dull a way.

Matti also was assisted by a younger brother, a somewhat surly fellow, but good-hearted enough, and to him fell the task of cooking their food on the verandah outside the office. For these Chaldeans of Mosul live day and night in their rooms, which are office and home combined ; and such men as Matti and Antoine had existed thus, in what we should call a small dark cellar full of merchandise, for two decades. In normal times, that is, when business was good, and passage after dark in the streets not dangerous, the Christians divided themselves into messes of five and six, each taking turn to cook ; but now, with the general insecurity forbidding intercourse between Matti's caravanserai, the Khan-i-'Ajam, and the caravanserai where the other merchants lived, and the terrible depression in trade, they had all retrenched, and with the exception of Matti and Habib, who still kept up the habit, each did for himself; and Habib might be seen every other day watching a sizzling pot anxiously while he sold cottons, or leaving a heap of half-prepared stuffed cucumbers to attend to a Kurdish buyer.

As often as they could induce me to stay, I would dine with Matti and Habib, but at first Matti had been very diffident, and had, in order to satisfy himself upon a certain point, ordered some lunch one day when I was present, and invited me to join. I had refused, but he continued to press, and I continued to excuse myself till at last he sighed, and said with signs of a little chagrin:

" I thought you were a liberal-minded Musulman, and would not consider me unclean, but I see that it is true that the Persians are more particular than the Sunni, and will not eat with a Christian."

The good man seemed so hurt in thus explaining himself, and it was so extremely ill-bred on my part to refuse and slight a man who did so much for me, that I speedily denied this bigotry, and dipped my hand into the dish with him, to his considerable satisfaction.

After this he would have had me dine every night with him, and was extremely difficult to refuse, but it would not have been politic for a Muslim, even though a Shi'a and no follower of the tenets of the Sunni Kurds, to become known as one who fed with Christians, and I restricted myself to feeding once a week with them. The Kurds have no scruples, for the caravanserai keeper, one Hama, a native of Aoraman, a bovine creature who served the Christians very faithfully, had the habit of consuming the considerable residue of their great meals.

I was surprised at first at the enormous quantities they ate at dinner. At sundown the caravanserai would be closed, and benches placed round a patch of garden they had made in the courtyard. On the benches, cushions and thick mattresses were arranged, and here Matti, Antoine, and Habib, the seniors, took their places, divesting themselves of their heavy turbans and loosening their waistbelts. They were usually joined here by a Bagdad Jew, a great handsome fellow, who kept everyone in a good humour by his jokes. Then the cry would go out, "Jib ul piala," and the younger brothers would bring forth each a little glass bottle, wrapped about with a damp napkin to keep the contents cool. As darkness fell, the same younger brothers, who performed the menial jobs, spread a carpet upon the courtyard floor and a coloured table-cloth upon it. As soon as the eatables had been turned out upon dishes the elder brothers left their couches, and squatting round the dishes, all set to work in the earnest fashion typical of Eastern diners, saying little till the meal was finished. The quantities of meat these Christians ate excited my wonder, and caused me to remark upon the fact to them. Habib, who always professed a knowledge of European thought and ideas, rather scorned me, for he accused me of having appropriated the European fallacy that unless a man took exercise he should not eat much meat, and he pointed out the futility of the argument by drawing attention to his and Matti's excellent health and condition.

Dinner was finished half an hour after sunset, and after a short interlude of conversation most of the company would sleep, to rise with the sun in the morning. One or two nights I slept there on one of the courtyard benches, but the sandflies were so numerous that I preferred my own roof, where there was usually a cool breeze.

One morning I was seated in my little upper room, upon my carpet, writing, when the courtyard door was thrown open and Mustafa Beg, accompanied by half a dozen Kurds, entered, and at my invitation ascended.

They all came crowding into the little room, and Mustafa Beg invited a youth to the highest place. The others took places anywhere, and two stood at the doorway, being servants. The old man introduced the lad as Sayyid Nuri, son of Shaikh Ahmad, a prominent member of the hated family of Shaikhs. Now, in Sulaimania a man who has escaped the notice of this family thanks Heaven, and prays for continued freedom from their acquaintance. Equally the day is accursed that one of the family discovers the unfortunate. It had been the boast of the quarter, too, that up to the present no shaikh had set his foot in its streets, for it was a respectable business quarter, well guarded, and too alert to be surprised by the night attacks of the shaikhs' roughs and robbers. Well did I know that the advent of Sayyid Nuri here would disturb the peace of the "mahalla" and make myself unpopular, for none were distrusted more than those whom the shaikhs treated in a friendly manner.

Sayyid Nuri himself was a mean but sharp-looking youth, a type of the mixture of Turkoman and Kurd that is found in Sulaimania, for he had the bravado look of the latter and the scanty moustache and long, wavy nose of a certain section of the former. He rustled in silk, and wore fine cotton socks. In his belt was stuck a huge knife, and a revolver dangled in its case from under his zouave jacket. Still, for all his unprepossessing appearance, for a member of the family from whom arrogance and all that is objectionable was to be expected, he was very polite.

Mustafa Beg seemed to think that, in bringing him there he had done me a great service, and sat beaming upon both of us, and listening to the Kurdish around him. The lad spoke excellent Turkish, for, as he explained, the family had plenty of dealings with the Turks. When he found that Mustafa Beg had not been wrong in describing me as a Persian, he was delighted, for all he desired to do was to air his knowledge of that language, which was not excessive.

From the first, however, he could not control his inquisitive nature, which led him to handle everything and turn over the most obvious things with a query

as to their use. From somewhere he had heard that
I was a doctor, and as ill-luck would have it, I had
arranged in the room—which I had fondly imagined to
be private—a row of nine or ten small bottles, containing
a few medicines I had accumulated on my passage from
Constantinople. These he saw at once, and reaching
up, pulled them down one by one, examining and
smelling them, and with the inspection of each, grew
more convinced that my denials were but lies, and that
I could cure as well as another. Mustafa Beg, however,
came in here to my rescue, by asserting that he knew
me not to be a doctor, although I possessed some
knowledge of the science. This hardly satisfied Sayyid
Nuri, so he took a couple of purgative pills, and two
of calomel that I added, saying that he would try them,
and would know afterwards whether I was a doctor
by the quality of the purgative !

Then he found one of the red india-rubber sponges
which are so common nowadays, and which had somehow escaped loss during my journeyings. This quite
upset him. Its use he appreciated at once, for I pointed
out that it was used in the bath for washing and rubbing
the skin. But by chance he smelled it, and the odour
of rubber that it gave out so disgusted him that he
left it alone at once. But what he had come to see
was the Mauser pistol, and to keep him quiet, for he
hopped around the room overturning all my papers and
books, I produced it. The weapon, however, did not
meet with the favourable reception I had hoped, for he
said he had seen and possessed one before. He found
a fine pastime provided in a charge of dummy cartridges
given by the sellers, with which to practise manipulating
the weapon without danger. His companions were
ignorant of their harmless nature, and watched with
interest his movements. Having loaded, he cocked his
pistol and covered the man who sat opposite him,
amusing himself by making him move this way and
that to be out of aim. Mustafa Beg regarded these
operations with dismay, and evidently thought that

Sayyid Nuri having trapped an enemy in another man's house, was going to kill and leave him there and let his death lie at my door, and he besought him in tones of earnest appeal to put down the pistol. His companions, seeing he did not desist, also joined in the protest, and he put it down, and then proceeded to enjoy the astonishment that followed his explanation of the nature of the cartridges.

Having exhausted the joke, he was at a loss for something to do, and explained his miserable existence, for he pointed out that as son of Shaikh Ahmad he had more money than he could spend — which was perfectly true — and was bound down to Sulaimania. He sighed for Kirkuk and its big, busy bazaars, and its proximity to Bagdad, which was his first aim, and stood in his eyes the first city of the world. His questions regarding Constantinople were few, and made more from a sense of thoroughness in his queries than a desire for information, and he thought it but a poor place compared even to Mosul. It took a long time to satisfy him as to the reason of my presence in Sulaimania, and I saw he did not believe that I was only remaining a short time, nor that my aim was the commerce in which I was engaged; for to him a merchant was inseparable from his office, and a man who spoke European languages and possessed medicines was obviously there for some other reason.

To my immense relief I at last got rid of him. Old Mustafa Beg had himself not anticipated the annoyance that would result from his visit, and was, I could see, very penitent and regretful, for in his own way he was jealous and did not wish others to be free of the house, a futile hope in Sulaimania, where the unmarried man who refuses free permission of entry to all and sundry is regarded as a lunatic, or an excessive evildoer who would conceal the actions that must be necessarily wicked because done behind closed doors.

The neighbours' protests against the visits were not long in coming. The old house-dame had been out at one of their houses and returned with a long complaint from several of them, the gist of which was that if this was the company I preferred I had better go elsewhere to enjoy it, for the advent of a shaikh in a quarter was the forerunner of all evil. Opposite to our house, however, a certain merchant lived, whose wife was one of the ancient family of the Hakkari religious chiefs, and bore the man's title of "Khan" that indicated her lineage. She was thus related to the shaikhs themselves, and I resolved to appeal to her when occasion should arise. So I kept a look-out for her husband, and when he arrived, called him in. He was a pleasant man, much respected in the quarter, and kept up the tradition of the Kurds that the stranger must be protected. I explained to him the circumstances of the visit, and he promised to send his wife to the shaikh house if the lad came again, and tell them that his presence was not required in the quarter. He lost no time in clearing my character of the blame that had attached to it, and took the most effective means to do so, for as it was sunset, and the women were spreading the bed-clothes behind the " chikha " or mat screens on the roofs, he ascended and announced in a loud voice that Ghulam Husain was more sorry than they at the visit, and had called him to witness his displeasure, and request his assistance in preventing any annoyance to the quarter. His emphatic utterance and assertion of going surety for my good intentions called forth expressions of gratitude from the people around, and I saw that by my action I had gained in their estimation.

In the bazaar and coffee-houses there was but one topic of conversation these days—the Hamavands. We heard rumours of their intention to raid Sulaimania, and at nights their riders came openly to the shaikhs' house to receive their orders. Once or twice they actually looted a few houses on the west side of the town. Not a soul dared venture forth. Matti used to tell me of happier times when the Christians and Kurds too used to go outside upon the low hills and spend days in the

cooler air picnicking to the accompaniment of music—
and I suspected, in the case of the Christians, too much
'araq. But now, to venture outside the fringe of houses
upon any except the north-east side was to court
robbery, if not destruction. And then the futile
talk of the "ta'qib," or punishment that was to be
dealt out to the tribe! We heard reports—and these
seemed true—of regiments of soldiers from Anatolia
and Mesopotamia collecting at Chemchemal, and judging from letters coming from Mosul and Bagdad, we
were able to keep a check upon rumour, and ascertained
that there were in reality some three or four thousand
military, foot and "mule-riders," gathered there—to
extinguish a couple of hundred rough horsemen. All
these troops were kept idle by the Mosul authorities
to wait for a commander, and as long as funds from
the shaikhs poured into the Mosul Vali's pocket, the
commander was kept engaged in pressing business
elsewhere, and the Hamavands redoubled their audacity,
actually raiding Chemchemal itself and killing some
soldiers.

Meanwhile the state of the district was becoming
worse, for travellers were threatened not only by roving
parties of Jafs and Hamavands, but by the local soldiery
also, for the "binbashis" had consumed what little cash
could be collected for their pay, and the "muhasibichis,"
or accountants, grew daily fatter upon sequestrated
funds. Soldiers were leaving for their native places, or
retiring over the frontier to Persia—taking with them
their new Mauser rifles; and in Halabja a colonel
commanded five half-tamed Kurdish levied men instead
of his usual fifty.

Then the affair occurred which threw ridicule and
despair alike upon the Turks of the district. A quarter
"tabur," or about one hundred men, was ordered to
replenish the Sulaimania garrison, which from a normal five
hundred men had fallen to thirty-four. These were also used
to convoy about seventy rifles and proportionate ammunition for distribution among the frontier posts. They started

from Chemchemal, commanded by a colonel ("binbashi") and two majors (or "yuzbashi"), and accompanied by several "'askar katibi" (accountants), and other Government officials with their wives and families. Across the Chemchemal plain they saw no signs of Hamavands, though they threw out scouts, and those sent forward to reconnoitre at the Bazian cleft through the hills saw no one. Consequently they approached the break, where the sundered hill presents a V-shaped entrance to the Bazian plain, without misgiving. The place is so formed that from the Chemchemal side it is impossible to see ahead very far, as the ground rises, and the break is only about ten yards wide at the bottom, sloping up and away to the hill-tops.

When they had passed the outcrop of rock that forms the break, and the last man had entered Bazian, the hills above them suddenly rang with the shouts of the Hamavands, and from each side they raced down helter-skelter, their hill-ponies leaping cleverly down the boulder-strewn slopes. At a distance of fifty yards they opened fire, and the first to fall was a "yuzbashi." The soldiers gathered in a bunch, and the non-combatants attempted to rush back through the gap, to find themselves confronted by three or four horsemen, who fell upon them and stripped them, leading away their loaded animals. The Turks were returning the fire, but, taken at a disadvantage, made no effect upon the quick-moving Hamavands, who wheeled around them. Yet they held out for a little, and attempted to push forward.

In point of numbers the Turks had the advantage, and their weapons were ten-shot Mausers as against Martini carbines, but their shooting must have been of the poorest, for they only succeeded in wounding one Hamavand. Several, too, tried to break away, and were immediately picked off. In a quarter of an hour the "binbashi" fell, shot through the chest, and twelve soldiers, too, were dead, and a score wounded. The remainder cast away their arms, seeing resistance futile, and the Kurds came upon them and stripped the caravan,

T

relieving it of all its rifles and ammunition, carrying
away or tearing off the soldiers' uniforms, and looting
the noncombatant passengers. There was an indescribable confusion; soldiers on foot and unarmed strove to
escape on all sides, and horsemen with the shouts of a
drover to his cattle rounded them up. Squads of
Hamavands, driving before them mules of the defeated
party, shouted at and encouraged their refractory and
frightened captives. As is usual in these cases, everything was being done with the utmost speed, and the
Hamavands, infuriated by the resistance they had met
with, were more merciless than usual to those whom they
stripped. The men they simply denuded, and scared
the women with fierce guestures and display of long
knives to make sure of their handing over anything they
might have concealed.

One of the women who had been robbed told me
that some of the Hamavands had brought their wives
with them, putting them behind rocks while the fight
proceeded, and calling them out afterwards to enquire
into the dress of the female captives more intimately
than a man could have done; for in these Muslim lands
even among the wildest Kurds, a man will seldom offend
a Musulman woman's modesty, and the Hamavand is
a singularly pious tribe, stopping even its raiding parties
to pray in a body at the appointed times.

The men they left in little more than a shirt—and
at last cleared off, taking with them the wife and
daughter of one of the majors, whom they subsequently
restored after having placed them in the care of the
chief's womenfolk for a time. The remains of the
caravan, twos and threes of half-naked men, and weeping women, proceeded on foot, reaching Sulaimania
next day, hungry and ashamed.

It was not unnatural that the possibility of such
catastrophes, and their actual occurrence, did a great
deal of damage to the Turkish name, and indeed in
the coffee-houses opinion was freely expressed. The
Turks were jeered at, and their soldiery ridiculed. The

shaikhs were rapidly becoming a terror to Sulaimania. Not a night passed without murders occurring, and in every case the assassins were known, and were shaikhs' men. One night an attempt was made upon the Khan-i-'Ajam, where Matti and my other Christian acquaintances lived. Some of them were sleeping on the roof, when sounds of scraping against the outer wall attracted their attention. They waited for a while, and Habib brought out his old Snider rifle. After some time one of the burglars had nearly succeeded in piercing the thick masonry, and at a certain moment, upon a signal, the occupants of the caravanserai raised a shout and fired a shot into the darkness, at which the robbers fled. They, however, became involved with a caravan just coming into Sulaimania, and a cry was raised among the muleteers. The people round about, sleeping on their roofs, woke at the noise, and in the surprise and confusion of the moment, imagining the Hamavands had at last carried out their threat of raiding Sulaimania, commenced a brisk fire upon the caravan, killing some mules and wounding a couple of muleteers who had not been able to convince the natives of their harmlessness in time. The robbers had taken advantage of the turmoil to get away, and by the time the caravan had once more got under way, half the people were beginning to find out the cause.

Such events would take place every night, the shaikhs taking advantage of the time to revenge themselves upon their enemies, and at the same time shout defiance at the Constitutional Government. It was seldom that we could sleep quietly from dark till dawn, for the firing around us, and the bullets that often buzzed overhead, kept us alert.

I was sitting in my courtyard a few days after the night attempt on the caravanserai when a moth-eaten creature in a kind of blue uniform with red shoulder-straps presented himself at the door. This was one of the four "policemen" of the place, a visit from whom I had been expecting for some time, for the fat police

commissaire had been annoying Habib with enquiries
as to my identity and reasons for staying in Sulaimania,
and it had occurred to me that he would at some time
demand my passport. The policeman now enquired
whence I had come, and why staying in Sulaimania;
and on my asserting that I was from Constantinople
and bound for Persia, but trying to do some business
in Sulaimania till the country settled a little, flatly
contradicted me, told me I was from Persia, and a
suspect, and demanded my passports. These I utterly
refused, and offered to come and see the mutasarrif
(governor) with him, claiming exemption from such
annoyance, as a subject of England, and pointing out
that now I had been six weeks in Sulaimania there was
time to have seen if I had any nefarious intentions,
and to have demanded proofs of my identity sooner.
The man was not, however, satisfied, and continued to
demand the papers, and I to refuse him, while the
people of the quarter gradually collected, and each, as
he or she learned, broke into protestations of my
respectability, and guaranteed my honesty. As the
policeman still remained, the women began to express
themselves somewhat freely regarding his behaviour, and
at length, seeing that no good could be done by staying
—only possible harm—for the people were inclined to
be unpleasant to him, he discontinued his demands and
returned to the bazaar. My good-hearted neighbours
urged me to complain to the mutasarrif, or at any rate
get the affair settled over the heads of the police, or,
they prophesied, I should have great trouble with them,
and the annoyance they would consider it their duty to
give me.

So I adopted their counsels, and went first to see
old Mustafa Beg and ask his views. I found him in
his cell, drinking a cup of coffee he had just brewed,
and on seeing me he beamed and gave the full salutation, as was his wont, the sonorous " Salamun 'alaikum
wa rahmatu'llah wa barikatahu." He insisted on my
taking coffee, which was a long operation, for he had to

make it over a little charcoal brazier, and having made it, find another cup, for he had but one in use, and only a single saucer in all when the second cup was found in a bag full of odds and ends.

I then told him what had happened, and as the recital proceeded, his indignation, never far to seek, burst forth in such phrases as "Adabsiz!" "Keupek ughlu!" "Tarbiatsiz!" (Mannerless! Sons of dogs! Ignorant creatures!), and then affirmed that he would at once see the commissaire of police and demand an apology. On second thoughts, however, he considered it wiser to seek assistance from the Mudir Effendi of the School. He bustled around, and having changed his trousers and coat—for he put aside his better clothes when in his cell, to save them—locked his door, and we went to the school, where we found the school-master on his bench in the garden. To him the old man poured out the tale in fluent Turkish, while the effendi nodded his head and played with his beads, and when he had finished, the old man banged with his stick upon the ground and once more abused the police. The Mudir Effendi then asked me why I had really come here, and I pointed out that even had I come as a "sayyah" or tourist, that no objection could be raised unless I be proved to engage myself in an undesirable pursuit. Further, that as far as circumstances permitted I had occupied myself in business, but that it was some-what difficult to trade in a place whence no roads were open to the neighbouring districts. This he agreed to, and having asked me to state that I was a British subject, said he would speak to the police. He said they had a right to demand the "ubur tezkere," or Turkish travelling passport, but none to remove other passports, nor were they authorised to annoy even a suspect in his own house.

As I could expect nothing more from him, I thanked him and left, and he with Mustafa Beg went towards the Serai or Governor's house to see the police commissaire, who had an office there.

CHAPTER XIII

LIFE IN SULAIMANIA (*continued*)

DURING this time Hama had returned once with a large number of mule-loads of "run" from Halabja, and was great with projects of a journey to Bagdad to buy sugar. The road to that place was still closed, and the only means of access to the south was by Halabja and Khaniqin, a large frontier town on the Bagdad Kermanshah road. All the merchants of the place were itching to be off and away to Bagdad, for the sugar that in April had cost two krans a loaf was now selling for five, and there were days at the coffee-house when one could not get tea, the sugar having run out, and people, from force of habit, sat there smoking cigarettes and discussing politics, tealess.

But in his commercial schemes, Hama, with all the characteristic of the Kurd to the fore, quite forgot that he had left outstanding at Halabja a number of debts which he must collect before more money was risked, and was hoping to rake in a good profit on a new undertaking, while disregarding the loss on the old one. So I had to send him back to Halabja, for he had disposed of the fifty pairs of shoes mostly on credit, and had but a hazy idea of who the buyers were. He sat at the edge of the tank twiddling his fingers and puzzling his brains to remember to whom he had given the shoes, while I tried to make a list, which was finely descriptive where he could not remember the names. One had taken a pair for twelve krans, "who was the second rider of

Majid Beg's men from Narinjalan"; another, "a big man
who sits at the corner of Shaul the Jew's shop, in the
bazaar"; another, "a man I met in the coffee-house, who
was talking to Hama Rasha of Ababail"; and so on.
Lady Adela herself had taken some, and there were
quite a number of her servants whose shoes, according
to Hama, were also chargeable to her, though apparently
she never consented to pay for them. So I sent him
away again to Halabja, and in his place engaged a
small boy, son of the Hama who was the caravanserai
keeper of Matti. This boy was content to serve for a
penny every three days, and his food. He was a child
of extraordinarily acute intelligence. He had picked
up some Persian in the bazaars, and displayed great
aptitude in learning it when spoken to him. But if his
intelligence helped him thus, it also assisted in making
him a great trial to both his father and the Christians in
the caravanserai. For he was the leader of several gangs
of small hooligans, was continually fighting, and obeyed
only in a small degree his father. His mother, a most
estimable soul, who came to make bread for me, was in
despair of him, for he was quite out of her hands, and
did just as he pleased with her. By making himself a
great nuisance to the Christians, he had instituted a
kind of toll, which he received on demand, a piastre or
two at a time. He would, for instance, come to Habib,
demanding his fee, and if it be refused, as it was sometimes, would jump upon the unfortunate man's back
and half throttle him, or sweep round and round his
office, overturning the wares and dealing destruction as
he went. If he were chastised, he returned, fortified
with genuine fury, to the fray, and the easiest way to
deal with him was to give him his twopence. When
he came to me, I naturally earned the gratitude of all
his victims, but he still found time to run round to the
caravanserai and hurl a taunt or two at its occupants.
He was a child of the Aorami, that tribe of Kurdistan
which is not Kurd, which claims descent from Rustam
himself, and counts its place of origin to be Demavend.

The neighbours were not particularly pleased at his advent, for he carried war into their territory, and from the roofs, the playground of children in the summer, he raided the courtyards, and taught all the quiet children of the quarter the wild games he delighted in. The women stood in dread of him, for he would, when sent upon an errand to borrow a pot or pan, a common enough errand in these parts, remain for an hour teasing.

According to the custom of Sulaimania, there were during the day none but women in the houses; and in our quarter, where small merchants and shopkeepers lived, the men were out from early morning to late evening. My interests took me but little outside on some days of the week, and as I became known, and the presence of the old dame rendered such a proceeding not indecorous, the female portion of the surrounding inhabitants would spend some part of their not too fully occupied time chatting. For the most part they were merry people, like all Kurdish women, free from any affectations of speech or manner, saying what they meant without an attempt at softening rough corners from the subject—saying it while they looked one straight in the eyes, so to speak—and laughing heartily at the pleasantries that abound in Kurdish conversation, with no sign of what we call "flirtation," nor self-conscious tricks of any kind.

Breadmaking days were the time for a regular meeting of such, and when, if at home, I would retire to my room. The professional woman baker would arrive early in the morning with a bag of flour, and Ghafur, the child of wrath, would be sent round to borrow a big copper pan from one of the neighbours, the capture of which he usually signalled by beating a tattoo upon its resonant sides all the way up the street. The woman baker was by this time drinking her tea with the old house-dame, listening to the oft-told tale of her son's death on the Bagdad road, and weeping a tear or two in sympathy. With the advent of Ghafur, she would speedily desert the tea—for she was, and I hope still is,

a busy woman—and get to mixing her flour. This operation was always performed under the little space of
roofing just inside the open courtyard door, so when
the neighbours, bound upon their multifarious house-to-
house errands, passed by, it was natural that they should
stroll in to assist. If they did not, then Ghafur would
be sent to beat them up, an operation which he fully
appreciated, for to bake the bread well required two or
three, and as we had no earth-oven, someone else's must
be heated, and then of course others who had a little
bread to bake would ask the favour of cooking theirs
after ours, in the still hot oven; for the heating costs
money, and the opportunity of baking at another's fire is
never lost by a good Kurdish housewife.

So as a rule we had as assistants at the game of
kneading and rolling into balls, ready for slapping into
thin flap-jacks, the carpenter's wife from opposite, a
sturdy creature, hard-worked and hard-working. She
had five children, whom she kept clean and tidy, two of
whom usually accompanied her, fair, curly headed
youngsters with pale blue eyes, and as rosy cheeked
as only a Kurd or a Persian is among the Middle Eastern
people. Then there were the two sisters from next door,
wives of two brothers who kept a coffee-house, lazy
creatures who sat about and smoked cigarettes. Occasionally one, Adela, wife of the ward of the children in whose
house I lived, would look in, but she was a haughty
creature, of velvets and golden ornaments and diamond
rings, the beauty of the quarter, who knew her own
importance. She certainly was very beautiful, and had
the added advantage possessed by many Kurdish women
over those of the neighbouring races—height, and a fine
straight height too.

But the best of these good-looking Sulaimanian
women — for they are a well-favoured people — was
Gulchin, flighty, good-hearted Gulchin. She was a tall
girl of about eighteen, a little pale for prettiness, but
of finely formed features. The gossips of the quarter
objected to her because she was light-hearted and ran

from house to house much as my serving-child Ghafur did, chaffing and teasing. She had quite a sad little history, too, and concealed under her frivolous manner lay a sorrow that broke out in tears sometimes when the other women returned her harmless badinage with a taunt, when she would fly to her house and sit in a corner sobbing till the natural buoyancy of her spirit asserted itself, and she came forth a little sobered, but still ready to meet the others.

She had been the young wife of a certain Taufiq, a handsome lad who had a good position under the local government, and a large house. With him she had been very happy, and had borne him a child. Unfortunately there were a mother-in-law and grand-mother, who, each detesting Gulchin, laid their wits together to eject her. So they spread rumours con-cerning her, to give a cause of irritation to her husband, and at the same time, with the assistance of a hedge-priest, discovered certain invalidities in her marriage bond. With this in hand, they continued the dissemina-tion of scandal, till the husband, hearing it from certain respectable people, came in wrath to Gulchin. She being a spirited girl, and moreover, innocent, naturally gave the retort very direct, and a quarrel occurred which for the time embittered one against the other. The old women now came to Taufiq with the defective bond, and taking the opportune moment of his resentment and wrath, induced him to divorce his wife.

So, disgraced and stripped of her good clothes and her ornaments, which, though she might have taken, she refused, Gulchin came to the house of her aunt Asima Khan, my neighbour, a descendant of the ancient priestly families of Hakkari, and as such bearing the masculine title " Khan."

Here Gulchin was reduced to the level of a superior maid, and had to do the housework, but her uncle gave her clothes and protected her, for he, Abdullah, was a grave, respected man, the senior of the quarter.

Had Gulchin's resentment against her husband con-

tinued, it would have been well for her, but unfortunately,
she was too good-hearted a girl to hate anybody, and
really loved him, so she wept tears of regret and
remembrance. And worst of all for her she had, in a
soft moment, confided her trouble to one of the other
women, and had become a subject for chaff, good-
humoured enough certainly, but hurtful all the same,
and had she not been naturally light-hearted would have
led a very sorry life.

What lost her the respect of her neighbours was
the habit she had on hot days of coming outside the
house without her turban, bareheaded except for a
tiny skull-cap, her thick, long hair exposing its ten or
twelve ropes of thick plaits uncovered by the veil that
accompanies the turban. But she was perfectly honest;
an immoral woman is the exception in Sulaimania, and
she scoffed at those who sacrificed comfort to false
modesty. Ghafur had succeeded, in a hunt for someone
to mend my clothes, in capturing her for the job, and
she would spend some of her mornings with the old
house-dame, often dropping her work to romp with
the child. Her methods were original sometimes, for
she had little patience. One morning she swept into
the courtyard at a moment when I had just discovered
a piece torn out of the sleeve of a shirt, and called to
her to mend it. She said she had no linen and no
money to buy any, and Ghafur not being there to get
some from the bazaar, she tore a piece from her own,
and then, seeing the expanse of white skin thus discovered, fled, blushing, to pin it up in a corner.

It was not long after my first visit from the police
that Sayyid Nuri again called. This time he came without
the knowledge of old Mustafa Beg, and was accompanied
only by a kind of confidential companion-servant and
a hideous old man whom he made the excuse for his
visit, for he said he wanted to introduce him to me
because he was a doctor, and I had considerable knowledge in the science. He was a horrible-looking old
creature, with a beaked nose and but three yellow teeth,

and had an intensely evil look in his small eyes. Like all of his class, and Sulaimanians in particular, he commenced asking a number of questions concerning myself; but his native suspicion did not allow him to believe most of the replies, and at last he asked if I had a passport, to which I answered in the affirmative. Sayyid Nuri here interrupted and objected to this inquisition, for though he himself had no scruples in asking the most intimate and offensive questions, he demurred when another would arrogate the privilege to himself. The old creature bent towards him and said, " If we could only see his passport, then we should know what he is "—but I interrupted him by telling him that had I a dozen passports in my pocket I should not display them to him, a remark which amused Sayyid Nuri and annoyed the old man. Then he put forward the proposition he said he had come to make. It appeared he possessed an old Arabic book setting forth the medical science as understood by the Arabs; the old Greek theory of heat and cold, the calorific and frigid temperament, with its diseases all classed under the two headings and cured by medicines antagonistic to such conditions of the body. He now proposed that he should produce this book, and with a stock of herbs purchased from the Jews, go into partnership with me, a proceeding which he asserted "would fill our pockets speedily enough, for a combination of European and Oriental skill will cover all the ailments of the people and provide an alternative to those cases which you cannot now touch, namely, the conservative part of the populace that objects to the " new Medicine " — the " Tibb-i-Jadid."

The more I protested the impossibility of such a combination, the component parts of which were too antagonistic to be possibly considered together, the more he pressed his point, affirming that I was a fool to let professional jealousy thus spoil my chances; to which I replied, that I was not even a doctor—an assertion they both laughed to scorn, and pointed to the bottles above their heads as incontrovertible proof. The "doctor" absolutely failed to understand why I should not join him, and exhibited very considerable chagrin at my consistent refusal, waving aside all my excuses— that I did not perform, even if I knew anything about medicine; that I had too small a stock; that I was very shortly leaving Sulaimania; and so on.

"No drugs!" he said, "buy some Epsom salts and phenacetin, that is as good a stock-in-trade as you can desire; and anything else you may require, why, we will make up some kind of concoction. Names are plentiful, and one looks no worse than another upon a bottle of the same stuff."

The creature pressed so hard that I did not know how to be rid of him, when a diversion came from Sayyid Nuri. He had been wandering about the room, and had discovered a small cube of yellowish-grey earth, the use of which he demanded. I explained to him that this was a piece of earth from the sacred tomb of the saint Ali, an apparatus of prayer not to be dispensed with by any good Shi'a Musulman.

"What! do you pray to this?" he cried.

"No," I replied, "but we place it before us on the ground. As you know, among the Sunni you place your foreheads upon the ground in praying, you prostrate yourselves upon any earth or any dust upon which you find yourselves. We do the same, but we see no harm in having a piece of consecrated earth between our foreheads and the ground, so that when we touch earth in our prostrations we may rest the head upon a spot more sacred than the place we are in, and at the same time have before us a reminder of the great man and saint and martyr whom even Sunni revere."

"Ah!" he exclaimed, "and that is how a Shi'a says his prayers! Why, I tell you, man, that such is idolatry and heathenism. Your prayers are worthless said over such a thing, and you stand in danger of terrible and eternal retribution for such a sin."

"And you Shi'a," he recommenced with some heat,

"are the folk that curse the name of Uthman, Umar, and Abu Bekr, and revile us, rising in the morning with abuse of us on your lips, and not slumbering till you have cursed us !"

The boy was losing his temper, and began to fumble with his dagger, but the "doctor" did his best to get him away out of the room, telling him that though some Shi'a might do as he said, I was not of the rampant kind, and at any rate should not be responsible for others' actions.

"Then let him renounce the schism," he grumbled ; but the old man had his answer ready to this :

"Shall not he follow his fathers? and be damned or saved with them ? Were he to desert now, he would fling off his new tenets directly he got away. Let him be, I say, he has not attempted to spread his doctrine ; let him pray in his fashion, the sin is upon him for continuing, and the merit yours, for you have pointed it out."

With that he rose and took his leave, and the boy seeing no further amusement in staying, followed him, bidding me adieu sullenly and with a bad grace. That was the last time he entered my house, for, a day or two after, Shaikh Ahmad was appointed Qaim Maqam of Chemchemal, and took his son with him.

But I was not to have peace for long. Only a few mornings after this, two policemen turned up, with a message from the commissaire of police, that he wished to see me at once. As I had imagined that he had ceased worrying about my passport, I followed them, wondering what he wanted. He was seated in a tailor's shop in the bazaar, a fat man, with a cunning look in his little blue eyes, and his mouth concealed under a heavy yellow moustache.

He spoke nothing but Turkish and Arabic, and as I reached him, addressed me in the former.

"Have you a passport?" he asked; "if so, why have you not submitted it to me?"

"Because so far you have not asked for it, nor done

anything except hint at the illegal objects of my visit here; had you asked reasonably for it I would have shown it."

"Well, I wish to know what you are doing here—why you came, why you do not go, where you came from, your name, your——"

"These," I broke in, "are known to everyone in Sulaimania but yourself. I came here to do business, and have done some, and would have done more had the place here been in a normal state of quietness. I came from Kirkuk, and as you were with the same caravan you should have known that; and as at Kirkuk my passport was seen and stamped, I am not going to volunteer details as to whence I came there, for it is not your business. As to why I do not go, I am hoping to leave very soon for Bagdad—as soon as your bold Turkish army can induce the Hamavands to leave a road open."

This kind of conversation in the open bazaar, and among a crowd of Kurds, half of whom understood, he had not expected, and appeared a little hurt at a tone he was not apparently used to.

"Well," he said, "at any rate I must see your passport, so you had better fetch it."

So, accompanied by a policeman I went back to the house and got my English passport, and the Turkish travelling passport issued to all who journey in that country. By now it had received ill-use, and the name was illegible, as well as particulars of religion and birthplace. These I brought to him there, and he inspected the travelling passport, and after humming and hawing, said :

"Yes, this is very well, but the essential thing is an identification passport. Where is it?"

I showed him the Foreign Office passport, which also interested the Kurds round about.

"This," he said, "is not a passport, it is merely a permit from your Government to travel."

"Well," I said, "can you read it?" a remark that elicited guffaws from the listeners.

"No," he answered, "of course I cannot."

"Then," I said, "you must either take my word or suspend the enquiry, you cannot blame me because you do not know English. I have stated that I am a British subject, and there is my British passport, with the visé of the Turkish Consul in London on the back, and there is my name, 'Ghulam Husain,' upon it," and I pointed to where my own name was written in English.

"Well, that may be," he said; "but yet it is not the personal passport such as we all carry, and which is essential for identification."

"Such a document," I said, "is before you."

Somewhat annoyed, he broke out:

"No! no! it is not, this is a travelling passport; where is the passport you were given when you had completed your time in the army?"

"Well," I said, "that I do not possess——"

"Oh! oh! why not?"

"Simply because we have the honour not to be Turkish subjects, do not have to serve in the army unless we please, and are not called upon to carry passports of identification everywhere with us; for we are not subject to the inquisition and annoyance enjoyed under Turkish rule, and there are too many of us, and we have too much to do, to waste our time and money on paying ornaments like yourself to harass us."

The poor police effendi had never been thus insulted before, and rose furious. The Kurds were enjoying the scene, and one or two advised the policeman to leave me alone, as it was evident that I was not to be scared sufficiently to bribe him.

He had my passports in his hand, and stood for a moment irresolute, so, thinking to bring matters to an end, I said:

"What do you want?—tell me, and perhaps we can conclude."

"What do I want?" he exclaimed; "why, satisfaction for the indignities you have put me to, your passport of identification, and a surety that you are not a seditious person: I must hold an examination!"

"Good," I said, "let us hold an examination, but not before I have seen the Governor. As a foreign subject I demand my right of appeal to him, and as you know, a British Consul is coming here in a few days (such was the bazaar rumour), and complaint of you and your ways will then be easy."

"Very well," and he shrugged in anger, "if you desire to increase your troubles, come along."

So together we left the bazaars and came through the long, busy street to the outside edge of the town. He became friendly. He took me by the hand, and we walked thus hand in hand while he began asking me again, and this time in a friendly, solicitous way, why I had wanted to come here.

"Why," I said, "in olden times, when there were Hamadan merchants here, you did not question them, and annoy them by such queries and doubts. They were buyers and sellers, and so would I be, were the country more secure. Meanwhile, what can I possibly do but wait the moment when peace will allow of commercial venture?"

"With what places would you trade?" he asked.

"With Saqiz and Bana, Keui and Kirkuk, Panjwin and Sina, as do others," I said.

"How do you know all these places, if you are a stranger, and where did you learn Kurdish? I am afraid you do not tell the truth about your past, my brother; were it not better to tell me at once why you are here. Your passports are defective. I have no personal animosity against you, and should like to see you often, but there are strong suspicions, and if we cannot be satisfied of your harmlessness, we shall have to deport you to Mosul."

"Good," I said, "I am not enchanted with Sulaimania, and such a step would put me in your debt, for as I am a foreign subject, you would have to provide me with guards there, and on my arrival your Govern-

U

ment would have to reimburse my commercial losses due to the abandonment of my business here, besides which, with the assistance of the Consul, I should be able to complain direct to the Vali of you and your methods."

With this we arrived at the Serai, or Government house, and he took me into a little office where three or four Turks were seated upon a bench, idle. These saluted me, and having asked the reason of my visit, and having been informed by the policeman, looked upon me with suspicion, and while he retired to make an appointment, asked if I had not a passport. I explained that I had all necessary passports, but that the ignorance of their officials apparently involved them in difficulties. At this they looked serious and offended, and held their peace.

Anon the effendi returned, and took me down a dark passage to another little office where was a fat Turk called the "Tabur Aghassi," and before him I was arraigned. Two or three Kurds were present, and as I knew one of them he took the opportunity to ask what the trouble was, while the policeman explained it in Turkish to the fat man. I suppose I expressed my disgust very freely, for the Kurds laughed heartily, and the policeman, who did not understand a word of Kurdish, turned sharply and asked what I was saying. Meanwhile the Tabur Aghassi was examining my English passport upside down, and looking grave. The various seals and endorsements upon the back interested him immensely, and at last he found a partially erased visé of the Turkish Consul in Kermanshah, which had been attached some time before I left that place for Bagdad.

The sight of a Turkish seal seemed to reassure him, so I pointed out the visé of the Turkish Consul in London, which he examined closely. These seemed to allay his suspicions, and in conjunction with the Turkish travelling passport appeared to put them at rest, and he told the policeman so. That individual—who had not been able to read the various endorsements—was somewhat chagrined, but thought to raise a difficulty by asking how I had got through Kirkuk without police inspection and seal upon my passport. I took the document from him and showed him the Kirkuk police seal, but he could not read it, and professed to believe it false; so I handed it to a Kurd, who with some gusto read out the inscription on the seal, at which even the Tabur Aghassi smiled, and the Kurds laughed, for I could not refrain from a complimentary expression upon the capabilities of a police commissaire who could not read the seals of his confrère and must rely on Kurds to do it for him. By now he had lost his temper, and I had too, for he continued to make fatuous remarks, and I commenced talking to him in a strain he was not used to hear, certainly not before Kurds, so he snatched up the passport and departed. The Tabur Aghassi was looking rather cross too, for he naturally did not approve of such procedure, but he sent a man after the police-man to tell him to seal and record my passports and let me get away, for I had done enough damage in the place already.

In five minutes he returned the document passed and sealed, and demanded half a mejidie, a last attempt. I took the paper from him, bade farewell to the Tabur Aghassi, and as I left the room told him in Kurdish that I would pay him in Mosul when I was deported. By the time this was translated I was away.

The whole place had heard of the affair, and I passed a row of sympathetic Kurds as I left, who made uncom-plimentary remarks anent all policemen and Government officials as I bade them good-morning.

From here I went to the caravanserai, and found Habib and Matti in a terrible stew, for they had already heard that I had been locked in a dungeon and fined heavily, and I was greeted by them and by the Kurdish merchants with a pleasant warmth as I entered the place, appearing to them as one who had escaped from certain disaster by a rare and wonderful luck.

Habib's fear had been doubled, for the policeman, before he sent for me, had been to his shop and held an examination of him, hinting that by his actions and friendliness with me, a suspect, he laid himself out to punishment and fines. Altogether, Habib was in a sore mood, for he, being a progressive fellow, talking Turkish, had cultivated an acquaintance with the Turkish officials, and the policeman had naturally annoyed him sooner than Matti, who spoke only Arabic and Kurdish, but who had a great deal more to do with me than had Habib. Besides, the Kurds and Christians held it a splendid opportunity to chaff Habib over the desire for Turkish favour and acquaintance that had thus led him near danger.

Despite the satisfactory ending of the affair, I knew that now I had definitely made enemies of the officials in the place, and should be worried whenever possible. Sulaimania possessed no particular charms, and as the country was getting more and more disturbed each day— for the Hamavands now burned the posts—the prospect of business was absolutely nothing ; so I began to consider the possibility of going away. Matti, to whom I carried most of my troubles, was gloomy, and predicted no good to anyone staying in Sulaimania. If they did not go now, he said, they would be forced to leave later, for with the shaikhs and Turks together, prices going up, taxes increasing, and security always doubtful, trade was ceasing to exist, and there would soon be no bread to buy, and no money to buy it with.

He was feeling very sore just then, for he had tried to get some carpets to Mosul by sending them *via* Keui Sanjaq, where the road was open, but they had been looted on the way. He now strongly advised me to leave Sulaimania if I could, but pointed out, at the same time, the impossibility of such a step, for several reasons. First, Hama was still at Halabja, the Jew not having fetched in the second consignment of "run," and dallying in the villages; secondly, if I left matters thus, Matti could not be responsible for getting the money back, for, as he truly said, " An absentee owner is the blessing of the dishonest debtor, and the despair of the agent "; and then, worse than all, there was no road to anywhere, except to Persia, and I was not keen just at that moment to go there. Had I been able to get to Kermanshah, I might have done so, but the road by Juanru was absolutely impassable, and the Kalhur country was upside down, so a journey there was out of the question. I could have got to Mosul, but my object was Bagdad, and the roads there either *via* Kifri or Kirkuk were absolutely closed, the Hamavands making it their business to see that none passed. The posts now only went at intervals, and refused to carry anything larger than letters, which could be concealed under the clothing of the peasant who carried them, and even then the Hamavands sometimes caught him and beat him, burning the letters. So all I could do was, like Matti and the rest of them, sit quiet and wait.

One morning Hama turned up unexpectedly with four loads of "run" that I had not been expecting, an instalment of the last amount. He also produced some tomans he had collected on account of the shoes. He had also had some interesting experience with the Shaikh ul Islam, that disagreeable person I had gone to Biara specially to see when I had been at Halabja. It appeared that one afternoon Hama had turned up as usual at Lady Adela's "divan," and had found the Shaikh ul Islam there. Without returning Hama's salutation, he asked what he had done with his Christian master. This created quite a sensation, and Hama hardly knew what to say. Lady Adela and Uthman Pasha, who were both there, demanded explanations, and the Shaikh ul Islam rose and denounced me, saying that he had met me in Constantinople, where I wore European clothes; that there I professed to be a European, while here in Musulman garments I claimed to be a Persian. In Constantinople, he said, he was convinced that I was not a European. He failed to understand what I was, but thought it probable that I was not a Musulman, and

I must have evil designs to have found my way in an unobtrusive manner thus to the heart of southern Kurdistan, with the Persian side of which I was familiar. He rose and denounced me as a spy, a maker of mischief and a danger to the country, and ended by cursing Hama for having anything to do with me. But he had been too hasty, for he received an unexpected rebuff from Lady Adela. She had apparently seen me saying my Musulman prayers on several occasions, and, with almost as much heat as the Shaikh ul Islam himself, defended me, saying that it was perfectly well known that I was a Persian of Shiraz, a fact which was evident also by my speech, and in this she was supported by Mansur, who strenuously denied that I was a Christian, for he also had seen me praying, and that in his own room. Others testified to my good faith, and the Shaikh ul Islam's position began to appear uncomfortable, when Hama put the cap upon his discomfiture by an extraordinary statement. He recalled to the memory of those present my journey to Biara, and said he would now explain the reason of the Shaikh ul Islam's enmity to me, and went on to describe how in Constantinople I had lent him a certain sum of money to help him to go back to his own country. This had never been repaid, and I had, on my way to Persia, purposely come by Sulaimania hoping to get back the loan, and for this purpose had visited the Shaikh ul Islam at Biara. He, wishing to evade his just debts, had repudiated it, and taken an attitude of enmity in order to scare me away; and now, finding that I was in the neighbourhood, doubtless hoped, by provoking a feeling hostile to me, to induce me to leave the district. The tables were now fairly turned, and Lady Adela, speaking for herself and the Pasha, signified their disapproval in forcible terms, and told the Shaikh ul Islam that unless he apologised to Hama there and then, they would eject him not only from their house, but from their lands. So with extremely bad grace he did so, and Hama came away covered with the glory that rests upon the vindicated and triumphant.

He was now the bearer of renewed invitations from Uthman Pasha, Lady Adela, and Tahir Beg, to stay with them at Halabja, and was full of schemes for extended trade under their protection.   But he also bore bad news, for he had been escorting several loads of " run " and had lost one, worth the—to him—immense sum of forty tomans, or about seven pounds. The caravan he had accompanied had arrived at Sulaimania very early in the morning, and his attention being taken to a mule that had fallen, he had let his other loads go ahead, through a village outside the town.

Here someone had taken advantage of the absence of a guardian quietly to lead a donkey and his load into a courtyard, and the caravan passed on, the absence of the animal not being discovered till they got into Sulaimania. Hama had spent a morning raising witnesses to the theft, a quite possible thing, although no one could possibly have seen it, and having fixed the crime upon certain villagers in collusion with a rival dealer in " run," he was going to find the police and have an enquiry held.   It did not appear to me of much use to do anything, for I knew the matter must go to the police commissaire, and I knew also that he would take such steps in the affair as would fulfil two aims : one, that I should not receive my goods again ; the other, that he should get out of this that emolument which he had hoped to gain by his prosecution of the passport scheme.   However, the owner of the donkey would do his best to assist Hama, if the stuff were to be found, of which I was doubtful, for it was a thousand to one by now that it had been disposed of in jars and pots, and the skins destroyed.   So I let Hama do what he could.   Matti and Habib were much perturbed, swearing that the whole affair was arranged out of revenge by the police commissaire, and urging me to represent the matter to the temporary mutasarrif or governor, a certain colonel who was replacing the senior while he was at Chemchemal waiting to condemn the Hamavands—when caught.

Old Mustafa Beg, too, who had never ceased his

morning calls, also came and insisted on being allowed to go and see the police commissaire himself and urge him to move in the matter. The old man always had a great sense of his own importance, and could not see what was so obvious, that he had been shelved, stowed away into this remote corner of the Turkish Empire to be allowed to wear out and give out gradually. He had received a fresh appointment in the last few days, which was equally a sinecure with the former one, for he could not get to the place, and had he done so the Kurds would have ejected him.

He was very keen for me to accept the invitation of the Mudir of the Military School to a great rejoicing to be held by the Turkish part of the population in honour of the anniversary of popular government in Turkey, and he showed me copies of telegrams received by various officials. There were orders for no less than one hundred and twenty guns to be fired; five hundred liras from the revenue were to be expended on a feast and upon decorations. All loyal subjects were called upon to place lamps upon their roofs at night, and flags over their doors by day.

The bazaar was to be closed, and a band was to play from morning till night, when the fireworks were to be let off in the big open space in front of the Serai. The band played, I remember, by fits and starts; but it was somewhat defective, for the bandmaster, whose pay was irregular and small, had pawned several of the brass instruments. Some ten guns were fired, the Tabur Aghassi, who was temporarily responsible for the affair, having abstracted the full amount of gunpowder from the armoury and sold the bulk to the gunmakers of the town. So the affair was a little ineffective, particularly as the Kurds refused to close the bazaars or decorate.

Mustafa Beg, however, did not foresee this, and imagined it was going to be a very fine affair, and his disgust afterwards was as loudly expressed as his praise before.

A night or two after this we were awakened, as we were nearly every night, by shots, but this time they were very close, and an uproar accompanied them. Two or three dark figures could be discerned running along the roof of the bazaar, and they ran the gauntlet of all the fire of the surrounding population, that was sleeping on the roofs with its guns beside it. Like all these affairs, however, it died down without anyone being the wiser, and we slept again. In the dusk of early morning I heard a voice calling from the street, "Agha Ghulam Husain!" and looking over the roof edge saw Matti, who had run from the caravanserai, and who was still doing up his waistbelt.

"Come quickly!" he said.

Snatching up my abba, I ran downstairs and joined him in the street. He was very agitated, and in reply to my questions could only gasp out "Khan-i-Ghafur Agha" —the Ghafur Agha caravanserai—towards which we were proceeding almost at a run.

Round the door a little crowd had gathered, and at the far side, near the room I had once stayed in, next door to Mustafa Beg, a knot, among whom I recognised the municipal and regimental surgeon, a little Greek. As I approached they beckoned, and I ran forward to see what they surrounded.

Lying where he had fallen was old Mustafa Beg, his face, always white, now a dreadful colour in the dusk of dawn, contrasting with the orgy of red his body displayed. A knife had entered the pit of his stomach, ripped it for nine inches, and allowed all that was inside to emerge. He lay in a pool of blood into which the bystanders stepped, and which made a little morass around him. He was conscious, but too feeble to do aught except move his eyes and whisper. He had asked for me, and now I had come, and leaned over, ear to his mouth, he whispered to me to undo his belt.

This I asked the surgeon to do, and as gently as he could he removed it. This was not all, for the old man had a little to say, which he could only do gradually. I caught the words as they came from his lips:

"Geundir Tarabulusda, har- . . . bir shai . . . var.

Allah! Allah! oghlu . . . oghlu . . . san insanidin . . . baqi . . . haivanlar. Tav . . . akkul . . . ullah, Allah, Al . . ."

His life passed, his last breath calling God.

"Send to Tripoli all that there is," he had said. "God, God . . . son! . . . son! . . . thou wert human . . . the rest . . . savages . . . I resign myself to God . . . God . . .!"

Matti, who stood a little distance away, was gulping and weeping, for he had a soft and true heart, and the little Greek snivelled as he began to prepare the body for removal. I sat a space away off and wept, for I had loved the old man. Only the Kurds stood around unmoved : they had seen worse than this, and might do or suffer it any day.

The surgeon, who was a capable little man, had already ordered a coffin, and this, hastily prepared, now arrived, and we left the caravanserai to the washers of the dead, who had arrived. We should return when the work was done. Because there is nowhere else to wait, we went to the coffee-house, and there heard how it happened.

Ghafur Agha, who owned the caravanserai, had been "Rais-i-Baladiyya," or Mayor, till a short time ago, and while holding that post had fallen out with the shaikhs. Now he had been deprived of his office, and the Shaikh family lost no time in showing him their open hostility by raiding his caravanserai. There were in the place one or two business offices, of which that of Haji Fattah was a prey they hoped to seize. The robbers had also known that one of the Jewish merchants had brought to his office the day before a thousand tomans in silver, and they hoped to loot this. How they got into the caravanserai no one seemed to know, the doorkeeper waking to find his heavy portals open. The noise of their breaking into the office of Haji Fattah had awakened Mustafa Beg, who slept in an old palanquin on the opposite verandah, and impetuous as he always was, he commenced shouting loudly for Hasan the doorkeeper. The robbers came to see who it was, and found him sitting there, and warned him if he made any more noise they would kill him. So for a moment he was silent. But he emerged from his palanquin, apparently to see that the door of his cell was locked, and could not restrain his inclination to advise the outside world of what was going on. So he shouted loudly for the night-watchmen of the streets; but before a moment had passed, a Turkoman, one of the robbers, had clasped him round the neck, and with his long, curved dagger ripped him and left him where he fell.

This we learned from the people in the coffee-house, one of whom had heard the deposition which the doorkeeper had made to the police; and we learned with considerable satisfaction that the robbers had got away with nothing of value, for the Jew's money had been too well concealed, and Haji Fattah's valuables were in a heavy iron box; and as the night-watchmen appeared soon after the murder of Mustafa Beg and roused the town by firing, they had been forced to climb to the roof and escape that way. The men were recognised by the doorkeeper, who had told their names to the police. This had been kept quiet, but it was known that they were shaikhs' people, so when one arrived and told us that the police commissaire effendi was examining the roofs for foot-marks, a smile of derision went round, for the roofs were almost as hard as stone, and no footmark could possibly leave a trace, and if it could, would have been obliterated by those of the people who had already passed and repassed the course of escape, for in Sulaimania the women use the roofs as a thoroughfare.

As no one came to inform us of the readiness of the body, we went to Matti's office there to wait. Matti was much affected by the sad event, and seemed to have no inclination for business that morning, and as the talk was bound to turn upon the ways and means of getting out of Sulaimania, we once more got to the subject of my leaving, and we arranged that if it were possible I should do so as soon as any opportunity offered, by caravan to Keui, whence I could get to Altun Keupri, or by one of the Shuan donkey-owners, who struck away from Sulaimania and reached Kirkuk by a long detour through their own country.

And in that way, things being thus settled, it came about that Matti brought himself to the point of asking a question I suppose he must have wanted to put many a time.

"Now, as you are soon going to leave us," he said, "I want to put a question to you, at which, if you do not approve, you must not be offended, and will not answer. It is some time now since you first came here, and we have come to know one another pretty well, and I have done my best to help you. But I have seen one thing, and that is, that you have never done business before in Kurdistan, and that even had you, you are not sufficiently interested in the getting of money to succeed. You do not seem to care whether your speculations render you a profit or not, and your conversation, unlike that of a merchant, is never of money, but of such subjects as those talk of who are at no need to study business. You seem at more pains to cultivate a knowledge of Kurdish and Kurdistan than of its business, and you put yourself at more pains to buy a book than to do anything else. Habib, too, has noticed this, and we have often wondered the reason for a Persian, and a Persian of Shiraz at that, coming here at all; for though there were Persians in the old days here, they were of Hamadan, and a Shirazi has never been seen before. Still, you never volunteered any information, and I have not ventured to put any questions, for fear of offending. I must say that it is this very characteristic, this neglect of business for which you are ostensibly here, that has caused the police to notice you, and had you not won your way out of their clutches, Habib and myself would have suffered severely, for they lose no opportunity of bleeding one, and we might have been put under suspicion and blackmailed unmercifully."

"The only reply to frankness," I said, "is frankness

itself, and I will tell what may possibly surprise you, and which will not, I hope, lead you to consider me an impostor. You, like all the rest, have been deceived into thinking me what I originally represented myself to be, and I have a satisfaction in feeling that while I shall leave the others still under the delusion, I shall have been able to pay you part of the debt of gratitude I owe you by putting you alone in possession of the truth.

"So I must tell you that I am neither Persian nor Turk, nor Kurd nor Chaldean, but an Englishman, born of English parents in England, and brought up in that land; and that fact will perhaps in itself go to partly explain my presence here, for you must know that people of my race are given to wandering over the face of the earth with no other reason than to see it and the people it supports. I have spent nine years of my life in Persia, and there acquired the language and a knowledge of the habits and customs. To gain an intimate acquaintance with the people of that land, I turned Musulman—ostensibly—and passed through a long course of theological training. Two years ago I found myself in Kermanshah, of south-eastern Kurdistan, and finding the people and language an interesting study, resolved to pursue it whenever possible. So, after having been in England last year for some time, I found the fascination of Kurdistan and its mountains upon me, and resolved to visit it once more for a time. But as a European it was impossible and undesirable; for, as you know, a European would be an alien, a stranger without acquaintance, in an isolated position and a dangerous one, hampered in his movements, and often enough not allowed to go from place to place. Moreover, had I desired to travel thus I could not have done so, for I possessed but little money; so you see, everything pointed to the fact that if I wished to see Kurdistan again, I must go humbly, and as a native. So from Constantinople I set out, disguised, and came away gradually here, where I had wished to remain, in order to learn the language of Sulaimania, which up to the present has been unknown to the Europeans. I have now accomplished this, and want to leave Kurdistan again for a while. But I cannot look over the months I have passed here, Matti, without realising that had you not been here, with your help, your sincerity, your advice, and brotherly friendship—all extended to a man of whom you knew nothing—I should have fared much worse, have fared hardly perhaps, instead of living comfortably with a feeling that when anything went wrong there was always Matti to go to. So, brother, you know now what I am, and why here, and all that remains is to ask your forgiveness, and to tell you that I am, like yourself, a Christian, and no Musulman."

"Allahu akbar!" cried Matti, using a Musulman phrase in his astonishment, "see the works of God, how inexplicable they are! Ghulam Husain, thou who art not Ghulam Husain, all that you tell me of being an Englishman I know to be true, for I see the truth in your eyes; but what matter it, if the friend be English or Russian, Turk or Kurd. What gives me greater joy than ever I felt before, is to think that he, in whom I found a friendly spirit, is of ourselves—of a Christian nation.

"Yet, had I known it before, how much more help I would have given you, for what I have done has been nought but the calling of mere courtesy, and the hospitable spirit incumbent upon all to the stranger, of whatever faith or race he be. Now, if you are resolved to go, I will give you letters to Khwaja Salim, my agent in Kirkuk, and to Matlub in Bagdad. But I place upon you an obligation, by your soul! that you will not, with the European clothes, put off the thoughts and remembrances of Kurdistan, nor let our names slip from your memory. For we are rough and savage, our ways are not yours—though you know ours, and follow them here like ourselves—what we deem comfort you deem savagery, and the European (I know this, for I have been in Beyrout and Aleppo and met the European) ever scoffs at the Eastern land; but we are still men, and if our lives are spent in a gloom of uncivilisation, it is not because we have refused to emerge from it, but because we cannot;

perhaps we should lose our few good points in the strong light of Westernism, and, taking to its comforts, spurn its obligations and become worthless—as I have seen so many become, who have been to Europe and returned. So you have taken us all by surprise; like an enemy in disguise you have penetrated the walls of our strongholds, and I for one am not going to tell the bazaar who has been amongst us."

Then he went on to ask details of my former life in Persia, and the way I had acquired sufficient knowledge of the land and life to pass in bazaar and mosque as I was doing.

During this conversation, one came to inform us that they were about to inter the body of Mustafa Beg. So, following him, we went outside to the graveyard on the southern hill, where on a bare stony slope three or four mulberry trees, bent double by the fierce "rashaba," find a footing among Sulaimania's dead. Here we met the coffin-bearers, who brought the coffin and without ceremony laid it in a shallow grave, covering it with stones and earth. There were but a few of us present, the master of the Military School, Matti, and myself, besides the people hired to bury him; nor could we stay, for the Hamavands were circling about on their ponies not far away.

The town surgeon had paid for his funeral out of the various almost worthless odds and ends he had possessed, together with his clothing, so that all that remained of the estate of the old Mustafa Beg was the four liras he had entrusted to my care. These I guarded, and would take to Bagdad, whence I could send them safely by postal remittance to Tripoli, and be reasonably certain of their getting to their proper destination.

The few of us who had seen the body buried were much affected by the death of the old man, though he was neither of our race nor countries; he was a stranger, and his horrible death in a place where he had lived an unhappy and lonely life, showed at once in a vivid manner the insecurity, and brought home to both Matti and the

master of the School the danger in which they lived, and
made them compare involuntarily their own positions in
the town with that of Mustafa Beg. For though they
were nothing like so friendless, they were equally unpro-
tected, and above all they were strangers in the land.
The sympathy of the Kurd and the people of Persia and
Kurdistan generally for the stranger is a lively one; in
these lands, to be away from home means more than in
countries where communication is rapid and intercourse
between distant points is frequent. The native place is
very dear indeed to the Turk, Persian, and Kurd. It is an
innocent enthusiasm that prompts the dweller in a pestilential and fever-ridden village with salt water, to extol it
as little less than Paradise itself, for the discomforts of life
in a strange land, far from his own language or dialect,
make the place he left appear far superior, and distance
lends an enchantment to his view that leads him to make
the most flattering descriptions of his native place. How
often had old Mustafa Beg told of the beauties of his
Tripoli, its fruits, its busy sea-coast, its climate, the hospitable nature of its inhabitants; and how often had he sighed
to go back, and counted the months to the time when he
should have sufficient money to return; and all his
eulogies had ended with a hope, expressed fervently, that
at least he might die among his own people; but here
we were burying his remains in a land which he hated,
whose people he hated, and of whose language he knew
not two words.

And as we saw the last shovelfuls of earth placed
upon his grave, the watchers on the hill-top cried out
to us to get away to town quickly, for over the valley
came a small party of horsemen, the Hamavands, shooting
at targets as they galloped; and we had to hasten back
lest the living should follow the new-buried dead.

At the house I found Hama, looking wretched. He
had not succeeded in finding the stolen "run," and had
called in the police, who were more disposed to work
up a case against him than help; for they heard whose
servant he was, and had some hope of getting out of

this business what they failed to get out of the passport affair—some money. I am afraid I did not care much, for I was resolved to leave very soon, and knew that it would be impossible to get satisfaction. But as he urged, I went to the acting Mutasarrif, whom I found in a little garden, surrounded by several colonels, all drinking coffee. Once more I had to go through the nuisance of introducing myself, hearing the same comments upon Persia, and answering the same questions regarding my native country, my travels, trade, and aims. Three or four spoke Persian, and were glad of the opportunity to display their knowledge to their more ignorant fellows, so with a few compliments upon their knowledge, I became friendly with them. In the middle of it the police commissaire came in, and seeing me upon the right hand of the deputy-governor, approached with smiles and compliments. The usual course of such things followed. The deputy-governor gave orders in a fierce voice that the stolen property should be immediately forthcoming. The commissaire assured him that that was the only aim in life of his four men, all at work on the affair, and bowed himself out to complete their operations. A soldier was sent to the scene of action, in town, "to make sure the stuff was produced immediately," and I took my leave perfectly satisfied that nothing would be done—as it most surely was not.

During the next two or three days I began to think how I could get away, and had almost settled a contract with a Shuan Kurd to go by donkey through the villages, and by making a detour to the Zab River, come at Kirkuk from the north. But hardly had I provisionally settled with him, than news and a caravan came direct from Kirkuk. The Hamavands had moved south, across the Bagdad road, and the Turks, who had not dared to come out of Chemchemal while they still remained in their country, were now scouring Bazian and its hills, and for the first time since March the road was passable; it was now the end of July.

X

The caravan was to go back in a day or two to bring some of the merchandise that had accumulated during the four months of insecurity. So I made haste to avail myself of this opportunity, and arranged to hire a mule from one Salih, a long-limbed Turkoman of Kirkuk. I paid the rent of my little house, and bade farewell to the various people with whom I had made friends. Asima Khan, the lady who had been instrumental in ridding me of the trouble caused by Sayyid Nuri, came with a number of the other neighbours' wives, and made the occasion of a call upon the old house-dame an opportunity for bidding me good-bye.

I was sorry to part from Gulchin, for she was the freest, most frank, and candid character of all, and her lighthearted ways and open sincerity had done a great deal to make the life in Sulaimania pleasant. She was looking very serious to-day in the company of her aunt Asima Khan, and presented the subdued and humble appearance due from a divorced girl in the presence of her seniors and superiors. So, since it would not be etiquette, even in free Kurdistan, to have held long conversation with the assembled company of women, I returned their farewell compliments and retired again to the house where I was settling with Hama, who tried to induce me by every means in his power to take him. But this I did not wish, for I intended, once clear of Sulaimania, to declare myself Christian, and see how one of that religion fared among the people of these parts, and Hama's attachment to me was greatly due to my piousness as a Musulman. Besides, he had sworn to my orthodoxy before Uthman Pasha and the assembled company, so I could not undeceive him, quite apart from the fact that did I ever return, I hoped to be welcomed again as Mirza Ghulam Husain.

In the custom of Sulaimania, we were to leave in the afternoon; not like the Persian habit, which enjoins rising in the cold, dark dawn. I had therefore to buy some food to last at least three days, for we were not going to Chemchemal, and between Sulaimania and our first inhabited stopping-place it might be three days. Gulchin had made me some road bread, sheets the size of a sheet of brown paper, and little thicker, of white, crisp bread. This with some pears was all I took, and all that would be considered necessary by any ordinary person in these parts. A little bowl for drinking-water completed the road outfit, with the exception of a cotton quilt, which served both for a cover at night and a softener over the hard páck-saddle.

I spent the morning bidding farewell to the numerous friends and acquaintances I had made during my stay in Sulaimania, and entrusted such affairs as were as yet unsettled to Matti. Then we had the usual "merchants' lunch" of kebab and bread together, and on foot set out on the road to walk a little way together, and join the caravan outside. It was the first time for months past that any one had dared venture outside the town on the Chemchemal side, for, but a week before, the Hamavands had been scouring the plain right up to the gates of the town.

Matti had not informed the muleteer who I was or of what creed and nationality, and I did not propose to him to do so. I should be asked, and that soon, and I could give such answer as I felt inclined. Habib, I think, had a notion that I was not what I pretended to be, for he was of a prying nature, and he had professed it difficult to believe several of my assertions in the face of the English and French books, and the maps he saw at my house, which to him suggested disguises and intrigues, because he could not understand them.

We came up to the waiting animals—a little group of three or four, for the main caravan had not arrived— and here took leave of one another, an incident of no little regret upon my part, and I hope, too, upon that of Matti; and before we left the brow of the hillock, I looked my last upon Sulaimania, a cluster of flat roofs in a hollow almost invisible a mile away, so well did the old pashas hide their town from the view of Turk and Kurd alike. I gazed, too, for a moment upon distant Aoraman, a frowning wall, black now, the snows invisible from the distance—the frontier of Persia, from which I once more receded.

CHAPTER XIV

TO KIRKUK

OUR caravan was a tiny one, and the muleteer, a long-legged Turkoman known as Ahmad Bash Chaush, was accompanied by a youth and a long-haired darvish, both natives of his town. This second was a quiet, cheerful man, short and stoutly built, as are many of the Turkomans, and he was the laughing-stock of many he met, for he had adopted the habit of wearing a Persian felt hat, which excited the ridicule of such of the local population as took him for a Persian at first sight.

We did not go far that day, but pushed along quickly till the village of Baba Murda, the inhabitants of which were encamped miles away in a pleasanter spot. Here upon a knoll we threw the loads, and while the youth took the animals to water, the darvish filled the jars at the spring, and Ahmad, as head-man, and entitled to ease first—though he had walked his twelve miles—sat with me and smoked.

It was hot this summer afternoon in Lower Kurdistan, though the heat was past its greatest, and we were glad to get that side of the loads where a light breeze played, and wait for the mules to be tethered, groomed, and finally given their barley, when the day's work was done. Then the darvish and the lad joined us, and we shared the pears I had brought, for they would not keep; and these with bread made the evening meal.

One is soon tired and sleepy after the jolting of the mule and the heat and air, and it is not usual to sit up long after sunset. The meal finished, we lay down where we were, upon a somewhat stony ground, and waited for the sleep that comes quickly. But the darvish sat upon his heels and commenced in a low voice chanting in monotone, "La allahu ill'allah," in rising cadence, drawing deep breaths with a groan, till his voice rang out in the still night. His breath shortened, and the curious exhaustion that accompanies these exercises overtook him, and with a groan he sank motionless upon the ground. Then, after a few minutes he recommenced, " Allahu akbar, allahu akbar," in sharp staccato, accentuat ing the last syllable of the word "akbar" so that it fell like a hammer-stroke upon the ear. Again till exhaus tion he continued, and once more he rose and started the cry upon " Allah." After this he lay prostrate and slept where he collapsed, and we slept too.

In the manner of caravan travelling it was yet pitch dark when we got under way in the morning, and the sun rose as we arrived at the foot of the ridge and pass, into Bazian—the now evacuated country of the Hamavands.

We struggled slowly and painfully up the long and stony ascent, and from the summit looked back again over Sulaimania—whose position was marked in the valley of Surchina by a white streak up the ridge of the opposite range—the road to Panjwin and Persia.

A turn behind a rock, and we left it all out of sight, and below our feet lay the narrow valley of Bazian, stretching right and left. Opposite it was bounded by the Bazian range, not high, but rising in a sheer cliff of several hundred feet, shutting in the land and giving the place an air of peaceful seclusion in the bright morning light, which changed to a gloomy prospect when the sun, going west, threw the cliff's shadow across the plain, and its face appeared a frowning wall, under whose lee the Hamavands had encamped, and from their camps watched the passage of caravans—and victims.

Now it was deserted, no smoke curled up quietly in the morning air, no horse neighed, and we had not heard the report of a single rifle since daylight. So, having nothing to apprehend, we picked our way leisurely down the slope, and at the bottom turned to the right along the valley, gradually making our way to the other side towards the pass of Darband-i-Bazian. We passed, as we went along, many a little garden that the Hamavands had left, little neat patches of cultivation on the hill-sides and in the bottom of the valley, which were now bearing fruit, and of which the travellers of another small caravan we had overtaken were busy cutting and carrying away the deserted produce.

About eleven o'clock, when we were well on the way towards Darband-i-Bazian, some alarm was caused by the sight of a small band of horsemen coming from behind us, along our road, and some were for getting their arms ready. But the general run of the passengers shared the opinion that if the approaching riders were Turkish irregular soldiery, there would be nothing to fear, and if they were Hamavands it would be useless to resist, so that our pace did not alter and we proceeded in the jogging way of caravans, apparently unconcerned. Nevertheless the relief was general when the riders were seen to be two irregular Turkish "mule-cavalry" and a handful of shaikhs' men. These, on coming up with the caravan, proceeded to scrutinise all very carefully, as if in search of someone, and one more officious than the others gave me a fright by holding the bridle of my steed the while he called his comrades, shouting :

"Amma niyya? piaeki bash nabi am kabra." ("Is this not he? this fellow appears not to be a good man.")

But my muleteer affirmed so loudly and strenuously that I was a trader, a friend of the Mosul traders, that they raised a laugh at the horseman's expense; so, changing his tone, he asked for a cigarette, and having obtained it, rode on with the others, and they passed ahead bound for Chemchemal. It is a long stretch from Baba Murda to Darband-i-Bazian, or it seemed so, for it was already noon—we had started at four in the morning —when we veered to the left, where the hills receded in a kind of bay, and crossed a large patch of cultivated land, where we threw the loads to give the beasts a rest.

This was where Rich, the East India Company's gifted resident at Bagdad in the early part of the 19th century, passed, and noticed in passing, that in 1808 there had been a Turkoman village named Derghezeen. There is nothing now but a little cultivation belonging to Bazian village; nor is there any sign of the ruins Rich mentions, and which he opined to be of Sasanian times; though, in view of the fact that this district was upon the borders of a province which in Sasanian times enjoyed great importance (Holwan), and in which there are still many relics of the Persian occupation of that period, there is every probability that Rich was perfectly right in his surmise.

The flanking wall of the valley here broadened greatly in depth from east to west, and became broken into spurs. This affords a passage westwards to get out of Bazian valley, and a long rising approach ends by passing through a neck, not twenty yards wide, whence one emerges as from a door, the hills finishing abruptly at the ridge in which the neck occurs, and which is left, as a wall, by the westwards bound passenger.

From the spot where we now rested to the neck was the danger place in times of peril, for the Hamavands had made this at once the impregnable gate of their secluded country, and the trap for those who would enter it. Upon these hill-sides and behind the rocks and boulders they had waited for their prey, and darted down and out upon the unfortunates; those who had entered the neck from outside and found themselves cut off from retreat, and those who would pass out and found themselves driven into the narrow funnel of the pass and assailed from all sides. Even now, when we could see in the distance the tent of the "bimbashi," who had pitched it by one of the streams that watered the Hamavand cultivations, we could not stray from the vicinity of our loads, for behind lay the folds of the hills where the Turks had not dared penetrate, and they might yet contain Hamavands.

At this neck of Darband-i-Bazian, Abdurrahman Pasha, one of the old Baba pashas of Sulaimania, made a brave stand in 1805, during the war by which he hoped to make this part of Kurdistan independent. He built a wall across the neck—the ruins of which are visible to-day —and fought there against Kuchuk Sulaiman Pasha of Bagdad, being defeated in the manner related by Rich.

" He placed here a wall and gate and three or four pieces of cannon, two of which were planted on the height in order to fire upon the Turkish camp below; and vain would have been Sulaiman Pasha's attack on this pass, had not a Koordish chief called Mahommed Bey, a son of Khaled Pasha who was united with the Turks, led a division of the Turkish troops and auxiliary Koords up the mountain, by a pass only known to some Koords, and which had been neglected as impracticable, so that Abdurraham Pasha found his position turned, and his guns on the height pointed against himself. He was then obliged to retreat, and the wall was razed by the Pasha of Bagdad, who afterwards advanced to Sulaimania." [1]

It was very hot that noontide, and do what we could, it seemed impossible to get any shade, though we piled the loads high and stretched a cloak over two sticks; so perforce we lay upon the stones sweating. Together we shared a meal of water-melon and bread—the former they had found in a Hamavand cultivation. Then the darvish and the youth had to go far away where the stream ran to attend to their animals, while I was left with the head-man, Ahmad. I had taken a great liking to him, for he was a quiet, respectable man, who minded his own business, and, while showing no distinction between himself and his passengers, assumed no hectoring bearing, as is so often the case with the muleteer and his native passengers. Together we sat and smoked our Kurdish cigarettes of chips, and he asked me, at length, my religion, for he remarked that he had not

[1] Rich, *Travels in Kurdistan*, vol. i., p. 58.

seen me pray, and supposed I could not therefore be a Musulman.

So, liking the character of my man, I resolved to try the truth upon him, and, quoting the words of a greater than myself, said:

"Thou hast heard that I am of Persia, thou speakest such of the tongue of that land as thou knowest to me; yet though I am of Persia in a measure, I am not Persian, and though I be not Persian, neither am I Kurd, nor Arab, nor Turk."

"What, then?" he asked.

"Nor yet am I of the tribe of the Nasara (native Christian), for I am of the land they call England, which is in Ferangistan."

"What! of Constantinople that is," he replied; "then you are a Turkish subject!"

"No," I said, "nor yet a Turkish subject. I am a subject of a land far from Turkey."

"And what God do they worship?"

"That same as the Nasara."

"Well, well," he said, with a doubtful cadence, "they are them I see in Bagdad, that wear such garments as the Constantinople Turk affects, but hats of various kinds, so that no man can tell from their headgear of what tribe and religion they may be. Why, then, do you not wear your country's headgear?"

"Because it pleases me," I said, "to adopt among these people their garments; for the Persian proverb truly says, 'He who would not be ashamed among the strangers, let him put upon himself their raiment and their speech,' and it would become neither me nor my circumstances to travel girt about with the unsightly swathings of a Ferangi, where I can avoid annoyance to myself and others by adopting the habits of the simple among the simple."

"Well, thou art come a long journey, doubtless, and sigh for your native mountains. Have they great hills and deserts there?"

"No," I replied; "it is a land of little hills and little

valleys, of no seclusion, of no peace and no rest, of incessant hurryings; in contravention of the word of Quran, that says, 'All haste is of Satan, and patience of God.' We are conveyed by rushing chains of carriages that run upon iron bars, that travel a day's march in an hour."

"'Haste is of Satan,' O true speaker," he replied; "it is a pity that you were not a Musulman, but each to his own faith, and the Nasara is of the people of the book and not damned; but tell me, have they there no muleteers and no caravans?"

"No, indeed, for where such carriages exist, what need for a muleteer?"

"What a land this, with never a caravan to traverse the country! Have you Kurds? and do they not rob these trains of carriages?"

"No, there are no Kurds, nor Arabs, nor Turks, nor are any of these tongues understood there."

"La allahu ill'allah!" he exclaimed, "what a land! and yet God made all men, brother, and all countries, in which are ever good and bad, and I trust that thou art of the better. What matter if man be Christian or Islam. Can he not follow the laws of his own prophet, and the ordinances of God? And thou, too, art a stranger, far from thy people, and it behoves both Turkoman and Kurd to treat such an one as his own brother."

With that he stretched himself in the four or five inches of shade that the boxes now cast, and composed himself for sleep; and I did likewise, my head in shadow and my body burning and sweating in the fierce sun.

Our rest was not for long. Half an hour afterwards we rose and loaded the mules, and once more set out. As the rocks drew closer on each side of the road the heat became intense. There was no wind, and we unwound the handkerchiefs that enveloped our heads, and tried to make miniature canopies of them, with little effect. It took us an hour to get over the stony track to the neck, the exit from which is not more than a few yards wide, a break in an otherwise uninterrupted line of hills that shows an almost perpendicular face to the outside world, a rampart—almost the last—of Kurdistan, to the west. Outside the Darband the ground fell away, and the plain of Chemchemal lay before us, no plain at all in reality. It is, so to speak, a long and broad valley filled with rolling hills intersected by deep ravines, but whose summits are so exactly of the same height that the country looks from afar but a flat plain.

Ahmad Bash Chaush had resolved to leave Chemchemal, and striking farther north take a more difficult but nearer route through the hills, stopping during the night, or what should remain of it, at a village he knew of. Our caravan was now a considerable one, for we had joined with two small parties, with a mixture of queer muleteers. There were three Arabs, men of the low country about Kifri, some Turkomans, a Shuan Kurd or two, and a Persian from Teheran, looking very out of place in his globe hat and short skirts among these men of turbans and long garments.

In company with these we jogged along, our faces to the now declining sun. Chemchemal was hidden behind the ridge formed by the ever-rolling hummocks and hills of the plain. From various spots great pillars of smoke arose; for the grass, dried with the summer heat, was burning furiously, and at night would shine like great beacons. A few miles further we saw Chemchemal—it was just sunset.

The little town lay in a great hollow, and above stands the mount, an artificial eminence similar in shape to the mounts seen at Erbil and other places once occupied by the Assyrians. The tents of the Turks were pitched around the foot of the mount, and made a gleaming white spot in the dusky scene.

Here, while yet Chemchemal lay indistinct, we left the road and the bulk of the caravan and proceeded in the gathering darkness, our way lit by a roaring furnace of flame that rushed up from a gully as from out of a

volcano. Beyond Chemchemal lies the last range of
hills westward on the Kirkuk road. This last is
approached by a gradual slope—formed by innumerable
little hills of rounded shape over and about which the
track winds. The village to which we were bound lay
well up in the eastern face of this range, and now our
difficulties commenced, for the track started forking and
branching, leading to the various villages of the Shuan
Kurds hereabout. At eight o'clock we separated in the
darkness from a large number of our companions, but,
relying upon the local knowledge of one of the Arabs,
who said he knew the road well, did not attempt to
follow them. We had passed no water since leaving
Bazian, and all were getting thirsty, but Jum'a, the
Arab, promised us to be at the village in an hour or
two. He had missed the right track, though, and we
commenced to wander among these low hills, a cloud of
dust accompanying us, and rendering our thirst considerably worse. From the dark ahead a shout arose
that we had come to water, and we sent the youth on
quickly to get our jar filled. A moment later we
ourselves arrived there, to find that the mules had made
a rush for the tiny stream and had hopelessly befouled
it before a single one of us could get a drink. And
now we knew that we were lost, for there is no spring
on the road we had expected to travel, besides which
this track was heading in a wrong direction. The Arab,
however, persisted that he knew the way, and a lively
discussion ensued as to whether we should throw the
loads there, where there was at least a drop of water,
or push forward. The fear of being attacked in the
night by Kurds overcame the greater part of the
company, and in deference to them we once more got
under way, heading for what we thought to be the right
direction. We were gradually rising, and the curious
effect of a dry climate and no breeze was well illustrated
here. We would descend into a hollow to a temperature that made us sweat, and a moment after, rising
again, come to the cool of the night, which struck chill.

We stumbled along thus for two or three hours, too tired to say much, the monotony of the dark night varied only by the falling of a mule, or the refusal of a donkey to proceed, till a volley of shots rang out, the bullets whizzing over our heads to the accompaniment of an inferno of barking from watchdogs. We stopped behind a protected hump and shouted to our assailants to desist. These to satisfy themselves of our harmlessness came running down from their village, and finding us what we affirmed—harmless travellers—put us on our way. But we must have missed in the darkness again, for we dragged on hour by hour, always rising gradually and never getting out of, or above, the knolls and hummocks. We seemed to wind round and round these interminable little hills. We had reached that stage where to sit on a mule is almost fatal, for one falls asleep—and off the beast. Most of us had walked some distance, and in the dark stumbled along tired and disgusted. We could see that it wanted but a few hours to morning, and yet, with the hope that pushes a man to foolishness, we went ahead. At last, however, we came to a point where the road definitely turned south—we wanted to go north—and there men and mules alike gave in. The beasts fell about, refusing a sharp, stony rise before us, and, disgusted with everything, we let them lie, loosening and casting off their loads where they stood or fell. The youth was parched, his tongue so swollen that he could not speak, but only grunted, and he, as well as Ahmad Bash Chaush, had been walking some fourteen hours without resting. Not stopping to arrange the loads or collect the nosebags and small gear that lay about, we fell upon the stones of the road, and, from the time we had stopped, during the process of throwing the loads and tying the animals to them, no one had spoken a word—though the process usually demands a great deal of talking.

I suppose we slept for a couple of hours or so, when the cold woke us. I was shivering, and chilled through. A morning breeze had risen and blew from the hills

above, lowering the temperature by many degrees in a
few seconds. The false dawn was just showing in the
east, and, with the unthinking simplicity of the land, we
sat up and smoked cigarettes in the hope of getting
warm. Far away, on the other side of the plain under
Bazian, we could see the big grass-fires still blazing, and
sighed not a little for some of their warmth. The silence
of the early morning was broken only by the swish of
the wind through the dry grass, and an occasional rifle
shot told of vigilant Kurds in their villages.

With the first light we began to load our animals,
and the Arab who was responsible for all the trouble
was made to go to the top of the hill where the breeze
blew strongest and spy the village up on the side of the
range, which he succeeded in descrying at no great
distance away. So we struck across the foothills, and
after an hour reached the place, which looked pretty
enough in the cool bright morning, for a thick clump of
fig-trees and a large willow grove, with several streams
and many green and grassy patches, made it look a
desirable spot for a halt. We found the bulk of the
caravan already encamped here, and had but little room
to dispose of ourselves in a place where shade should
cover us when the sun rose higher. As we approached,
the villagers, some of whom were working at the fig-
garden, greeted us with the laconic Kurdish salutation,
" Ma nabi ! " (" May you not be tired "), and one or two
ran off to get us a skin of "du," and some barley for
the mules.

Under a willow-tree we threw the loads, and arranged
them in a wall to keep off the fast warming sun-rays,
and having entrusted them to the care of a traveller
near by, they took the mules away to water, while Ahmad
Bash Chaush and myself retired to a tiny spring of clear
cold water and indulged in a good wash—the first since
Sulaimania—and filled our water-pots.

From the grove there was a fine view of the borders
of Kurdistan, for we were high enough to see the hills
behind Bazian, and the greater mountains behind them.

Pir-i-Muguran, or Omar Gudroon, as it is called by
Rich, the great rock of Sulaimania, stood up like a
sentinel of the mounted army—on its outskirts, with the
outlines of Aoraman just visible on one side, and the
Kandil Dagh over Ravanduz and Keui Sanjaq on the
other side. Immediately below us the plain of Chemchemal, like a sea of lumpy billows, stretched away to
Bazian, the break in the range at Darband giving a
glimpse of the hills on the other side of the valley of
evil fame.

During the morning a cousin of the Shuan chief to
whom this plain belonged came in, a gaudy young Kurd,
rich in striped silks and scarlet riding-boots, a good
rifle over his shoulder, and a Mauser pistol in his belt,
and having said a word or two to all, a question as to
destination and journey, he departed again, followed by
three or four men.

We had bought a great handkerchief full of fresh
figs, like small green pears in appearance, for a kran,
and having soaked a little of our bread—for it was as
hard as an iron plate—we all sat round and made a
great meal, and then, our troubles and labour over for
the time being, sprawled about, to rest till the afternoon,
when we must once more take to the road.

Upon a knoll above, under a canopy of leaves, sat
three Kurds, whose sharp eyes saw everyone approaching, and now and then a hoarse cry of " Karvani, oh,
Karvani," would come down, and a muleteer would run
out to collect his mules nearer home, for they were
grazing on the hill-side.

Once they shouted to all to bring their mules into
camp, and a rush ensued, followed by an invasion of
trotting mules kicking up clouds of dust. And the
reason we saw a little while after, for down below a
great army of men and beasts filed slowly across the
plain, like a string of ants—Kurds shifting their camp—
and a band of thirty or forty horsemen rode by the
grove-men from over the Rania side, Pishdir and
Bilbas, in the short velvet coats and rakish turbans

THE KURDISH FRONTIER MOUNTAINS.

[To face p. 336.

of those people, as wild a lot as any might wish to meet.

Soon after noon a move was made to leave again, and, as is so often the case, when one beast had been loaded everyone else displayed the utmost activity in the hope of being away first. Half the caravan and more, having got ready, left, but took a path along the hill-side, which would lead them through a break in the range later. We, however, with a few others, made a line straight for the hills, and were soon among them, passing through some fine valleys where plentiful streams ran swift and strong. In one of these a camel caravan was camped, the camel-men being at first invisible, till feet were seen protruding from between pairs of bales arched over with a cloth, forming a kennel in which the Arab camel-men retired during the day. These caravans travel very slowly and by short stages, and stop where-ever there is thorn for the camels, never putting up at a village. They are thus always met with in deserted places, and, as the Arabs are unpopular with the Kurds, and *vice versa*, one of the former may pass from Bagdad to Kirkuk and Sulaimania without ever seeing a Kurd at close quarters, or ever exchanging a word with him.

The range, as seen from the Bazian, where it forms a high sky-line, appears to be but a single ridge of hills, but it took us five hours to get clear of it. The track was ever on an up-grade; one ascended through valleys and over ridges to the very top, where there was a fine view. Looking back, Kurdistan and its mountains stood up high; and forward, the vast Tigris plain stretched away, unbroken, except for the low ranges towards Altun Keupri, and the single mountain that stands up due west of Kirkuk, which we could see yellow in the afternoon sun, at a great distance.

Around us the hills of the range, a wonderful red and yellow, earth and stones twisted into queer shapes, stretched away on either side, and below; and after half an hour of level mountain-top, we began the descent. Darkness overtook while yet we were in the mountain,

Y

and as there was no moon, the going was retarded, for the shadows of the hills made the darkness yet more sombre.

Our caravan was now very small, as many of the others had taken other tracks through the hills, and we pushed forward as fast as possible to get into Kirkuk before midnight, when the gate would be closed against passengers, and a long detour would have to be made to get into the town by another entrance. All the way across the plain we were descending, by steps in the plain formed of rocky outcrop, very bad going for the mules, and as we approached the town it grew warmer and warmer.

About midnight, having been ten hours on the march, we passed the gate, and turned into the long street of Kirkuk, a full mile from end to end. I had a letter to one Salim, a Mosul Christian, and to his business caravanserai we proceeded. Our way took us through the silent-domed bazaars, and by the light of a single lamp we picked our way under the sombre vaults of the bazaar till we came to the door of the serai, our blows upon whose door resounded through the whole place.

A sleepy guardian opened to us, and after Ahmad Bash Chaush had announced who we were, we had permission to pass in. In the dark I could not see what kind of a place it was, except that it was an ordinary business caravanserai, but without any cloisters round it, on the ground floor. Instead there was an upper storey, the rooms of which stood back from the level of the wall, making a verandah all round the serai-yard.

There came from above a small man in the slack garments of night, a handkerchief about his head. He introduced himself as Khaja Salim, and hearing that I was recommended to him, showed me a bench on the upper floor where I might sleep, and where, without further talk, I soon lay upon the hard boards in sound slumber.

In the morning I had my effects brought up and disposed in an empty room, and proceeded to the coffee-house for a cup of tea. Here I met Salim, and joined him in a cup of hot sweetened milk, which it is the custom to take early in the morning in these parts. I returned with him to his office, a little room, where he—more advanced than his co-religionists in Sulaimania—sat upon a chair behind a table. I did not care for the looks of the man. He was a tiny fellow, rather fat and pale, and with a very sharp and shifty look. However, he was polite enough and welcomed me to Kirkuk, asking my nationality. I told him I was English, and he made no remark, except to ask if I had met his neighbours in the caravanserai. As I had not, he took me round to half a dozen rooms like his own, each of which harboured a pair of Mosul merchants. Unlike the Mosuliots of Sulaimania, who were an exceptionally pleasing set of men, the looks of none of these were reassuring, nor was my further experience of them conducive to a better opinion. One of them in particular, a youth who wore European clothes, collar and cuffs complete, was unusually unpleasant in appearance. His eyes were those of the habitual drunkard, and his sloppy mouth and greasy face were quite repellent. This was the son of a very rich merchant of Mosul.

Salim's lack of curiosity was no feature of the behaviour of these men. They pestered me with questions, and were loth to believe me English, taking me for a Persian; for I had to speak to Salim in Kurdish, and as I had not the appearance of a Kurd (I was now wearing a short coat, European trousers, and a fez), they opined I must be a Persian. However, on being told that they might please themselves as to what they believed, they put me a question or two from the New Testament, and receiving satisfactory replies, became convinced that at any rate I was a Christian, and dubbed me "Saun Effendi."

They pressed me to stay, and Salim told me that

he would not permit me to make any arrangements for dinner while I was there, that I must share with the rest of them, and fend for myself during the day. He promised meanwhile to try and find me mules in the Bagdad caravan, which would leave a few days hence.

So, having nothing to do, I bethought me of that resort of the idle, the bazaar, and took a stroll there, refreshing my memories of the place, where I had stayed sixteen days four months before.

It was extremely hot here. The end of August in Kirkuk is probably as ʰhot as in any town of Mesopotamia, and, fresh from the hills of Kurdistan, great drowsiness overtook me, and hardly was I back in my room than I lay and slept—till sunset, being awakened by Salim, who, thinking I must be ill, came in to see what was the matter.

We went and sat in the verandah outside, where Salim's brother was cooking a meal, and Salim himself having divested himself of his business garments—the long striped tunic, Aleppo gold-threaded belt and fez— donned loose clothing, and enveloped his head in a handkerchief.

For a time he rummaged about in his room, and at last came forth with two little glasses and a bottle wrapped in wet rags, to keep the contents cool—and I perceived that I had met a drinker. The drink was araq, a fiery spirit flavoured with aniseed and aromatic gum, and he insisted on my joining him in three or four glasses of the stuff, followed by morsels of sweet watermelon, which is taken to remove the unpleasant aftertaste from the mouth, and quench the thirst the spirit generates.

As it grew darker, we repaired to the roof, where benches were set about. The sun had just set, and from the roof one could see over Kirkuk, with its flat roofs, to the great desert westwards, where the gold of the setting sun was blotted ʼby the shape of the big mountain, standing lonely and unsupported by foothills or rising slope, in the west.

How little did these lineal descendants of the Assyrians know that the very prospect they looked over, the town in which they lived, had been founded by their ancestors, and the mount under which the caravan-serai lay, called "Qala debeit Seluk"—"The fortress of the Seleucids."

There was but little time to enjoy the prospect, for the sun having set, it grew dark almost immediately, and the chatter of the Christians and their invitation to drink prevented any attempt at a stroll in the cool breeze. Every one of them was provided with a little bottle of the araq, and by the bench of each was a pail of water in which they kept their bottles cool.

I created, I fear, a bad impression by refusing to drink with them, and finding their conversation of very little interest, relapsed into silence, at which they were not a little surprised, for the spirit moving them, they grew extraordinarily loquacious, and failed to understand why their merriment was not shared by me. Salim besought me to join them, for, he said, "It creates a bad impression upon your hosts to refuse their drink, for which we live, counting it our only pleasure in a wretched life. Besides, what kind of an Englishman will it be that does not drink, and drink level with the rest?"

I replied that it was no longer considered an accomplishment and sign of good breeding to drink another man under the table, and that popular opinion condemned the practice, and therefore I could not join them; neither could my stomach, unused to alcohol for so long, endure the spirit. Yet he did not desist, and at last, at the risk of seriously offending him, I told him that if the presence of a stranger and a guest who did not drink was repugnant to him and his companions, I would not force my company upon them, at which he became very apologetic and left me in peace, and the dinner arriving just then—many dishes of pilau and baked meats—the discussion closed, and we drew round a table they set, and dipped our fingers into some

particularly savoury dishes. Here, again, I was unpopular, for having been used for a long time to eat
little more than dry bread and fruit, a diet I found
sufficient in every way, I could not eat much of these
dishes, and made a meal from the bread that accompanied them, much to the disgust of my hosts, who,
like all these sedentary Christians, put away enormous
quantities. Unpopularity, however, among such people
is of no disadvantage, for it permitted me to say I was
tired, and retired to my bench, where I lay smoking
and looking up at the stars, thinking, while I listened
to the rising voices of the Christians, who were growing more noisy as the drink got into them, of the
contrast between them and the Musulman; and rather
wishing I had continued as a Musulman, among whom
I made and kept good friends, and lived in the reasonable manner possible among people the preservation of
whose self-respect was at least a factor in their character.

As the night drew on these creatures began to get
drunk, and shouted dirges and ditties in monotonous
Arabic, hiccupping and breaking into screams of laughter,
an inane and futile gathering of sots. The night was
made hideous by their clatter, and, as no one slept till
drink overcame him on the ground or couch, it was late
before I could sleep, and the last sound I heard was of
violent vomiting over the roof edge into the courtyard.

I had caught a cold in the head, a very bad one, too,
and in the morning I woke with a strong fever, and
crawled to my room out of the sunlight and lay down
on my bed, a piece of thin carpet on the bricks. Here
I lay all day burning in the heat of both fever and climate.
Kirkuk is a place where temperatures at this time of the
year are over one hundred and ten degrees in the shade,
and that little room, which had no outlet to the air except
the door, just stored up the heat reflected from the walls
of the caravanserai, and never felt the breeze to cool it.

About sunset the fever left me, and Salim appeared,
to ask why I had not come out during the day. He
quite refused to believe that there was anything the

matter with me, thinking my conduct but a continuation of that of the previous evening. But I induced him to leave me alone at last, and he went away to his araq in dudgeon, and I dozed again.

So for three days I kept in the room, creeping to the bazaar once a day to buy a piece of bread and some water-melon. The Christians, convinced that I was an unsociable fellow, shunned me, for which I was rather thankful than otherwise, and devoted their time after sunset to that form of amusement which appeared to be their only resource.

The fourth day, the cold and fever were a good deal better, and I bethought me of the coffee-house where they sold warm milk, entered in there, and ordered my drink. This I consumed and paid for, when one came forward with coffee, and would have poured out some of the bitter stuff for me. When I refused he looked astonished, and retired to where the owner of the place was making the nasty beverage, holding a conversation with him, of which, to judge by the glances they cast in my direction, I must be the subject. The owner himself now came forward with coffee and poured out for me, and I again refused, at which he grew wroth.

"Who are you," he exclaimed, "that comes into a coffee-house and refuses what it serves to its customers? Either take your coffee or go."

"Why," I replied, "I drank your milk, and paid for it, must I drink coffee as well? By what right or custom do you force your coffee down your customers' throats?"

"By the right of the owner of the coffee-house; the milk-seller is nothing to do with the coffee-house, and his customers have no right to sit in the coffee-house. Now that you have done so, you must have the coffee and pay for it."

"Never!" I replied, feeble and excessively angry; "pour your coffee in the gutters, where the filth were well left. You trap strangers in your shop by allowing them to be attracted by one of another trade, and then force them by harsh words and the bestial manners of the Turk to buy your wares."

The coffee-seller had poured out a cup of coffee and held it still towards me. With an exclamation of disgust at my stubbornness he thrust it at me, and in the annoyance of the moment I took it and flung the contents in his face and walked out of the shop, to the astonishment of several Turkish officers, who had been close by and listened to what was going on. One of these, an elderly man in the uniform of a "yuzbashi," followed me out and caught me by the arm as he left.

"Brother, brother," he said, "wherefore this unseemly rage, this insult of the Turk? True, you are a stranger and apparently sick, to judge by your looks, but that is the way to start blood-feuds and rebellions. You have my sympathy, but I deprecate your haste. But you must come to my house and rest awhile, for you are feeble,"—and in truth I was, for I was stumbling at every step and fits of giddiness took and held me, rolling me up against walls and corners, where I had to lean till my head cleared.

The old man lived in a little house by the mosque of Kirkuk, a mean mud and stone building, and had his wife spread a carpet on the shady side of the yard. Here we sat down, and he called for tea and proceeded to ask me those leading questions I was so used to hearing.

I could see that he did not believe that I was English, and interpreted my statement to mean that I was a British subject. Hearing that I was going to Bagdad, he told me that there were no caravans going for a long time yet, and I should have to stay in Kirkuk for many days if I intended to go with the caravan. I had no intention of doing this, however, and told him so, when he proposed a very practical scheme, that I should go to Altun Keupri and thence by kalak, or raft, to Bagdad. This sounded excellent, and at least afforded an opportunity of getting away from Kirkuk, the climate of which is abominable.

He, however, pressed me to stay with him for a few

days till I should be stronger, but the idea of quitting
the uncongenial air of Kirkuk was too good to be
abandoned, even for a day or two more than necessary.

So I took my leave of him and went to a caravanserai
near the western gate and river-bed, where the Altun
Keupri and Keui Sanjaq muleteers gathered. Here I
found one, Umar, willing to take me to Altun Keupri
for two mejidies—a high rate, but one at which I was
not disposed to cavil, for I wanted to go. He promised
to leave in two days, and having paid him a mejidie in
advance, I came back to my room feeling more pleased
with life than I had done for several days.

Salim I informed of my pending departure, and he
begged me to dine with them that evening, calling in
his neighbours to help his cause. So I consented, as these
were probably the last two evenings in Kirkuk, though
I made it a condition which was near to severing our
friendship once for all, that I should not be pressed to
drink. They at last agreed, though, and we parted on
better terms than had existed since my arrival.

Next morning I was going out of the serai to the
bazaar, when to my astonishment and dismay I heard
someone calling "Ghulam Husain" from right opposite
the caravanserai door, and turning, saw sitting in a
saddler's shop Sayyid Nuri, the youth, son of Shaikh
Ahmad, who had annoyed me so in Sulaimania.

I trembled lest one of the Christians should see me
with him, or hear him talking to me, for he spoke in
a loud voice, and called me by name at every second
sentence.

His style of conversation was as ever, a string of
questions, and his first was as to why I had changed
my style of clothing. I was now, as previously mentioned,
wearing a European suit of clothes and a fez unadorned
by any handkerchief. Needless to say, my dress included
no collar or cuffs, and I still wore the locally made shoes,
and carried an abba or camel-hair cloak. I explained
to Sayyid Nuri that I was bound for Bagdad, and
answered as shortly as possible in order to get away with

all expedition. He asked me where I was staying, and
I replied, " In a caravanserai near," for I did not mention
that I lived in the place from whose portals he had seen
me emerge, lest he should call there, and calling, ask for
Ghulam Husain, when my friends the Christians would
curse me for a traitor and an enemy in their midst, and
I should lose caste with the Musulman for consorting
with such people.

Fortunately no one emerged from the caravanserai
while we sat in the saddler's shop, and I managed to
get away to the bazaar, where I had been going. I had
not expected to meet Sayyid Nuri, for I had thought
him to be in Chemchemal with his father, but apparently
being unable to rest so near to Kirkuk without being
in it, every few days he undertook the arduous journey
between the two places for the pleasure of lounging in
the bazaar.

I met him again, but hurried by with scarcely a word,
leaving him astonished at my haste, and somewhat hurt
or offended. Most of that last day I spent with the
old Turkish yuzbashi who had befriended me the previous
day; and, as I had promised, I dined with the Christians,
enduring once the sight of their transition from staid
merchants to boisterous idiots, and through all the
stages of drivelling till they lay quiet.

Next morning I was occupied with getting my few
things together, and purchasing some bread for the road.
The journey was not a long one, but the one stage in
which it was done was very weary, and is usually
reckoned at ten to twelve hours, if one does not stop
nor dismount.

The muleteer came after me at mid-day, and I bade
farewell to the Christians who gathered in Salim's office
and bade me good-bye with great cordiality. Our
starting-point was a long way from the caravanserai,
and we had to hire porters to take my baggage to a
large ruinous place at the extreme western edge of the
town, where a large caravan of donkeys was loading for
Altun Keupri. As usual, a number of travellers were not

ready, so I sat in an archway in the portico of the serai
and got into conversation with a long Mukri Kurd, very
like my own Hama I had left behind, who was exercised
as to how he should bind his head with a piece of twine.
On being asked the reason for this strange anxiety, he
said that he had missed the road from Keui Sanjaq to
Kirkuk, two days before, and getting among the hills,
had been attacked by Hamavands, and thrown off his
donkey down a ravine, hitting his head. He now bound
it together to keep the pieces of his skull in contact till
they should stick again, but as he felt his head aching
in all kinds of places he was seeking advice as to how
to make one piece of twine bind all the aching spots
together. In the middle of the confusion of loading, a
couple of Turkish mule-mounted soldiers pushed their
way into the place, upsetting donkeys, bursting loads,
and creating damage and confusion generally. They
then found some five mules in the stable somewhere,
and proceeded to drive them out of the caravanserai,
ignoring the heaving mass of donkeys, loads and men
they had just thrown into turmoil. The mules, urged
by the points of the soldiers' hangers, came trotting
forward, mixed up in the rack and riot, and a fight
followed between our caravan and the soldiers, who
persisted in trying to force their way through. All the
people around seemed to be joining in the fight, and
the situation was only saved by a stampede of donkeys
into the street, leaving a free passage for the mules and
soldiers, who got away, somewhat the worse for wear,
to meet a yuzbashi outside who cursed and swore at the
delay.

It took another hour before we were loaded, and as
we were starting I remembered I had left something
with Salim, so I ran back all the way to the bazaar to
get it, the muleteer saying he would keep my mule.
It took me, I suppose, twenty minutes or more to
return, to find the caravanserai empty, so I started out
on foot, walking quickly. They must have started immediately after I left, for I walked right through the

outskirts of Kirkuk, through Quria the suburb village, and for a couple of miles along the plain before I found them, and as I was carrying a large water-melon I had bought, and was walking at my quickest under the hot August sun, I was not sorry to get astride my beast and open out my clothing to let the sweat dry a little. The sun temperature in these parts at this time is about one hundred and forty degrees.

There was the usual mixed crowd of travellers. Almost the first I addressed was a native of Sina, of Persian Kurdistan, going to Bagdad. He had, for a Kurd, travelled widely, having followed six or seven trades anywhere from Teheran to Bushire on the Persian Gulf. He offered to come with me as a servant and companion to Bagdad, on the terms usual in such engagements, the price of his passage and his food. I assented to this, but as it turned out, I left Altun Keupri before he was ready, and so missed him.

There was also an Armenian of Aleppo returning to his native place, a man of some intelligence and tremendous verbosity, who launched into a long eulogium of the English and their behaviour during the Armenian massacres. He was an unsavoury creature, though, like most of his race, so I entered into an argument with a Sulaimanian in Kurdish—of which the Armenian was ignorant—to rid myself of him.

We jogged along for hours and hours, through the low hills, across them, and to the plain on the other side. There was no moon, and the usual straining of eyes was accompanied by drowsiness, and the state of semi-unconsciousness that overtakes one on long night journeys. Once we were all brought to a halt by being bombarded from a village, bullets flying around and over us, killing a donkey, whose owner, a Shuan Kurd, calmly shifted its load to another beast and went on without a word, for we had decided to go on through the firing and get away out of it, which we did after a bit, the bullets—flying wide in the dark—hitting nothing else.

I made the slight acquaintance during the journey of a queer pair of people. One was a young man of singularly foolish appearance. His garb was of Sulaimania or Kirkuk, and at first I took him for a Sulaimanian, only finding my mistake when, on addressing him in Kurdish, he replied in Turkish. His companion was his father, an elderly man of sturdy build and firm demeanour, who rode upon a small donkey immediately behind his son, urging them both along. To hear their conversation, one would imagine that the youth was the victim of a harsh parent who sternly rebuked him for everything he said and did, but a few moment's conversation with him was convincing evidence of his stupidity, and of the justice of his father's admonitions.

What attracted my attention to them at first was the crash of a water-pot the lad had let drop, because he tried to drink from its wide mouth while riding in the thick of the caravan. The inevitable result occurred— a mule jostled him, and, putting out his occupied hand to save himself, the jar fell. Not ten minutes after, he asked me for a drink from mine, but as I was unhooking it from my pack-saddle his father intervened.

"No, brother, give not to the foolish; for he that goes thirsty from the breakage of his water-jar deserves no chance to smash another's."

Nor would he permit it at all, but turned upon his son and rebuked him for his folly, and for his ill manners in thus addressing a stranger, asking for the little water that another possessed.

The old man was not of a conversational nature, and rode in absolute silence except when some foolishness of his son urged him to speech, so I saw little more of him before we arrived at Altun Keupri, which we did an hour before daybreak.

I had to rely upon my muleteer, Umar, for a place to sleep, and he said he knew of such a one, and would take me there. The caravan melted away as soon as we crossed the high-peaked bridge, and we with two

Kirkuklis who had a load of "run," made our way along the long main alley to a caravanserai, at whose door we beat in vain for some time, to be told at last that four "Aistr-sawar," or mule cavalry, had taken the place and would let no one in. We succeeded in persuading them to do so, however, and stumbled, in the dark, into the small courtyard. Here the muleteer threw our loads and drove off his beasts, before I realised that he did not intend to stable them there, or that the place possessed no "Darban" or "Khanchi" men to look after travellers and the caravanserai. The place was, moreover, a ruin. A flight of mud stairs, so worn as to be little more than a smooth-backed buttress to its wall, led up to the stable roof, and three or four rooms which I did not explore. The soldiers were sleeping on the roof, so making the best of a bad job, I shouldered my goods and got them up the stairs somehow to the stable roof, and casting a sack upon the floor, lay down beside the soldiers and slept for a couple of hours.

CHAPTER XV

TO BAGDAD

At daybreak I woke, and immediately went to look at the rooms, one of which I required to put my things in. Two were locked, a third and a fourth had the roofs fallen in upon the floor, and a fifth I found I could lock after a little repair, which I effected with a horse-shoe nail from the courtyard and a piece of wood broken from another door. I dragged my things in, avoiding the holes in the verandah that looked through into the stable below, and padlocked the door.

The bazaar was not yet open, and as I went out of the caravanserai door the soldiers were just waking, and shouted at me to shut it again after me. I turned to the right down the street, continuing the direction of my journey of the night before, and came out upon the wide beach of the north branch of the loop of the Lesser Zab, which makes Altun Keupri an island. Here I had a good wash and a drink in the cold, sweet water, and ate a scrap of bread I found in my pocket. I was rather hungry, for except for a little bread and half a melon, I had had nothing since the morning before in Kirkuk.

Turning back, I came again into the town and sought a coffee-house, where I might glean some information as to how and where to find a raft going to Bagdad.

There are four coffee-houses in the main street of Altun Keupri, of which the largest and most popular sells only coffee. So I left this on my right, desiring

tea, and stayed at another. The attendant told me that
to get a kalak—or raft—I must address myself to the
people beyond the grain market, and instructed me how to
go. The proprietors, he said, were to be seen in a coffee-
house by the beach, where the rafts loaded.

So having paid my reckoning, I again went along
the little main street to the beach, at which I had
washed earlier, but turned to the left outside the town,
and keeping along its outskirts came to the grain market,
a busy space where heaps of fine wheat lay upon the
ground neatly marked with the impression of a spade
or some special implement to prevent thieving, and
picking my way among these came to two great coffee-
houses on the beach of the southern branch of the river.
Here under a pleasant canopy of green leaves outside
the coffee-house I sat, and, drinking tea, looked about
me. There were many Arab kalak-owners here, but the
coffee-house proprietor, who spoke Persian, told me of
one that would leave during the morning. As I was
talking my acquaintances of the previous day entered,
the stern father and silly lad, and hearing our talk, said
they were upon the same errand, and that we might
search together. At this I was extremely grateful, for
the stranger in a strange land hails with delight the
prospect of a travelling companion.

At the recommendation of the coffee-house keeper
we sought, and soon found, one Haji Uthman, a surly
Arab, whom we found contemplating the loading of a
kalak from the shelter of a canopy of boughs upon the
beach. Upon asking him if he had a kalak leaving
that morning, he replied in the affirmative, and pointed
to one just before him—then turning his back upon us
he entered into conversation with a dirty Arab upon
some trivial matter. He refused for some time to
recognise that we existed, till we turned to go away
in disgust, when he shouted over his shoulder that he
would give us a passage to Bagdad if we wanted one.
The price he quoted as four mejidies a man, and when
we protested at this large sum, he again ignored us and

engaged himself with other matters. Once again we turned away, and this brought the price down to three mejidies, but it required another rehearsal of the same act to bring him to the proper price, two mejidies. Even then he only consented with the most perfect ill-manners possible, telling us we must sleep on our own luggage and not spread it about the raft on the cargo.

He further demanded a mejidie from each of us, which we paid, and told us to go away as quickly as possible and buy ourselves provisions, for the kalak might start in a few minutes, and would wait for no one. Hurried off in this abrupt manner, we separated, each to seek food and luggage. On the way to the caravanserai I hired an old man with a donkey, and together we went to the room and loaded my things on the beast's back, and entrusting him with the transport and custody of the luggage, I left him to go to the bazaar, where I met the muleteer of yesterday, Umar.

Him I pressed to my assistance, and as he heard that I was leaving immediately, he thought of the most necessary thing, bread, so calling a boy (he seemed to know everyone in the place), he told him to run to his mother and tell her bake a large quantity of bread, and while it was making to have a bag made to put it in. We then turned our attention to the purchase of anything else the bazaar could supply for the journey, and found the only lasting fruit to be small pears. After much haggling we decided upon the goods of a certain man, and asked for a huqqa of them, and in view of the fact that we were thus purchasers on a large scale, were allowed to inspect each pear before accepting it. So we joined in together in the task, biting one here and there, feeling each and examining it for bruises and rot, and after what seemed an hour, having made our version of the weight agree with that of the seller, poured our purchase into a handkerchief, and set forth to find cheese. Various kinds we saw and tasted, unsavoury lumps of what would appear to be grey stone, and chose some the vendor swore was at least a year old, and so

z

warranted not to deteriorate with keeping. To eat such, it must be soaked in water for half an hour to soften it and expel some of the salt with which it is impregnated. We poured the cheese in with the pears, and my food for the journey—when I should have my bread—was complete, and I should have laid out, fare included, about four mejidies (or thirteen shillings) for a journey of eleven days to Bagdad.

All things being now ready, except the bread, we returned to the coffee-house, the terminus, so to speak, for all kalaks, and called for tea. While discussing this, I heard "Ghulam Husain," and was joined in a moment by a tall Arab, who had accompanied me on the journey in the spring to Sulaimania. Now I was not certain whether Umar knew what I purported to be, and was glad that the old man and his son were not present, for they knew me for a Christian, and to appear in a false light before either them or the Arab would have been very undesirable, particularly as the latter was an extremely fanatical fellow, with whom I had had many a religious argument on the right of Shi'a and Sunni.

He ran upon me, and embraced me with the greeting of Islam, a kiss upon either cheek, and talking in a loud voice in Turkish, began to ask me where I had been, and what doing. All the time I was keeping a weather eye lifting for the old man and his son, and endeavoured to get away, but the Arab refused to let me go, saying that by a chance God had thrown us together and we must not lose the time thus given us for brotherly conversation. And so he held me talking, speaking of Shiraz and Persia, subjects that attracted the idle in the vicinity, making us the centre of a listening group. In the thick of it a kalak-man came running to say that they were just leaving, and it occurred to me at the same moment that I had not yet got my bread, so entreating him to wait a few minutes I rushed off, glad to get away from the Arab, and full of the new fear of being left behind to kick idle heels in Altun Keupri for another week or so.

My shoes I had left on the kalak to mark the particular bales which I claimed as my place, and I ran through the streets of Altun Keupri, my feet scorching on the hot earth. I was wearing my old dressing-gown and a Kurdish headgear, a distinguished costume, and as I ran the tail caught between two donkeys' pack-saddles, and I left half a yard behind. Sweating, I arrived at the door of the baker, to find the housewife counting out the flaps of bread and putting them into a bag. I snatched it up and threw it across my back, astounded at its weight and bulk; and still wondering how I could ever eat this mountain of bread, I stumbled out of the yard, regardless of the good woman's cries to count the bread, and arrived at the beach just in time to get myself and my load aboard by wading through four feet of water, and mark my Arab friend emerging from the coffee-house to bid me a farewell that he shouted as he ran. The current was full here, though, and we were soon carried beyond earshot, and my attention was drawn to my immediate surroundings by the congratulations of the old man, who had installed himself at the opposite end of my row of bales, and sat viewing my torn skirts with sympathy.

For a half hour or so I was occupied in arranging a place upon the bales, spreading my cotton quilt under me, making a pillow of my bread, trying to arrange some means of forgetting that under me was not even level ground, but what I have called bales, bundles of knobby sticks of the hardest and spikiest wood on earth, I was sure, being taken to Bagdad for sale.

This I managed to a certain degree, and at last sat quiet to fry under the August sun, in a breathless day—and feel the sweat running down. The raft turned round and round slowly, veritably roasting us all like kebabs on a skewer. The temperature in these quiet reaches of the river between low red hills was immense, and to think of it was but to remember that worse was certainly to come when we reached the Mesopotamian plains.

About an hour before sunset we tied up at a little village

of Kurds where we were to take more loads of roots, and
all our nice arrangements were upset, for we had to take
our goods ashore to allow of the shifting of cargo. The
place was at the end of a long, still reach of the river; and
entrusting my goods to the old man, I retired to a
secluded spot and indulged in a bathe, the first swim I
had taken for a year, and the first bath of any sort for
well over a month.

We ate our simple meals of bread and fruit there
upon a stony beach, and lay down to sleep upon the
pebbles until early morning. And so for three days
we progressed, our way winding among low hills along
the picturesque Lower Zab through an almost deserted
land. That we had left Kurd and Turkoman behind
was now evident, however, for we saw none but Arabs,
and very few of them.

At intervals along the bank would be tiny patches
of cultivation of melons, where the falling summer river
left a damp bank of silt, and occasionally the owner
would be there tending the fruit, but often enough we
would not see any signs of habitation for miles and miles
near a cultivation, which seemed ownerless and deserted.
The day heat was intense. As the river was too low to
navigate at night, we were enabled to sleep on the banks,
and early morning saw us once more afloat enjoying the
half-hour of light before the sun rose. Then, too, two
hours followed of cool, the breeze overcoming the sun's
heat, but during the morning this would drop, and we
floated unsheltered from a sun that seemed to scorch the
bare flesh, and sent the perspiration rolling down among
the hair and into the eyes. Then one afternoon, following a day during which we had been nearing a forbidding
and perpendicular ridge of mountain, we spun round
a corner, across a bar, and out into a very lake—the
Tigris—which crept round a great bend and flowed
under the Jabal Hamrin range, a barren and desolate
mountain that harboured nought but Jabaur Arabs.
Now we tied three of our small rafts together, and there
would be no more nights ashore. Till we got to Bagdad

we must sleep on our bundles of roots, and bear the
ever-increasing heat through days of still slower progress.

The stream carried us under the great red bare
rocks of the mountain, and from behind them sprang
out a score of Arabs, who ran along the bank shouting to
us to stop. One, stripping, swiftly dived and swam off
to us. He was a savage-looking creature, and swimming
with a strong, determined stroke, he overtook one of the
rafts. Naked he sprang upon it, and—like all the robbers
of the East, in a terrible hurry—he demanded tobacco
and bread. These were given him and he pushed off to
another raft, taking toll again, when finding it drifting
afar he sprang off, and holding his spoil above his head,
swam rapidly to shore. Meanwhile his mates continued
to threaten, and our Arab kalak-men, intimidated, propelled their clumsy craft near the side, and to satisfy the
shrieking Arabs, collected a little tobacco from each of
us and swam ashore with it, considering themselves
fortunate to be allowed to go on without suffering further
loss. These same Arabs had and have a bad reputation,
and will fire upon a kalak till the craft comes alongside,
when they will strip it, carrying away even the skins and
poles of which it is made.

The current took us away gradually from them, and
the last we saw of them was a fight going on for shares
of the tobacco.

We had taken as a passenger at the Kurdish village
a queer old man, wizened and bent, clad in curious
garments, flowing and old, who carried a little bag and
a tin water-pot. He had appeared on the beach that
evening when we had first halted, and announced himself
a native of Samarqand. In truth, he had a Mongol
appearance. His little eyes went up at an angle from
the bridge of his flat nose, and his beard grew in that
straggly, meagre way typical of the Turkoman and
Mongol races. He spoke Turkish, Kurdish, and Arabic,
but was so old that he had forgotten which was which,
and, mixing them up, was utterly unintelligible to the
Arab kalak-men. All day he muttered to himself,

fingering his water-pot, or mending ancient garments
with a wooden needle. He had no bread, and ate
sparingly of what we gave him. He made this out to
be his fifteenth journey to Mecca, but had quite forgotten
the pilgrim season. His talk was of many people and
places, jumbled together. Relics he had of each: a
penknife from Meshed, a piece of wax from Aleppo, a
knob of some aromatic gum from a village in the
remoter wilds of northern Kurdistan.

"That," he would say in his mouthing way, "is what
they call in my language a knife—'buchaq,' or Arabic
'sikkin'—those Kurds call it 'kiard.' It is a good one,
and I bought it for two metallik (a small Turkish coin)
in Meshed bazaar, near the Imam Reza mosque, of a good
Musulman that never let pass a day but he gave bread
to such as myself. It was here in this Bagdad I
bargained for the knife of him, a tall Kurd of Diarbekr,
when—" and he would break off, and in the middle of
the morning, having forgotten his ablutions, stand up—
back to Mecca, instead of face to it—and say afternoon
prayers.

On being addressed, he would give an answer to
some thought in his reminiscent brain, as like as not
in Turkish, and finished in Kurdish, which he spoke
often enough—the rough Kurdish of Bayazid that we
southerners hardly understood. He reckoned to get to
Mecca in a year's time, begging his way from serai to
serai, or perhaps getting a passage from Busreh to
Jedda by a pilgrim ship. "Oh," he said, "I found my
way from Bagdad to Palmyra and Medina twice, perchance I may do it again, who knows?"—and he would
ramble off into reminiscences of thirsty days in the
Arabian desert, mixed with the memory of the defiles
of Kurdistan and the freezing winter plains of Turkistan,
lapsing now and again into a queer dialect we could
only suppose to be that of his native place.

So this strange company floated to where a cliff
cropped out of the flat desert, and we came to dirty
Tekrit, upon a slope under its lee, a desert town, isolated

in a barren stretch of nothingness upon the loneliest river surely that ever ran. Filthy Tekrit, with its thirteen shops which it calls a bazaar, and its two coffee-houses, one full of Turkish parasites, who sit upon a little verandah high on a rock to catch the warm evening breeze.

Hideous straight-sided houses, a town of ugliness, full of well-dressed Arabs sitting in the shade doing nothing —the favourite pursuit of all Arabs—their women filing down in strings to fill the narrow-necked, big-bellied water - pots the Arabs use from Mosul to the Gulf. Pretty girls some of them were, that stopped carefully to wash their feet and the water-pot before carrying it back. The young bride might be seen there, soon entered upon the life of drudgery that would age her at twenty-five, bearing gold ornaments hanging about her; and the hag, who lived upon the charity of an idle and arrogant son, and gathered her dirty rags about her shrivelled and blackened limbs. Essence of barren-ness, this Tekrit, a scorpions' nest of venomous Arabs, a city of dust built in the dust. Not a blade of grass, no sign of a green leaf. Yet from somewhere came one selling fresh dates, and we bought the sticky, half-ripe things as a luxury, while we crouched among the Arabs under a falling wall to get away from the sun's rays.

It has a kind of history, and its antiquity is undoubtedly great, like that of most of the Mesopotamian towns. Persian and Arab historians tell that it was built by Ardashir Babakan, the Persian king who ruled in the 3rd century of the Christian era, and founded the great Sasanian dynasty that ruled till Muhammad upset the growth of Christianity and spread of civilisation, under the Persians. Others say that the founder was a niece of that Bekr that built Diarbekr, but this can be little but a fable.

On the cliff above Tekrit there are ruins, and in the vicinity of the town there are signs of the time when Birtha, as the place was called in ancient times, was a large and important place. During early Christian times it was the residence of an important Christian official, and is said to have contained as many as twelve churches. At any rate, during the time of the khalifas of Bagdad it was important enough to possess a good bridge, no relic of which now remains, and it withstood a siege against Timur Lang.

Here, hoping to enter by the bridge into Mesopotamia and approach Bagdad from the west, Hulagu Khan, the leader of the Mongol horde that blighted all the Middle East, advanced upon Tekrit, but the Khalifa Al Musta'sim b'Illah destroyed it before he reached the place, and a great battle occurred between the two armies around the place. This was in the first half of the 9th century.

Now it is a place of some fifteen hundred houses, whose inhabitants, says a Persian traveller, "are a people friendly to darvishes," and of the Hanafi branch of the Sunni Musulman.

Here we took as a passenger an old woman going to Bagdad, a relation of one of the kalak-men, who looked after her with great care. She, on her part, took the ancient man under her special protection and provided him from her plentiful store of bread. She pressed such delicacies as sweet thin wheat cakes and dates upon us, and was extremely sympathetic when she found I spoke but little Arabic and was a stranger from a far land. It was she, too, that rigged up a shelter from the sun between two rows of bales, and gave me some of her sticks, with which to do the same, for which I was grateful, for the mid-day sun was now almost past bearing without some shelter.

Next morning we woke to see the spire of Imam Daur, a small town upon the left bank of the river, backed by one of the ancient mounts. This Daur, or Dura as it was anciently called, has a very old history indeed, for we read of it in the Bible :—"Nebuchadnezzar the king made an image of gold, whose height was threescore cubits and the breadth thereof six cubits: he set it up in the plain of Dura, in the

province of Babylon;" and here the story of Shadrach,
Meshach, and Abednego was enacted. Here the Roman
army, after Julian was dead, attempted the passage of
the Tigris, and part actually waded and swam across;
and here Jovian, who succeeded Julian, having retreated
from Ctesiphon, made a treaty with the Persians which
gave them back the northern Mesopotamian provinces.
Here at the same ford attempted by the Romans, we
saw a caravan of asses being swum across the river,
their drivers effecting the transit by wading part of the
way and swimming the rest.

The third or fourth day out of Tekrit we saw the
golden domes of Samarra—" Surra-man-ra " ("That maketh
glad the heart of him who espies it"). It is a big place
upon a cliff that juts out into the broad Tigris; tawny,
like the desert out of which it rises, its great mosque
standing clear above all, with that clean, new appearance
that any strong building must possess in this clear, dry
atmosphere. No trees adorn its streets, they are as
desert as the plain outside. Only upon the opposite
side are a few gardens, and the remains of a bridge
of boats, which affords sufficient excuse for the Turks
to take a toll from all who pass down the stream.

The ancient fame of Samarra is departed, the crowds
of Persians that once inhabited it are departed, leaving
behind a mixed population, noted for its immorality
and rascality.

Persian historians affirm that Samarra was built by
Shapur the Sasanian in the middle of the 3rd century
A.D., but that after the power of the Sasanians waned
and disappeared in the 7th century before the rising
might of Muhammad, the town fell to ruins and was
neglected till the reign of Al Mu'tasim, khalifa.of Bagdad,
who made it his capital, and one of the famous cities
of the East. This position it held till the time of the
Khalifa Mu'tamid, who re-established the Khalifate at
Bagdad. The period of the occupation of Samarra by
the khalifas was a decadent one. Following immediately
the brilliant times of the famous Harun ar Rashid and

Al Ma'mun,[1] who died in A.D. 813, Mu'tasim, whose mind was fanatical and his ambitions those of a rapacious plunderer, by his employment of Turkish mercenaries took the first step upon that road that led to the decline of the dynasty, which, however, was never extinguished till the Mongols sacked Bagdad and murdered Al Musta'sim in A.D. 1240.

Here Mu'tasim built a great mosque, and enlarged the city so much that the Persian historians describe it as having "stretched its length and breadth, so that they said it was seven leagues long and a league broad."[2]

Here, too, was the famous minaret of Mu'tasim, which figures in the romantic stories of Wathiq, of whom the most fantastic tales have been told.

The fanatical nature of Mu'tasim has already been mentioned, and this was the moving factor in the pursuit of one of the greatest heresiarchs that ever threatened early Islam. This was Babak, who was known as the Khurrami, and who defeated in battle many of the bravest and most accomplished generals of the Khalifate. He was, however, captured by Afshin, a leader of great renown and bravery. To arrive at a knowledge of what the tenets of Babak were is now almost impossible, as the only record we have is the prejudiced accounts of Musulman writers, who naturally endeavour to fix upon him every loathsome and repulsive doctrine that is possible. At any rate, it would appear that Babak was supported in his wars by the northern Kurds, many of whom, not converted from the corrupt form of Zoroastrianism they had originally professed, were perfectly ready to throw the weight of their arms against any power that would force upon them new rulers and a new religion, particularly when those same were their hereditary enemies, the Arabs.

---

[1] It is noticeable that the mother and wife of Ma'mun were both Persian, and during the period of the khalifas of Abbasid extraction—the most brilliant—it was the Persian influence which contributed a great deal towards its liberality and high literary standards.

[2] *Bustan us Siaha.*

Professor Browne, one of the greatest authorities, writes at length on the subject of his beliefs,[1] which appear to have included the doctrines of metempsychosis, and a pretension to divinity.

When captured, he was sent to Samarra, where he was killed, his body being crucified on the cliff that overlooks the Tigris. And the grimmest feature of the whole tragedy is the ultimate fate of Afshin, the conqueror and captor of Babak, for he was suspected of having abetted the rebel Mazyar (who was crucified beside Babak), and was tried at Samarra on the charge of himself being a follower of Babak, and of pretending to the Divine Title. He was found guilty of these and other crimes, and while Mazyar was executed and his body hung next that of Babak, the unhappy Afshin languished in a prison. Then he too, dead, took his place between them, and his ashes—for the body was subsequently burned—were cast upon the waters of the Tigris.

These things happened in the years A.D. 839 and 840, and with the accession of Mutawakkil (A.D. 847), a tyrant and profligate, the dynasty declined, and Samarra began to acquire that name for evil that it has never lost.

Yet it ranks high among the holy cities of Arabian Iraq, for here the tenth and eleventh saints of the Shi'a succession lived and died. During the time of the Khalifate at Samarra, there lived the saint Ali bin Muhammad bin Ali bin Musa bin Jafar bin Muhammad bin Zain ul Abidin bin Husain bin Ali, the son-in-law of the Prophet himself. This was the "Tenth Imam," and he was succeeded by his son Husain al Askari, the Eleventh Imam, whose offspring Muhammad "as Saghir" ("the Lesser"), is that Twelfth Imam, the mysterious saint who has passed from the living, but upon whose coming again the Shi'a waits, and around whose second advent are clustered such masses of prophecies and tales as would fill volumes. He is the "Mahdi," at the mention of whose name the Persian rises and bows, for—who knows—he may see, as he is in the world of spirits, invisible but extant. He disappeared

[1] *A Literary History of Persia,* vol. i., pp. 323-328.

in the year 873 in a cellar in Samarra—a place where the dwellers retreat during the heat of the day. According to some he departed in Hillah, near Bagdad.

These religious circumstances, combined with an ancient fame and a present very fine mosque, make Samarra a favourite place of pilgrimage for Shi'a and Sunni alike—particularly the former—but all will agree with the Persian traveller who says, " The numbers of Sayyids[1] and beggars passes all description "|; and again, " The inhabitants of Samarra are said to be Hanafites, but it is really impossible to assert of what race or of what belief they be, for they are of an extreme meanness and servility of character, and of an avarice such that the beggars of Samarra are a bye-word in all Islam."[2]

As the golden dome faded from sight in the distance and the growing night, I realised that my journey as a poor man was nearly over, for we were approaching Bagdad. During the succeeding two days we passed cultivations, and gardens, and date groves, signs of the city we were approaching. From afar we sighted Kazemain, that holy place, too often described to call for mention here, and at last, one evening, our kalak-man told us that midnight would see us at the bridge above Bagdad, below which kalaks may not pass.

I began to think how I might enter Bagdad as a European, for I wished to go straight to the only hotel, and appear next day among the Europeans, with some of whom I had affairs, and some acquaintance. So, behind the bales, in the dark, I donned a suit of white clothing I had kept ready, minus a collar—for it was summer, and heat excuses many such details. I donned a pair of socks, a luxury to which I had long been a stranger, and had a soft felt hat, much squashed and battered—but still a Ferangi hat—ready in a handkerchief. Drawing the old dressing-gown around me, I climbed up on my bundles of roots and lay down and slept awhile. About two in the morning I woke, for the kalak bumped against a bank, and

---

[1] Persons claiming direct descent from the prophet.
[2] *Bustan us Siaha*, p. 303.

I saw we had arrived. My friends were collecting their goods, and the old Kirkukli asked me how and where I proposed to go? to which I replied, I would depart in a "quffa," or round bitumen-covered coracle, to the house of a friend lower down the river. This craft one of the kalakmen found for me after some minutes, and I took a farewell of my friends, the last friends I should have in a world I was leaving—not without pangs, for I had become one of them, and found myself often enough contemplating with disgust the prospect of striding about as a Ferangi—the "vulgar and blatant abomination" at which Turkoman, Turk, Arab, Kurd, and Persian stand astonished.

I slipped into the quffa, my fez still upon my head, still "effendi," and sat quiet, waiting till we should arrive at the back-stairs of Bagdad's only hotel, a humble house kept by a Christian. When we arrived I hurried to the door, and standing in the shade of the portal, bade the men of the quffa wait beside my luggage. In the dark and shadow I slipped the European hat upon my head, threw the dressing-gown over my arm like an overcoat, and stood, a European in appearance, if somewhat shabby.

The door opened, I entered, and pleading fatigue sat in a dark corner while the baggage was brought in and the boatman paid. I was shown to a room, and slept for an hour, and woke in the morning to a hot bath and a meal of European bread, milky tea, and boiled eggs, the sight of which discomfited me, so that I passed them away and called for tea from a tea-shop—milkless, and in a small glass—not a footbath of a cup.

I spent most of the day trying to get used to sitting upon a chair, but it was horribly uncomfortable, and my legs would gather under me in spite of myself.

I felt stranger and more lonely than I had done ever before. Gone was the coffee-house and the bazaar, of the multitudes of which I was one, and equal, with whom I spoke and laughed, and fought and wrangled. They were far away, and I must learn to look upon them as upon strange and inferior beings, if such were now possible, and taking place again on the platform of Western birth, once more go on my way affecting to ignore their joys and sorrows—which had so lately been my own.

CHAPTER XVI

OF KURDS AND THEIR COUNTRY

"Shedders of blood, raisers of strife, seekers after turmoil and uproar, robbers and brigands ; a people all malignant, and evil-doers of depraved habits, ignorant of all mercy, devoid of all humanity, scorning the garment of wisdom ; but a brave race and fearless, of a hospitality grateful to the soul, in truth and in honour unequalled, of pleasing countenance and fair cheek, boasting all the goods of beauty and grace."—*Bustan us Siaha,* p. 459.

THE race of Kurds is so little known, and so maligned when mentioned, that some idea of their origin and history, as well as an attempt at a vindication of their character, is not out of place here. Within recent years they have probably never come before the eye of the British public except in their traditional character of rapacious and furious fiends, fantastic figures of savagery pouring out from impregnable mountains and carrying desolation before them, slaying Christian and Musulman alike, resisting all efforts by princes and powers to subdue or even coerce them.

Of what they may be, their origins and history, I suppose less is known than of any other race in the East, so numerous and powerful, and it may come as a surprise to many that Kurdistan has a history, and an ancient one, noble families, and a fine—if somewhat limited—literature. So well have the secrets of the race been guarded, that one at least of the many travellers who have remained among them for some time goes so far as to state definitely that " they are as destitute of annals as the wolves and jackals among whom they have lived in the high mountains from immemorial time,"[1] a statement which reflects more upon the ignorance of the writer than upon the Kurds, whom he would thus brand as being but little removed from the denizens of the hill-sides.

The Persian legend has it that Kurds are descendants of those young men who were saved from the voracity of the serpents of the monster Zohak of the Persian mythology, which were fed upon human brains at the devil's suggestion, and which were deceived by having the brains of goats substituted for those of the two youths who were to become the progenitors of the Kurdish race.

Another and less known legend is that Solomon, having sent for four hundred virgins from the East, and they having arrived in the country now called Kurdistan, were deflowered by the devils therein, whereupon Solomon resigned them to those devils, and their offspring were called Kurds.[2]

It is a long retrospect back to 1200 to 1500 years B.C., for it is there we are to see the kings of Nairi, who appear to be the forbears of those Medes who later gained renown, and again later, under the name of Kurd, remained a word of terror in the ears of the neighbours.

In those days the Assyrians reigned in the lands about Mosul and between the rivers Zab. Following the course of the Greater Zab, from its middle to its source, was an obscure, little-known land, and here was the heart of the Nairi land. Here, too, later, were the Medes established, and here is still the heart and centre of Kurdistan.

Armenia, or Urartu, was tucked away north of all this, behind the mountains and Lake Van, upon its plateau, and the kings of Urartu are not to be confounded with the men of Nairi. Nor were the Nairi lands confined to the upper waters of the Great Zab, for the people between the

---

[1] Creagh, *Armenians, Koords, and Turks*, vol. ii., p. 167.

[2] One of the many stories invented on account of the fear and dread they inspire in the people around them.—*Sharaf Nama.*

Tigris headwaters and the Euphrates north of Mount Niphates, that is, in modern times, Kharput and Darsim, in Bitlis and the Taurus range, were mentioned by Tiglath-Pileser and his successors (1100 to 600 B.C.), as the Nairi; that same land that later harboured the Invincible Gordyene, whose name appeared immediately after the disappearance of the name Mede at the middle of the Achæmenian dynasty of Persia (about 400 B.C.), and in reference to races inhabiting the lands of modern Kurdistan—which was Media.[1]

And since that time it has been Kurdistan, home of wild races speaking a language the purity of whose ancient forms is one of the best proofs of the occupation by the Kurds of their great mountains ever since the Aryan horde started from its "land of the Dawn" to people Persia, Media, and part of Europe—of which we ourselves are the descendants, through the Saxons, and so kin to the Kurd, who has never mixed his blood with that of the Arab or Turk, but kept it as pure as his unmixed speech.

Assyria, that conquered its world, found in these people of the mountains a more difficult problem than any they had yet encountered. We are told[2] that there is no reason to believe, although the Assyrians passed through the Zagros (the mountains *par excellence* of the Kurds) that they subdued any but the people immediately upon their route, a characteristic of Kurdistan and the attempts to invade it so like the tales of modern Persia and Turkey, that it might be the story of any of the sultans and shahs of the last two centuries.

Professor Ragozin, in the work referred to below,[3] remarks: "It is impossible not to notice the remarkably

---

[1] Speculation has had its day even with the origin of the Kurds, in the theory put forward by some that they are the descendants of the Parthians, a theory quite impossible to consider, now that the Parthians are known to be of Scythian race, of a type ethnologically and linguistically different from the modern Kurd, who is a pure Aryan.

[2] Ragozin, *Assyria*.   [3] P. 54.

2 A

mild treatment which Tiglath-Pileser awarded to the kings of Nairi, a treatment so strongly contrasting with his usual summary proceedings as plainly to indicate a conciliatory intention."

And again, speaking of the mountains above Erbil: " An expedition into the south-east, into the outposts of the Zagros mountains, is mentioned indeed as successful and profitable, but without much emphasis, which, in view of the tremendous stress always laid upon any victory by the inscriptions, points to a somewhat abortive expedition."[1]

Nor was it always a case for aggression by the Assyrian king, for the great amount of the time spent by some of their monarchs in fighting with the Kurds seems to indicate that the Assyrians may even have been defending themselves rather than adopting an aggressive part.

Shalmaneser II., in the records of whose reign (860 to 824 B.C.) all the lands which he conquered are set out in detail, must have failed to make any impression upon the Zagros hills, for no mention is made of the Nairi whatever.

And when a tribe, important or unimportant, was subdued or vanquished, it was reckoned so great a feat of arms and courage, that it was worthy of particular record in the king's annals. Thus we find Sennacherib, who performed so many great deeds, marching against a tribe in Zagros called Kasshu, and actually subduing them. Care is taken to mention in the record that this tribe had never before been conquered.

As the Assyrian dynasty grew old and feeble, the Medes were gaining in strength. Their tribes were in unison of purpose, and at last were gathered under the first Median king, who established himself at Hamadan (the Biblical Ecbatana), situate upon the eastern border of his kingdom, and protected from Assyria by great mountain ranges.

This was a member of the " House of Dayaukku," a family with which the Assyrians had fought before in the neighbourhood of Van.[2]

---

[1] Ragozin, *Assyria*, pp. 54-5.   [2] *Ibid.*, p. 420.

His son, Fravartish, and his son after him, too, Uvakshatara, spent their days in organising an army, the younger man, when he succeeded his father, altering the formation of the army from that of a disconnected mass of small tribes fighting independently, to a homogeneous force. And as long as the Medes held thus together they carried all before them, to which fact there is no better evidence than the Bible itself.

But Mede and Persian fell again; the Persians were subdued, and the Medes, deprived of the support of these their kinsmen, retired to their fastnesses and commenced the later period of history of their race—under the name of Gordyene, or Kurd.

Xenophon found them—his Karduk—to his cost, as all who read the " Retreat of the Ten Thousand " may learn, and he found them there in Anti-Taurus, or as we call it to-day, Hakkiari, Central Kurdistan.

When it is remembered that this part of Western Asia has been subject to the most wholesale revolution, to invasions by the armies of every nation that ever acquired fame and name in the Eastern world's history—Assyrian, Parthian, Greek, Roman, Persian, the Arabs under Muhammad, and the Mongols—the fine stability of the race stands out, for among all the people of these lands they alone have withstood every army, and retained pure their language and blood, and claim with a pride of race to which none can grudge admiration, that they are the pure Aryan, the " holders of the hills, and the possessors of the tongue."

Within the last century the national spirit awoke four times and asserted itself in attempts to throw off the yoke of the Turks. The first occurred in 1806, when Abdurrahman Pasha, the Baban of Sulaimania, fought long and bravely against the Turks for the independence of southern Kurdistan, being defeated at Darband-i-Bazian in 1808 by the Bagdad Pasha, who, assisted by one of the Kurdish Pasha's relations at feud with him, succeeded in taking him in flank.

A few years later, Muhammad Pasha, also of the Baban

stock, at Rawanduz, acquired great power, and he too made a bid for national independence, and actually possessed himself of Upper Mesopotamia, Erbil, and Kirkuk. His rule was of so cruel and inflexible a nature as to subdue even the most turbulent, and his power such that, aided by his large army of irregular cavalry, he kept his provinces in absolute subjection and excellent order. He was eventually, at an advanced age, lured by the Turks into a snare, and after a journey to Constantinople, where he had been received with great honour, and a restitution, his murder was contrived on his return journey to his provinces.

Yet once again, one of the last of the Sulaimania pashas, Ahmad, attempted a revolution against the Turks, and went out to battle against them, marching on Bagdad, to fail.

The fourth event, which can be hardly termed quite a bid for independence, was the revolution under Badar Khan Bey in 1847, mention of which has been made in the chapter dealing with the history of the Chaldeans.

In recent times, commencing some five hundred years back, and as their surroundings have become accessible, as well as owing to the very gradual increase of their numbers, they have spread north and west. Their southern limit always was, and still is, the ancient road from Kermanshah to Qasr-i-Shirin, but in Turkish territory they have established themselves in Armenia, and have pushed their way west from Darsim and Kharput, so that now there are villages of the Milli Kurds a day out of Aleppo and away up in the mountains of the north-west.

So little is known of their history, that it is hardly realised that among them there are ancient tribes and noble families, some of whom it will not be out of place briefly to mention here. To attempt an adequate treatment of the history of the tribes, so far as it is possible to learn it, would be to write another volume.

Turning first to the centre of ancient Kurdistan,

Bitlis and the Hakkari[1] country (the upper Great Zab and the mountains south of Lake Van to the Tigris at Jazira ibn Umar), we find the tribe of Hakkari, that has sent its philosophers as far north as Bayazid, and peopled to a great extent that city, and given princes to Rawanduz and the south.

After the conquest of Diarbekr by Timur-i-Lang (Tamerlane) in the 14th century, a governor was placed over the district of Hakkari, named Amir Qara Uthman (the Black Lord Uthman), who, finding the country impregnable and access to it impossible, took the politic line of seeking in marriage the hand of a lady of the noble Hakkari clan of feudal lords. In doing so he identified himself with the tribe, and when the hand of Timur-i-Lang grew weak in the environs of Kurdistan, this Amir Qara Uthman became to all intents and purposes a Kurd, and his descendants founded or rather exalted the old Hakkari family, adopted the title of Prince, and ruled in great state at Bitlis, where the princes of the Hakkari ruled up to the 19th century.

They became so powerful, and contracted such wise alliances with the tribes, that at Jazira ibn Umar, Amadia, Julamark, and Rawanduz, the beys and princes were of the Hakkari, ruling independently of all outside powers, and never troubling about the claims of Turkey and Persia to the possession of their land, which were inaccessible.

Under its princes Bitlis became a very important centre, and Edrisi, the brilliant minister of Sultan Selim, himself a Hakkari Kurd, was responsible for expanding the territories held by some of the tribes under Hakkari rule.

He moved the Haidaranlu and the allied tribes northward into the Armenian country to guard the Persian frontier, and there they have stayed, till now Kurds of these, the most savage of all the Kurds, are domiciled

[1] This word is often spelt Hakkiari, the first "i" providing the word with the vulgar and the Turkish pronunciation.

across Armenia, and as far west as Erzerum, living in
such numbers as almost to warrant the application of the
name Kurdistan to these provinces.

The princes of Bitlis reached their greatest power
in the 16th, 17th, and 18th centuries, when they
were independent, sometimes acknowledging a kind
of suzerainty of Persia or Turkey, and at others denying the right of any Power to claim them as subject
rulers. The last of the line, Sharif Bey, held out against
the Turks for several years during the first half of the
19th century, when Turkish effort was concentrated to
bring Kurdistan to subjection. He was captured by
the Turks in 1849 and taken to Constantinople, and
Bitlis has since been ruled by a Turkish governor.

Though their capital has been taken from them, the
Hakkari are still a very powerful and famous tribe, and
remain unmolested in the highlands of their country.
The Turks have also adopted a more conciliatory attitude
towards them, as, being on the frontier, it is highly advisable that they should be favourably disposed to Turkey.[1]

In the neighbourhood of the Hakkari—to the west and
north-east in Darsim—are the Kurds of the Zaza, a
curious tribe, of the history of which nothing is known
except that they have been in these mountains for ages.
I regret exceedingly not having stayed among them,
for their dialect is of extraordinary interest, Aryan of
the Persian and Kurdish group, but differing from both.
The tribe inhabit mountainous regions in most of the
least-known parts of the lands about the Tigris headwaters and in Darsim. By travellers they have been
described as " shy, impish little people," and those of
them I met, while shy, certainly were of a genuine and

---

[1] A curious custom is told of in connection with the succession
to the Khanate. This was, and is, hereditary, but if the khan be not
considered equal to his exalted post, a meeting of important men
is called. If after deliberation the khan is deemed unworthy, a pair
of shoes is placed before him, and he is expected to don them and
quit the room, thereby consenting to the transfer of the succession
to the next candidate. The deposed khan's lands and property are
not taken from him.

simple type, courageous and hard-working little men, with a large proportion of blue-eyed, fair-haired people among them.

Turning once more south-east, we come by the Hakkari to the tribes south and south-east of them, the Mukri and Ardalan of Persia, and the Jaf of Turkish territory, three famous tribes—and yet farther south the Kalhur and Guran.

The Mukri tribe, which inhabits Persian territory south of Lake Urumia, is the southern arm of what may be termed the northern branch of the race, that speak the Kurdish language in all its purity of accent and grammatical form. The Mukri claim that their dialect is the most ancient of all, and while its antiquity is probably not greater than that of its neighbours, its excellent preservation of ancient forms gives it a claim to be considered the standard by which to compare other dialects.

The tribe is not now a large one, but is allied to those surrounding it, particularly to the west and south-west, and enjoys a great name, which it has won for itself by the bravery of its people and the power of its sardars, or rulers, who at their curious little capital, Sauch Bulaq, have reigned for several hundred years. Shah Abbas, Nadir Shah, and Fath Ali Shah have all relied upon the Mukri for assistance in their various wars, and the first mentioned and greatest of them— who relied upon the Kurds to a very great extent for his fighting forces—made many of them high officers in his army, and it is said owed many of his victories— particularly in the west—to the Kurds in his army. This was the case in 1624, when the bulk of Shah Abbas' army was composed of Mukri Kurds, who defeated the Turks in a considerable battle. The tribe has always been kept in good fighting form by the proximity of the renowned robber tribe of the Bilbas, with whom they have often been to battle, and whose depredations in Persia they have not infrequently been called upon to punish. The Mukri and Bilbas are of almost exactly the same stock, and probably are two branches of the same tribe.

It is interesting to note that in the territory of the Mukri is the place where Zoroaster, the great prophet of old Persia, was born and first taught.

Here in their northern boundaries lies an interesting ruin, which—now known as Takht-i-Sulaiman—is said to be ancient Shiz, and capital of Media.[1]

The Mukri, thus knowing many of the legends that hang around this place, indicate it as evidence to support their assertion that they are original Kurdish stock. They have, however, did they know it, a more notable proof of their descent from the Medes in the very language they talk, for it is the nearest of all the dialects to the Avestic of Zoroaster himself.

Their southern neighbours are a more famous race in modern times, and have played a more important part in Persian history than have the Mukri. These are the Beni Ardalan, whose capital is the beautiful little town of Sina, in the province known in Persia as Kurdistan—the Kurdistan *par excellence* of Persia. Here in the province of Ardalan ruled a noble and gifted family, which was founded, so it is said, in the 14th century, before which the old Ardalan chiefs reigned. The family claims descent from no less a person than Saladin himself, a Kurd of the Hasan Kaif, sub-tribe of the Hakkari.

That Sina is of great antiquity is evidenced by the number of inscriptions near and around it, mostly of the Sasanian period, when the district to its south-west, Holwan, the Zohab, and Qasr-i-Shirin of to-day, were seats of the Sasanian kings.[2]

The khans of Ardalan, after ruling in absolute

---

[1] For a detailed description of the place and full references regarding it, see Prof. Williams Jackson, *Persia, Past and Present*, pp. 123-143.

[2] The present town of Sina was built about A.D. 1633, beside the old town, which was on a flat space, whereas the present town is on a slope.

independence for some centuries, accepted the title of Vali of Ardalan from the Persian shahs, and identified the province with Persia, to which state Ardalan has always been very loyal. The independence of the khans at Sina was hardly affected by the change, for the only proof of allegiance they were called upon to supply was men for war, which they did. Up till the time of Khosru Khan, son of Amanullah Khan—a famous chief whose name lingers yet in these districts—Ardalan had preserved almost intact its independence, working with Persia in her wars more as an ally than as a vassal.

The little kingdom had extended its borders during the preceding centuries to include all the provinces and weaker tribes up to the borders of the Jaf, Mukri, and Rawanduz rulers.

These provinces were Juanru, Aoraman, Merivan, Bana, Saqiz, and the Persian districts of Hasanabad and Isfandabad.

Of these, undoubtedly the most interesting is Aoraman. This tiny province was practically independent, living under its own rulers, a proud family claiming descent from Rustam, the Persian national hero, speaking a language of their own, not admitting themselves Kurds, but " Aorami."

These Aoramani live in a knot of great mountains, guarded on every side by the mighty walls of Nature, and their habit and temperament is as exclusive as their country. According to their legend, Darius the Mede expelled the original Aoram from his native place near Demavend, in northern Persia, and he fled with his brother Kandul[1] to Media, finding in the recesses of these mountains a refuge. Here he established himself and founded the Aorami tribe.

At times during the ascendency of the Ardalan khans attempts were made to dislodge and subdue the Aoramani, but they were fruitless, and alone among the small tribes of the Perso-Turkish frontier Aoraman can

[1] Whose descendants are said to be the Kandula tribe, east of Kermanshah, speaking a similar dialect.

still look over its own mountain slopes to-day, and bid defiance to all and sundry, for the ruler, Ali Shah, of Aoram Castle, is to-day independent in all but name.

The sub-provinces of Merivan and Bana, which lie to the north of Aoraman, were under their respective beys and khans, and never gave the trouble that Aoraman did, being purely Kurdish, and also possessing but little strength. The begs of Merivan had a habit of fighting with the sultans of Aoraman (as they have to-day), but so long as the Ardalan family retained their normal power the whole province was kept in good order.

The Court at Sina was kept up till well into the last century, and probably one of the most noted of all the Sina khans was Amanullah Khan, vali of Ardalan in the first two decades of the 19th century, who kept regal style in his little capital.

The family had, however, thrown in its lot to a great extent with the Qajar tribe of Persia when it first began to contest the Persian throne, and had made treaties of friendship and alliance. And once having given their allegiance to the Qajar dynasty (the present reigning one of Persia),[1] they kept true to their word, and assisted with men in the battles against the unfortunate Lutf Ali Khan Zend, whose defeat and death left the throne in Qajar hands.

Khosru Khan married a daughter of Fath Ali Shah, who, being a woman of strong character, still continued to hold the reins of government after her husband's death, and was succeeded by Ghulam Shah Khan in 1865.

Upon the demise of this, the last Ardalan vali, Nasir ud Din Shah took advantage of his power both as relative and sovereign, to introduce such factors into the succession as should render the candidate uncertain, and in the meantime, while the young khans were

---

[1] This commenced with Agha Muhammad Shah, who grasped the throne in 1794, and was succeeded by Fath Ali Shah, contemporary of Amanullah Khan.

waiting a decision, he by a coup established his own uncle, Mu'tamed ud Douleh, a strong man, as governor of Kurdistan.

The people of Ardalan made little resistance, for they had become accustomed to the rule of the Qajar princess, and moreover the dynasty had lost a great deal of its influence and power, and become decadent. So Mu'tamed ud Douleh found it an easy task to retain his seat at Sina. But when he turned his attention to Aoraman he found himself confronted by a very different situation. The Aoramani, who had found it hard enough to have to submit to the Ardalan family, discovered in Persian suzerainty a condition of life to which their natures could not consent without a struggle.

Mu'tamed ud Douleh had a long and hard struggle before he could subdue Hasan Khan, sultan of the Aorami; and even when he did so, the respect the tribe had gained for itself was so considerable that the government was given into the hands of the son and his brother.

At the present time Aoraman lies part in Turkish and part—the greater—in Persian territory, and while the rulers on both sides are nominally subjects of those powers, they are to all intents and purposes independent, particularly Ali Shah, the Persian Aorami, who owns allegiance to none. An expedition is at the time of writing being sent against him from Sina to collect taxes and attempt to bring him to order.

The Ardalan family, though shorn of their power, are still a noteworthy family, and holders of position under the Persian Government. Fakhr ul Mulk, the present head of the family, an old man of great culture and learning, is Governor of Shushtar and Dizful, in Arabistan, and has an heir who is about twenty-five years of age.

From this advanced and powerful family we have to turn aside to their neighbours, of a different stamp—the Jaf, known throughout southern Kurdistan for their ability and ferocity in war. Up to the present little if

anything has been known of their history, and it is
given here upon the authority of a member of the
ruling family, Muhammad Ali Beg Pushtamala, of Qizil
Rubat, in extreme southern Kurdistan.

The tribe lays claim to having been domiciled in
Juanru, one of the sub-provinces of Ardalan already
mentioned, from the earliest times till about A.D. 1700,
and there they lived under the rule of the valis of
Ardalan. It appears, however, that either the Ardalan
valis cast jealous eyes upon the extremely fertile
province of Juanru, or, piqued by the growing strength
of the Jaf, made an attempt to bring the government of
the land more directly under their own hands. This
was not accomplished without fighting, and after a battle
in which the chief of the Jaf with his brother and son
were caught and slain, the remaining chiefs of the tribe
fled to the protection of the Kurdish pasha of Sulaimania, except a few sub-tribes whose attachment to the
land was greater than their detestation of the conquerors.

Some of these, however, the Qadir Mir Waisi, Taishai,
Qalkhani, Yusif Yar Ahmadi, Kuyik, Nirji, and Gurgkaish,
unable to submit to the rule of the arrogant Ardalan
valis, took refuge with the Gurans and adopted the
name also, being to-day known as the Jaf Guran.

The Kurdish pasha of Sulaimania gave the chiefs
protection, and granted their tribes the right to migrate
in the spring and autumn on the routes they still occupy,
namely, northward towards Panjwin, and south as far
as Qizil Rubat and Khaniqin. They thus became
Turkish subjects, and have remained so ever since.

The tribe is estimated to number some hundred
thousand people, and the pasha—Mahmud Pasha is the
head now — claims to be able to put four thousand
horsemen into the field at a few hours' notice.

One of the late chiefs, Uthman Pasha, who died in
the autumn of 1909 (to whom reference is made in the
chapters on Sulaimania and Halabja) strengthened and
enriched the tribe by his marriage with Adela Khanum,
who was a lady of the old Ardalan family of ministers

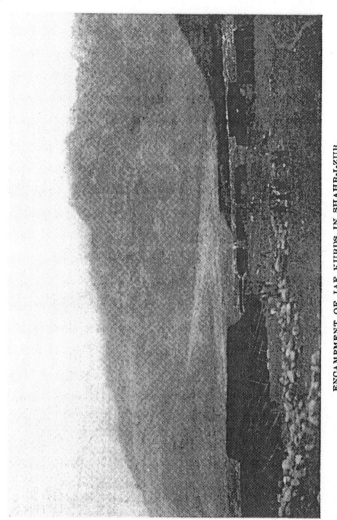

ENCAMPMENT OF JAF KURDS IN SHAHR-I-ZUR.

[To face p. 380.

to the valis, and at once drew upon himself the displeasure of the Turks and the approval of the Persians, who granted him a sword and title as a mark of the recognition of his having chosen a Persian subject to wife.

The pashas of the Jaf are a proud and haughty class of men, speaking little, but prompt to act, and they have, during the last hundred years, whenever trouble occurred in the tribe, taken such swift and effective action that since the first division of the tribe none further has taken place. Almost alone among the greater tribes of the Kurds this one of the Jaf has been able to live in good interrelation, for, as the heads of the various families have worked in concert, the tribe has grown wealthy and strong.

This is a remarkable feature of Kurdish life, for the reason why Persia and Turkey have been safe from the great invasions by Kurds that would otherwise have occurred, is the inability of the tribes to live at peace with one another—a not uncommon feature of the temperament of mountain races in all parts of the world.

The tribe seldom passes the Persian frontier, except at its northern migration limit near Bana, for over their southern border lies the territory of the Guran, an ancient and renowned tribe, which, while not so strong as it used to be, still commands a sufficient respect to keep in check its turbulent neighbours in Turkish territory.

Of all Kurdish tribes, perhaps the Guran has been best known and has excited most interest among those who have travelled in western Persia and southern Kurdistan. If, however, ethnological research could be brought to bear upon the tribe, it is possible that the Guran would be discovered to be not Kurdish, but either Lurish or Persian. Along the border that separates Kurdistan from Luristan, are a number of tribes that are neither Lur nor Kurd, and speak a dialect which is imagined to be the relic of the old Persian Tajik.

It is now thought that this country was peopled by

a sedentary population called Guran, speaking the dialect above referred to, and which is still spoken with variations by the Aoraman, Kanduleh, and Rizho settled tribes. The tongue was, and still is in a measure, the classical language of the Ardalan family, and is used in all the very extensive poetry that was and is written in and about Sina. It is now called Aorami, or Shahrazuri.

This theory accounts for the fact that a large portion of the Guran tribe—the sedentary section—still speaks the language. The nomadic section speaks a definitely Kurdish dialect, but this is readily accounted for by the circumstances which led certain Jaf and Kalhur sub-tribes to put themselves under the protection of the Guran and adopt their name.

The original tribe, which, governed by families of " Sultans," is a very ancient one, and claims direct descent from Bahrum Gur, whose name is familiar to those who have read FitzGerald's translation of *Omar Khayyam.*

After 1639, when the least indefinite of all the frontier treaties between Persia and Turkey was concluded and when the Jaf and other tribes joined them, the Gurans ruled with great power from their old capital at Gahwara, and made more famous their ballads and poems—which have given rise to the Kurdish name for certain kinds of poems—" Gurani."

They have lost their power recently owing to the weakness of their rulers, and have in the last few years quite retired into the background, leaving the field in possession of the Kalhur tribe, now stronger than ever before, a compact amalgamation of the sub-tribes bearing the generic name.

The Guran are the professors of that curious and obscure cult the Ali Illahi, those who have ostensibly accepted Ali, the son-in-law of the Prophet, as the personification of the Deity, and worship him as such.

It is impossible even to mention generally the mass of report and rumour that has grown up around the tenets of this faith. Every traveller, Persian and European, failing to find out what it is, yet desiring to place information on record, has advanced as fact what have sometimes been nothing but his own theories. Among the mass it is difficult to select any one that bears signs of even probable approach to the truth.

It would appear from reading through a collection of theories on the Ali Illahi sect that some have confused them with the Yazidis, of whom a description is given in Chapter IV., for they are accused by some of nocturnal congregation at which orgies occur, the very same accusation as was brought against the Yazidi. Among many of these descriptions the report of the Shi'a Muhammadan is evident, for it is common with him, when endeavouring to describe a sect of which he is ignorant, to attribute to it a leaning towards the things unlawful in the Muhammadan code, as well to make a narrative as to impress his hearers with the extent of the schismatics' backslidings. Thus—" In their own villages they do not deny themselves the use of wine or spirits, nor do they abstain from the prohibited food of the Quran; on the contrary, they indulge freely in swine's flesh and intoxicating liquors."

Be their customs what they may, their tenets at any rate include a great reverence for the Baba Yadgar, who was reckoned by them as one of the incarnations of God, for they apparently held such to be possible, and to have occurred in the case of Benjamin, Moses, Elias, David, Jesus Christ, and Ali; and seven "bodies," one of whom was the saint, who is buried at Baba Yadgar, the place of pilgrimage.[1]

They frequently invoke David, and the name Daud is a popular one among the Guran and Kalhur tribes; and it is said that before going to war, sacrifices of sheep are made to David.

Once a year a feast is observed, before winter commences, at which Ali is worshipped, and during the

---

[1] Sayyid Rustam, who is head of the sect, is asserted by a great many of them to be an incarnation of the Almighty.

summer is the feast of "Birkh,"[1] when sheep and fowls are sacrificed. A reverence is undoubtedly paid by them to fire, as is done to a great extent among many other tribes all over Kurdistan.

Their holy places are, besides the Baba Yadgar above mentioned, Zarda, which is quite near, in the Dalahu Mountain, and Dukkan-i-Daud. This last is an ancient Persian sculpture representing a religious ceremony by Zoroastrians.

It is evident that there is no definite code which can be described as Ali Illahism. It appears rather to be, as in the case of the Yazidis, an agglomeration of certain of the customs of many religious systems, some of which have been adopted to give an appearance of conformity with the religion of the ruling races in order to avert persecution for the rites they practise in secret. There is no guarantee even that Zoroastrianism was the original faith, though there are strong traces of it among them. Islam has obviously never touched them to such an extent as to convert them, and the reverence paid to Ali was doubtless the same as granted to other "incarnations of the Deity," and adopted for the reasons given above. The people are quite as ignorant of Musulman tradition as of Jewish, though certain travellers, Rawlinson in particular, thought certain of their habits to be Judaic.

The Persian opinion of their sect is as follows, as expressed in the most impartial works. It will be noticed that they give them a purely Muhammadan origin.

Their principal belief is that Ali is God, and, like the Nusairi sects, they say that to know God is impossible, because the essential entity and the non-essential (God and man) are in no way related one to the other, unless the essential entity descend from its inaccessibility and by beneficence guide men. The Divine matter and command may then become visible and cognate in order to be appreciable by man, and did

---

[1] "Birkh" in Kurdish = a lamb.

so in the case of the Virgin Mary, who was made the receptacle of such a manifestation.

In every cycle some spirit is vouchsafed to guide men,[1] that of this present age being Ali bin Abu Taleb, "to whom all creatures of Heaven testify," and him they call Qasim ul Arzaq (the Giver of Blessings).

There is current among them a belief that God Himself actually becomes visible in the most perfect men, and that He is visible in Ali.

A sect of them assert "that the saint is continuous with God, as the ray with the sun, but is not God, and yet is not other than God, neither is he separated from God nor commingled."

Abdulla ibn Saba, an Arab, and contemporary of Ali himself, first proclaimed him to be God, declaring, "God shall not appear but in Ali abu Taleb: prophecy pointed to him and the saints were inspired by him, taking all knowledge from him, who was creator and enricher, and in whom all limitations ceased." Ali himself, who execrated their beliefs, seized this Abdulla, and caused his followers to be cast into a pit, and fire thrown upon them. But so stubborn was their belief that as the burning brands descended they cried: "Now is the certainty of all certainty that thou art God, for the Prophet has said, 'None but God shall punish with fire.'"

This action did not exterminate the sect among the Arabs, for after the death of Ali they asserted that he was but temporarily absent, perchance in heaven, and that the lightning was a visible sign of his presence, and the sun his manifestation.

The Persian or Kurdish section say that Ali appeared three hundred years ago and renewed their faith and law.

They have given secondary names to their saints, and thus designate Ali the Sahib-i-Karam, Ibn Yamin they call Pir, Imam Reza they name Daud, Imam Husain they know under the name of Yadgar.

Their own people they term "yar," and strangers

---

[1] One of the Shi'a axioms.

"jouz," and when a convert is made he must bring a nutmeg (jouz), which is a sign of his renunciation of all other beliefs. They abhor shaving the beard or clipping the moustache.[1]

Their chief men are called Sayyid; they are known as a manifestation of the Sahib-i-Karam, and they have the power to decide what is lawful and what is unlawful.

One Persian writer, Mirza Muhammad Husain Isfahani, Zaka ul Mulk, says:—

"The author has been for years among them, and—while refuting their doctrines—he is bound to say that though they do not veil their women there is little or no immorality among them."

Such are the opinions of the best Persian authors regarding the origin of the sect, and it is evident that they explain very inadequately the curiosities of their beliefs, and have been led to commit some errors by attempting to give the Ali Illahi a purely Muhammadan origin.

There remains for notice the tribe of Kalhur, which is hardly within the province of this book, and to which therefore the briefest reference will suffice.

The tribe is to-day the most powerful of southern Kurdistan, and has for several centuries inhabited the lands near the frontier, upon the extreme southern border of Kurdistan and towards Kermanshah. Their leader is Daud Khan, an extremely powerful man, who from being a pedlar has risen to chief, and up to a month or two ago exercised the sway of an almost independent chief from Kermanshah to the Turkish frontier, as he has dispossessed the Guran of some of their power, and subjected entirely some small tribes, such as the Senjabi.

All kinds of curious theories have been put forward to account for the origin of the Kalhur, none being more fantastic than that of Rawlinson, that they are the

---

[1] The Musulman clips the "sharib," that part of the moustache liable to dip into liquids when drunk from a cup or bowl.

descendants of the Jews carried into captivity by Nebuchadnezzar.

They themselves are fond, like one or two other of the southern tribes, of asserting that they originated near Shiraz, and are southern Persians.

There is no particular reason to believe that they are other than Kurds, of the Kurdish race, mixed certainly with Lur blood, but of no other origin than the race among whom they are reckoned.

So much information has been collected about the tribe, that it is redundant to detail any here. From its situation along the Bagdad-Kermanshah road, the intercourse its chiefs have with Persia, and the fact that it is Shi'a by religion, the Kalhur is probably the most accessible of all the tribes of Kurdistan, and by no means the most interesting, either from the point of view of language, customs, or history.

As to the Kurdish language, so little is known of it that it has been described as a corrupt dialect of Persian and Arabic, "a kind of dog-Persian," and "a degraded old Persian dialect."

It is none of these.

Probably the Persian of to-day, beautiful language as it is, and perfect—the most euphonious and complete of all the Aryan tongues—cannot show such manifest signs of antiquity as does Kurdish. For there is a Kurdish language, a complete tongue, having rich grammatical forms, distinct syntax, and a total freedom from those Arabic importations which have, while enriching Persian, thrown into abeyance the old words of pure Aryan origin which were formerly used.

Ranging side by side the many dialects of Kurdistan, which differ in pronunciation and form so much as to be practically different languages, we find that one among them shows a regularity of form, a perfectly developed grammatical scheme, with a conciseness and clarity of construction and pronunciation.

This is the Mukri language, spoken in Lahijan of Persia, south of Lake Urumia, and at Sauch Bulaq, a little town in the mountains, capital of the Mukri tribe.

This is not the place for an excursion into investigations of the similarity of Kurdish roots to those of the Zendavesta; it is sufficient to say that the Mukri people, living where Zoroaster commenced his teaching, and where was possibly his native place, and speaking the language most nearly approaching the archaic form, have some good claim to be considered the preservers of one of the best specimens of a pure Aryan tongue extant.

Investigation of the Kurdish language generally shows it to be a pure language which has suffered only from the erosion of form and corruption of pronunciation inevitable in a language not "fixed" by possessing a generally used literature.

From the point of view of the interest of the student, it is most regrettable that Kurdish has so little literature; indeed, it is commonly supposed to have none. As has been mentioned before, however, there is a large amount of written matter.

Nor has the Kurdish nation, popularly supposed to be so obscure and savage, been deficient in supplying eminent men to the Government and army of Turkey. Probably few people know that the famous Saladin was a Kurd, or that Edrisi, the minister of the Sultan Selim, was of the same race.

As to their part in military affairs, the instinct of the race has given its members pre-eminence wherever as leaders they have sought it, and Turkey has counted among its bravest generals several Kurds of the north.

Bayazid, the frontier town of Turkey in Asia, close under Mount Ararat, is nowadays practically a Kurdish town, and as early as 1591 there was resident there one of the most celebrated Kurds of his time, Ahmadi Khani of the Hakkari, who built a mosque, wrote a number of philosophical, religious, and poetical works in his native tongue, and conducted a large school at which Kurds were the students, and their own language the chief subject of instruction.

One of the first books was a curious little vocabulary of Arabic, written in verse, as he says himself, for the instruction of " Kurmanj," *i.e.* Kurdish, children when they have finished their course of the Quran, "when it is well that they become acquainted with reading and writing." The little volume begins with the admonition :

> " If your grammar and lessons you fail to construe,
> No fame nor renown is in store for you."

The text is cleverly written in various metres, the name of which the author states at the head of each stanza, and which it is impossible to imitate in translation :—

> " ' Man ' and ' woman ' of the Arabs, we call mīr and zhin.
> ' Father,' bāb ; and ' mother,' dā ; ' brother ' we call brā.
> ' Son,' say we kurra ; ' daughter,' kich ; and ' uncle,' mām.
> ' Aunt ' is mata ; ' turban,' shāsh ; ' grandfather ' goes like pīra-dā.
> ' Rent ' is kirā ; ' a pledge,' kīrū ; ' loss,' ziān ; and durū, ' lie.'
> ' Selling ' we say firūhtin ; ' giving,' dān ; and ' buying,' kirrin
> ' Neck ' is mil or ustū ; ' heart ' is dul ; shāhīna is ' gay.' "

In this manner some two thousand words are taught to the child, and, with the excellent memory of the Aryan, this style of teaching (a popular one throughout the East) is less automatic and "parrot-like" than might be imagined.

From Ahmadi Khani we may turn to the *Sharaf Nama*, a famous history of the Kurds written by Sharaf ud Din Bey Hakkari of Bitlis, a rare and eagerly sought after volume, of which there is a copy in the British Museum. This is the best known of the literary works of Kurds, the fact, however, of its not being written in Kurdish denying it a place in Kurdish literature.

Sulaimania, during its short life of two centuries, has produced a great number of poets, who have contributed in verse to the literature of Kurdistan, generally in Kurdish, and some have progressed so far as to have written very bulky volumes.

The best known was Nali, who was the author of most

of the various styles of poems that go to make up a complete "Divan," or, as it may be called, "set of Works."

The subject of the Sulaimania poet is like that of nearly all the poems of townsmen, love ; page after page of fanciful allusion and play upon words, quite in the Persian style, which the Kurd always allows to influence the poem when it is of one of the forms used in Persian. The Kurdish poets of Sulaimania have, however, committed to writing some of the peculiar Kurdish chorus poems, which have a grace all their own. To translate such is to lose all the beauty of the original, which depends for its charm upon the language and the turn of the phrases more than upon the idea, for the love poems are much restricted in their simile, using all the stereotyped metaphor that Persian prosody allows, and little else, so close does the Kurdish taste in literature run to the Persian, unconsciously. Still, I only speak of the Sulaimania poets here. Outside, in the plain and upon the mountain-side one hears myriad songs, simple and pretty, for the Kurds are a race naturally gifted with all the kindred abilities to the linguistic sense, and it is extremely infrequent to meet one whose memory (unweakened by the use of memoranda and the art of writing, and unburdened by too many ideas) is not a storehouse of ancient folk-songs.

My bovine Hama was very fond in quiet moments of singing to a curious tune the old Mukri song, that of the fighter leaving his wife to go to the blood-feud :—

"I would across the hills and far away, wife,
    Say, shall I go, or shall I stay, wife ?

"If you would go, God guard you on the track,
    And I will watch you from the pass, till you look back ;
    I shall stand there in the sun until your clothes are shining white,
    Till you overtake the pilgrims that are travelling towards the night.

"What like of wife am I if I should weep or wail for you ?
    Or leave neglected home and field to make a child's ado ?
    Christian, Turk, and Persian whimper thus, and fear.
    Come, kiss me, and go swiftly, man and Mukri, Ah ! my dear."

There are many hundreds more of this kind of song, some of love, some of war, and others of nothing more than comic histories, such as the Kurds love, and a collection, once started, would never end.

Of the written poetry there is a large quantity—from Sina—written in the old Guran dialect by Kurds who learned it at the Court of Sina, and the following verses are taken from a manuscript volume containing some of the poems of the most celebrated poets of Sina, Aoraman, and Sulaimania, mostly written about A.D. 1750.

From the poems of Zain ul Abidin Palangani:—

THE EARLY DAWN OF SPRING.

"I look around upon the pearl drops of the dew
Suspended from the branch, and from the foliage new.

"The purple budlets show a new year's wounds are nigh,
And tears are dropping from the mist—itself a sigh.

"The buds and flowers are laughing at the nightingale,
For though they're wingless, yet they live within the flowery pale.

"From out the turf, the narcissus seems like a scar
Upon the ground, of winter—who still has not passed far."

From Shaik Ahmad Takhti, about A.D. 1770:—

"Come with me and view the forest's treasury now,
The silver's turned to gold, and yet the trees in sorrow bow.

"The treasury and I, we both are weak and desolate,
It, for its turn is come, and I, for grief's my autumn mate."

———

"Autumn goes
And winter's storms will leave the forest no repose.

"The weeping, whining wind is singing for the autumn forest's death,
The golden trees are weeping leaves of gold into the mountains' chilly breath.

"Some of them now are shedding all their blood-stained cloaks, and soon
Each one shall stand denuded, brave and stark as Bisitun.[1]

---

[1] A famous rock in southern Kurdistan.

"Their boughs displayed—not long ago—tints a hundred thousand
    fold,
So that the hot blood-feud, hunting in their glades, from awe grew
    cold.

"Then, catching them all unprepared, a wind arose and blew,
And cast away their ropes of foliage, their glory overthrew.

"And tore their leaves asunder, stripping off their raiment green
So poured away their gaudy glory, and left their stature mean.

"And where the autumn's gorgeous temples stood, was left forlorn
A melancholy company of mourners with garments rent and torn."

An old song of the Mukri :—

"A three-fold anklet jingles in thy skirt,
    Ah, Amina, then turn about this way ;
Dancing forward, rustling here and there, O flirt,
    Shake thy bangles, naughty one, in play.

"But love will catch thee while thou yet mayst dance,
    And catching thee, will stay the tripping feet
That turn thee round, to meet a sudden fiery glance :
    The head will whirl, the feet stand still, the heart will beat.

"Ah, Amina, thy budlike mouth awhile will sing thy song,
    Ah, Amina, then turn about this way ;
But love will take his toll, before so very long,
    And age, that poor old hag, will have her day."

These are not scraps and doggerel as it appears here,
owing to the translator's poor English: the originals are
sweet, and go far enough to show that the nation is not
devoid, as is popularly imagined, of all poetry or any idea
beyond savage and insensate war and killing.

The race certainly is, these days, a savage one, and
many tribes fully merit the execration that has been poured
upon them for outrages and massacres ; that is, they fully
merit the execration of modern European times. Yet, if
justice be done, we must for purposes of comparison place
Kurdistan side by side with the Europe of six hundred
years ago, and then it requires but little comparison to
show very conclusively that in point of mercilessness,
lawlessness, and savagery, this people of a militant creed
stand out in almost creditable relief against the black

deeds of the Middle Ages in a land where the religion of submission was supposed to be the guiding motive of life. Nor, in the present day, does the Kurd appear unfavourably in comparison with the European, judging him by the gauge of ideal and precept, upon the adherence to which alone a man can be judged, having in mind the exalted nature of each, or, as is too often the case, their absence. There is less crime of a despicable nature among any thousand Kurds, picked at random, than among the same number of Europeans taken in the same manner.

Yet the character of the Kurds is one on which the would-be writer is to experience enough difficulty, for the tribal character differs so much as to make one summary quite inadequate for the whole nation.

In the north, circumstances have to a great extent made the Kurd what he is, a brigand. Among the tribes of Hasananlu, Sipkanlu, Haidaranlu, Adamanlu, and Zirkanlu, who inhabit the mountains of Armenia and the country on the Turkish frontier, the character resultant from the precarious life of a robber is developed to the full. With the tribes on the frontier, who have always lived a life of duplicity, by the nature of the stratagems they adopt to escape the wrath of the countries whose frontiers they ravish, the man becomes suspicious, wary and unscrupulous. Their mountains, too, are not such as to lend to much cultivation, nor are there any commercial towns. So they are driven back to the horse and rifle, and as is natural, such a life demands scheme and counter-scheme, which speedily becomes a treacherous habit. Of their bravery there is little doubt, though I take it that it is more the bravery of "derring-do" than a calm, cool courage against steady odds. This, however, is a feature of many mountain peoples and guerilla fighters.

The true feudal spirit is strong in the race. Devoted to the mountains, to his own clan, intensely proud of being a Kurd, the northerner will take to arms at the word of his chief, never asking to hear his reason. Fraser, a traveller in the early part of the 19th century, observes: "The similarity between these Kurds as they are, and the Highland (*i.e.* Scottish) clans as they were not many centuries ago, is wonderfully strong."

The fighting Kurd is, like the Highlander of old, looking about him ever for the enemy, always on the defensive, and the character developed by these circumstances, coupled with the wild and terrible country in which the northern Kurd lives, has gone to make that character, composed of suspicion, bravery, an intense alertness, and highly developed faculty of observation.

In considering the criminal characteristics of a race or class, the conditions among which it exists must always be regarded, as also the amount of instruction in what we may call recognition of the existence of others.

Self-sacrifice, except that of the mother for the child, which is an instinct, is a purely artificial quality, and one instilled with great difficulty, and easily lost by those who fail to hold before them an ideal or principle. Now Islam provides no such ideal. The Christian has the highest incentive to this quality, which must be the foundation of all true civilisation, and yet even he is extraordinarily apt to forget it as time goes on.

The Kurd has not even the strict commands of Islam before him, and so is fain to learn by hard experience how he must live his life if he is to exist, and this, as among most rough communities, is a pure selfishness; and since the man thinks of nought but himself, there is no occasion for the birth of those qualities by which we are apt to appraise men. Moreover, it may be said, though it be a platitude, that the decadence and backward condition of the Islamic states generally is due to this omission in the religious code, for every public improvement is fundamentally due to the recognition of the existence of others.

If, then, we are to find in the Kurdish character any quality that falls within our Western category of good qualities, it must be ascribed to a nature which, fundamentally possessing such tendency, would be capable of development along those lines to the ultimate good of the community.

And we do find it.

A steady faithfulness, a recognition of the given word, a generous affection for the near relatives,[1] a manlier treatment (among the southern and middle Kurds) of his women than is seen among any other Musulman race, a keen literary sense and love of poetry, a ready willingness to sacrifice himself for his tribe, and a fine pride of country and race. With what a fine air does the Kurd draw himself up and say, according to his dialect, "Az Kurmanjam," or "Min Kurdim" ("I am a Kurd.")

If, then, one can hardly acquiesce in the eulogistic description by a French traveller, that "en somme les Kurdes sont des beaux hommes, forts, intelligents, d'un joli type, et lorsque la civilisation les aura policés, ils seronts supérieurs à leurs voisins les Turcs et les Persans,"[2] one can still see that there is more good in them than in many races at present preening themselves in the sunshine of "civilisation."

They have a terrible temper, suddenly roused—consequence again of the violent and precarious life they lead —and with it all, among the southerner, an extraordinarily keen sense of humour. They are always ready to tell stories against themselves of this very characteristic.

There was once a khan of the Herki of Oramar (in the Hakkari), who being bitten by a fly, scratched the place, five minutes afterwards it irritated still, and again he scratched. Yet again it commenced, and he snatched a pistol from his belt, and cursing the father of flies, shot his finger off.

Two Kurds were discussing the position in which the star Sirius (which marks the end of the warmest

---

[1] This may not occur to the reader in Europe as anything but what must be in the nature of all, like maternal love, perhaps ; but it is an unusual thing in the East, where the nearer the relative also means the greater enemy.

[2] Henry Binder, *Au Kurdistan*, p. 110.

weather) might be expected in the firmament. Without any abusive language they disagree as to the position, stop upon the road, and fall upon one another. One remains there dead.

Such is, as briefly as possible, the character of the Kurd. In the south the same description holds good, except that the furious savageness of the northerner is absent, tempered to a steadfastness, a humour of determination in any business he undertakes.

Yet of course there is the terrible ignorance of the mountain tribesman. How many among them even know their own age? or have any idea of what is outside Kurdistan? They learn swiftly enough, given the opportunity, and the Kurd learning is as rapacious for knowledge, as robbing he was for loot. The linguistic ability is remarkable, and, as has been mentioned, the literary instinct inherent.

Among the people of the south, where a large population has become sedentary, a very good type has been evolved, mostly recruited from the Kalhur, Bajlan, and Jaf tribes, and they have had an opportunity for discovering their natural aptitude for mechanical work with an Oil Concession, which commenced boring near Qasr-i-Shirin. Here these men were employed on the well-rigs and in the machine shop, and displayed such ability that when the company transferred its work to the present oil-field in south-western Persia, a number of Qasr-i-Shirin Kurds were taken there, and still remain one of the most satisfactory and skilled sections of the workers, some having attained great proficiency in technical and mechanical work. The type is steady and quiet, hard-working, with a great enthusiasm for all things appertaining to engineering.

The Kurd from north to south is monogamous, and the family seldom exceeds three or four. The wife has a remarkable freedom, and the Kurdish women are a fine class of unaffected, brave women, deserving as much praise for their domestic qualities as for the physical beauty that is so often theirs. Many are fine, bold riders, and can handle a rifle, and among the more warlike tribes the women themselves join in the fray.

Millingen, a traveller among the Kurds, quotes a fantastic story of how the Kurdish women form them- selves into bands for the decoy and robbery of the unfortunate traveller.[1]

In the house they look after everything, and while they are, particularly among the sedentary tribes, forced to do excessively arduous manual labour, such as the fetching and carrying of water, they get through all their labours with a jovial and hearty spirit, and keep the family and flocks in excellent order, taking the severest hardships as but a trivial incident in a life in which they seem to find plenty of enjoyment.

Many a time in villages has the housewife, in the absence of her man, entertained the writer, sat with and talked to him, never displaying any of the false shame or modesty of the Turk or Persian, and sharing cheerfully with him whatever the house had to eat and drink; and when the man came in, ignoring him in the attention to the guest, till having bestowed his horse, the husband comes in and joins the guest. Mind, I speak of their attitude towards those they consider humble like themselves. Towards the European I understand there is a different attitude.[2]

As a result of this frank nature and free life, it may be credited that in the Kurmanj language the only words for "prostitute" are Turkish and Persian, and those only understood in towns. Adultery among the country Kurds is looked upon as a remarkable and unnatural lapse from all reason and tradition, and is punished by death.

Many and many a marriage is one of mutual attraction—an example of which I have quoted in the chapter dealing with my stay in Halabja. Genuine affection between husband and wife (so rare among the Islamic nations) is by no means unknown among the

[1] Millingen, *Wild Life among the Koords*, p. 244.
[2] Not always, however; see Layard, *Nineveh*, vol. i., p. 153.

less savage tribes, and there is no finer feature of the
race than its open intercourse and good understanding
between the sexes. Witness the example of Lady
Adela,[1] of the widow of Ghulam Shah, khan of Sina;
of the women of the ancient Hakkari family—who are
entitled "Khan"—whose power is equal to, nay, greater
than many of the men of their own families; and many
others all over central and southern Kurdistan. Such
can be solely the result of an understanding between
the sexes more nearly approximating to our English
ideas than obtains among any other Oriental race, and
at the same time goes to show how little Islam has
affected what must be the habit of ancient times.

Judged as specimens of the human form, there is
probably no higher standard extant than that of the
Kurds. The northerner is a tall, thin man (obesity is
absolutely unknown among the Kurds). The nose is
long, thin, and often a little hooked, the mouth small,
the face oval and long. The men usually grow a long
moustache, and invariably shave the beard. The eyes
are piercing and fierce. Among them are many of
yellow hair and bright blue eyes; and the Kurdish
infant of this type were he placed among a crowd of
English children, would be indistinguishable from them,
for he has a white skin. In the south the face is a
little broader sometimes, and the frame heavier. Of
forty men of the southern tribes taken at random there
were nine under six feet, though among some tribes
the average height is five feet nine. The stride is long
and slow, and the endurance of hardship great. They
hold themselves as only mountain men can do, proudly
and erect, and look what they are—the Medes of to-
day, worthy, were they only united, of becoming once
again a great military nation, whose stern, hard nature
could keep in hand the meaner races among whom
they live. Many and many a man have I seen among
them who might have stood for the picture of a

---

[1] Also the ladies of Kerind, who each keep a little court.

Norseman. Yellow flowing hair, a long drooping moustache, blue eyes, and a fair skin—one of the most convincing proofs, if physiognomy be a criterion (were their language not a further proof), that the Anglo-Saxon and Kurd are one and the same stock.

In dress they have always been fantastic, and I cannot do better than quote from travellers the style of the Kurds of a hundred and of seventy years ago :—

"In front, on a small, lean, and jaded horse, rode a tall, gaunt figure, dressed in all the tawdry garments sanctioned by Kurdish taste. A turban of wonderful capacity, and almost taking within its dimensions horse and rider, buried his head, which seemed to escape by a miracle being driven in between his shoulders by the enormous pressure. From the centre of this mass of many-coloured rags rose a high conical cap of white felt. This load appeared to give an unsteady rolling gait to the thin carcase below, which could with difficulty support it. A most capacious pair of claret-coloured trousers bulged out from the sides of the horse, and well-nigh stretched from side to side of the ravine. Every shade of red and yellow was displayed in his embroidered jacket and cloak; and in his girdle were weapons of extraordinary size, and most fanciful workmanship." [1]

The following refers to the dress of the northern Mukri Kurds, south of Urumia :—

"On their heads they wear a large shawl of striped silk, red, white, and blue, with fringed ends, which is wound in the most graceful manner round their red skull-cap. Its ample folds are confined with some sort of band, and the long fringes hang down with a rich fantastic wildness; their true Saracenic features, and bright black eyes, gleam with peculiar lustre from under this head-tire. Their body garments consist of a sort of ample vest and gown, with magnificent wide Turkish sleeves, over which is worn a jacket, often richly

---

[1] Layard, *Nineveh*, vol. i., pp. 206-7 (description of a Hakkari), 1848.

embroidered and furred, according to the owner's rank. Their lower man is enveloped in ample *shulwars*, not unlike those of the Mamlucs, into which, in riding, they stuff the skirts of their more flowing garments. Around their waist, instead of a shawl, they wear a girdle fastened with monstrous silver clasps, which may be ornamented according to the owner's taste with jewels, and in which they stick not only their Kurdish dagger, but a pair of great brass or silver-knobbed pistols. From this, too, hang sundry powder-horns and shot-cases, cartridge-boxes, etc., and over all they cast a sort of cloak or *abba*, of camel's hair, white, or black, or striped white, brown, and black, clasped on the breast, and floating picturesquely behind."[1]

The costume here described has changed not at all, except perhaps that the big pistols have given place to revolvers, and a carbine swings over the shoulder, four and sometimes even five rows of cartridge-belts, one above the other, encircling the horseman's body.

Of the southern Sulaimanian and Jaf, J. C. Rich gave the following description:—

"His gown was of a rich flowered gold Indian stuff; he had a superb cashmere shawl, ornamented with gold fringe, on his head, put on in a wild, loose manner; his upper dress was a capot, or cloak of crimson Venetian cloth, with rich gold frogs, or bosses, on it.

"The Jaf men wore a dress belted round their middles, light drawers, with the worsted shoe, which is a comfortable covering for the feet, and a conical felt cap on their heads."[2]

Describing the costume of the northern Hakkari, Binder, a modern traveller, says:—"ils . . . se coiffent d'un bonnet de feutre blanc conique autour duquel ils enroulent d'énormes turbans; leur pantalon, d'une largeur demesurée, est en tissu de poil de chèvre rouge et souvent bariolé de dessins; ils portent une petite jaquette de-

---

[1] Fraser, *Travels in Koordistan*, p. 86, 1835.

[2] Rich, *Residence in Koordistan*, vol. i., pp. 77 and 181, 1820.

scendant à peine à la taille, pardessus laquelle ils mettent souvent un manteau, pas plus long que la jaquette en poil de chèvre, garni sur le devant de grossières passementeries ; comme chaussures, ils ont des bottes en cuir rouge, avec de fortes ferrures au talon."[1]

The Mukri and Rawanduz Kurds have exchanged the pointed white cap for one in green, and of cloth, and not so high, but with a little stiff tassel sticking up from the point. The turban is smaller, and wound so that the fringes conceal both sides of the face. They have adopted the Persian "qaba," a short tunic not reaching to the knee, and over it often wear the "sardari" or plaited frock-coat, but made in a bright-coloured velvet.

As one comes south the dress becomes more like that of the Arab. The workmanlike costume of the north, where the man is, so to speak, in his shirt-sleeves all the time, is replaced by a long tunic reaching to the ankles, over a white shirt, the sleeves of which, made like "bishop-sleeves," touch the ground. A "salta" or zouave jacket is worn, generally of some sober-coloured cloth ornamented with gold-thread work, and according to the tribe different kinds of turbans are worn, the skull-cap usually being of cotton cloth embroidered.

In addition to this costume all tribes of the south wear the typical Kurdish felt waistcoat, which is sleeveless, and about half an inch thick.

It may be said that in the south the Kurd has preserved no prejudices in the matter of dress, except the turban, which is his distinguishing feature.

The costume of the women is simple. In the north, a long coloured shirt, and full trousers, or full skirts, supplemented in cold weather by more shirts, and perhaps a felt, constitutes the dress. A large turban is worn.

In central and southern Kurdistan, however, the dress becomes more complicated. The Mukri and Sina women enjoy the reputation of wearing the biggest turbans of any tribes, huge masses of coloured silk handkerchiefs

---

[1] Binder, *Au Kurdistan*, pp. 109-10, 1887.

cocked to one side. Earrings, bracelets, strings of gold coins around their foreheads, are all common enough features of their dress. Among the Mukri the women often wear the "sardari," and if not that, the "charukhia," a kind of heavy cloth thrown over one shoulder.

The veil is absolutely unknown to the Kurds, and the women never hide their faces.

The dress adopted by the Sulaimania women is, while Kurdish in character, yet influenced by the Arab style.

The underclothes are a short shirt and baggy trousers, the upper parts of which are made of white cotton and the lower of some striped material. Over this is a long shirt reaching to the feet, with small bishop-sleeves of white cotton, and open at the neck. Over this again is the "kawa," a long coat—also reaching to the feet— buttonless, not meeting at the front, of some heavier stuff, the sleeves of which are tight, but slit on the inner side for a few inches from the wrist.

The headgear consists of, first, a little ornamented skull-cap, over which is thrown the "jamana," a coloured handkerchief, which hangs behind and is often brought once round the neck. The Kurdish turban has given place to a long thick cord with pieces of black cloth fastened in it, in contact with one another, making an apparatus more like a "boa" than anything else. This, the "pushin," is wound round the head over the jamana, and the costume altogether is graceful and dignified, particularly when the wearer is tall, as are most of the women of Sulaimania.

The Kurds are by no means devoid of the superstition and folklore that is to be expected among such a people.

Like the Persians, whose Islamiyyat has not expelled the ancient fables, they still believe in the fairies, and although the Jinn of the Arabs have taken a large place in the scheme of beings of the underworld, Peri and Shait still hold their own. There is too the Pir or saint, the origin of whom is wrapped in obscurity, and who is popularly supposed to exist in certain spots and tombs, where the votive offering of rags is made, just as in Persia—relic of a custom surely older than Islam.

The Shaits are a curious class of supernatural beings, for among them are classed all the martyrs of Islam and many Kurds who have fallen in defence of their tribe, and they, like the living, are a wandering tribe of beings, beneficent, and desirous of helping the mortal Kurd to his desires. In fact, they are regarded in a light very similar to the Pir, and may be appealed to at their halting-places—often enough great trees on the hill-sides.

The Peri—whence our own word and idea of fairies —are essentially the same beings as our own folklore teaches us, for as our lore has come from the northern Aryans, so are our fairies the same little folk as the Peri.

As to the Jinn, they have adopted the unfortunate Arabic fellow, just as Muhammad, perhaps in his turn borrowing from tradition, introduced him, "a being made of fire, but like men, dependent upon food for existence, and like men, some malignant and some well disposed, and not all malignant like the devils."[1]

As to the Div—devils—they exist, as they did in the days of Zoroaster, but the Kurd, living the strenuous life he does, seems to think but little of them.

[1] From a little book on the Fundaments of Faith, Shiraz, 1902.

APPENDIX

KURDISH TRIBES

THE following table includes the main tribes upon the Turkish and Persian frontier. Numbers 1 to 9 term themselves generally " Kurmanj," " Kurdmang," *i.e.*, Kurds, while the rest use the designation "Kurd" to signify their race. Those using the first appellation are of the purest Kurd blood.

No.	Name of Tribe	Sub-tribes.	Situation of Country.
1	Haidaranlu	Zilanlu, Hasananlu, Adamanlu, Sipkanlu, Jibranlu, Zirkanlu, Shadi, Milan, Mamanlu.	The Armenian plateau, and up to the Persian frontier.
2	Shekak	.	Persian frontier near Salmas.
3	Hakkari	Oramar, Shamisdinan, Jelu, Herki, Zebari, Ruzhaki (an ancient clan of which the princes of Bitlis were members), Shernakli, Khizan, Barzan, Girdi, Bahdinan (from which the powerful religious families and Shaikhs came), Missuri, Bohtan, Hasankaifan, Nauchai, Jelali, Rawan, and many other small sections.	Bitlis, the Great Zab valley, the Tiyari, Amadia, Jazira ibn Umar.
4	Mukri	.	Sauj Bulaq and the district around, up to the Turkish frontier.
5	Pishdir	Nuraddini and others	Upper Lesser Zab River valley.
6	Bilbas	.	The Kandil Dagh in Central Kurdistan.
7	Rawanduz	.	Rawanduz.
8	Shuan	.	South of the lower Lesser Zab, N.E. of Kirkuk.
9	Baban	.	Sulaimania.
10	Bana	.	Bana.

11	Merivan	.	Merivan.
12	Jaf	Pushtamala, Amala, Jaf-i-Sartik, Tilan, Mikaili, Akhasuri, Changani, Rughzadi, Tarkhani, Bashaki, Kilali, Shatiri, Haruni, Nurwali, Kukui, Zardawi, Yazdan Bakhshi, Shaikh Ismaili, Sadani, Badakhi, Musai Tailaku.	From Qizil Rubat along the west bank of the Sirwan River as far as Shahr-i-Zur, Panjwin.
13	Hamavand	.	Qaradagh, near Sulaimania.
14	Sharafbaiani	.	Haorin, on the south of the Sirwan River, in Persian territory.
15	Bajlan	Jumur, Shirawand, Hajilar Gharibawand, Dandawand, and Qazanlu.	Immediately south of the Sharafbaiani.
16	Aoram or Haoram	Haoram-i-Ali Shah, Haoram-i-Ja'far Sultan	The Aoraman Mountain.
17	Salahi	.	Kifri, Salahi district.
18	Guran	Gahwara, Baziani, Nerzhi, Qalkhani, Buyani, Kalleh Zanjiri, Qadir Mir Waisi, Taishai, and other small sections.	The western part of the province of Kermanshah.
19	Kalhur	Shuan, Kuchimi, Charzrbari, Alawand, Khaledi, Shiani, Sia-Sia, Kazem Khani, Khamman, Kalajubi, Harunabadi, Baidaghbagi, Kerkah, Mansuri, Vermizyari, and others.	The province of Kermanshah.
20	Sinjabi	.	Near the Turkish frontier, in the Kermanshah province.

BIBLIOGRAPHY

THE undermentioned are the principal works which have been used for purposes of reference and comparison :—

The Bible.

A Literary History of Persia, Prof. Browne, M.A., M.B., F.B.A. Unwin, 1906.

A Year among the Persians, Prof. Browne, M.A., M.B., F.B.A. Murray.

Bustan us Siaha, Haji Zainu'l 'Abidin Shirwani.

Haqaiqu't Taraiq, Haji Mirza Ma'sum Shirazi, Naibu's Sadr. Teheran, 1314 A.H.

Treaties between Persia and Turkey, Aitchison.

Ghayyath ul Lugha. Bombay.

Dictionary of Islam, Hughes. Allen, 1895.

Athar-i-'Ajam, Fursat Shirazi. Bombay, 1314 A.H.

Persia, Past and Present, Prof. T. Williams Jackson. MacMillan, 1906.

Nineveh and its Remains, Layard. Murray, 1850.

Dabistanu'l Mazahib, A.H. 1267.

The Qur'an.

Commentary on the Quran, Wherry. Paul Trench Trubner, 1896.

Sale's *Quran.*

Persia, Lord Curzon.

Assyria, Ragozin. Unwin, 1898.

Parthia, Rawlinson. Unwin, 1893.

Armenia, H. F. B. Lynch. Longmans, 1901.

Travels in Koordistan, Fraser. Bentley, 1835.

Residence in Koordistan, Rich. Duncan, 1836.

Armenia, Koordistan, etc., Kinneir. Murray, 1818.

Wild Life among the Koords, Millingen. Hurst & Blackett, 1870.

Au Kurdistan en Mesopotamie, Binder.   Paris, 1887.

Travels in Persia, etc., Wagner.   Hurst & Blackett, 1856.

Armenians, Koords, and Turks, Creagh.   Tinsley, 1887.

History of Persia, Malcolm (Persian translation).

Assyrian Life and History, Harkness.   R. T. Soc.

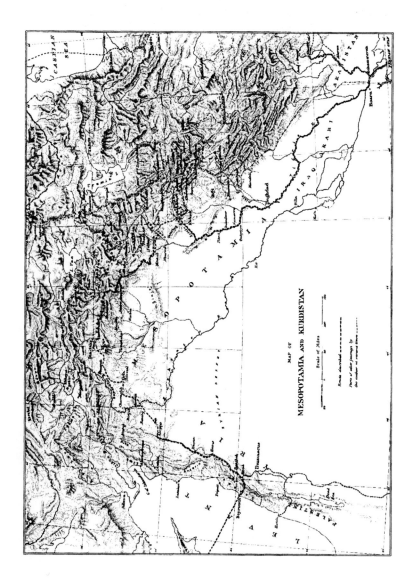

MAP OF

MESOPOTAMIA AND KURDISTAN

Scale of Miles

Route described

Parts of other journeys by
the author or compiled from

INDEX

411

COSIMO is a specialty publisher of books and publications that inspire, inform, and engage readers. Our mission is to offer unique books to niche audiences around the world.

COSIMO BOOKS publishes books and publications for innovative authors, nonprofit organizations, and businesses. **COSIMO BOOKS** specializes in bringing books back into print, publishing new books quickly and effectively, and making these publications available to readers around the world.

COSIMO CLASSICS offers a collection of distinctive titles by the great authors and thinkers throughout the ages. At **COSIMO CLASSICS** timeless works find new life as affordable books, covering a variety of subjects including: Business, Economics, History, Personal Development, Philosophy, Religion & Spirituality, and much more!

COSIMO REPORTS publishes public reports that affect your world, from global trends to the economy, and from health to geopolitics.

FOR MORE INFORMATION CONTACT US AT
INFO@COSIMOBOOKS.COM

❈ if you are a book lover interested in our current catalog of books

❈ if you represent a bookstore, book club, or anyone else interested in special discounts for bulk purchases

❈ if you are an author who wants to get published

❈ if you represent an organization or business seeking to publish books and other publications for your members, donors, or customers.

COSIMO BOOKS ARE ALWAYS
AVAILABLE AT ONLINE BOOKSTORES

VISIT COSIMOBOOKS.COM
BE INSPIRED, BE INFORMED